# Retracing
# the
# Past

# Retracing the Past

## Readings in the History of the American People

### VOLUME ONE · TO 1877

**Second Edition**

**EDITORS**
**GARY B. NASH**
*University of California, Los Angeles*

**RONALD SCHULTZ**
*University of Wyoming*

1817

**HARPER & ROW, PUBLISHERS, New York**
Grand Rapids, Philadelphia, St. Louis, San Francisco,
London, Singapore, Sydney, Tokyo

Sponsoring Editor: Lauren Silverman
Art Direction: Heather A. Ziegler
Cover Coordinator: Mary Archondes
Cover Design: A Good Thing, Inc.
Photo Research: Joan Scafarello
Production: Willie Lane

**Cover Illustration:** Benjamin Henry Latrobe, *View of the Baliye, at the Mouth of the Mississippi . . . ,* watercolor inscribed in ink. Courtesy Maryland Historical Society.
**Part-Opening Illustrations: Page 1:** *Dutch Seascape* (Thought to be departure of the Pilgrims from Delfthave on the 'Speedwell') Attributed to W. van de Velde, seventeenth century. Courtesy of the Pilgrim Society, Plymouth, Massachusetts. **Page 85:** *Surrender of Lord Cornwallis at Yorktown* by John Trumbull, © 1828. Copyright Yale University Art Gallery. **Page 175:** *California News* by William Sidney Mount, 1850. The Museums at Stony Brook; gift of Mr. and Mrs. Ward Melville, 1955

**RETRACING THE PAST: Readings in the History of the American People, VOLUME ONE, TO 1877, Second Edition.**
Copyright © 1990 by Harper & Row, Publishers, Inc.

Library of Congress Cataloging-in-Publication Data

Retracing the past : readings in the history of the American people
  editors, Gary B. Nash, Ronald Schultz. — 2nd ed.
    p.  cm.
  Contents: v. 1. To 1877 — v. 2. Since 1865.
  ISBN 0-06-044744-3 (v. 1). — ISBN 0-06-044745-1 (v. 2)
  1. United States—History.  I. Nash, Gary B.  II. Schultz,
Ronald, 1946-  .
E178.6.R45  1990
973—dc20                          89-20053
                                         CIP

89 90 91 92 9 8 7 6 5 4 3 2 1

# CONTENTS

PREFACE   vii

## PART ONE
## A COLONIZING PEOPLE   1

## PART TWO
## A REVOLUTIONARY PEOPLE   85

v

# PART THREE
# AN EXPANDING PEOPLE  175

# PREFACE

This two-volume reader has been designed to accompany the second edition of *The American People: Creating a Nation and a Society* (New York: Harper & Row, 1990), but we hope it will also prove a useful supplement to other books in American history. The essays have been selected with three goals in mind: first, to blend political and social history; second, to lead students to a consideration of the role of women, ethnic groups, and laboring Americans in the weaving of the nation's social fabric; and third, to explore life at the individual and community levels. The book also means to introduce students to the individuals and groups who made a critical difference in the shaping of American history or whose experience reflected key changes in their society.

A few of the individuals highlighted are famous—Benjamin Franklin, Abraham Lincoln, and Jackie Robinson, for example. A number of others are historically visible but are not quite household names—Squanto, Tecumseh, Samuel Gompers, W. E. B. Du Bois, John Muir, and Elizabeth Blackwell. Some will be totally unknown to students, such as "Long Bill" Scott, a Revolutionary soldier, and Absalom Jones, who bought his way out of slavery and became a leader of Philadelphia's free African Americans after the American Revolution. Often the focus is on groups whose role in history has not been adequately treated—the Chinese in the building of the transcontinental railroad, the grass-roots black leaders during Reconstruction, and the Hispanic agricultural laborers of this century.

Some of the essays chosen take us inside American homes, farms, and factories, such as the essays on the Springer family of Delaware farmers before the Civil War and the transcontinental migrants of the nineteenth century. Such essays, it is hoped, will convey an understanding of the daily lives of ordinary Americans, who collectively helped shape their society. Other essays deal with the vital social and political movements that transformed American society: the debate over the Constitution in the 1780s; abolitionism and reform in the antebellum period; populism and progressivism in the late nineteenth and early twentieth centuries; and the civil rights and women's movements of our own times.

Readability has been an important criterion in the selection of these essays. An important indicator of readability, in turn, is how vividly and concretely the past has been brought alive by the authors. The main objective has been a palpable presentation of the past—one that allows students to sense and feel the forces of historical change and hence to understand them.

Gary B. Nash
Ronald Schultz

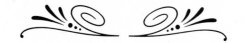

# Retracing
# the
# Past

# PART ONE

# A
# COLONIZING
# PEOPLE

# 1

# SQUANTO: LAST OF THE PATUXETS

## NEAL SALISBURY

By the beginning of European colonization in the seventeenth century Native American tribes had inhabited the eastern seaboard of North America for more than 6,000 years. Until recently, historians have paid little attention to the contributions of the Powhatans, Mahicans, Abenaki, and many other tribes in shaping the course of American history. In this essay Neal Salisbury recasts the familiar story of Squanto in light of this new historical scholarship and in the process reveals the complex interaction that took place between the original inhabitants and the Europeans who explored and settled along the New England coast.

The central event of Squanto's life was the virtual destruction of his people by European diseases. From the time of Columbus's landing in the New World, Native American peoples, who had lost their immunities to Euro-Asian diseases through centuries of geographic isolation, were devastated by the introduction of smallpox, cholera, and even such relatively minor European diseases as measles and chicken pox. As Salisbury points out, the horrible decimation of the Native American population that followed European contact had profound effects upon those who, like Squanto, survived. With mortality rates as high as 80 percent in a single generation, normal social relations became impossible, the mixed economy of hunting and planting was disrupted, political alliances were shattered, and long-standing cultural systems were destroyed. Survivors were left vulnerable to the designs of European settlers and to the new economic system that they brought with them.

In spite of this devastation and cultural dislocation, the history of early European–Native American contact was more than a tale of death and destruction. It was also the story of the several ways in which early settlers depended on the Native Americans' presence: for the sites of their settlements, for their crops, and for the pelts of indigenous animals with which they paid for their imported goods. As this essay reveals, successful interaction between Native Americans and Europeans depended on the skills of cultural mediators who worked to bring the disparate cultures together. Without Squanto and other Native American mediators, New England might have developed very differently.

As every American schoolchild knows, a lone Indian named Squanto rescued the Pilgrims from the wilderness by teaching them how to plant corn and introducing them to friendly natives. In so doing, the textbooks imply, he symbolically brought about the union of the European colonizers and the American land. Though contemporary events and critical historical inquiry are now undermining this myth, Squanto's story retains some significance. For when placed in its historic and cultural context, it reveals the range of truly human, if prosaic, qualities called forth among Native Americans during the early colonization of New England.

As befits a mythic hero, the time and circumstances of Squanto's birth are unknown. His birth date can only be inferred from what the sources say and do not say. The firsthand descriptions of him, written between 1618 and his death in 1622, do not suggest that he was strikingly young or old at that time. All we can safely conclude is that he was probably in his twenties or thirties at the time he was forcibly taken to Europe in 1614.

Though Squanto's early years are obscured by a lack of direct evidence, we know something of the cultural milieu that prepared him for his unexpected and remarkable career. Squanto and his fellow Patuxet spoke an Algonquian dialect that they shared with the other natives around Plymouth Bay and west as far as the near shore of Narragansett Bay. Moreover, its differences from other dialects in what is now southern New England were minimal, so that the Patuxet could communicate with the natives throughout this region. Like other coastal villages below the mouth of the Saco River, Patuxet was positioned to allow its inhabitants to grow crops, exploit marine resources, and have easy access to wild plants and animals. In accordance with the strict sexual division of labor maintained by virtually all eastern North American Indians, Squanto's major activities would have been to hunt game and to engage in certain kinds of fishing. He would also have fashioned a wide variety of tools and other material items and participated in the intensely ritualized world of trade, diplomacy, religious ceremonies, recreation, warfare, and political decision making that constituted a man's public life.

The training of young men in precontact southern New England was designed to prepare them for that world. Of the Pokanoket, closely related to the Patuxet, the Plymouth leader Edward Winslow wrote, "a man is not accounted a man till he do some notable act or show forth such courage and resolution as becometh his place." A New Netherland official noted that young Pokanoket men were left alone in the forest for an entire winter. On returning to his people in the spring, a candidate was expected to imbibe and vomit bitter [poisonous] herbs for several days. At the conclusion of his ordeal, he was brought before the entire band, "and if he has been able to stand it all well, and if he is fat and sleek, a wife is given to him."

As a result of such training, young Algonquians learned not only how to survive but also how to develop the capacities to withstand the severest physical and psychological trials. The result was the Indian personality type that Euroamericans came to characterize as stoic, the supreme manifestation of which was the absolute expressionlessness of prisoners under torture. Though the specific content of such training did little to prepare Squanto for his later experiences in Malaga, London, or Newfoundland, it imparted a sense of psychological independence and prepared him for adapting to the most demanding environments and situations.

Patuxet men such as Squanto also exercised their independence in making political judgments and decisions. As elsewhere in southern New England, the band, consisting of one or more villages, was the primary political unit. Its leader, the sachem, was drawn from one of a select group of lineages elevated in prestige above the rest. The sachems distributed garden plots to families and exercised certain judicial prerogatives. They also represented the band on diplomatic and ceremonial occasions. But a sachem's power was derived directly from the band members. To secure economic and political support he or she needed leadership ability as well as a family name. Band members could oblige a faltering sachem to share the office with a relative or step down altogether. Moreover, major political decisions were reached through a consensus in meetings attended by all adult males. Squanto came from a world, then, where politics was a constant and integral component of a man's life.

Squanto was even better prepared for his unusual career if, as seems probable, he was a *pniese* in his band. In preparation for this position, young men were chosen in childhood and underwent unusually rigorous diets and training. The purpose of this preparation was not simply to fortify them and develop their courage but to enable them to call upon and visualize Hobbamock, a deity capable of inflicting great harm and even death on those he did not favor. Hobbamock appeared in many forms to "the chiefest and most judicious amongst them," in Winslow's words, "though all of them strive to attain to that hellish height of honor." It is clear that those who succeeded in the vision quest had developed the mental self-discipline demanded of all Indians to an extraordinary degree. By calling on Hobbamock, the *pnieses* protected themselves and those near them in battle and frightened their opponents. They constituted an elite group within the band, serving as counselors and bodyguards to the sachems. They were universally respected not only for their access to Hobbamock and for their courage and judgment but for their moral uprightness. Because of his psychological fortitude, his particularly astute grasp of Indian politics and protocol, and his continued sense of duty to his band after its demise, it is quite likely that Squanto was a *pniese.*

The few recorded observations of Patuxet during Squanto's early years show that it was a very different place from the "wilderness" the Plymouth colonists later found there. Both

Samuel de Champlain, in 1605 and 1606, and John Smith, in 1614, noted that most of the coast between Massachusetts and Plymouth bays was under cultivation. The colonists were told, probably by Squanto himself, that in Plymouth Bay "in former time hath lived about 2,000 Indians." The population of the surrounding area—that is, of the Indians with whom the Patuxet maintained the closest relations—was probably between twenty and twenty-five thousand in 1615. Most of these natives were concentrated in village communities ranging in size from five hundred to fifteen hundred individuals. Squanto was thus accustomed to a more densely settled environment than we might expect and was probably as comfortable in the European cities he later visited as in the tiny colonies.

Though no one could have known it at the time, Squanto was born at a turning point in the history of his people and his region. For a century Europeans had been trading and skirmishing with, and sometimes kidnapping, Indians along the coast. At the time of Squanto's birth, however, these activities had not been extended south of Canada on a regular basis. Infrequent visits from European explorers and traders and the natives' own well-established exchange routes brought some iron tools and glass beads to Patuxet. But these were too scattered to induce any economic or cultural changes of a substantive nature. Unlike the fur-trading Indians to the north, the Patuxet and their neighbors had not become dependent on European trade items for their survival.

The turn of the century marked an intensification of French and British interest in New England's resources. The differing economic goals of the colonizers from the two countries gave rise to differing attitudes and policies toward the natives. The French were concerned primarily with furs. Following Champlain's explorations of the New England coast in 1605 and 1606, French traders using his descriptions and maps began to visit the Indians annually and to cultivate an extensive trade as far south as Cape Cod. Their goals encouraged the maintenance of friendly relations with stable Indian bands and even the development of broad regional ties among the natives.

For the English, however, furs were at best a useful by-product of more pressing interests. Beginning with Bartholomew Gosnold's expedition in 1602, they showed a preference for resources such as fish and sassafras that did not require the cooperation of the natives. Moreover, they thought in long-range terms of making Indian land available to Englishmen for farming, a goal that virtually guaranteed eventual conflict with the natives. Indian allies were cultivated, but only for purposes of assisting the English in establishing themselves, and the methods used were generally more coercive than those of the French. Nearly every English expedition from Gosnold's to that of the Mayflower generated hostility with the Indians. By 1610 taking captured Indians to England had become routine. Would-be colonizers such as Sir Ferdinando Gorges hoped to impress their captives with the superiority of English culture, to learn as much as they could about the lay of the land, and to acquire mediators with the local Indians. They also displayed their captives prominently in order to attract financial and public support for their projected colonies.

John Smith, the former Virginia leader, witnessed the results of the competition between the two colonial strategies when he explored the coast from the Penobscot River to Cape Cod in 1614. Smith found that he had arrived at the end of an active trading season. Aside from one Englishman's cozy monopoly at the mouth of the Pemaquid River, all the ships were French. Though the better-endowed region north of the Pemaquid had yielded twenty-five thousand skins that year, Smith judged the south capable of producing six to seven thousand annually. He himself had retrieved thirteen hundred pelts, mostly beaver, in the wake of the French departure. He also found that all the Indians in the region he visited were friendly with one another through three loose regional alliances. Ostensibly

formed to resist incursions from the Micmac in eastern Canada, the friendship chain had an economic function as well, for Smith noted that some primarily horticultural Indians in southern New England traded corn to Abenaki hunting groups farther north whose concentration on the fur trade was apparently leading to food shortages. In return the horticulturalists obtained some of the Abenaki's supply of European trade goods. Though only minimally developed by 1614, this trade was already fostering a specialized division of labor among France's clients in New England.

The extent of Patuxet's participation in the corn trade is unknown. But Squanto and his people were producing substantial fur surpluses by the time of Smith's visit in 1614 and had gained at least some acquaintance with the Europeans. From the visits of Champlain, Smith, and the traders, Squanto had learned something of European approaches to trade, diplomacy, and military conflict and had witnessed some of their technological accomplishments. But the regularized trade was less than a decade old. And the ease with which groups of Patuxet men were manipulated by Smith and his officer, Thomas Hunt, in 1614 suggests that they had not developed the wariness toward Europeans, particularly the English, of the more experienced Indians to the north.

Squanto's life reached a sudden and dramatic turning point with Hunt's visit. Smith had returned to England, leaving Hunt in charge of his fishing crew to complete the catch and carry it to Malaga, Spain. Before departing, Hunt stopped at Patuxet. Using his association with Smith, who had left on friendly terms, he lured about twenty natives, including Squanto, aboard. Quickly rounding Cape Cod, he drew off seven more from Nauset and then turned east for Malaga. Hunt's action indelibly marked the English as an enemy of all the Indians in the Patuxet-Cape Cod region. In the words of Sir Ferdinando Gorges, Hunt's action resulted in "a warre now new begunne betweene the inhabitants of those parts and us," and John

Smith condemned Hunt for moving the Indians' "hate against our Nation, as well as to cause my proceedings to be more difficult."

Native outrage at Hunt's action was reinforced by the near-simultaneous return of an earlier Indian captive, Epenow, a sachem of Capawack (Martha's Vineyard). Epenow had been seized three years earlier and taken to Gorges in England. On constant public display, he learned English well and impressed Gorges and others as "a goodly man of brave aspect, stout and sober in his demeanour." Thus his tales of gold on Capawack were eagerly seized upon, and in 1614 Gorges commissioned a voyage under Nicholas Hobson, accompanied by Epenow as a guide. Epenow had apparently planned his escape all along, but the news of Hunt's deed hardened his desire for revenge. As the ship drew near his island, Epenow escaped under a cover of arrows from the shore. A fierce battle ensued with heavy casualties on both sides. Among the injured was Hobson himself, who returned to England emptyhanded. Epenow thereafter constituted one source for the anti-English sentiment that would persist in the region to the founding of Plymouth colony six years later.

Meanwhile Squanto and his fellow captives reached Malaga, where Hunt tried to sell them as slaves. A few had already been sold when, according to Gorges, "the Friers of those parts took the rest from them and kept them to be instructed in the Christian faith." What happened to Squanto in the next three years is not clear. Particularly intriguing are questions about the extent and influence of his Catholic instruction and the means by which, in William Bradford's words, "he got away for England." We know only that by 1617 he was residing in the London home of John Slany, treasurer of the Newfoundland Company, where he learned or at least improved his English and his understanding of colonial goals. In the following year he went to Newfoundland itself, presumably at Slany's instigation. Here he met for the second time Thomas Dermer, an officer with Smith in 1614 who now worked for Gorges. Dermer was so impressed with Squanto's tales of Patuxet that he took him back to England to meet Gorges. Though the strategy of employing captive Indians as guides had backfired several times, Gorges was ready to try again. He saw in Squanto the key to countering the recent successes of the French and reestablishing England's reputation among the Indians. For his part Squanto knew, as had earlier captives, how to tell Gorges what he wanted to hear in order to be returned home. In March 1619 he and Dermer were bound for New England.

Moving in the circles he did, Squanto undoubtedly knew something of the epidemic that had ravaged New England, including Patuxet, during his absence. A Gorges expedition under Richard Vines had witnessed what Vines called simply "the plague" at Sagadahoc in 1616 and reported on its effects. Most notable was the immunity of the English; while most of the Indians were dying, Vines and his party "lay in the Cabins with those people, [and] not one of them ever felt their heads to ake." This immunity and the 75 to 90 percent depopulation among the Indians make it clear that a virgin soil epidemic of European origin had been planted in New England's isolated disease environment. Though the specific instigator cannot be identified because of the frequency with which Europeans were visiting New England, it is noteworthy that the stricken zone, as reported by Dermer in 1619, was the coast from the Penobscot to Cape Cod—precisely the area encompassing the loose coalition of Indian groups engaged in trade with the French and each other. At its southern extremity the epidemic spread west to the Patuxet's allies, the Pokanoket, at the head of Narragansett Bay, but not to their Narragansett rivals on the western side. Such an outline suggests that the epidemic spread via established exchange routes that were shaped to a great extent in response to the fur trade and the accompanying developments.

Squanto found his own village completely vacated. Most of its inhabitants had died, but some had fled inland to other villages. He surely noticed, as did others, the undergrowth that had overtaken the formerly cultivated fields and the vast numbers of unburied dead whose "bones and skulls," in one Englishman's words, "made such a spectacle. . . . it seemed to me a new found Golgotha." The depopulation was so great that the Narragansett were able to force the weakened Pokanoket to abandon their position at the head of Narragansett Bay and to retain only the eastern shore.

The Narragansetts' avoidance of the epidemic gave them a greater advantage than that derived from numbers alone. In the view of their stricken neighbors, the Narragansetts' good health reflected their faithful sacrifices to the deity, Cautantowwit. The ritual worlds and belief systems of the stricken Indians, however, had been badly shaken by the epidemic. The usual practice of gathering with the *pow-wow* (shaman) in a sick person's wigwam could only have served to spread the disease more rapidly. With even the *pow-wows* succumbing, the Indians could only conclude that their deities had aligned against them. And being unable to observe the proper burial rituals, the survivors had to fear the retribution of the dead. The Indians' perception that they had lost touch with the sources of power and that others controlled the access to them would be a critical factor in facilitating Squanto's later political success.

As Dermer's expedition traveled overland from Patuxet in the summer of 1619, Squanto's presence and diplomatic skill enabled the English to break through the antagonisms toward them and to make friendly contacts at Nemasket (near Middleboro) and Pokanoket (near Bristol, Rhode Island). For once an Indian captive had performed as Gorges hoped. But as Dermer returned to his ship and prepared to sail around Cape Cod, Squanto took his leave to search for surviving Patuxets. On his own, Dermer was unable to persuade the Indians at Monomoy (now Pleasant Harbor) of his good intentions. He was captured and barely succeeded in escaping. After a seemingly cordial meeting on Martha's Vineyard with Epenow, the former Gorges captive, Dermer was attacked off Long Island and again managed to escape. Returning to New England in the summer of 1620, he was captured by his newly made friends at Pokanoket and Nemasket and released only after Squanto interceded on his behalf. Dermer, with Squanto, then proceeded to Martha's Vineyard, where they were attacked by Epenow and his followers. Most of the crew was killed this time, while the luckless captain escaped with fourteen wounds and died in Virginia. Squanto was again made a captive, this time of the Indians.

In a letter written after his release at Nemasket, Dermer attributed his reception there to his hosts' renewed desire for revenge. He noted that another English crew had just visited the area, invited some Indians on board their ship, and then shot them down without provocation. The incident could only have revived the Indians' suspicions of the English that had prevailed before Squanto's return. These suspicions were now focused on Squanto himself, as Dermer's accomplice, and led to his being turned over to the Pokanoket with whom he remained until he was ransomed by the Plymouth colonists in March 1621.

The Patuxet-Pokanoket-Cape Cod region was vastly different in the autumn of 1620 from a decade earlier when French traders had begun to frequent it regularly. Fewer than 10 percent of its twenty thousand or more former inhabitants were still living, and they were now consolidated into a few bands. The region was vulnerable as never before to exploitation by outsiders. The once-powerful Pokanoket and their sachem, Massasoit, had been subjected to a humiliating tributary relationship with the Narragansett, who were emerging as the most powerful aggregation in New England because of their size and their control of Indian-European trade links east of Long Island. Moreover, the decimated Indians could no longer count on the fur trade as a means of compensating for other weaknesses. Always limited in both the quality and quantity of its fur resources, the region's loss of most of its hunters now made it an unprofitable stop for traders.

Though a captive, Squanto was able to capitalize on the Pokanokets' despair. "He told Massasoit what wonders he had seen in England," according to a future settler, "and that if he could make English his friends then Enemies that were too strong for him would be constrained to bow to him." He did not have to wait long to be proved right. In December 1620, less than six months after Dermer's departure, word reached Pokanoket that a shipload of English colonists had established a permanent settlement at Patuxet.

Like the other Puritans who later settled New England, the group at Plymouth (for so they renamed Patuxet) was motivated by a combination of religious and economic motives that shaped their attitudes toward the natives. Their experience with persecution in England and exile to the Netherlands had sharpened their desire to practice their exclusionary, intolerant separatism without external interference. Moreover, though seeking distance from English ecclesiastical authorities, the settlers were attempting to reinforce their English identities. They had abandoned their Dutch haven for fear that their children would be assimilated there. Finally, though ostensibly migrating to fish and trade for furs, the colonists sought land to improve themselves materially and, they supposed, spiritually. Though Plymouth lacked the sense of divine mission of the later nonseparatist Puritan colonies, its goals of religious and ethnic exclusivity and an abundance of land had obvious implications for its relations with the natives.

These implications were apparent in Plymouth's early policies and attitudes toward the Indians. In a major promotional pamphlet published in 1622, Robert Cushman restated what had already become a familiar justification for dispossession of native lands:

Their land is spacious and void, and there are few and do but run over the grass, as do also the foxes and wild beasts. They are not industrious, neither have art, science, skill, or faculty to use either the land or the commodities of it, but all spoils or rots, and is marred for want of manuring, gathering, ordering, etc. As the ancient patriarchs therefore removed from straiter places into more roomy . . . so is it lawful now to take a land which none useth, and make use of it.

Cushman's statement was consistent with the emerging European doctrine of *vacuum domicilium,* by which "civil" states were entitled to the uncultivated lands of those in a "natural" state. Though Plymouth's own "civility" was formalized by the hastily contrived *Mayflower* Compact, its financial backers had anticipated its need for more than an abstract principle to press its claim—among its own people as well as among any natives they might encounter. Accordingly, they had hired Miles Standish, a soldier of fortune fresh from the Dutch wars, to organize the colony militarily. It was Standish who would shape Plymouth's Indian policy during its first generation.

Standish began to execute this policy even before the *Mayflower* arrived at Patuxet. Landing first at Cape Cod, the settlers aroused native hostilities by ransacking Indian graves, houses, and grain stores. At Patuxet they also stirred suspicions during the first four months of their stay. But their own situation grew desperate during their first New England winter. They lost half their numbers to starvation and disease, and as inexperienced farmers they were ill-prepared for the approaching planting season. In this condition they could no longer expect to alleviate their shortages through pilferage with impunity. The impasse was broken one day in March 1621 by the appearance of Samoset, a sachem of the Pemaquid River band, which had been trading with the English for more than a decade. Samoset learned the needs and intentions of the colony and returned a few days later with Squanto.

The Pokanoket had been watching the Plymouth group throughout the winter. With

Samoset and the newly useful Squanto offering advice and experience, they concluded that the time was ripe to befriend the settlers instead of maintaining a hostile distance. Such an alliance would enable them to break from the hold of the Narragansetts, whose haughty demeanor stung even more than that of the English. Nevertheless, the decision was not to be taken lightly. Bradford wrote that the Indians did first "curse and execrate them with their conjurations" before approaching the settlers. But this description betrays his fear of witchcraft as it was understood by Europeans, rather than his comprehension of Indian rituals. More likely the Pokanoket were ritually purging themselves of their hostilities toward the English.

Samoset and Squanto arranged the meeting between the Pokanoket and Plymouth colony that resulted in their historic treaty. In it each side agreed to aid the other in the event of attack by a third party, to disarm during their meetings with each other, and to return any tools stolen from the other side. But in addition to these reciprocal agreements, several others were weighted against the natives. Massasoit, the Pokanoket sachem, was to see that his tributaries observed the terms; the Indians were to turn over for punishment any of their people suspected of assaulting any English (but no English had to fear being tried by Indians); and, the treaty concluded, "King James would esteem of him [Massasoit] as his friend and ally." The meaning of the last honor was made explicit by the colony's annalist, Nathaniel Morton, who wrote that by the treaty Massasoit "acknowledged himself content to become the subject of our sovereign lord the King aforesaid, his heirs and successors, and gave unto them all the lands adjacent to them and theirs forever." Morton made clear that among themselves the English did not regard the treaty as one of alliance and friendship between equals but as one of submission by one party to the domination of the other, according to the assumptions of *vacuum domicilium.*

For the Pokanoket, however, the meaning of a political relationship was conveyed in the ritual exchange of speeches and gifts, not in written clauses or unwritten understandings based on concepts such as sovereignty that were alien to one party. From their standpoint, the English were preferable to the Narragansett because they demanded less tribute and homage while offering more gifts and autonomy and better protection.

The treaty also brought a change in status for Squanto. In return for his services, the Pokanoket now freed him to become guide, interpreter, and diplomat for the colony. Thus he finally returned to his home at Patuxet, a move that had, as we shall see, more than sentimental significance. Among his first services was the securing of corn seed and instruction in its planting, including the use of fish fertilizer, which he learned from his own people or from the Newfoundland colonists.

Squanto also enabled Plymouth to strengthen its political position in the surrounding area. He helped secure peace with some bands on Cape Cod and guided an expedition to Massachusetts Bay. His kidnapping by anti-English Indians at Nemasket and subsequent rescue by a heavily armed Plymouth force speaks compellingly of his importance to the colony. Moreover, this incident led to a new treaty, engineered in part by Squanto, with all the Indian groups of Massachusetts Bay to the tip of Cape Cod, including even Epenow and his band. By establishing a tributary system with the surrounding Indian bands, the colony was filling the political vacuum left by the epidemic and creating a dependable network of corn suppliers and buffers against overland attack. But it also incurred the resentment of the Narragansett by depriving them of tributaries just when Dutch traders were expanding their activities in the bay. The Narragansett challenged Plymouth's action in January 1622 by sending a snakeskin filled with arrows. On Squanto's advice Plymouth's leaders returned the skin filled with powder and shot. The Narragansett sachem, Canonicus, refused to accept this counterchallenge, in effect acknowledging the colony's presence and political importance.

However effective in appearance, Plymouth's system of Indian diplomacy was fraught with tensions that nearly destroyed it. A Pokanoket *pniese,* Hobbamock (named for his patron deity), became a second adviser to Plymouth in the summer of 1621. Whether the English thought that Hobbamock would merely assist Squanto or would serve to check him is unclear. In any event, Squanto was no longer the only link between the colony and the Indians; indeed, as a Pokanoket, Hobbamock had certain advantages over him. As one whose very life depended on the colony's need for him, Squanto had to act decisively to check this threat to his position. His most potent weapon was the mutual distrust and fear lingering between English and Indians; his most pressing need was for a power base so that he could extricate himself from his position of colonial dependency. Accordingly, he began maneuvering on his own.

Squanto had been acting independently for several months before being discovered by the English in March 1622. As reconstructed by Edward Winslow:

> his course was to persuade [the Indians] he could lead us to peace or war at his pleasure, and would oft threaten the Indians, sending them word in a private manner we were intended shortly to kill them, that thereby he might get gifts to himself, to work their peace; . . . so that whereas divers were wont to rely on Massasoit for protection, and resort to his abode, now they began to leave him and seek after Tisquantum [Squanto].

In short, he sought to establish himself as an independent native political leader. At the same time he endeavored to weaken the Pokanoket's influence on Plymouth by provoking armed conflict between the two allies. He circulated a rumor that Massasoit was conspiring with the Narragansett and Massachusett to wipe out the colony. The English quickly verified the continued loyalty of the Pokanoket but, though angry at Squanto, were afraid to dispense with him. Instead they protected him from Massasoit's revenge, which brought tensions into the Pokanoket-Plymouth relationship that were only finally assuaged when Squanto died later in the year.

In seeking to establish his independence of Plymouth, Squanto was struggling for more than his survival. As Winslow put it, he sought "honor, which he loved as his life and preferred before his peace." What did honor mean to Squanto? For one thing, of course, it meant revenge against the Pokanoket, not only for threatening his position at Plymouth but for his earlier captivity. But it meant more than that. Squanto appears to have made substantial inroads among Indians loyal to Massasoit in a short period of time. Winslow indicated, unknowingly and in passing, the probable key to this success. The news of Massasoit's alleged treachery against Plymouth was brought, he said, by "an Indian of Tisquantum's family." Contrary to the Plymouth sources (all of which were concerned with establishing the colony's unblemished title to the land around Plymouth Bay), there were certainly a few dozen Patuxet survivors of the epidemic at Pokanoket, Nemasket, and elsewhere. Though Squanto undoubtedly sought the loyalty and tribute of others, it was to these relatives and friends that he would primarily have appealed. The honor he sought was a reconstituted Patuxet band under his own leadership, located near its traditional home.

Squanto's hopes were shattered when his plot collapsed. With Massasoit seeking his life, he had, in Bradford's words, "to stick close to the English, and never durst go from them till he dies." This isolation from other Indians and dependence on the colonists helps explain the latter's willingness to protect him. In July, Squanto again engineered an important breakthrough for Plymouth by accompanying an expedition to Monomoy, where suspicion of all Europeans persisted. The Indians here had attacked Champlain's party in 1606 and Dermer's in 1619. Standish's men had taken some of their corn during their stop at Cape Cod in November 1620. Now, as Winslow phrased it, "by Tisquantum's means better persuaded, they left their jealousy, and traded with them." The colony's take was eight hogsheads of corn and beans. But as the expedition prepared to depart, Squanto "fell sick of an Indian fever, bleeding much at the nose (which the Indians take for a symptom of death) and within a few days died there."

By the time of Squanto's death, Plymouth colony had gained the foothold it had sought for two and a half years. The expedition to Monomoy marked the establishment of firm relations with the last local band to withhold loyalty. Moreover, the trade in corn was no longer an economic necessity, remaining important primarily as a means of affirming tributary relationships. These accomplishments would have been infinitely more difficult, if not impossible, without Squanto's aid. But it is questionable whether his contributions after the summer of 1622 would have been as critical. Thereafter, the colony's principal dealings were with the hostile Massachusett and Narragansett Indians beyond Patuxet's immediate environs. Moreover, the world in which Squanto had flourished was vanishing. A rationalized wampum trade had begun to transform Indian-European relations in southern New England. And the end of the decade would bring a mighty upsurge in English colonization that would surround and dwarf Plymouth. Within the restrictions imposed by his dependence on Plymouth's protection, Squanto would have adapted to these changes. But his knowledge and skills would no longer have been unique nor his services indispensable.

It is difficult to imagine what direction the life of this politically and historically isolated man, who valued "honor" above all else, might have taken in the coming decades. It is in this light that we should read his well-known deathbed conversion wherein he requested Bradford "to pray for him that he might go to the Englishmen's God in Heaven; and bequeathed sundry of his things to sundry of his English friends as remembrances of his love." He was acknowledging that after eight years of acting with honor in alien settings, he had been cornered. Dying so ignominiously, the last Patuxet would have found it ironic that later generations of Americans celebrated him as a hero.

# 2

# LOOKING OUT FOR NUMBER ONE: CONFLICTING CULTURAL VALUES IN EARLY SEVENTEENTH-CENTURY VIRGINIA

## T. H. BREEN

Emigration to the New World in the seventeenth century was an arduous undertaking. The journey required two to six months at sea, with passengers huddled in cramped quarters with little provision for privacy. During the long voyage one could expect minimal, and at times rotten, provisions. Seasickness, fevers, contagious diseases, and boredom afflicted most sojourners. Death itself often awaited the very young, the old, and the infirm. For those who set sail for the Chesapeake, the voyage was only the first part of their ordeal. Once ashore, virtually every immigrant contracted yellow fever, malaria, or other parasitic diseases from the mosquitoes that thrived in the low-lying tidewater swamps. Contemporary records suggest that up to half of all English immigrants died of disease within a few years of reaching Virginia or Maryland.

Yet despite the rigors and dangers of such a crossing, thousands of English men and women left their homeland for the Chesapeake in the first half of the seventeenth century. In this essay, T. H. Breen explores the character of those who made this fateful choice. What drew these people to the Chesapeake, most of them as indentured servants? And what, he asks, were these people like that they would risk disease and death to come to a region with so little in the way of typical English social and family life?

The answer, Breen suggests, was a simple one. Wave after wave of immigrants came to the Chesapeake to make money from the tobacco crop that was the sole reason for colonization of the region. The well-off and poor alike arrived in Virginia with the hope of obtaining the land and labor that would enable them to rise in the expanding economic world of the seventeenth century. The stakes and risks were both high, Breen concludes, and those who attempted to follow the Chesapeake's quick way to wealth were "adventurers"—atypically individualistic, competitive, and materialistic Englishmen with few concerns other than their own advancement.

Despite their common English background, the thousands of European men and women who migrated to Barbados, Virginia, and New England during the seventeenth century created strikingly different societies in the New World. As one historian, Thomas J. Wertenbaker, explained of Virginia, it "developed a life of its own, a life not only unlike that of England, but unique and distinct." Certainly, for anyone analyzing the founding of these colonies a major problem is accounting for the appearance of diverse social forms.

This essay examines the creation of a distinct culture in Virginia roughly between 1617 and 1630. Although early Virginians shared certain general ideas, attitudes, and norms with other English migrants, their operative values were quite different from those that shaped social and institutional behavior in places such as Massachusetts Bay. Virginia's physical environment, its extensive network of navigable rivers, its rich soil, its ability to produce large quantities of marketable tobacco, powerfully reinforced values which the first settlers carried to America. The interplay between a particular variant of Jacobean culture and a specific New World setting determined the character of Virginia's institutions, habits of personal interaction, and patterns of group behavior that persisted long after the early adventurers had died or returned to the mother country.

An ethnographic reconstruction of Virginia between 1617 and 1630 begins with an analysis of the values that the settlers carried with them to the New World. Here the distinction that social anthropologists make between "dominant" and "variant" values becomes relevant. The men and women who sailed for the Chesapeake Bay in the early seventeenth century were certainly part of a general English culture. They shared a set of views, customs, and expectations with other Jacobeans, with New Englanders and Barbadians, with those persons who remained in the mother country. Historians of colonial America have closely analyzed this common cultural background,

and there is no need to repeat their findings in detail.

From these accounts we learn that the crucial formative values transferred to Virginia were religious and political. Their constitutional heritage provided the colonials with civil and legal imperatives; their religion with a world view that structured their daily lives. Perry Miller has reminded us that the Virginians were products of the English Reformation. Both Virginians and New Englanders, he argued, were "recruited from the same type of Englishmen, pious, hard-working, middle-class, accepting literally and solemnly the tenets of Puritanism—original sin, predestination, and election—who could conceive of the society they were erecting in America *only* within a religious framework." Miller claimed that without knowledge of this theological system, the history of Virginia was no more than "a bare chronicle." Other writers, without denying the importance of Calvinistic Protestantism, have stressed the role of English legal and political precedents in shaping institutional behavior. Wesley Frank Craven explained that the Chesapeake migrants brought "their identification with the traditions of the Common Law, a decentralized system of local administration, and parliamentary usages of government for the development of the colony's political institutions."

Early Virginians undoubtedly subscribed to these general constitutional and religious values and, whenever feasible, attempted to translate them into action. Anyone who has read the colony's history knows the first settlers saw God's hand behind human affairs, marched to church to the beat of a drum, and formed a representative legislative body called the House of Burgesses. But this sort of analysis does not carry us very far in understanding why Virginia society was unlike those formed by English migrants in other parts of the New World, or why despite the presence of common dominant values various groups of settlers created distinctive patterns of social and institutional behavior.

Such problems are reduced when we realize that the early settlers in Virginia were an unusual group of Jacobeans. In no way did they represent a random sample of seventeenth-century English society or a cross section of English values. While little is known about the specific origins or backgrounds of most settlers, we do have a fairly clear idea of what sort of inducements persuaded men and women to move to Virginia. The colony's promotional literature emphasized economic opportunity, usually quick and easy riches. In his "True Relation of the State of Virginia" written in 1616, for example, John Rolfe pitied England's hard-working farmers who barely managed to make ends meet. "What happiness might they enjoy in Virginia," Rolfe mused, "where they may have ground for nothing, more than they can manure, reap more fruits and profits with half the labour." And in 1622 Peter Arundle, overlooking the colony's recent military setbacks at the hands of the Indians, assured English friends that "any laborious honest man may in a short time become rich in this Country." It was a compelling dream, one which certain Englishmen were all too willing to accept as truth. Indeed, so many persons apparently risked life and possessions in the illusive search for the main chance that John Harvey, a future Royal Governor of Virginia, begged men of integrity on both sides of the Atlantic to control "the rumors of plenty to be found at all tyme[s] in Virginia."

The lure of great wealth easily obtained held an especially strong appeal for a specific type of seventeenth-century Englishman, individuals who belonged to a distinct subculture within Jacobean society. By all accounts, early Virginia drew a disproportionately large number of street toughs, roughnecks fresh from the wars in Ireland, old soldiers looking for new glory, naive adventurers, mean-spirited sea captains, marginal persons attempting to recoup their losses. If contemporaries are to be believed, Virginia found itself burdened with "many unruly gallants packed thether by their friends to escape ill destinies." Even Sir

Thomas Dale, himself a recent veteran of English military expeditions in Holland, was shocked by the colony's settlers, "so prophane, so riotous, so full of Mutenie and treasonable Intendments" that they provided little "testimonie beside their names that they are Christians."

Even if Dale exaggerated, there is no reason to question that the colonists were highly individualistic, motivated by the hope of material gain, and in many cases, not only familiar with violence but also quite prepared to employ it to obtain their own ends in the New World. By and large, they appear to have been extremely competitive and suspicious of other men's motives. Mutiny and anarchy sometimes seemed more attractive than obeying someone else's orders. Few of the colonists showed substantial interest in creating a permanent settlement. For the adventurer, Virginia was not a new home, not a place to carry out a divine mission, but simply an area to be exploited for private gain. It was this "variant" strain of values—a sense of living only for the present or near future, a belief that the environment could and should be forced to yield quick financial returns, an assumption that everyone was looking out for number one and hence that cooperative ventures of all sorts were bound to fail—that help to account for the distinctive patterns of social and institutional behavior found in early Virginia.

The transfer of these variant values, of course, only partially explains Virginia's cultural development. The attitudes, beliefs, and ideas that the founders brought with them to the New World interacted with specific environmental conditions. The settlers' value system would certainly have withered in a physical setting that offered no natural resources capable of giving plausibility to the adventurers' original expectations. If by some chance the Virginians had landed in a cold, rocky, inhospitable country devoid of valuable marketable goods, then they would probably have given up the entire venture and like a defeated army, straggled home. That is exactly what happened in 1607 to the unfortunate men who settled in Sagadohoc, Maine, a tiny outpost that failed to produce instant wealth. Virginia almost went the way of Sagadohoc. The first decade of its history was filled with apathy and disappointment, and at several points, the entire enterprise seemed doomed. The privatistic values that the colonists had carried to Jamestown, a tough, exploitive competitive individualism were dysfunctional—even counter-productive—in an environment which offered up neither spices nor gold, neither passages to China nor a subject population easily subdued and exploited. In fact, before 1617 this value system generated only political faction and petty personal violence, things that a people struggling for survival could ill-afford.

The successful cultivation of tobacco altered the course of Virginia's cultural development. Clearly, in an economic sense, the crop saved the colony. What is less obvious but no less true, is that the discovery of a lucrative export preserved the founders' individualistic values. Suddenly, after ten years of error and failure, the adventurers' transported values were no longer at odds with their physical environment. The settlers belatedly stumbled across the payoff; the forests once so foreboding, so unpromising, could now be exploited with a reasonable expectation of quick return. By 1617 the process was well-advanced, and as one planter reported, "the streets, and all other spare places planted with Tobacco . . . The Colonie dispersed all about, planting *Tobacco.*"

The interplay between the settlers' value system and their environment involved more than economic considerations. Once a market for tobacco had been assured, people spread out along the James and York Rivers. Whenever possible, they formed what the directors of the Virginia Company called private hundreds, small plantations frequently five or more miles apart which groups of adventurers developed for their own profit. By 1619 forty-four separate patents for private plantations

had been issued, and by the early 1620's a dispersed settlement pattern, long to be a characteristic of Virginia society, was well established. The dispersion of the colony's population was a cultural phenomenon. It came about not simply because the Virginia soil was unusually well suited for growing tobacco or because its deep rivers provided easy access to the interior, but because men holding privatistic values regarded the land as an exploitable resource, and within their structure of priorities, the pursuit of private gain outranked the creation of corporate communities.

The scattering of men and women along the colony's waterways, their self-imposed isolation, obviously reduced the kind of ongoing face-to-face contacts that one associates with the villages of seventeenth-century New England. A migrant to Virginia tended to be highly competitive and to assume that other men would do unto him as he would do unto them—certainly an unpleasant prospect. Dispersion heightened this sense of suspicion. Because communication between private plantations was difficult, Virginians possessed no adequate means to distinguish the truth about their neighbors from malicious rumor, and lacking towns and well-developed voluntary organizations, without shared rituals, ceremonies, even market days, they drew increasingly distrustful of whatever lay beyond the perimeter of their own few acres.

The kind of human relationships that developed in colonial Virginia graphically reveal the effect of highly individualistic values upon social behavior. In this settlement only two meaningful social categories existed, a person was either free or dependent, either an exploiter or a resource. There was no middle ground. Those men who held positions of political and economic power treated indentured servants and slaves not as human beings, but as instruments to produce short-run profits. As a consequence of this outlook, life on the private plantations was a degrading experience for thousands of men and women who arrived in Virginia as bonded laborers. Whatever their expectations about the colony may have been before they migrated, the servants' reality consisted of poor food, meager clothing, hard work, and more often than not, early death. The leading planters showed little interest in reforming these conditions. The servants were objects, things to be gambled away in games of chance, beaten or abused, and then, replaced when they wore out.

But dependence has another side. In Virginia dominance went hand in hand with fear, for no matter how tractable, how beaten down, the servants may have appeared, both masters and laborers recognized the potential for violence inherent in such relationships. In the early 1620's several worried planters complained that Captain John Martin, a long-standing troublemaker for the Virginia Company, "hath made his owne Territory there a receptacle of Vagabonds and bankerupts & other disorderly persons." Whether the rumors of Martin's activities were accurate is not the point. In such a society a gathering of "Vagabonds" represented a grave threat, a base from which the exploited could harass their former masters. The anxiety resurfaced in 1624 when the Virginia Company lost its charter and no one in the colony knew for certain who held legitimate authority. In shrill rhetoric that over the course of a century would become a regular feature of Virginia statute books, the colony's Assembly immediately ordered that "no person within this Colonie upon the rumor of supposed change and alterations [may] presume to be disobedient to the presente Government, nor servants to theire privatt officers masters or overseers, at their utmost perills."

The distrust that permeated Virginia society poisoned political institutions. Few colonists seem to have believed that local rulers would on their own initiative work for the public good. Instead, they assumed that persons in authority would use their office for personal gain. One settler called Governor George Yeardley, a man who grew rich directing public affairs, "the right worthy statesman for his own profit." William Capps, described simply as an old planter, referred to the governor as an "old smoker" and claimed that this official had "stood for a cypher whilst the Indians stood ripping open our guts." Cynicism about the motives of the colony's leaders meant that few citizens willingly sacrificed for the good of the state. In fact, Virginia planters seem to have regarded government orders as a threat to their independence, almost as a personal affront. William Strachey, secretary of the colony, condemned what he labeled the general "want of government." He reported, "every man overvaluing his owne worth, would be a Commander: every man underprising anothers value, denied to be commanded." Other colonists expressed agreement with Strachey's views. During the famous first meeting of the House of Burgesses in 1619, the representatives of the various plantations twice commented upon the weakness of Virginia's governing institutions. Toward the end of the session, they declared that whatever laws they passed in the future should go into immediate effect without special authorization from London, "for otherwise this people . . . would in a shorte time growe so insolent, as they would shake off all government, and there would be no living among them."

The colonists' achievements in education and religion were meager. From time to time, Virginians commented upon the importance of churches and schools in their society, but little was done to transform rhetoric into reality. Church buildings were in a perpetual state of decay; ministers were poorly supported by their parishioners. An ambitious plan for a college came to nothing, and schools for younger children seem to have been nonexistent. The large distances between plantations and the pressure to keep every able-bodied person working in the fields, no doubt discouraged the development of local schools and parish churches, but the colony's dispersed settlement plan does not in itself explain the absence of these institutions. A colonywide boarding school could have been constructed in Jamestown, a Harvard of Virginia, but the colony's planters were incapable of the sustained, cooperative effort that such a project would have required. They responded to general societal needs as individuals, not as groups. Later in the seventeenth century some successful planters sent their sons at great expense to universities in England and Scotland, but not until the end of the century did the colonists found a local college.

An examination of Virginia's military policies between 1617 and 1630 provides the clearest link between social values and institutional behavior. During this important transitional period, military affairs were far better recorded than were other social activities, and the historian can trace with a fair degree of confidence how particular military decisions reflected the colonists' value system. And second, in any society military efforts reveal a people's social priorities, their willingness to sacrifice for the common good, and their attitudes toward the allocation of community resources. Certainly, in early Virginia, maintaining a strong defense should have been a major consideration. Common sense alone seemed to dictate that a group of settlers confronted with a powerful Indian confederation and foreign marauders would, in military matters at least, cooperate for their own safety. But in point of fact, our common sense was not the rule of the seventeenth-century Virginian. The obsession with private profits was a more compelling force than was the desire to create a dependable system of self-defense. This destructive individualism disgusted John Pory, at one time the colony's secretary of state. In 1620 he reported that Governor Yeardley asked the men of Jamestown "to contribute some labor to a bridge, and to certaine platformes to mounte greate ordinance upon, being both for the use and defense of the same Citty, and so of themselves; yet they repyned as much as if all their goods had bene taken from them."

Virginians paid dearly for their failure to work together. On March 22, 1622, the Indians of the region launched a coordinated attack on the scattered, poorly defended white settlements, and before the colonists could react, 347 of them had been killed. The details of this disaster are well known. The Massacre and the events of the months that followed provide rare insight into the workings of the Virginia culture. The shock of this defeat called into question previous institutional policies—not just military ones—and some colonists even saw the setback as an opportunity to reform society, to develop a new set of values.

Virginia's vulnerability revealed to some men the need to transform the privatistic culture into a more tightly knit, cooperative venture. Local rulers bravely announced that "this Massacre will prove much to the speedie advancement of the Colony and much to the benifitt of all those that shall nowe come thither." No longer would the planters live so far apart. Shortsighted dreams of tobacco fortunes would be laid aside, and the people would join together in the construction of genuine towns. And most important, the settlers would no longer evade their military responsibilities. As the members of the Virginia Council wrote only a month after the Massacre, "our first and princypall care should have beene for our safetie . . . yet its very necessarie for us yett at last, to laye a better and surer foundation for the tyme to come." But despite the death and destruction and despite the bold declarations about a new start, the colonists proceeded to repeat the very activities that contemporary commentators agreed had originally caused the people's immense suffering.

Even though the Indians remained a grave threat to security throughout the 1620's, the settlers continued to grumble about the burden of military service. Each person seemed to assess the tragedy only in personal terms—how, in other words, had the Indian Massacre affected his ability to turn a profit. By the end of the summer of 1622, there were unmistakable signs that many people no longer regarded the defeat of the Indians as a community responsibility. Few men talked of the common good; fewer still seemed prepared to sacrifice their lives or immediate earning power in order to preserve the colony from a second disaster.

Even as the governor and his council were weighing the various military alternatives, colonists were moving back to their isolated frontier plantations. The dispersion of fighting men, of course, seemed to invite new military defeats. But the danger from the Indians, although clearly perceived, was not sufficient to deter Virginians from taking up possessions which one person declared were "larger than 100 tymes their Number were able to Cultivate." In a poignant letter to his parents in England, a young servant, Richard Frethorne, captured the sense of doom that hung over the private plantations. "We are but 32 to fight against 3000 [Indians] if they should Come," he explained, "and the nighest helpe that Wee have is ten miles of us, and when the rogues overcame this place last [Martin's Hundred], they slew 80 Persons how then shall wee doe for wee lye even in their teeth, they may easily take us but that God is mercefull." Frethorne wrote this letter in March 1623, just twelve months after the Massacre had revealed to all the survivors the consequences of lying in the Indians' teeth.

The Virginia Council protested to colonial administrators in England, "It is noe smale difficultie and griefe unto us to maintaine a warr by unwillinge people, who . . . Crye out of the loss of Tyme against their Commanders, *in a warr where nothinge is to be gained.*" By contrast, the village militia in Massachusetts Bay provided an effective fighting force precisely because the soldiers trusted those persons who remained at home. In theory, at least, most New Englanders defined their lives in terms of the total community, not in terms of private advancement, and the troops had no reason to believe that their friends and neighbors would try to profit from their sacrifice. But in Virginia long before the massive enslavement of black Africans, human relationships were regarded as a matter of pounds and pence, and each day one man chased the Indi-

ans through the wilderness or helped build a fortification, another man grew richer growing tobacco. When William Capps in 1623 attempted to organize a raiding party of forty men to go against the Indians, he was greeted with excuses and procrastination. Almost in disbelief, he informed an English correspondent of the planters' train of thought, "take away one of my men, there's 2000 Plantes gone, thates 500 waight of Tobacco, yea and what shall this man doe, runne after the Indians. . . . I have perhaps 10, perhaps 15, perhaps 20, men and am able to secure my owne Plantacion; how will they doe that are fewer? let them first be Crusht alittle and then perhaps they will themselves make up the Nomber for theire own safeties." Perhaps Frethorne's anxiety grew out of the knowledge that no one beyond Martin's Hundred really cared what the Indians might do to him and his comrades.

Such foot-dragging obviously did nothing to promote colonial security. Regardless of the planters' behavior, however, Virginia leaders felt compelled to deal with the Indians. After all, these appointed officials did not want to appear incompetent before the king and his councillors. But the Virginians soon discovered that in the absence of public-spirited citizen soldiers, their range of military responses was effectively reduced to three. The governor and his council could make the business of war so lucrative that Virginians would willingly leave the tobacco fields to fight, entrust private contractors with the responsibility of defending the entire population, or persuade the king to send English troops at his own expense to protect the colonists from their Indian enemies. Unfortunately, each of these alternatives presented specific drawbacks that rendered them essentially useless as military policies.

The first option was to make the conditions of service so profitable that the planters or in their place, the planters' servants, would join in subduing the common enemy. In times of military crisis, such as the one following the Great Massacre, both Company and Crown officials tried their best to persuade the settlers that warfare was not all hardship and sacrifice—indeed, that for some men, presumably not themselves, Indian fighting could be an economic opportunity. For the majority, however, such arguments apparently rang hollow. The colonists had learned that local Indians made poor slaves, and in a spacious colony like Virginia, the offer of free land was an inadequate incentive for risking one's life. The promise of plunder drew few men away from the tobacco fields, and with typical candor, Captain John Smith announced in 1624, "I would not give twenty pound for all the pillage . . . to be got amongst the Salvages in twenty yeeres."

A second possible solution for Virginia's military needs was to hire someone to defend the colonists. The merits of this approach seemed obvious. The state could simply transfer public funds to groups of enterprising individuals who in turn might construct forts along the rivers, build palisades to ward off Indian attacks, and even in some cases, fight pitched battles along the frontier. Unlike the New Englanders, who generally regarded matters of defense as a community responsibility, much like providing churches and schools, Virginians accepted the notion that private contractors could serve as an adequate substitute for direct popular participation in military affairs.

In this belief the Virginians were mistaken. A stream of opportunists came forward with schemes that would compensate for the colony's unreliable militia. Without exception, however, these plans drained the public treasury but failed to produce lasting results. Indeed, Virginia's social values spawned a class of military adventurers—perhaps military profiteers would be a more accurate description—who did their best to transform warfare into a profitable private business.

Some of the private military schemes of the 1620's were bizarre, others humorous, almost all misallocations of public revenues. In the summer of 1622 a sea captain named Samuel Each, whose military qualifications remain obscure, offered to construct a fort of oyster shells to guard the mouth of the James River. Each's project seemed a convenient way to secure the colony's shipping from possible foreign harassment. For his work, the captain was promised a handsome reward, but as was so often to be the case in the history of seventeenth-century Virginia, the contractor disappointed the settlers' expectations. The proposed site for the fortification turned out to be under water at high tide and "at low water with everie wynd washed over by the surges." One colonist sardonically described Each's pile of sea shells as "a Castle in the aire" and suggested that the captain had wisely died on the job "to save his Credit."

During the 1620's other adventurers followed, but their performance was no more impressive than Each's had been. These men sometimes couched their proposals in rhetoric about the common good. There was no question, however, about what considerations motivated the contractors. In 1628, for example, two of the colony's most successful planters, Samuel Mathews and William Claiborne, presented the king of England with what they called "A Proposition Concerning the Winning of the Forest." They humbly informed Charles I that their plan grew "not out of any private respects, or intent to gaine to our selves, but because in our owne mindes wee perceive [?] our selves bound to expend both our lives and fortunes in so good a service for this Plantation." One may be justly skeptical about the extent of their anticipated personal sacrifice, for in the next paragraph, the two Virginians demanded 1200 pounds "in readie monye" and 100 pounds sterling every year thereafter. Governor Francis Wyatt gave the project begrudging support. He explained that because of the planters' "too much affection to their private dividents" and their unwillingness to alter their pattern of settlement in the interest of defense, Mathews and Claiborne should be encouraged to construct a fortified wall running six miles between the Charles and James Rivers. The two men promised to build a palisade and staff it with their own armed servants. There is no record of what happened to this particular plan, but if it had been accepted, the servants most likely would have spent their days planting tobacco for two men already quite wealthy.

The reliance on military adventurers held dangers of which the Virginians of the 1620's were only dimly aware. As long as the price of tobacco remained relatively high, the colonists ignored much of the waste and favoritism associated with lucrative military contracts. But high taxes caused grumbling, even serious social unrest. In the early 1620's the members of the Virginia Council reported that when it came time to reimburse Captain Each, there was "a general unwillingness (not to say an opposition) in all almost but ourselves." As tobacco profits dropped over the course of the seventeenth century, small planters and landless freemen showed an increasing hostility to private military contractors, and a major precipitant of Bacon's Rebellion was Governor William Berkeley's expensive frontier forts which appeared to do little good except for a few of the Governor's friends engaged in the Indian trade.

A second difficulty with the adventurers was no bigger than a man's hand during the 1620's. The colony needed every able-bodied defender that could be found, and no one seems to have worried much about arming indentured servants and poor freemen. But in later years, Virginians would have cause to reconsider the wisdom of creating mercenary bodies composed largely of impoverished recruits. The leading planters discovered, in fact, that one could not systematically exploit other human beings for private profit and then expect those same people to risk their lives fighting to preserve the society that tolerated such oppressive conditions. As privatism became the way of life, the colony's leading planters were less and less certain whether internal or external enemies posed a greater threat to Virginia's security.

A third possible solution to the settlement's early military needs lay in obtaining direct English assistance. During the 1620's Virginia leaders frequently petitioned the mother country for arms, men and supplies. In 1626—four years after the Massacre—the royal governor informed the Privy Council that the security of Virginia required "no less nombers then five hundred soldiers to be yearly sent over." On other occasions officials in Virginia admitted that as few as 50 or 100 troops would do, but however many men England provided, the colonists expected the king to pay the bill. Free protection would remove the necessity for high taxes. Understandably, the English administrators never found the settlers' argument persuasive, and royal policy makers may well have wondered what several thousand colonists were doing to defend themselves.

Before the 1670's not a single English soldier was dispatched to Virginia. Nevertheless, despite repeated failures in gaining English assistance, the dream of acquiring a cheap, dependable military force remained strong. Had the colony's own citizens been more involved in Virginia's defense, more willing to live closer together, there would have been no reason to plead for outside support. But the spirit of excessive individualism ironically bred a habit of dependence upon the mother country, and as soon as internal problems threatened the peace, someone was sure to call for English regulars.

Virginia's military preparedness was no more impressive in 1630 than it had been a decade earlier. The colony's rulers still complained that the planters "utterly neglected eyther to stand upon their guard or to keepe their Armes fitt." The Council admitted helplessly that "neyther proclamations nor other strict orders have remedied the same." The settlers were incorrigible. Forts remained unbuilt; the great palisade neither kept the colonists in nor the Indians out. And in 1644 the local tribes launched a second, even more deadly attack, revealing once again the fundamental weakness of Virginia's military system.

Virginia's extreme individualism was not

an ephemeral phenomenon, something associated only with the colony's founding or a peculiar boom-town atmosphere. Long after the 1620's, values originally brought to the New World by adventurers and opportunists influenced patterns of social and institutional behavior, and instead of providing Virginia with new direction or a new sense of mission, newcomers were assimilated into an established cultural system. Customs became statute law, habitual acts tradition.

The long-term effects of these values upon society are too great to be considered here. It should be noted, however, that seventeenth-century Virginians never succeeded in forming a coherent society. Despite their apparent homogeneity, they lacked cohesive group identity; they generated no positive symbols, no historical myths strong enough to overcome individual differences. As one might expect, such a social system proved extremely fragile, and throughout the seventeenth century Virginians experienced social unrest, even open rebellion.

Nor should the grand life style of the great eighteenth-century planters, the Byrds, the Carters, the Wormeleys, mislead one into thinking that their value system differed significantly from that of Virginia's early settlers. These first families of the early eighteenth century bore the same relationship to Captain John Smith and his generation as Cotton Mather and his contemporaries did to the founders of Massachusetts Bay. The apparent political tranquility of late colonial Virginia grew not out of a sense of community or new value-orientations, but out of more effective forms of human exploitation. The mass of tobacco field laborers were now black slaves, men and women who by legal definition could never become fully part of the privatistic culture. In Byrd's Virginia, voluntaristic associations remained weak; education lagged, churches stagnated, and towns never developed. The isolation of plantation life continued, and the extended visits and the elaborate balls of the period may well have served to obscure the competition that underlay planter relationships. As one anthropologist reminds us, "in a society in which everyone outside the nuclear family is immediately suspect, in which one is at every moment believed to be vulnerable to the underhanded attacks of others, reliability and trust can never be taken for granted." In the course of a century of cultural development, Virginians transformed an extreme form of individualism, a value system suited for soldiers and adventurers, into a set of regional virtues, a love of independence, an insistence upon personal liberty, a cult of manhood, and an uncompromising loyalty to family.

# 3

# THE HEART OF PERFECTION: THE CHURCH

## KENNETH A. LOCKRIDGE

The early communities of southern New England were dominated by family agriculture and the Puritan church. The English Puritans were staunch critics of the established Church of England, which they thought insufficiently reformed in structure and doctrine. Taking their beliefs from the French reformer Jean Calvin, the Puritans criticized not only the doctrines of the established church, but also its elaborate ceremonials and especially the inclusive nature of its membership. To be born English was to be born into the Church of England, to be expected to pay its tithes and fees, and to accept such ministers as the church hierarchy saw fit to appoint. Against this idea of a national church, the Puritans believed in a locally controlled church with a voluntary membership of faithful believers who elected and paid their own ministers. By the 1620s the growing number of Puritan communities became a threat to the established church as well as to Charles I's plans for an absolutist state. Under the tenure of Archbishop William Laud, the titular head of the national church, Puritan ministers and their congregations were harshly persecuted as heretics as well as enemies of the state. It was against this backdrop that over 16,000 Puritan men, women, and children uprooted themselves between 1630 and 1641 and set sail for the wilderness of New England, where they sought to create the kinds of locally oriented communities that English conditions prevented them from achieving.

In this article, Kenneth A. Lockridge recounts the private soul-searching and painstaking deliberations that led to the gathering of the village church in Dedham, Massachusetts. Above all else, he points out, the town's founding elders were concerned with assuring that church membership would be limited to those men and women who could demonstrate that they had received that gift of grace which set the "saints" apart from the unregenerate. Since church membership alone conferred social and political rights within the town, this attempt to create an exclusive church was at heart, Lockridge argues, an attempt to preserve a pure and perfect community.

"The Heart of Perfection: The Church" is reprinted from *A New England Town, the First Hundred Years, Dedham, Massachusetts, 1636–1736,* by Kenneth A. Lockridge, by permission of W. W. Norton & Company, Inc. Copyright © 1970 by W. W. Norton Company, Inc.

Dedham was not to be a theocracy. By law, the Puritan clergy could not become officers of the civil society here or elsewhere in the colony. In some ways, the local church actually came to occupy a position of isolation. A good many of the lay elders of the congregation would play no role in the leadership of the town, while the town government, though it shared control of the business affairs of the church, had so little to do with religious beliefs that references to the Lord appeared in its records only twice in fifty years.

This superficial isolation did not mean that the church was irrelevant to the life of the new community. Quite the contrary, it was in several ways central to the settlers' experience. In the first place, these Englishmen had not left their homes merely to organize their own township. John Allin, their first minister, spoke for most of them when he wrote that only "the hope of enjoying Christ in his ordinances" could have persuaded the emigrants to "forsake dearest relations, parents, brethren, sisters, Christian friends and acquaintances, overlook the dangers and difficulties of the vast seas, the thought whereof was a terror to many, and . . . go into a wilderness where we could forecast nothing but care and temptation." Even before a church was organized, this overriding concern for the implementation of true Christian faith had been written into the town Covenant, ensuring that the townsmen would be Christians in secular life as well as in church. Once the church was formed, the inhabitants of the town would assemble several times each week to hear sermons or lectures in practical piety, most of them would become members of the church, and church and town officers together would keep watch over the moral tone of the community. So, if anything, the church was to be the focus of that revived Christian spirit which had brought the settlers to America and was to illumine every aspect of their communal life.

At the same time, the church was intimately related to the community of Dedham in that both were organized around the principles of autonomy, exclusiveness, and unity. The local church emerged as an autonomous congregation whose membership excluded persons who could not prove they had received saving grace and in which the members were united by a covenant of love. Although these features were eventually expected of all churches by the religious authorities of the colony, the idea of a self-governing corporation of the saved was not just imposed from above. Founding their church in the years when the spiritual leaders of Massachusetts were still groping their way toward a definition of the true Church, the Dedham townsmen contributed to the growing insistence on what came to be called "congregationalism" and "the church of saints." Their church was organized according to their own vision of religious perfection, a vision which in this respect was very like their vision of social perfection. Both town and church partook of a common utopian form whose sources lay with yet beneath Puritan Christianity, in the Bible yet also in the ancient enduring motives of peasant communities.

\*   \*   \*

Founding a church was more difficult than founding a town. For the town, it had been enough to write down the skeletal social ordinances of the Covenant, whereupon admissions and allotments had gone forward, but months of painstaking discussion had to pass before a church covenant could be agreed upon. The basic principles were probably clear from the beginning, since they were largely the principles already written into the town Covenant. But in seeking to establish a true church the townsmen were trying to discover the exact means of salvation, a task whose implications were of the utmost importance. When it came down to the fine points of theology, their only authoritative guide was the Bible, a diffuse, obscure, sometimes contradictory book. It is no wonder that the process took time.

They began late in 1637, with a series of

meetings open to "all the inhabitants who affected church communion . . . lovingly to discourse and consult together [on] such questions as might further tend to establish a peaceable and comfortable civil society and prepare for spiritual communion." The townsmen, "being from several parts of England," sought to become "further acquainted with the tempers and gifts of one another." The meetings were held on the fifth day of every week at several houses in rotation. After the man of the house had opened proceedings with a prayer, each person asked questions or talked as he felt the need, all "humbly and with a teachable heart not with any mind of cavilling or contradicting." "Which order," wrote John Allin, "was so well observed as generally all such reasonings were very peaceable, loving and tender, much to edification." The weeks of mutual exploration probably spared them many later contentions.

"After which," Allin noted, "we proceeded to such as more properly concerned the scope of our meetings." Facing the task of gathering a church, those in attendance hammered out thirteen questions and answering propositions containing the doctrinal base of the proposed congregation. They began with a clean slate. Did they, as a collection of Christian strangers in the wilderness, have any right to assemble with the intention of establishing a church? The answer was positive. As they understood the meaning of the Bible, "the right to pray, fast, consult, and institute a church" flowed from the relation of individual believers to Christ; they did not have to be either members of or under the supervision of an existing church in order to begin a new one. Assured of the legality of their endeavor, the participants went on to list the canons of the perfect church.

The second proposition set forth the universal "duties of Christian love," these being "to exhort, admonish, privately comfort, to communicate and improve any gift . . . to relieve the wants of each other." Typically, the rule of love was placed before the complexities of doctrine. But the third question forced them to leave behind a simple fellowship of love; it asked "whether having these privileges of Christian communion [question one] and being bound by such duties [of love, question two], we may not rest in such a condition and look no further?" The reply was firm: "Negatively, we may not, but [must] seek for a further union even such as may . . . convey unto us all the ordinances of Christ's instituted worship, both because it is the command of God . . . and also because the spiritual condition of every Christian is such as stand in need of all instituted ordinances for the repair of the spirit." The Quakers would one day shrink back from this conclusion, resting content with a loving fellowship of believers, leaving to each man the details of his own worship. The Puritans were more skeptical about the ability of the individual to find a valid form of worship. Putting their faith instead in the church institutions which the Bible seemed to demand, they moved beyond.

The essential feature of "Christ's instituted worship" was spelled out in the answer to the fourth question. The church fellowship was to be restricted to "visible saints . . . agreeing to live together in spiritual communion . . . in the use of all the holy instituted ordinances . . . of the gospel." Only congregations of saints could exercise the ordinances of Christian worship, since by the word of Christ only they were pure enough. How then were visible saints to be distinguished from other men? The fifth proposition replied, "a profession of faith and holiness [and] the fruit of it as makes it visible makes a man fit matter for a visible church." God alone knew the identity of the saints, knew who had received grace and who would one day be elected to join the company of the saved. But a person's public behavior and his profession of faith—his spiritual autobiography—could serve to identify him as a visible saint, almost surely one of the elect of God. By measuring candidates' lives and experiences against their own, the members of a church could select those who were "fit matter" to join. The rest, excluded, would attend dutifully the sermons delivered in the meetinghouse, awaiting the spiritual quickening that might come to carry them past the examination and into the inner communion. The sixth proposition provided that the saints thus selected were to sign a covenant which would knit them "firmly in the bond of love . . . and a sweet communion," serving also as a contract with God for the observance of the forms ordained in the Bible.

Yet how could those present examine candidates or write a church covenant if there were among them no proven saints? To ask a neighboring congregation to select the first saints and founding members would be unthinkable, since each congregation was responsible directly to Christ for the purity of its standards. The problem was solved by asking a few likely men to "join by way of confession and profession of faith" to one another in order to assure themselves that they were suitable founders of a church. After testing each other for sainthood, these pillars of the church could then sign a covenant and judge the spiritual qualifications of applicants. "But," it was added, "the number and what persons should first join is not much material, so they be such as are living stones . . . and also be of that innocency of life as may invite others more willingly to join to them."

The remaining six questions and propositions filled in the broad spaces of this framework, listing the ordinances of the church (baptism, communion, marriage, preaching), naming its offices. At the end the faith in "brotherly love" was reaffirmed. Doctrines had been spun out with infinite care and legalistic turns of speech, but before and after all doctrine came the rules of the spirit which were to lead the way to an enduring church.

The search for doctrine having ended, the search for the "living stones" on which to found the church began. In the early Spring of 1638, ten men chosen by all present began to meet separately "after solemn invocations and humiliation . . . before the Lord, . . . to open

their conditions and declare the workings of God in their souls . . . [and to] approve or leave out as the Lord should give us to judge of every one's conditions or fitness for the work." The goal was a lengthy mutual testing of the men who had been chosen likely candidates for "soundness of grace." Each was to speak all he knew of himself or the others with neither ambition nor reticence. After "many meetings" six of the ten were found suitable, as was John Hunting, a new arrival in the town, while Edward Alleyn was considered a strong possibility. Of the remaining three, Joseph Kingsbury, still "stiff and unhumbled," and Thomas Morse, "not being able to hold forth anything that might persuade the company of a work of saving grace," agreed to suspend their candidacies for the moment.

The eight most likely submitted themselves to "a meeting or conference of the whole town," asking the inhabitants, "if they had any offences or grievances in their spirits from any of us and knew any just cause which might move us to leave out any, that now they would faithfully and plainly deal with such a one." Though there were no bruised feelings in Dedham, several men from out of town arose to complain of offenses at the hands of Edward Alleyn. His replies satisfied everyone, so all eight men gained the unqualified approval of the meeting. John Allin, Ralph Wheelock, John Luson, John Frary, Eleazer Lusher, Robert Hinsdell, John Hunting, and Edward Alleyn were the products of six months of doctrinal debate followed by six months more of intense mutual examination. A wrong step, the misreading of the Word or of a man's character, could have threatened the purity of the church. Now, in November of 1638, nearly two years after the General Court had created the new township and a year after the first exploratory meetings of the settlers, the covenant could be signed and the church instituted.

Preparations for the ceremony went forward in an atmosphere of joyful expectation. Invitations were sent out to the churches and magistrates of the colony, asking them to send representatives to see "that nothing might be done therein against the rule of the gospel." The men of Dedham had every reason to ask the "advice and counsel of the churches" and "countenance and encouragement of the magistrates," for they had been careful in searching out the rule of the gospel. They did not expect objections. In case the authorities should decide to object, Dedham reminded them that strict congregational theory meant that each congregation was responsible only to Christ, implying that any objections which were not couched as advice would be looked upon as unwarranted interference. On the chosen day John Allin read aloud the founders' profession of faith. He asked that it be criticized "faithfully and plainly." No criticism was voiced. The covenant, which included a promise "to live together . . . according to the rule of love in . . . faithful mutual helpfulness in the ways of God for the spiritual and temporal good and comfort on one another," was likewise approved by all present. The eight pillars signing the document, the church was begun at that moment.

Not even this ended the process. Though candidates for regular membership could now be heard and admitted, there were no officers. Without a minister, a teacher, or an elder there could be no preaching and no communion. Still another "tender" search began; after more months of humble discussions another ceremony followed, at which Allin was ordained as minister, John Hunting as elder, and the church was fully constituted.

So the utopian theory behind the foundation of the church proved much the same as that behind the foundation of the town; it is summarized in the words autonomy, exclusiveness, and unity. But the parallel had not been exact. In the case of the town, exclusiveness and unity were complementary virtues; strangers were kept off in order that the inhabitants might live undisturbed under the rule of love. The theory did not work that simply in the case of the church. While religious exclusiveness protected the pure church and fostered a close fellowship among the saints, it was potentially disruptive in the wider context of the town, since some of the inhabitants of the town might not meet the spiritual standard required for membership in the church. What if tension should arise between those inhabitants who were members and those who were not? The drive for perfection in the church could lead to conflict in the town! Recognizing this source of dissonance in their utopian scheme, the townsmen had taken great care to balance the exclusiveness of the church with a larger unity. They had created not only a pure church whose members were closely bound together, but also a church which the whole town had helped to create, could agree to support, would regularly attend, and perhaps could expect one day to enter. Should that day come, church and town, co-existent creations of the same impulse, would become virtually identical, no more than two aspects of one perfect Christian community.

\*　\*　\*

Harmony continued to prevail as the congregation was formed and settled into the life of the town. The inherent exclusiveness of the church was all but forgotten for the first twenty years. Admissions during this period were frequent enough to make the membership of the congregation and the town substantially the same. Seventy percent of the adult men in town in 1648 had become members, as had many of their wives; in other families wives alone were members. Eighty percent of the children born in Dedham between 1644 and 1653 were baptized, the membership of one or both parents qualifying them for the sacrament. Women joined in equal numbers with men. Servants joined their masters in the company of saints, and men of modest means mingled freely in the fellowship with men of substance. When the wife of Robert Hinsdell became "fearful and not able to speak in public, . . . fainting away there," the church refused to let the customary public examination keep out a shy saint; she was admitted on the basis of a private conference. The congregation may have preferred "tender-hearted and hopefull" Christians such as Daniel Fisher or the "tender and brokenhearted" Henry Phillips, but the proud were gathered in as well: "Jonathan Fairbanke, notwithstanding he had long stood off from the church upon some scruples about public profession of faith and the covenant, yet after divers loving conferences . . . he made such a declaration of his faith and conversion to God and profession of subjection to the ordinances of Christ in this church that he was readily and gladly received by the whole church." Even "stiff" Joseph Kingsbury was not left out; rejected as a founding member in 1638, he entered the fold in 1641. Though nonmembers were consequently rare, the town did not discriminate against them; John Haward and Samuel Morse were elected to public offices before they had joined the congregation. In view of the high rate of admissions, the townsmen may have assumed that Haward and Morse would be members soon enough.

Much of the good order of the church was attributable to John Allin, who had steered the townsmen through the complications of their search and urged on them the humility which had eased the way. His account of the process and his public writings in defense of New England Puritanism reveal that Allin valued Christian love above theological perfection. It was no accident that the sermon which his parishioners later chose to reprint as a memorial was entitled, "The Lord Jesus, His Legacy of Peace." The sermon stated the theme of Allin's career: ". . . all troubles and all dangers shall not hurt this peace, but all shall work together to the furtherance of their everlasting peace, which . . . will guard your hearts against all evil whatsoever."

While he lived, Dedham's first minister was given material proof of the respect of the town. His salary of sixty to eighty pounds yearly was a handsome sum in a society in which a total estate of 500 pounds meant wealth. On each division of public land his name was near the top of the list, his share one of the largest. More important to Allin was the fact that this generosity was entirely voluntary. Not a word about the sordid details of collections or arrears in salary could be found in the records during his tenure. Both members and nonmembers gave silently, freely, as the spirit moved them.

Fifteen years after the founding of the church, Edward Johnson remarked that the religious community in Dedham had "continued in much love and unity from their first foundation." The record bore him out. No open disputes had flared within the congregation, no one in the town had criticized the saints. Johnson's observation was included in his *Wonder Working Providence,* a breathless account of the achievements of the Puritans in New England. Considering the religious quarrels which had divided men in England, it is possible to understand why Johnson added Dedham's "love and unity" to his list of the many wonders wrought by God in the northern wilderness.

*   *   *

Despite the success in establishing harmony, it was ultimately an attachment to exclusiveness which most marked the Dedham church. Throughout the colony the second half of the seventeenth century brought challenges to the doctrine of a church of saints. Most of the men and women of the emigration had been seekers after God with their whole hearts, as their actions testified. The experience of grace had come to them often, if not easily. But what about their children, brought young to America or born there never having known the heresies and persecutions of Anglican England? Would they be so ready to feel the work of divine grace on their sinful souls? If they did not, they could not become members of the church. What would become of their children in turn, for the children of nonmembers could not even be baptized? And what would become of the Puritan Church in the colonies as fewer became members and fewer still were introduced into its traditions by baptism? As the first generation died off, the covenants would lack adherents and the Church would dwindle to a handful of saints. Along with many other communities, Dedham came face to face with this dilemma. From 1653 to 1657 only eight inhabitants were admitted to membership; none joined from 1657 to 1662. The young men and women of the second generation were coming of age but were not joining the church. They were not hostile; they simply failed to undergo the profound emotional conversion required for sainthood. By 1662 nearly half the adult men in town were not members and their numbers were growing steadily as ever more young men grew to maturity. Since their children were not eligible for baptism, the proportion of infants baptized into the church fell from eighty to forty percent. Yet, while the ministers of the colony took steps to head off disaster, the Dedham congregation clung to the church of saints.

The ministers convened a Synod in 1662. Retreating from advocacy of the pure church of saints, they created an additional "half-way" membership bound by a "half-way" covenant of its own. Under the new covenant the children of the saints could become members entitled to all ordinances except communion if they would show that they understood, believed, and would try to obey the word of God as revealed in the Bible. By avoiding the requirement of an inner experience of grace, the new membership opened the churches to the second generation and guaranteed that the third generation would be baptized. John Allin volunteered to defend the new doctrine against its conservative critics, having seen in his own town the pernicious effects of the old way. But, alas for Allin, his own congregation would not compromise its desire for perfection. The members refused to allow "half-way" members to join the saints in the church so that the Dedham church narrowed still further. The disagreement never became a dispute; Allin stayed on to the day of his death, honored if not always heeded. But there could be no

doubt that the congregation was determined to preserve the pure church that the members had so carefully constructed. Other reluctant congregations abandoned resistance in 1671, when an overwhelming majority of the town's representatives to the General Court voted support of the doctrinal authority of the clergy, but Daniel and Joshua Fisher, representatives from Dedham, dissented.

Though it never brought either the congregation or the town to open argument, the path of resistance was a hard one. A temporary reverse followed Allin's death late in 1671. Remorse and repeated refusals from ministers offered the vacant pulpit persuaded the congregation to back down. The change of heart was sincere: "We acknowledge the fault to be ours, not that of our pastor, who brought us up properly and showed the way and the word clearly and long . . . [especially the] church duty to the children of the covenant born of us and growing up with us as members of the church by divine instruction and so the proper subjects of . . . church privileges. . . . We are now under the conviction of our total neglect of the practice of this doctrine. . . . We do therefore hereby solemnly and in the fear of God . . . acknowledge all such children of the covenant . . . to be joint members of this particular visible church together with ourselves. . . . We apply and cry earnestly unto God for his spirit and grace whereby we may be all enabled to stand fast in one spirit with one mind striving together not only in faith but the order of the gospel that both may abide with us from generation to generation forever."

But the issue did not rest there. From 1685 to 1692 the church was once more without a minister. Once again likely young Harvard men were offered the pulpit and once again they refused. Late in 1691 the congregation at last put an end to all resistance: "The church of Christ in full communion . . . do now by their vote declare . . . that the declaration of the synod [of 1662] and the doctrine of their late reverend pastor is according to the mind of Christ and do resolve through his help and grace to practice accordingly." A minister was soon found and the issue never arose again.

Such enduring exclusiveness is a formidable mark of the intensity with which the men of Dedham sought perfection in their religion. The attachment to a pure church was not easily loosened by time and circumstance; fathers passed on to their sons the adherence to the old principle of membership, and the sons who did not become saints did not object to the narrowness of the church. Originally justified by Puritan ideology, the commitment to exclusiveness gained its persistence from what has been called "tribalism," the eternal desire to protect the ways of the community against the encroachment of change. Like the town, the church sprang from a thirst for perfection whose origins were deep and whose complex effects permeated every part of the common existence.

# 4

# THE SOCIAL CONTEXT OF DEMOCRACY IN MASSACHUSETTS

## MICHAEL ZUCKERMAN

During the 1950s many historians were concerned with demonstrating the colonial origins of American democracy. For them democracy and America were synonymous. The most influential work to come from these historians was Robert E. Brown's *Middle-Class Democracy and the Revolution in Massachusetts* (Ithaca, N.Y.: Cornell University Press, 1955). In his book Brown used a wide variety of sources, both quantitative and nonquantitative, to show that landownership and the suffrage that it conferred were much more broadly distributed in colonial Massachusetts than had been previously thought. From this Brown argued that colonial Massachusetts and by implication the other American colonies were democracies long before the American Revolution.

In this essay Michael Zuckerman accepts Brown's findings but argues that the extent of suffrage was by no means the most important criterion of a democratic society. For Zuckerman the more important consideration is the social context in which political participation takes place. New England towns, he argues, allowed widespread political participation, not so much from democratic principle as from the need to bring about a consensus in all public matters. This need for unanimous agreement derived, in turn, from the Puritan concept of community. The Puritan town was a convenanted community composed of religious saints whose actions were guided by the hand of God. Dissent or discord in such a community would have called into question the omniscience of God and the saintliness of the town's residents. Thus, as Zuckerman shows, the town meeting, while formally democratic, was in fact a mechanism for enforcing consent.

From *William and Mary Quarterly,* 3rd ser., 25; pp. 523–44 (1968). Reprinted by permission of Michael Zuckerman and William and Mary Quarterly.

For at least a decade now, a debate has passed through these pages on the extent of democracy in the old New England town. It began, of course, with Robert E. Brown, and it did not begin badly: Brown's work was a breath of fresh air in a stale discussion, substituting statistics for cynicism and adding figures to filiopietism. But what was begun decently has degenerated since, and findings that should have provoked larger questions have only produced quibbles and counterquibbles over methodology and quantification. The discussion has not been entirely futile—few would now maintain the old claim that the franchise was very closely confined in provincial Massachusetts—but neither has its apparent potential been realized. We are, ultimately, as far from agreement as we ever were about whether eighteenth-century Massachusetts was democratic. Somehow, the discussion has stalled at the starting point; a promising avenue of inquiry has not developed beyond its initial promise.

Perhaps a part of that failure was implicit in Brown's initial formulation of the problem; but one man cannot do everything, and Brown did advance our consideration of the New England town as far as any one man ever has. If he did not answer, or even ask, all the questions which might have been raised, other students could have done so. Brown's work made that possible. But since *Middle-Class Democracy and the Revolution in Massachusetts* (Ithaca, 1955) no comparable advances have been made. Indeed, the discussion seems to have stopped conceptually where Brown stopped, and one is forced to wonder not merely whether the right questions are being asked but whether any significant questions at all are being asked, other than those of how better to compute voting percentages. Certainly the terms of the debate have been, and are, inadequate to its resolution. Most obviously, figures on the franchise simply cannot serve to establish democracy. In our own time we have seen too many travesties on universal suffrage in too many non-democratic regimes to continue to take seriously in and of itself such an abstract calculus. Yet on both sides the discussion of New England town-meeting democracy has often assumed that the franchise is a satisfactory index of democracy, and the recourse to the seeming solidity of the voting statistics has depended, if only implicitly, upon that dubious premise.

Even those few critics who have challenged the contention that the issue of eighteenth-century democracy could be settled by counting heads have generally acquiesced in the far more fundamental assumption that in one way or another the issue of the eighteenth century was what the Browns have declared it to be: "democracy or aristocracy?" But democracy and aristocracy are probably false alternatives in any case for provincial Massachusetts; and in this case they are surely so, because they have been made initial tools of inquiry instead of end terms.

Of course, the Browns have hardly been alone in their strategy of frontal assault. On the contrary, it is indicative of how thoroughly their work established the contours of subsequent study that others have also rushed right into the issue of democracy without even a pause to ponder whether that issue was quite so readily accessible. Yet it would be admitted on most sides that democracy was hardly a value of such supreme salience to the men of provincial Massachusetts that it governed their conscious motives and aspirations; nor, after all, did it provide the framework for social structure in the towns of the province. In application to such a society, then, a concept such as democracy must always be recognized for just that: a concept of our own devising. It is not a datum that can be directly apprehended in all its immediacy; it is an abstraction—a rather elevated abstraction—which represents a covering judgment of the general tenor or tendency of social relations and institutions. As such, it can carry its own assurance of validity only if it proceeds out of, rather than precedes, analysis of the society to which it is applied. To rip it out of its social context is to risk exactly the disembodied discussion of democracy we have witnessed over the past decade.

If we would study democracy in provincial Massachusetts, we cannot plunge headlong into that issue without sacrificing the context which conferred meaning on whatever degree of democracy did exist. Since democracy was incidental to the prime purposes of provincial society, we must first confront that society. Democracy, to the extent that it existed, was no isolated element in the organization of the political community, and problems of political participation and inclusion cannot be considered apart from the entire question of the nature of the provincial community. Even if most men in eighteenth-century Massachusetts could vote, that is only the beginning, not the end, of inquiry. What, then, was the *function* of a widely extended suffrage, and what was the function of voting itself in the conduct of the community? Who specifically was admitted to the franchise, and who was denied that privilege, and on what grounds? For ultimately, if we are to understand the towns that made the Revolution in Massachusetts, we must find out not only *whether* most men could vote but also *why*.

It is particularly imperative that we place provincial democracy in its social context because nothing else can plausibly account for its development. The founders of the settlement at Massachusetts Bay came with neither an inclusive ethos nor any larger notions of middle-class democracy. In 1630 a band of true believers had entered upon the wilderness, possessed of a conviction of absolute and invincible righteousness. Their leaders, in that first generation, proudly proclaimed that they "abhorred democracy," and, as Perry Miller maintained, "theirs was not an idle boast." The spirit of the founders was set firmly against inclusion, with the very meaning of the migration dependent for many on an extension of the sphere of ecclesiastical exclusivity. The right of every church to keep out the unworthy was precisely the point of the Congregationalists' difference with the established church,

and it was a right which could not be realized in England. Yet, without any English prodding and within about a decade of the first settlements, the original ideals of exclusion had begun to break down at the local level. Until 1692 the colonial suffrage extended only to freemen, but by that time nonfreemen had been voting in town affairs for almost half a century. The ability of the settlers to sustain suffrage restrictions at the colonial level so long after they were abandoned in the towns not only indicates the incomplete coincidence of intellectual currents and local conduct in early New England but also contradicts any contention that the pressures for democratic participation derived from Puritan theology or thought. The New England Puritans were pressed to the popularization of political authority only in grudging adjustment to the exigencies of their situation.

Their situation, quite simply, was one that left them stripped of any *other* sanctions than those of the group. The sea passage had cut the new settlement off from the full force of traditional authority, so that even the maintenance of law and order had to be managed in the absence of any customarily accepted agencies for its establishment or enforcement. Furthermore, as the seventeenth century waned and settlement dispersed, the preservation of public order devolved increasingly upon the local community. What was reluctantly admitted in the seventeenth century was openly acknowledged in the eighteenth, after the arrival of the new charter: the public peace could not be entrusted to Boston, but would have to be separately secured in each town in the province. And though this devolution of effective authority to the local level resolved other difficulties, it only aggravated the problem of order, because the towns even more than the central government were without institutions and authorities sanctioned by tradition. Moreover, the towns had relatively limited instruments of enforcement, and they were demonstrably loath to use the coercive power they did possess.

Nonetheless, order was obtained in the

eighteenth-century town, and it was obtained by concord far more than by compulsion. Consensus governed the communities of provincial Massachusetts, and harmony and homogeneity were the regular—and required—realities of local life. Effective action necessitated a public opinion approaching if not attaining unanimity, and public policy was accordingly bent toward securing such unanimity. The result was, to be sure, a kind of government by common consent, but government by consent in eighteenth-century Massachusetts did not imply democracy in any more modern sense because it required far more than mere majoritarianism. Such majoritarianism implied a minority, and the towns could no more condone a competing minority by their norms and values than they could have constrained it by their police power. Neither conflict, dissent, nor any other structured pluralism ever obtained legitimacy in the towns of the Bay before the Revolution.

Thus, authority found another form in provincial Massachusetts. Its instrument was the town meeting, which was no mere forum but the essential element in the delicate equipoise of peace and propriety which governed the New England town. In the absence of any satisfactory means of traditional or institutional coercion, the recalcitrant could not be compelled to adhere to the common course of action. Therefore, the common course of action had to be so shaped as to leave none recalcitrant—that was the vital function of the New England town meeting. To oversimplify perhaps, the town meeting solved the problem of enforcement by evading it. The meeting gave institutional expression to the imperatives of peace. In the meetings consensus was reached, and individual consent and group opinion were placed in the service of social conformity. There the men of the province established their agreements on policies and places, and there they legitimized those agreements so that subsequent deviation from those accords became socially illegitimate and personally immoral as well, meaning as it did the violation of a covenant or the breaking of a promise. In

the town meetings men talked of politics, but ultimately they sought to establish moral community.

In the context of such a community, the significance of an extended franchise becomes quite clear: governance by concord and concurrence required inclusiveness. In communities in which effective enforcement depended on the moral binding of decisions upon the men who made them, it was essential that most men be parties to such decisions. Not the principled notions of the New Englanders but the stern necessities of enforcement sustained town-meeting democracy in Massachusetts. The politics of consensus made a degree of democracy functional, even made it a functional imperative. Men were allowed to vote not out of any overweening attachment to democratic principles *per se* but simply because a wide canvass was convenient, if not indeed critical, in consolidating a consensus in the community.

Under this incentive to inclusion, most towns did set their suffrage almost as liberally as Brown claimed. To seek the social context of the suffrage, then, necessitates no major quarrel with Brown's figures on franchise democracy; what it may provide is an explanation for them. It also offers the possibility of accounting for more than just the figures. As soon as we see that the high degree of participation permitted in the politics of the provincial town was not an isolated phenomenon but rather an integral aspect of the conduct of the community, we are in a position to go beyond a disembodied study of electoral eligibility and a simple celebration of middle-class democracy in Massachusetts. We are in a position to convert polemics into problems, and to press for answers.

In many communities, for example, a substantial and sometimes an overwhelming proportion of the people were *not* technically entitled to vote. Brown did not discuss some of these places, and the ones he did discuss were added to his evidence only with the special explanation that sometimes even the ineligible were admitted to the ballot box. But in the context of community such lapses would not necessarily invalidate his larger conclusions, nor would such *ad hoc* expedients be required; for the same imperatives impinged on towns where few were legally qualified as on the others, and the same results of wide political participation obtained because of the same sense that inclusiveness promoted peace while more rigorous methods threatened it. The town of Douglas, with only five qualified voters in its first years, flatly refused to be bound by a determination confined to those five, declaring its conviction "that the intent of no law can bind them to such ill consequences." Mendon, in its "infant state" in 1742, voted "to permit a considerable number of persons not qualified by law to vote . . . being induced thereto by an apprehension that it would be a means of preserving peace and unity amongst ourselves." Princeton, incorporated in 1760 with forty-three settlers but only fourteen eligible to vote according to provincial regulations, established a formal "agreement among themselves to overlook" those regulations, and the General Court upheld that agreement. "The poor freeholders" in the early days of Upton were also "allowed liberty to vote in town meeting," and it had produced "an encouraging harmony" in local affairs until 1746, when a few of the qualified voters, momentarily possessed of a majority of the ten in town, sought to upset the customary arrangements and limit the franchise as the law required. The rest of the town at once protested that "such a strenuous method of proceeding would endanger the peace of the town" and begged the General Court "to prevent the dismal damages that may follow" therefrom. The Court did exactly as it was asked, and at the new meeting the town reverted to its old form: "everyone was admitted to vote, qualified or not."

The principle which governed such universalism was not deliberate democracy; it was merely a recognition that the community could not be governed solely by the qualified voters if they were too few in number. Such a situation was most likely to occur in new communities, but it was not limited to them. Middleton had been established for almost a quarter of a century when it was conceded that in the local elections of 1752 "there was double the number of votes to the lawful voters." In a variety of towns and at other times, requirements for the franchise were also ignored and admission of the unqualified acknowledged explicitly. Thomas Hutchinson's wry lament that "anything with the appearance of a man" was allowed the vote may have been excessive, but it was not wholly fabricated. And even towns whose political procedures were more regular resorted to universalism in cases of conflict or of major issues. Fitchburg, for instance, voted in 1767 that "every freholder be a voter in Chusing of a minestr," while twenty years earlier, in a bitterly contested election in Haverhill, "there was not any list of valuation read nor any list of non-voters nor any weighting of what name or nature whatsoever by which the selectmen did pretend to show who was qualified to vote in town affairs."

The question of inclusiveness itself sometimes came before a town, not always without challenge but generally with a democratic outcome. Dudley, more than a decade after the incorporation of the town, voted "that all the freeholder of sd town should be voters by a graet majorytie and all agreed to it." In Needham in 1750 it was also "put to vote whether it be the mind of the town to allow all freeholders in town to vote for a moderator," and there too the vote carried in the affirmative. And that verdict for inclusion was not even as revealing as the method by which that verdict was reached, for in voting *whether* to include all in the election, Needham *did* include all in the procedural issue. Every man did vote on the question of whether every man was to be allowed to vote.

Of course, absolute inclusiveness never prevailed in provincial Massachusetts—women could not vote at all, and neither could anyone under 21—and property and residence qualifications, introduced in 1692, were

probably adhered to as often as they were ignored, so that even the participation of adult
males was something less than universal. It
was an important part of Brown's achievement
to show that, in general, it was not *very much*
less than universal, but, by the nature of his
research strategy, he could go no further than
that. If we are to penetrate to particulars—if we
are to ask who was excluded, and why, and
why the suffrage standards were what they
were—we must consider not only numbers
but also the conditions of community.

The men who were not allowed legitimately
to vote with their fellow townsmen were commonly tenants or the sons of voters; as Brown
discovered, it was these two groups against
which the property requirement primarily operated. But where the controversialists seek to
*excuse* these exclusions, or to magnify them, a
broader perspective allows one to *explain*
them, for against these two groups sanctions
were available that were far more effective
than those of the generalized community.
Stringent property qualifications were clearly
self-defeating in a society where consensus
was the engine of enforcement, but overly gen-
erous qualifications were equally unnecessary.
Where some men, such as tenants and dependent sons, could be privately coerced, liberal-
ity on their behalf, from the standpoint of
social control, would have meant the commission of a sin of superfluity.

Similarly, almost nothing but disadvantage
could have accrued from a loose residence
requirement enabling men not truly members
of the community to participate in its decision-
making process, since voting qualifications in
provincial Massachusetts were connected to
the concept of community, not the concept of
democracy. The extensions and contractions
of the franchise were significant to the townsmen of the eighteenth century primarily as a
means of consolidating communal consensus.
All those whose acquiescence in public action
was necessary were included, and all those
whose concurrence could be compelled otherwise or dispensed with were excluded, often

very emphatically. Sixty-six citizens of Water-
town, for example, petitioned against the al-
lowance of a single unqualified voter in a 1757
election because he was "well known to belong
to the town of Lincoln." In many towns such as
Sudbury the town clerk "very carefully warned
those that were not legally qualified not to vote
and prayed the selectmen to be very careful
and watchful that nobody voted that was not
legally qualified." Even in disputes over specific qualifications, both sides often agreed on
the principle of exclusion of the unqualified;
contention occurred only over the application
of that principle.

Consciousness of voting qualifications colored the conduct of other town affairs as well
as elections, as indeed was natural since the
meaning of the franchise went so far beyond
mere electoral democracy. Protests by men
recently arrived in a town could be discred-
ited, as they were in Haverhill in 1748, without
any reference to the justice of the protest itself,
simply by stating that "many of their petitioners are not qualified to vote in town affairs as
may be seen by the selectmen's list of voters,
and some of them were never known to reside
in town or did we ever hear of them before we
saw their petition." Similarly, in the creation
of new communities qualification for the
franchise could be crucial. Inhabitants of
Bridgewater resisted their own inclusion in a
precinct proposed by thirty-seven men dwelling in their vicinity by pointing out that "there
is not above eleven or twelve that are qualified
to vote in town meetings as the law directs."
Many towns in their corporate capacity made
much the same plea when confronted with an
appeal for separation from the community. As
Worcester once noted in such a case, more
than half the petitioners were "not voters and
one is a single Indian."

Such consciousness of qualifications sometimes appeared to be nothing more than an
insistence on a "stake in society" in order to
participate in the society's deliberations and
decisions, but the stake-in-society concept, despite its popularity in the West and its conver-

gence with certain conditions of public life in the province, was not precisely the notion which controlled those restrictions of the franchise which did persist after 1692. It was not out of any intrinsic attachment to that concept, but simply out of a fear that those without property were overly amenable to bribery or other such suasion, that the men of Massachusetts clung to their voting qualifications. As the Essex Result was to state the principle in 1778, "all the members of the state are qualified to make the election, unless they have not sufficient discretion, or are so situated as to have no wills of their own." Participation in community decisions was the prerogative of independent men, of *all* a town's independent men, but, ideally, *only* of those. Indeed, it was precisely because of their independence that they had to be accorded a vote, since only by their participation did they bind themselves to concur in the community's chosen course of action. The town meeting was an instrument for enforcement, not—at least not intentionally—a school for democracy.

This logic of competence governed the exclusion of women and children and also accounted for the antipathy to voting by tenants. The basis of the prohibitions which were insisted upon was never so much an objection to poverty *per se*—the stake-in-society argument—as to the tenant's concomitant status of dependence, the pervasive assumption of which emerged clearly in a contested election in Haverhill in 1748. There the petitioners charged that a man had been "refused as a voter under pretense that he was a tenant and so not qualified, when the full reason was that he was a tenant to one of their [the selectmen's] opposers and so at all hazards to be suppressed," while another man, a tenant to one of the selectmen themselves, had been received as a voter though "rated at much less in the last year's taxes than he whom they refused." The protest was thus directed primarily against the abuses of the selectmen: that tenants would do as their landlords desired was simply taken for granted. And naturally the same sort of assumption controlled the exclusion of sons still living with their parents. The voting age of twenty-one was the most rudimentary expression of this requirement of a will of one's own, but the legal age was not very firm at the edges. Like other laws of the province, it could not stand when it came up against local desires, and the age qualifications were often abrogated when unusual dependence or independence was demonstrable, as in the case of the eighteen-year-old who voted in a Sheffield election of 1751 because his father had died and he had become head of his family. As the town's elected representative could declare on that occasion, quite ignoring the legal age requirement, the lad "had a good right to vote, for his estate rested in him and that he was a town-born child and so was an inhabitant."

Of course, the townsmen of the eighteenth century placed no premium on independence as such. Massachusetts townsmen were expected to be independent but not too independent; ultimately, they were supposed on their own to arrive at the same actions and commitments as their neighbors. Any *genuine* independence, excessive *or* insufficient, was denigrated if not altogether denied a place in the community. Thus, when a number of inhabitants of a gore of land near Charlton faced the threat of incorporation with the town, they submitted "one word of information" about the townsmen who had asked for that incorporation. The note said only:

| | |
|---|---|
| Baptist signers | —7 |
| Churchmen | —3 |
| Tenants | —4 |
| Neither tenants nor freeholders but intruders upon other men's property | —15 |
| The whole of the petitioners in Charlton consisting of 35 in number. | |

In other words, tenants were tainted, but so too were all others who were their own men, such as squatters and those who dared to differ in religion. In denigrating them, the inhabitants of the gore drew no distinctions: tenant and Baptist were equally offensive because equally outside of orthodoxy, beyond the confines of consensus.

Ultimately almost *any* taint on membership in the homogeneous community was a potential basis for derogation. Some inhabitants of Rutland once even attempted to deny the validity of a town decision merely because many of its supporters were "such as were and are dissenters from the public worship of God in the old meeting-house." And though Rutland's religious orthodoxy was a bit exquisite even for eighteenth-century New England, it was so only in degree. For example, when Sutton opposed the erection of a new district out of parts of itself and several other towns in 1772, the town actually deducted the Anabaptists from the number of signatories to the application— Baptists simply did not count as full citizens. Worcester did the same thing and indeed went even further. Several of the signers of the petition for separation were not heads of families but mere "single persons, some of them transient ones," and so, said the town, were not to be "accounted as part of the number of families the petitioners say are within the limits of the proposed district." Whereas excessively reliable bonds confined the tenant, no reliable bonds at all attached a single man to the community, and either alternative evoked suspicion.

Ultimately, however, the insistence on orthodoxy did not directly exclude any excessive number, and neither did the property and residence requirements disqualify any great proportion of the province's adult males. In the perspective of the English villages from which the New Englanders came, these very dimensions of disqualification may be better seen, in fact, as defining a broader qualification than had previously prevailed in English practice. Far more fundamentally, the criteria of exclusion were measures of the inclusiveness of the communities of early Massachusetts.

The most fundamental shift that had occurred was the one from property to residence as the irreducible basis of town citizenship. In England, several classes of property-holders were "technically termed inhabitants even though they dwelt in another town"; property defined political citizenship, and only those who held the requisite property in the community directed its affairs. In provincial Massachusetts such stake-in-society notions never prevailed for reasons that had little to do with any abstract attachment to democracy or antipathy to absentee ownership. They never prevailed because the point of the town meeting was not so much the raising of a revenue as it was political government, especially the maintenance of law and order. In Massachusetts it was necessary to act only on the individuals living in each town, and it was imperative to act upon all of them. Of course, taxation as well as residence provided the basis for the ballot in Massachusetts, but that was of a piece with the residence requirement. As early as 1638 "every inhabitant of a town was declared liable for his proportion of the town's charges," in sharp contrast to the towns of England where only a few were so taxed.

The democracy of the Massachusetts towns was, then, a democracy despite itself, a democracy without democrats. But it was still, so far as anything yet said is concerned, a democracy, at least in the simple sense of a widely diffused franchise. Such democracy is admitted—indeed, required—in the analysis advanced above; the objection urged against the defenders of that democracy is not that they are wrong but that they are right for the wrong reasons, or for no reasons at all. When they examine electoral eligibility apart from its social setting and when they place franchise democracy at the center of provincial social organization instead of in the peripheral position it actually occupied, they do not condemn their findings to invalidity, only to sterility. They may be correct about the degree of diffusion of the vote, but they can go no further. Within their original terms, they cannot systematically study the purposes of participation, the relative importance of inclusiveness when it confronted competing values, the limits of eligibility and the reasons for them, or, more broadly, the particular texture of the electorate as against abstract statistics.

But if the analysis urged thus far has basically buttressed Brown's position by extending and explaining his statistics, that analysis also has another side. For when we see franchise democracy as a mere incident in the central quest for concord and concurrence among neighbors, we must also observe that the same concern for consensus which promoted wide participation also imposed very significant limitations on the democracy of the provincial community, limitations sufficiently serious to suggest that the democratic appellation itself may be anachronistic when applied to such a society.

For one thing, the ideal of "townsmen together" implied the power of each town to control its own affairs, and that control not only extended to but also depended upon communal control of its membership. From the founding of the first towns communities retained the right to accept only those whom they wished, and that right persisted without challenge to the time of the Revolution. "Such whose dispositions do not suit us, whose society will be hurtful to us," were simply refused admission as enemies of harmony and homogeneity. Dedham's first covenant, "to keepe of from us all such, as ar contrarye minded. And receave onely such unto us as be such as may be probably of one harte," was typical. For inhabitancy was a matter of public rather than private concern, and among the original settlers it scarcely had to be argued that "if the place of our cohabitation be our own, then no man hath right to come in to us without our consent." Consent meant the formal vote of the town or its selectmen, and none were admitted without one or the other. Not even inhabitants themselves could entertain outsiders—"strangers," they were called—without the permission of the town, and any who violated the rule were subject to penalties. And, of course, the

original thrust of congregational Puritanism to lodge disciplinary powers with the individual churches rather than with bishops also aimed at more local control of the membership of the local community.

Most of these practices continued unabated into the eighteenth century. Swansea's "foundation settlement" of 1667 provided that "if any person denied any particular in the said agreement they should not be admitted an inhabitant in said town," and half a century later seventy-eight townsmen reaffirmed their commitment to the ancestral covenant. Cotton Mather's manual of 1726, *Ratio Disciplinae Fratrum Nov-Anglorum* (Boston, 1726), described a process of "mutual Conferences" by which men came to "a good understanding" which might be subscribed to by any applicant. And even in the crisis of the dissolution of a church, as at Bellingham in 1747, the congregation could not simply disperse to the nearest convenient towns. Each of the congregants, for all that he had already met the tests of church membership and partaken of communion, had to be accepted anew into the nearby churches and approved by their towns, and in 1754 Sunderland claimed that this right of prior approval was "always customary."

Another customary instrument for the stringent control of access to the town which was also sustained throughout the provincial era was the practice of "warning out." Under this aegis, anyone who did secure entry to the town and was then deemed undesirable could be warned and, if necessary, lawfully ejected from the community. Such a policy was, in some part, a device to escape undue expenses in the support of paupers, but it was also, and more importantly, the product of the powerful communitarian assumptions of the early settlers, and those assumptions did not decline in the eighteenth century. William Weeden found the invocation of warning procedures so common that "the actual occurrences hardly need particular mention," and he concluded that "the old restrictions on the admission of freemen to the municipality, and on the sale of land to outsiders, do not appear to have been relaxed generally" as late as the era immediately preceding the imperial crisis. Town records such as Worcester's were studded with such warnings, from the time of the town's founding to the time of the Revolution itself. In other towns, too, penalties were still imposed for violation of the rules of inhabitancy.

The result was that fundamental differences in values were rarely admitted within a town, while differences of race, nationality, or culture scarcely appeared east of the Hudson River before the Revolution. Massachusetts was more nearly restricted to white Anglo-Saxon Protestants than any other province in English America, with the possible exception of its New England neighbors, Connecticut and New Hampshire. Less than 1 per cent of the quarter of a million Germans who came to the English colonies between 1690 and 1770 came to New England, and the proportion of Irish, Scotch, and Scotch-Irish was little larger. There was no welcome whatsoever for French Catholics and very little encouragement, according to Governor Bellomont, even for the Huguenots. Negroes never attained significant numbers at the Bay—by 1780 they accounted for only 2 per cent of the population of the province and a bare 1 per cent of all the Negroes in the Confederation—and the Indians, who once were significant, were on their way to extinction well before the Revolution broke out. Committed to a conception of the social order that precluded pluralism, the townsmen of Massachusetts never made a place for those who were not of their own kind. The community they desired was an enclave of common believers, and to the best of their ability they secured such a society, rooted not only in ethnic and cultural homogeneity but also in common moral and economic ideas and practices. Thus, the character of the community became a critical—and nondemocratic—condition of provincial democracy; for a wide franchise could be ventured only after a society that sought harmony had been made safe for such democracy. In that society it was possible to let

men vote precisely because so many men were not allowed entry in the first place.

Thus we can maintain the appearance of democracy only so long as we dwell on elections and elections alone, instead of the entire electoral process. As soon as we depart from that focus, the town meetings of Massachusetts fall short of any decent democratic standard. Wide participation did obtain, but it was premised on stringently controlled access to eligibility, so that open elections presupposed anterior constriction of the electorate. Similarly, most men could vote, but their voting was not designed to contribute to a decision among meaningful alternatives. The town meeting had one prime purpose, and it was not the provision of a neutral battleground for the clash of contending parties or interest groups. In fact, nothing could have been more remote from the minds of men who repeatedly affirmed, to the very end of the provincial period, that "harmony and unanimity" were what "they most heartily wish to enjoy in all their public concerns." Conflict occurred only rarely in these communities, where "prudent and amicable composition and agreement" were urged as preventives for "great and sharp disputes and contentions." When it did appear it was seen as an unnatural and undesirable deviation from the norm. Protests and contested elections almost invariably appealed to unity and concord as the values which had been violated; and in the absence of any socially sanctioned role for dissent, contention was generally surreptitious and scarcely ever sustained for long. The town meeting accordingly aimed at unanimity. Its function was the arrangement of agreement or, more often, the endorsement of agreements already arranged, and it existed for accommodation, not disputation.

Yet democracy devoid of legitimate difference, dissent, and conflict is something less than democracy; and men who are finally to vote only as their neighbors vote have something less than the full range of democratic options. Government by mutual consent may have been a step in the direction of a deeper-going democracy, but it should not be confused with the real article. Democratic consent is predicated upon legitimate choice, while the town meetings of Massachusetts in the provincial era, called as they were to reach and register accords, were still in transition from assent to such consent. The evidence for such a conclusion exists in an abundance of votes from all over the province on all manner of matters "by the free and united consent of the whole" or "by a full and Unanimous Vote that they are Easie and satisfied With What they have Done." Most men may have been eligible to vote, but their voting did not settle differences unless most men voted together. In fact, differences had no defined place in the society that voting could have settled, for that was not in the nature of town politics. Unanimity was expected ethically as well as empirically. Indeed, it was demanded as a matter of social decency, so that even the occasional cases of conflict were shaped by the canons of concord and consensus, with towns pleading for the preservation of "peace and unanimity" as "the only occasion of our petitioning."

This demand for unanimity found its ultimate expression in rather frequent denials of one of the most elementary axioms of democratic theory, the principle of majority rule. A mere majority often commanded scant authority at the local level and scarcely even certified decisions as legitimate. In communities which provided no regular place for minorities a simple majority was not necessarily sufficient to dictate social policy, and many men such as the petitioners from the old part of Berwick were prepared to say so quite explicitly. Since its settlement some eighty or ninety years earlier, that town had grown until by 1748 the inhabitants of the newer parts easily outnumbered the "ancient settlers" and wished to establish a new meetinghouse in a place which the inhabitants of the older parts conceived injurious to their interest. Those who lived in the newer parts of town had the votes, but the "ancient settlers" were icily unimpressed

nonetheless. Injury could not be justified "merely because a major vote of the town is or may be obtained to do it," the petitioners protested. They would suffer "great hurt and grievance," and "for no other reason than this: a major vote to do it, which is all the reason they have for the same." Equity, on the other hand, required a "just regard" for the old part of town and its inhabitants. They "ought" to retain their privileges despite their loss of numerical preponderance. And that principle was no mere moral fabrication of a desperate minority. Six years earlier the Massachusetts General Court had endorsed exactly the same position in a similar challenge to the prerogatives of numerical power by the "ancient part" of another town, and in the Berwick controversy the town majority itself tacitly conceded the principle upon which the old quarter depended. Accusing the old quarter of "gross misrepresentation," the rest of the town now maintained that there had been a disingenuous confusion of geography and population. There could be no question as to the physical location of the old town, but, as to its inhabitants, "the greatest part of the ancient settlers and maintainers of the ministry do live to the northward of the old meetinghouse and have always kept the same in times of difficulty and danger." The newer townsmen, then, did not deny that ancient settlers were entitled to special consideration; they simply denied that the inhabitants of the old quarter were in fact the ancient settlers.

Antiquity restricted majoritarianism elsewhere as well in demands of old settlers and in determinations of the General Court. In Lancaster as in Berwick, for example, a "standing part" could cite efforts to disrupt the old order which had been rejected by the Court as unreasonable, "and now though they have obtained a vote from the town the case still remains equally unreasonable." In other towns, too, a majority changed nothing. Consensus comprehended justice and history as well as the counting of a vote. In such a society a case could not be considered solely in its present aspects, as the original inhabitants of Lunenburg made quite clear. "What great discouragement must it needs give to any new settler," those old ones inquired,

> to begin a settlement and go through the difficulties thereof, which are well known to such as have ever engaged in such service, if when, so soon as ever they shall through the blessing of heaven upon their diligence and industry have arrived to live in some measure peaceably and comfortably, if then, after all fatigues and hardships undergone, to be cut to pieces and deprived of charter privileges and rights, and instead of peace and good harmony, contention and confusion introduced, there will be no telling what to trust to.

Nor was history the only resort for the repudiation of a majority. Other men offered other arguments, and some scarcely deigned to argue at all. In a contested election in Haverhill, for example, one side simply denied any authority at all to a majority of the moment. It was, they said, nothing but the creature of "a few designing men who have artfully drawn in the multitude and engaged them in their own cause." That, they argued, was simply "oppression." The merchants of Salem similarly refused to accept the hazards of populistic politics, though their refusal was rather more articulate. The town meeting had enacted a tax schedule more advantageous to the farmers than to themselves, and the merchants answered that they felt no force in that action, because "the major part of those who were present were [farmers], and the vote then passed was properly their vote and not the vote of the whole body of the town." That legitimacy and obligation attached only to a vote of the whole community was simply assumed by the merchants, as they sought a subtle separation of a town ballot—sheer majoritarianism— from a "vote of the whole body of the town"—a notion akin to the general will—for which the consent of every part of the population was requisite.

Disdain for direct democracy emerged even more explicitly and sweepingly in a petition from the west precinct of Bridgewater in 1738. The precinct faced the prospect of the loss of its northern part due to a town vote authorizing the northern inhabitants to seek separation as an independent town, and the precinct feared that the loss would be fatal. Accordingly, the parishioners prayed the General Court's intervention, and after briefly disputing the majority itself, the precinct allowed that, whether or not a majority in the town *had* been obtained, such a majority *could* be contrived. "We own it is easy for the two neighboring parishes joining with the petitioners to vote away our just rights and privileges and to lay heavy burdens upon us, which they would not be willing to touch with the ends of their fingers." Yet for all the formal validity of such a vote, the precinct would not have assented to it or felt it to be legitimate, "for we trust that your Excellency and Honors will not be governed by numbers but by reason and justice." Other men elsewhere urged the same argument; perhaps none caught the provincial paradox of legality without legitimacy any better than the precinct of Salem Village, soon to become the independent town of Danvers. After a recitation of the imposition it had suffered from the town of Salem for no reason but superior numbers, the village came to its indictment of the town: "we don't say but you have had a legal right to treat us so, but all judgment without mercy is tedious to the flesh."

Typically in such cases, the defense against this indictment was not an invocation of majority rights but rather a denial of having employed them oppressively. Both sides, therefore, operated upon an identical assumption. One accused the other of taking advantage of its majority, the other retorted that it had done no such thing, but neither disputed the principle that majority disregard of a minority was indefensible.

This principle was no mere pious protestation. In Kittery, for instance, the parent parish complained that the men who later became the third parish had "long kept us in very unhappy circumstances . . . counter-acting us in all our proceedings" until finally "we were obliged to come into an agreement with them for dividing the then-lower parish of Kittery into two separate parishes," yet it was conceded on both sides that the old inhabitants enjoyed an easy numerical supremacy. Had they been disposed to employ it, almost any amount of "counter-acting" could have been contained and ultimately quashed, so far as votes in public meeting were concerned. But the parish clearly did not rely upon simple majoritarian procedures. It was more than morality that made consensus imperative; it was also the incapacity for coercion without widespread consent. It was the same incapacity which shaped a hundred other accommodations and abnegations across the province, which enabled some "aggrieved brethern" in Rehoboth to force the resignation of a minister, which paralyzed the town of Upton in the relocation of its meetinghouse. "All are agreed that it should be removed or a new one built," a town petition explained, "but cannot agree upon the place." In the absence of agreement they could see no way to act at all on their own account; there was never any thought of constructing a coalition within the town or contending for a majority.

Ultimately almost every community in the province shared Upton's determination "to unite the people." Disputes, when they arose at all, were commonly concluded by "a full and amicable agreement" in which all parties "were in peace and fully satisfied," and the conflicts that did occur evoked no efforts at resolution in a majoritarian manner. "Mutual

and general advantage" was the condition of town continuance in "one entire corporate body." But that corporate ethos was something distant indeed from democracy, and electoral eligibility is, therefore, an unsatisfactory index even of political participation, let alone of any more meaningful democracy. Most men may have been able to vote in the eighteenth-century town, but the town's true politics were not transacted at the ballot box so much as at the tavern and all the other places, including the meeting itself, where men met and negotiated so that the vote might be a mere ratification, rather than a decision among significant alternatives. Alternatives were antithetical to the safe conduct of the community as it was conceived at the Bay, and so to cast a vote was only to participate in the consolidation of the community, not to make a choice among competing interests or ideals.

Accordingly, the claim for middle-class democracy in provincial Massachusetts simply cannot be sustained from the figures on electoral eligibility; relevant participation resided elsewhere than in the final, formal vote. And yet, ironically, local politics may have been democratic indeed, at least in the limited terms of political participation, since a politics of consensus required consultation with most of the inhabitants in order to assure accord. In little towns of two or three hundred adult males living in close, continuing contact, men may very well have shared widely a sense of the amenability of the political process to their own actions and attitudes, and the feeling of involvement may well have been quite general. But to find out we will have to go beyond counting heads or tallying the town treasurers' lists.

# 5

# PATTERNS OF BLACK RESISTANCE

## PETER H. WOOD

As English colonists gained a foothold on the mainland of North America and began the process of establishing permanent communities, the need for labor became increasingly acute. The small farmers of New England and the Middle Atlantic colonies needed labor to clear land, harvest crops, and maintain livestock. In the South large plantations required flocks of fieldhands to tend labor-intensive crops, such as tobacco and rice. And in the growing seaport cities labor was needed to handle a growing volume of goods, to build houses for a burgeoning population, and to augment the production of local craftsmen. During the colonial period much of this labor was supplied by indentured servants, who exchanged four to seven years of their labor for passage to America.

But by the end of the seventeenth century colonists began to turn to a new source of labor: African slaves. Slavery was not new to the Americas; Spain and Portugal had been conducting a profitable slave trade since the sixteenth century. English mainland colonists could also draw upon the experiences of their West Indian counterparts, whose sugar plantations depended on a constant supply of slaves for their operation. By the early eighteenth century southern plantation owners as well as northern artisans and merchants had turned to large-scale importations of slaves in order to maintain their tobacco and rice plantations, their shops, and their homes.

While the importance of early American slavery has long been recognized, historians have only recently turned their attention to the lives of the slaves themselves. One of the most important outcomes of this research is our growing understanding of the Afro-American response to enslavement. In this essay Peter H. Wood explores one aspect of this response, the subtle and varied ways in which slaves resisted their bondage. Slave resistance was continuous, he suggests, and took place along a continuum that ranged from collective violence at one extreme to individual acts of defiance and dissimulation on the other. While America witnessed no successful large-scale rebellions, Afro-American slaves nonetheless engaged in a continuous struggle with their owners and overseers throughout the colonial and antebellum periods.

It is by no means paradoxical that increasingly overt white controls met with increasingly forceful black resistance. The stakes for Negroes were simply rising higher and the choices becoming more hopelessly difficult. As the individual and collective tensions felt by black slaves mounted, they continued to confront the immediate daily questions of whether to accept or deny, submit or resist, remain or flee. Given their diversity of background and experience, it is not surprising that slaves responded to these pressures in a wide variety of ways. To separate their reactions into docility on the one hand and rebellion on the other, as has occasionally been done, is to underestimate the complex nature of the contradictions each Negro felt in the face of new provocations and new penalties. It is more realistic to think in terms of a spectrum of response, ranging from complete submission to total resistance, along which any given individual could be located at a given time.

As in any situation overladen with contradictory pulls, there were those few persons who could not be located on such a spectrum at all; that is, their personalities "dis-integrated" in the face of conflicting pressures—internal and external—and their responses became unpredictable even to themselves. The Negro Act of 1751 made provision for local parishes to relieve poorer masters of the cost of confining and maintaining "slaves that may become lunatic." This category of individuals is not easy to define, for mental illness, like physical illness, became an element in the incessant game of deception developing between masters and slaves; Negroes pretended outright insanity upon occasion, and owners readily called such bluffs, perhaps more frequently than they occurred. Deception aside, it is no easy matter to define rational behavior within an arbitrary social system. Certain acts of resistance such as appropriating goods and running away, usually involved prior calculation by their very nature, as did poisoning, arson, and conspiracy, which will be examined [here]. Many other actions represented impromptu responses to trying situations, but even reactions which seemed most irrational in terms of straightforward appearances and consequences rested upon a rational appraisal of the slave environment.

At one end of the spectrum of individual resistance were the extreme incidents of physical violence. There are examples of slaves who, out of desperation, fury, or premeditation, lashed out against a white despite the consequences. Jemmy, a slave of Capt. Elias Ball, was sentenced to death in 1724 "for striking and wounding one Andrew Songster." The master salvaged the slave's life and his own investment by promising to deport Jemmy forever within two months. For others who vented individual aggression there was no such reprieve. In August 1733 the *Gazette* reported tersely: "a Negro Man belonging to Thomas Fleming of Charlestown, took an Opportunity, and kill'd the Overseer with an Axe. He was hang'd for the same yesterday." An issue during 1742 noted: "Thursday last a Negro Fellow belonging to Mr. Cheesman, was brought to Town, tried, condemn'd and hang'd, for attempting to murder a white lad."

Such explosions of rage were almost always suicidal, and the mass of the Negro population cultivated strict internal constraints as a means of preservation against external white controls. (The fact that whites accepted so thoroughly the image of a carefree and heedless black personality is in part a testimony to the degree to which black slaves learned the necessity of holding other emotional responses in outward check.) This essential lesson of control, passed on from one generation to the next, was learned by early immigrants through a painful process of trial and error. Those newcomers whose resistance was most overt were perceived to be the least likely to survive, so there ensued a process of conscious or unconscious experimentation (called "seasoning" or "breaking" by the whites) in which Africans calculated the forms and degrees of resistance which were most possible.

Under constant testing, patterns of slave resistance evolved rapidly, and many of the most effective means were found to fall at the low (or invisible) end of the spectrum. For example, for those who spoke English, in whatever dialect, verbal insolence became a consistent means of resistance. Cleverly handled, it allowed slaves a way to assert themselves and downgrade their masters without committing a crime. All parties were aware of the subversive potential of words (along with styles of dress and bearing), as the thrust of the traditional term "uppity" implies, and it may be that both the black use of this approach and the white perception of it increased as tensions grew. In 1737 the Assembly debated whether the patrols should have the right "to kill any resisting or saucy Slave," and in 1741 the Clerk of the Market proposed that "if any Slave should in Time of Market behave him or herself in any insolent abusive Manner, he or she should be sent to the Work-house, and there suffer corporal Punishment."

At the same time traits of slowness, carelessness, and literal-mindedness were artfully cultivated, helping to disguise countless acts of willful subterfuge as inadvertent mistakes. To the benefit of the slave and the frustration of the historian, such subversion was always difficult to assess, yet considerable thought has now been given to these subtle forms of opposition. Three other patterns of resistance—poisoning, arson, and conspiracy—were less subtle and more damaging, and each tactic aroused white fears which sometimes far exceeded the actual threat. All three are recognized as having been methods of protest familiar in other slave colonies as well, and each is sufficiently apparent in the South Carolina sources to justify separate consideration.

African awareness of plants and their powers [was widespread], and it was plain to white colonists from an early date that certain blacks were particularly knowledgeable in this regard. In 1733 the *Gazette* published the details of a medicine for yaws, dropsy, and other distempers "for the Discovery whereof, a Negroe Man in Virginia was freed by the Government, and had a Pension of Thirty Pounds Sterling settled on him during his Life." Some of the Negroes listed by the name "Doctor" in colonial inventories had no doubt earned their titles. One South Carolina slave received his freedom and £100 per year for life from the Assembly for revealing his antidote to poison; "Caesar's Cure" was printed in the *Gazette* and appeared occasionally in local almanacs for more than thirty years.

In West Africa, the obeah-men and others with the herbal knowledge to combat poisoning could inflict poison as well, and use for this negative capability was not diminished by enslavement. In Jamaica, poisoning was a commonplace means of black resistance in the eighteenth century, and incidents were familiar on the mainland as well. At least twenty slaves were executed for poisoning in Virginia between 1772 and 1810. In South Carolina, the Rev. Richard Ludlam mentioned "secret poisonings" as early as the 1720s. The administering of poison by a slave was made a felony (alongside arson) in the colony's sweeping Negro Act of 1740. No doubt in times of general unrest many poisoning incidents involved only exaggerated fear and paranoia on the part of whites, but what made the circle so vicious was the fact that the art of poisoning was undeniably used by certain Africans as one of the most logical and lethal methods of resistance.

The year 1751 was striking in this regard. The Rev. William Cotes of Dorchester expressed discouragement about the slaves in St. George's Parish, a "horrid practice of poisoning their Masters, or those set over them, having lately prevailed among them. For this practice, 5 or 6 in our Parish have been condemned to die, altho 40 or 50 more were privy to it." In the same year the assemblymen attempted to concoct a legal antidote of their own. They passed an addition to the existing Negro Act, noting that "the detestable crime of poisoning hath of late been frequently committed by many slaves in this Province, and notwithstanding the execution of several criminals for that offence, yet it has not been sufficient to deter others from being guilty of the same." The legislation declared that any Negroes convicted of procuring, conveying, or administering poison, and any others privy to such acts, would suffer death. A £4 reward was offered to any Negro informing on others who had poison in their possession, and a strict clause was included against false informers.

Three additional clauses in the measure of 1751 suggest the seriousness with which white legislators viewed the poisoning threat. They attempted belatedly to root out longstanding Negro knowledge about, access to, and administration of medicinal drugs. It was enacted "That in case any slave shall teach or instruct another slave in the knowledge of any poisonous root, plant, herb, or other poison whatever, he or she, so offending, shall, upon conviction thereof, suffer death as a felon." The student was to receive a lesser punishment. "And to prevent, as much as may be, all slaves from attaining the knowledge of any mineral or vegetable poison," the act went on, "it shall not be lawful for any physician, apothecary or druggist, at any time hereafter, to employ any slave or slaves in the shops or places where they keep their medicines or drugs." Finally, the act provided that "no negroes or other slaves (commonly called doctors,) shall hereafter be suffered or permitted to administer any medicine, or pretended medicine, to any other slave; but at the instance or by the direction of some white person," and any Negro disobeying this clause was subject to "corporal punishment, not exceeding fifty stripes." No other law in the settlement's history imposed such a severe whipping upon a Negro.

A letter written five years later by Alexander Garden, the famous Charlestown physician, sheds further light on the subject of poisonings. The outspoken Garden was forthright in criticizing his own profession, observing to his former teacher in Edinburgh that among South Carolina's whites, "some have been actually poisoned by their slaves and hundreds [have] died by the unskilfulness of the practitioners in mismanaging acute disorders." He claimed that when local doctors confronted cases

proving both too obstinate and complicated for them, they immediately call them poisonous cases and so they screen their own ignorance, for the Friends never blame the doctors neglect or ignorance when they think that the case is poison, as they readily think that lies out of the powers of medicine. And thus the word *Poison* . . . has been as good a screen to ignorance here as ever that of *Malignancy* was in Britain.

Nevertheless, actual instances of poisoning intrigued Garden, and he put forward a scheme "To examine the nature of vegetable poisons in general." He took the association with Africa most seriously and requested from his colleague "assistance in giving me what information you could about the African Poisons, as I greatly and do still suspect that the Negroes bring their knowledge of the poisonous plants, which they use here, with them from their own country." Perhaps most conclusive of all is the fact that Garden listed explicitly as part of his plan "To investigate the nature of particular poisons (chiefly those indigenous in this province and Africa)."

But apparently neither strict legislation nor scientific observation could be effective in suppressing such resistance, for in 1761 the *Gazette* reported that "The negroes have again begun the hellish practice of poisoning." Eight years later several more instances were detected, and although the apparent "instigator of these horrid crimes,' a mulatto former slave named Dick, made good his escape, two other Negroes were publicly burned at the stake. According to the account in a special issue of the *Gazette,* Dolly, belonging to Mr. James Sands and a slave man named Liverpool were both burned alive on the workhouse green, "the former for poisoning an infant of Mr. Sands's which died some time since, and attempting to put her master out of the world the same way;

and the latter (a Negro Doctor) for furnishing the means." The woman was reported to have "made a free confession, acknowledged the justice of her punishment, and died a penitant," but the man denied his guilt until the end.

In 1770 the colony of Georgia passed a law similar to South Carolina's, but the practice was not curtailed. The Rev. Muhlenberg, living in the region in 1774, entered in his journal for October 1: "Visit from Mr. J[acob] M[ack], a neighbor of the Rev. Mr. Rabenhorst, who told me with sorrow that some time ago a household negress had given poison to Pastor Rabenhorst and his wife." The next week Muhlenberg recorded (October 10):

He also told me the circumstances of the poisoning of Mr. Rabenhorst and his wife. One evening about six weeks ago an old, sullen house negress had taken some arsenic, which she had been using to kill rats, and put it into the coffee, seeking to kill her master and mistress. As soon as Mr. Rabenhorst drank the first cup of it he became dizzy and sick and had to vomit. Mrs. R, supposing it to be caused by something else, also drank a cup, whereupon she immediately suffered the same violent effects. When the contents of the coffee-pot were examined, the poison was discovered in the grounds. They were in extreme peril of death, but by God's grace were saved by the use of powerful medicines. The negress is said to have betrayed herself by saying to the other negress [an informer?], "I thought my master and mistress would get enough, but it was not sufficient." The negress fell into the hands of the authorities, was condemned, and after several weeks burned alive.

The act of arson, highly destructive and difficult to detect, provided another peculiarly suitable means of subversion. Early in the century, with considerable forced labor being used to produce naval stores, the governor urged the Assembly "to make it ffelony without benefitt of Clergy, willfully to Sett ffire to any uncovered Tarrkiln or Pitch and Tarr in Barrells, as in like cases, ffiring Houses and Barnes." In later decades arsonists also fired stores of rice, and the Negro Act of 1740 was explicit in declaring death for "any slave, free negro, mulattoe, Indian or mustizoe, [who] shall wilfully and maliciously burn or destroy any stack of rice, corn or other grain."

Indeed, as rice production intensified, the number of barns which burned between the months of October and January (when the majority of slaves were being pressed to clean and barrel the annual crop) increased suspiciously. A telling letter to the *Gazette* in October 1732 reads:

Sir,
I Have taken Notice for Several Years past, that there has not one Winter elapsed, without one or more Barns being burnt, and two Winters since, there was no less than five. Whether it is owing to Accident, Carelessness, or Severity, I will not pretend to determine; but am afraid, chiefly to the two latter. I desire therefore, as a Friend to the Planters, that you'll insert the following Account from Pon Pon, which, I hope, will forewarn the Planters of their Danger, and make them for the future, more careful and human.

*About 3 Weeks since, Mr. James Gray work'd his Negroes late in his Barn at Night, and the next Morning before Day, hurried them out again, and when they came to it, found it burnt down to the Ground, and all that was in it.*

Several years later, just after Christmas, "the Barn of Mr. John Fairchild at Wassamsaw, with all his Crop was burnt down to the Ground," and in November 1742, "a Barn, belonging to Mr. Hume, at Goose-Creek, was burnt in the Night, and near 70 Barrels of Rice consumed."

Undoubtedly Negroes were occasionally made the scapegoats for fires which occurred by chance. The Rev. Le Jau relates vividly how a woman being burned alive on the charge of setting fire to her master's house in 1709 "protested her innocence . . . to the last." But as with accusations of poisoning, numerous

Negroes charged with burning their masters' homes had actually resorted to such sabotage. Moreover, arson could occur in conjunction with other offenses, serving to cover evidence or divert attention. Runaways sometimes resorted to setting fires, and arson was occasionally linked to crimes of violence as well. The following news item from South Carolina appeared in Ireland's *Belfast News Letter,* May 10, 1763:

*Charlestown, March 16.* A most shocking murder was committed a few weeks ago, near Orangeburg by a Negro fellow belonging to one John Meyer, who happened to come to Charlestown; the cruel wretch murdered Mrs. Meyer, her daughter, about 16 years of age, and her sucking infant; he then dressed himself in his Master's best cloaths and set fire to the house, which was burnt to the ground; three other children of Mr. Meyers made their escape and alarmed the neighbors, some of whom did not live above half a mile distant. The murderer was taken up next day and by a Jury of Magistrates and Freeholders condemned to be burnt alive at a stake which was accordingly executed. The unfortunate husband and father, we are told, is almost, if not entirely distracted by his misfortunes; it is said both he and his wife used the barbarous destroyer of their family and substance with remarkable tenderness and lenity.

It was fires within the town limits which aroused the greatest concern among white colonists, for not only were numerous lives and buildings endangered, but the prospect of subsequent disorder and vandalism by the city's enslaved residents was obvious. A fire engine was purchased by public subscription in the 1730s. But it proved of little use in 1740, when the Carolina colony, having experienced several epidemics and a series of slave conspiracies in rapid succession, added a severe fire to its "Continued Series of misfortunes." On the afternoon of Tuesday, November 18, flames broke out near the center of Charlestown, and, whipped by a northwest wind, burned out of control for six hours, consuming some three hundred houses, destroying crucial new fortifications, and causing property losses estimated at £250,000 sterling.

Even though 2 P.M. seemed an unlikely hour for slave arson, there were strong suspicions about the origin of the holocaust. Not long before, in the strained atmosphere following the Stono Uprising, a slave had been accused of setting fire to the home of Mr. Snow and had been burned to death for the crime. Officials suspected the Spanish of instigating arson by Negroes as one form of resistance, for an act passed the previous April charged the Spaniards in St. Augustine with, "encouraging thither the desertion of our Slaves and . . . exciting them to rise here in Rebellion and to commit Massacres and Assassinations and the burning of Houses in divers parts of this Province of which practices there have of late been many proof[s]."

Word of the November fire reaching northern ports was accompanied by rumors of arson and insurrection. In January a Boston paper had to print a revised account of the fire, saying the story "that the Negroes rose upon the Whites at the same Time, and that therefore it was supposed to be done by them, turns out to be a Mistake, it happening by some Accident." The story finally reaching London was that the flames were "said to have begun among some Shavings in a Saddler's Shop."

Whatever the actual cause of the fire, the white minority feared Negro violence in the aftermath of the blaze. "It is inexpressible to relate to you the dismal Scheme [scene?] . . . ," Robert Pringle wrote to his brother in London, "the best part of this Town being laid in Ashes." He blamed his "Incorrect Confus'd Scrawl" on the fact that he had hardly slept in the three days since the fire. He cited as an explanation "the great Risque we Run from an Insurrection of our Negroes which we were very apprehensive off but all as yet Quiet by the strict Guards & watch we are oblig'd to keep Constantly night & Day." In a letter the next week he mentioned that much property had been stolen and concealed, apparently by freemen and slaves alike. But large-scale disorder was prevented, and Negro labor was soon at work "pulling down the Ruins of Charles Town" and clearing away rubble for the arduous task of rebuilding.

Regardless of its true origins, the November fire could only have confirmed to slaves the effectiveness of arson. Moreover, there was word the following spring of Negro incendiaries at work in the northern colonies, supposedly with Spanish connections. On July 30, 1741, the *Gazette* contained a front-page story about a rash of barn-burnings in Hackensack, New Jersey. The next page was given over to details of an arson plot in New York City, for which nine Negroes had already been burned at the stake. The conspiracy, stated the report from New York,

was calculated, not only to ruin and destroy this City, but the whole Province, and it appears that to effect this their Design was first to burn the Fort, and if Opportunity favoured to seize and carry away the Arms in store there, then to burn the whole Town, and kill and murder all the Male Inhabitants thereof (the Females they intended to reserve for their own Use) and this to be effected by seizing their Master's Arms and a general Rising, it appears also as we are informed, that these Designs were not only carried on in this City, but had also spread into the country. . . . And so far had they gone that the particular Places to be burnt were laid out, their Captains and other Officers appointed, and their places of general Rendezvous fixed, and the Number of Negroes concern'd is almost incredible, and their barbarous Designs still more so. . . .

It may not be coincidence that within five days after these lurid reports appeared in Charlestown several slaves attempted to kindle another fire in the city. After dark a mulatto slave woman named Kate and a man named Boatswain entered Mrs. Snowden's house in Unity Alley, climbed to the roof, and placed a small bundle of straw on the shingles so that it rested under the gables of the adjoining house, belonging to Moses Mitchell and fronting on Union Street. They lit the tinder with a brand's

end, and the fire they started might have been capable "of burning down the remaining Part of the Town," had not Mrs. Mitchell, walking in her yard, spotted the blaze so promptly that it could be dowsed with several pails of drinking water.

An old Negro woman who heard one of the arsonists stumble descending the stairs testified against Kate, and within forty-eight hours she had been tried, convicted, and sentenced to die. At the eleventh hour, upon promise of pardon, Kate named Boatswain as a co-conspirator, and he in turn was sentenced to burn alive. According to the *Gazette*'s account, "On his Tryal after much Preverication and accusing many Negroes, who upon a strict Examination were found to be innocent, he confessed that none but he and *Kate* were concerned." Since Boatswain "looked upon every white Man he should meet as his declared Enemy," his prosecutors concluded that the incident stemmed from "his own sottish wicked Heart," and that there was probably no larger plot. The same people may have been somewhat less sanguine several months later, when two slaves were found guilty of attempting to set fire to the city's powder magazine.

Arson, real and suspected, remained a recurring feature in eighteenth-century South Carolina. In 1754, for example, a slave named Sacharisa was sentenced to burn at the stake for setting fire to her owner's house in Charlestown. Two years later a suspicious fire started on a town wharf in the middle of the night. In 1797 two slaves were deported and several others were hanged for conspiring to burn down the city. In some ways the protracted Charleston Fire Scare of 1825 and 1826, which came four years after the Denmark Vesey Plot, was reminiscent of the concern for arson which followed in the wake of the Stono Uprising of 1739.

While poisoning and arson rarely involved more than one or two compatriots, organized forms of resistance, which involved greater numbers (and therefore higher risks), were not unknown in the royal colony. In fact uprisings appear to have been attempted or planned repeatedly by slaves. For obvious reasons, published sources are irregular on these matters—the *South Carolina Gazette* refrained from mentioning the Stono incident, which occurred within twenty miles of Charlestown—but a number of conspiracies were recorded. In these instances it is sometimes difficult to categorize the objectives of the insurgents, since often a will to overpower the Europeans and a desire to escape from the colony were intertwined in the same plot. The province's first major conspiracy, uncovered in 1720, provides a case in point. "I am now to acquaint you," wrote a Carolina correspondent to the colony's London agent in June, "that very lately we have had a very wicked and barbarous plott of the designe of the negroes rising with a designe to destroy all the white people in the country and then to take the town in full body." He continued that through God's will "it was discovered and many of them taken prisoners and some burnt some hang'd and some banish'd." At least some participants in the scheme "thought to gett to Augustine" if they could convince a member of the Creek tribe to guide them, "but the Savanna garrison tooke the negroes up half starved and the Creeke Indians would not join them or be their pylott." A party of whites and Indians had been dispatched to "Savanna Towne," where fourteen captives were being held, and it was planned that these rebels would "be executed as soon as they came down."

This incident, or perhaps another similar one, was mentioned in an official representation sent to the king late in 1721. His majesty was informed that the "black slaves . . . have lately attempted and were very near succeeding in a new revolution, which would probably have been attended by the utter extirpation of all your Majesty's subjects in this province." Not surprisingly, the Negro Act of the following year spelled out more fully than ever the punishments to be inflicted on any slaves attempting to rebel or conspiring together or gathering up "arms, powder, bullets, or offensive weapons in order to carry on such mutiny or insurrection." A minister's letter from Goose Creek Parish in 1724 ascribed "secret poisonings and bloody insurrection" to certain Christian slaves.

Another scantily documented incident occurred in mid-August 1730. A letter written five days after the episode and published in Boston conveyed the initial shock and fatalism felt by many whites. It mentioned the prominent causes of failure in such attempts—divided leadership, insufficient recruitment, and premature discovery.

> I shall give an Account [the correspondent wrote from Charlestown] of a bloody Tragedy which was to have been executed here last Saturday night (the 15th Inst.) by the Negroes, who had conspired to Rise and destroy us, and had almost bro't it to pass: but it pleased God to appear for us, and confound their Councils. For some of them propos'd that the Negroes of every Plantation should destroy their own Masters; but others were for Rising in a Body, and giving the blow at once on surprise; and thus they differ'd. They soon made a great Body at the back of the Town, and had a great Dance, and expected the Country Negroes to come & join them; and had not an overruling Providence discovered their Intrigues, we had been all in Blood. . . . The Chief of them, with some others, is apprehended and in Irons, in order to a Tryal, and we are in Hopes to find out the whole Affair.

What few details came to light may have been embroidered with time, for it seems likely that this foiled rebellion provided the basis for the tale told during the Revolution concerning a narrowly averted "Sicilian Vespers." Although the Hessian officer, named Hinrichs, who recorded the story mistakenly placed it in 1736, the scheme he described, like the one narrated in the Boston letter, unfolded in August and involved conflicting plans for plantation murders and an attack on Charlestown. Moreover, it took the form of a large gathering several miles outside the city two days before the intended coup and ended only "when fate was merciful and betrayed the horrible plot." Since all these details conform with the letter sent to Boston, there seems little doubt that Hinrichs was referring to the incident of 1730. There is probably substance to his concluding remark that "Through torture and punishment their leaders were found out ... and ... tortured to death, while many others were subjected to severe bodily punishment."

Despite harsh reprisals, however, secret gatherings of slaves, sometimes exceeding one hundred people, were again reported within several years. In February 1733 the Assembly urged the slave patrols to special watchfulness and ordered a dozen slaves brought in for questioning, but there is no sign that any offense was uncovered. Late in 1736 a white citizen appears to have sought a reward for uncovering a Negro plot. Early in the following year the provost marshal took up three Negroes "suspected to be concerned in some Conspiracy against the Peace of this Government," and although the Assembly cleared and released the most prominent suspect, it did not deny the existence of a plot.

By September 1738 the government had completed "An Act for the further Security and better Defence of this Province" and given instructions that the two paragraphs relating to slaves were to be reprinted in the *Gazette.* The paper complied several days later by publishing the section which ordered that within a month every slaveowner in the colony was to turn in to the militia captain of his local precinct "a true and faithful List, in Writing, of all the Slaves of such Persons, or which are under their Care or Management, from the Age of 16 Years to the Age of Sixty Years." Each list was required to specify "the Names, Ages and Country of all such Slaves respectively, according to the best of the Knowledge and Belief of the Persons returning the same."

The statute imposed a heavy fine of £100 upon any master who neglected or refused to comply, so that the required local lists (if collected and sent to the governor annually as authorized) must have constituted a thorough census of the colony's adult slaves. The unlikely reappearance of even a portion of these lists would be a remarkable boon to historians, in light of the unique request for the original country of all slaves. This detail appears to bear witness to the fact that masters were generally interested and informed as to the origins of the Negroes they owned. It may also reflect the belief, commonly accepted in the Carolinas as elsewhere, that new slaves from Africa posed the greatest threat to the security of the white settlers. John Brickell explained at this time, "The Negroes that most commonly rebel, are those brought from Guinea, and who have been inured to War and Hardship all their lives; few born here, or in the other Provinces have been guilty of these vile Practices." When country-born slaves did contemplate rebellion, Brickell claimed, it was because they were urged to it by newcomers "whose Designs they have sometimes discovered to the Christians" in order to be "rewarded with their Freedom for their good Services."

The thought that newcomers from Africa were the slaves most likely to rebel does not appear to have been idle speculation, for the late 1730s, a time of conspicuous unrest, was also a time of massive importation. In fact, at no earlier or later date did recently arrived Africans (whom we might arbitrarily define as all those slave immigrants who had been in the colony less than a decade) comprise such a large proportion of South Carolina's Negro population. By 1740 the black inhabitants of the colony numbered roughly 39,000. During the preceding decade more than 20,000 slaves had been imported from Africa. Since there is little evidence that mortality was disproportionately high among newcomers, this means that by the end of the 1730s fully half of the colony's Negroes had lived in the New World less than ten years. This proportion had been growing steadily. In 1720 fewer than 5 per cent of black adults had been there less than a decade (and many of these had spent time in the West Indies); by 1730 roughly 40 per cent were such recent arrivals. Heavy importation and low natural increase sent the figure over 50 per cent by 1740, but it dropped sharply during the nearly total embargo of the next decade, and after that point the established black population was large enough so that the percentage of newcomers never rose so high again.

Each of the lowland parishes must have reflected this shift in the same way. In St. Paul's for example, where the Stono Uprising originated, there were only 1,634 slaves in 1720, the large majority of whom had been born in the province or brought there long before. By contrast, in 1742 the parish's new Anglican minister listed 3,829 "heathens and infidels" in his cure, well over 3,000 of whom must have been slaves. Of these, perhaps as many as 1,500 had been purchased in Charlestown since 1730. A predominant number of the Africans reaching the colony between 1735 and 1739 have been shown to have come from Angola, so it is likely that at the time of the Stono Uprising there were close to 1,000 residents of St. Paul's Parish who had lived in the Congo-Angola region of Africa less than ten years before. While this figure is only an estimate, it lends support to the assertion in one contemporary source that most of the conspirators in the 1739 incident were Angolans. The suggestion seems not only plausible, but even probable.

European settlers contemplating the prospects of rebellion, however, seem to have been more concerned with contacts the slaves might establish in the future than with experience that came from their past. White colonists were already beginning to subscribe to the belief that most Negro unrest was necessarily traceable to outside agitators. Like most shibboleths of the slave culture, this idea contained a kernel of truth, and it is one of the difficult tasks in considering the records of the 1730s and 1740s to separate the unreasonable fears of white Carolinians from their very justifiable concerns.

Numerous anxieties were intertwined. It was all too clear, for example, that internal and external threats to white security were likely to coincide and reinforce each other, if for no other reason than that the militia with its dual responsibilities for defense and control was divided and thereby weakened in times of trouble. Even if not linked beforehand, hostile elements inside and outside the colony could be expected to join forces during any alarm, so Europeans were as anxious about foreign infiltration as domestic conspiracy. For this reason Indians often appeared to be the slaves' likeliest allies. For example, suspicion of a Negro plot had scarcely died in 1733, when an Indian slave was brought before the Assembly. He testified "that an Indian Woman had told him that all the Indians on the Continent design'd to rise and make War, against the English." Had such word contained any substance it might have triggered slave impulses to rise against the English as well, but this particular rumor apparently lacked foundation, and the informant was dismissed.

The following spring the Assembly sent a memorial to the king, outlining the threats posed by the Indians, Spanish, and French and asking assistance in defense. This document from 1734 stressed that white colonists faced "many intestine Dangers from the great Number of Negroes" and went on to observe, "Insurrections against us have been often attempted, and would at any time prove very fatal if the French should instigate them by artfully giving them [the Negroes] an Expectation of Freedom." The next ten years were filled with enough dangers—real and imagined—from these various quarters to keep the English in a constant state of agitation. In 1748 James Glen, thinking back to this period, summarized the sea of anxieties which had beset white Carolinians:

> Sometime ago the People of this Province were Annually alarmed with accounts of intended Invasions, & even in time of profound Peace they were made believe that the Spaniards had

prepared Embarkations for that purpose at St. Augustine & the Havanna, or that the French were marching by Land from Louisiana with more Men than ever were in that Country to drive us into the Sea. Sometimes the Negroes were to rise & cut their Masters Throats at other times the Indians were confederating to destroy us.

Of the various sources of outside agitation none seemed so continually threatening after 1720 as St. Augustine, for the abduction and provocation of slaves by the Spanish were issues of constant concern. While London and Madrid were reaching a peace settlement in 1713, Charlestown and St. Augustine had renewed their agreement concerning the mutual return of runaways, but Spanish depredations continued long after the conclusion of the Yamasee War. During the 1720s Spanish ships, "stiling themselves Guarda-Costas on Pretence of searching," plundered or captured English vessels bound for southern ports. Often Africans were aboard these boats, as in the case of the sloop *Ann,* seized in 1721 coming from Barbados to South Carolina with a cargo of sugar, rum, and Negroes. The disappearance to the southward of slaves owned in South Carolina continued also. In December 1722 a committee of both Houses concerned with the return of slaves from St. Augustine urged higher rewards for taking up runaways. To guard against infiltrators who might encourage such defections, the committee also suggested that "a Law be passed to Oblige all Persons possessing Spanish Indians and Negroes to transport them off the Country." A mission sent to Florida in 1726 to confirm the agreement about returning fugitives seems to have accomplished little, for the Assembly soon received a petition from Thomas Elliott and several other planters near Stono seeking government action since they had "had fourteen Slaves Runaway to St. Augustine."

In June 1728 Acting Gov. Arthur Middleton sent a formal complaint to authorities in London that not only were the Spanish "receivie-

ing and harbouring all our Runaway Negroes," but also, "They have found out a New way of sending our own slaves against us, to Rob and Plunder us;—They are continually fitting out Partys of Indians from St. Augustine to Murder our White People, Rob our Plantations and carry off our slaves," Middleton stated, "soe that We are not only at a vast expence in Guarding our Southern Frontiers, but the Inhabitants are continually Allarmed, and have noe leizure to looke after theire Crops." The irate leader added that "The Indians they send against us are sent out in small Partys . . . and sometimes joined w[th] Negroes, and all the Mischeife they doe, is on a sudden and by surprize."

These petty incursions soon subsided. Nevertheless, rumors reached South Carolina in 1737 from the West Indies of a full-scale Spanish invasion intended, in the words of Lt. Gov. Thomas Broughton, to "unsettle the colony of Georgia, and to excite an Insurrection of the Negroes of this Province." He reported to the Lords of Trade that the militia had been alerted, "and as our Negroes are very numerous An Act of the General Assembly is passed, to establish Patrols throughout the Country to keep the Negroes in order."

The threatened assault never materialized, but in the meantime a new element was added to the situation. Late in 1733 the Spanish king issued a royal *cédula* granting liberty to Negro fugitives reaching St. Augustine from the English colonies. The edict was not immediately put into effect, and incoming slaves continued to be sold, but in March 1738 a group of these former runaways appealed successfully to the new governor for their freedom and obtained it. Seignior Don Manuel de Montiano established them on land two and a half miles north of St. Augustine at a site called the Pueblo de Gracia Real de Santa Terese de Mose, which soon became known as "Moosa." With the approval of the Council of the Indies, the governor undertook to provision this settlement of several dozen families until its first harvest and arranged for a Catholic priest to offer them instruction. He may also have urged other slaves to join them, for the captain of an English coasting schooner returning to Beaufort the following month testified that "he heard a Proclamation made at S$^t$ Augustine, that all Negroes, who did, or should hereafter, run away from the English, should be made free." As a result, according to the captain, "several Negroes who ran away thither, and were sold there, were thereupon made free, and the Purchasers lost their Money."

In November 1738 nineteen slaves belonging to Capt. Caleb Davis "and 50 other Slaves belonging to other Persons inhabiting about Port Royal ran away to the Castle of St. Augustine." Those who made it joined the Negro settlement at Moosa. It was apparently at this time that the Catholic king's edict of 1733 was published (in the words of a South Carolina report)

by Beat of Drum round the Town of St. Augustine (where many Negroes belonging to English Vessels that carried thither Supplies of Provisions &c. had the Opportunity of hearing it) promising Liberty and Protection to all Slaves that should desert thither from any of the English Colonies but more especially from this. And lest that should not prove sufficient of itself, secret Measures were taken to make it known to our Slaves in general. In Consequence of which Numbers of Slaves did from Time to Time by Land and Water desert to St. Augustine; and the better to facilitate their Escape carried off their Master's Horses, Boats &c., some of them first committing Murder; and were accordingly received and declared free.

When Capt. Davis went to St. Augustine to recover his slaves he was pointedly rebuffed, a sign for Carolina's legislature that this difficulty might grow worse in the coming year. Any premonitions which colonial officials might have felt were to prove justifiable, for the year 1739 was a tumultuous and decisive one in the evolution of South Carolina. Only the merest twist of circumstances prevented it from being remembered as a fateful turning point in the social history of the early South.

# 6

# THE SMALL CIRCLE OF DOMESTIC CONCERNS

## MARY BETH NORTON

Throughout the colonial period, American women lived their lives in a world dominated by men. Subject to the will of their fathers from birth until marriage, once married they became wards of their husbands with no legal rights of their own. Yet as Mary Beth Norton reveals in this essay, despite their subordinate status, women formed a vital and indispensable part of the family economy. Whether their fathers and husbands farmed, traded, or crafted manufactured goods, women spent their days near the household, cooking, cleaning, rearing children, making cloth and clothing, tending vegetables, and maintaining the pigs, chickens, and cows that supplemented the family diet.

But, while domestic concerns dominated the lives of all early American women, the character of their lives varied considerably depending upon their race and class as well as the region in which they lived. Thus Norton shows that while everyday life on the frontier was dominated by an unremitting round of daily and weekly chores with little chance for recreation and sociability, the markets and density of urban life permitted middling-class women a much greater measure of leisure and conviviality. Equally, while northern wives might oversee the work of an apprentice or household servant as part of her family duties, the wives of southern planters were veritable managers of a household that extended far beyond the Great House to encompass the welfare of all those who lived on the estate. Domesticity, this essay demonstrates, took many different forms in seventeenth- and eighteenth-century America.

The household, the basic unit of eighteenth-century American society, had a universally understood hierarchical structure. At the top was the man, the lord of the fireside; next came the mistress, his wife and helpmate; following her, the children, who were expected to assist the parent of their own sex; and finally, any servants or slaves, with the former taking precedence over the latter. Each family was represented in the outside world by its male head, who cast its single vote in elections and fulfilled its obligations to the community through service in the militia or public office. Within the home, the man controlled the finances, oversaw the upbringing of the children, and exercised a nominal supervision over household affairs. Married men understandably referred to all their dependents collectively as "my family," thereby expressing the proprietary attitude they so obviously felt.

The mistress of the household, as befitted her inferior position, consistently employed the less proprietary phrase "our family." Yet she, and not her husband, directed the household's day-to-day activities. Her role was domestic and private, in contrast to his public, supervisory functions. As the Marylander Samuel Purviance told his teenaged daughter Betsy in 1787, "the great Province of a Woman" was "Economy and Frugality in the management of [a] Family." Even if the household were wealthy, he stressed, "the meanest Affairs, are all and ought to be Objects of a womans cares." Purviance and his contemporaries would have concurred with the position taken in an article in Caleb Bingham's *The American Preceptor,* a textbook widely used in the early republic: "[N]eedle work, the care of domestic affairs, and a serious and retired life, is the proper function of women, and for this they were designed by Providence."

Of course, such statements applied only to whites, for no eighteenth-century white American would have contended that enslaved black women should work solely at domestic tasks. But the labor of female slaves too was affected by their sexual identity, for they were often assigned jobs that differed from those of male slaves, even though such tasks were not exclusively domestic. Appropriately, then, an analysis of black and white women's experiences in eighteenth-century America must begin with an examination of their household responsibilities.

**I**

"I have a great and longing desire to be very notable," wrote a Virginia bride in 1801, declaring her allegiance to the ideal of early American white womanhood. In this context, the adjective "notable" connoted a woman's ability to manage her household affairs skillfully and smoothly. Thus the prominent clergyman Ezra Stiles asked that his daughter be educated in such a way as to "lay a founda[tion] of a notable Woman," and a Rhode Islander wrote of a young relative that she "Sets out to be a Notable house Wife." When the Virginian Fanny Tucker Coalter exuberantly told her husband, John, "I'm the picture of bustling notability," he could have had no doubt about her meaning.

The characteristics of the notable wife were best described by Governor William Livingston of New Jersey in his essay entitled "Our Grand-Mothers," which was printed posthumously in two American magazines in the early 1790s. Decrying his female contemporaries' apparent abandonment of traditional values, Livingston presented a romanticized picture of the colonial women of the past. Such wives "placed their renown" in promoting the welfare of their families, Livingston asserted. "They were strangers to dissipation; . . . their own habitation was their delight." They not only practiced economy, thereby saving their husbands' earnings, but they also "augmented their treasure, by their industry." Most important, "they maintained good order and harmony in their empire" and "enjoyed happiness in their chimney corners," passing on these same qualities to the daughters they carefully raised to be like themselves. Their homes, in short, were "the source of their pleasure; and the foundation of their glory."

Although other accounts of the attributes of notable housewives were couched in less sentimental form, their message was the same. Ministers preaching funeral sermons for women often took as their text Proverbs 31, with its description of the virtuous woman who "looketh well to the Ways of her Household and eateth not the Bread of Idleness." So too drafters of obituaries and memorial statements emphasized the sterling housewifely talents of the women they eulogized. Such a model of female perfection did not allow a woman an independent existence: ideally, she would maintain no identity separate from that of her male-defined family and her household responsibilities. A man like James Kent, the distinguished New York lawyer, could smugly describe himself as "the independent . . . *Lord of my own fireside,"* while women, as William Livingston had declared, were expected to tend the hearth and find "happiness in their chimney corners."

These contrasting images of autonomy and subordination were translated into reality in mid-eighteenth-century American household organization. Although the mistress directed the daily life of the household, her position within the home was secondary to that of her husband. She was expected to follow his orders, and he assumed control over the family finances. In 1750, the anonymous author of *Reflections on Courtship and Marriage,* a pamphlet long erroneously attributed to Benjamin Franklin, told men that it "would be but just and prudent to inform and consult a wife" before making "very important" decisions about monetary matters, but evidence drawn from a variety of sources indicates that few colonial husbands followed this advice. Instead, they appear to have kept the reins of financial management firmly in their own hands, rarely if ever informing their wives about even the basic details of monetary transactions.

The most comprehensive evidence of this phenomenon comes from an analysis of the claims for lost property submitted by 468 white loyalist refugee women after the Revolution. The claims procedure as established by Parliament and carried out by a commission appointed for the purpose required that American loyalists prepare detailed written statements of their losses of property and testify orally about those statements. Because each claimant wanted to receive the maximum possible return on her claim, there was no reason for her to withhold any information from the commission or to feign ignorance of a particular item of property that had belonged to her family. As a result, claims prepared by female refugees, the vast majority of them widows of loyalist men, accurately depict the dimensions of the world in which they had lived prior to the war. If they had participated in economic decision making, the claims documents would demonstrate that fact by revealing their knowledge of their families' financial status. But instead the claims uniformly disclose loyalist women's insulation from the external affairs of the household and their confinement to a wholly domestic realm.

The evidence of women's ignorance of financial affairs takes a variety of forms in the claims records. Rural wives often were unable to place a precise value on tools, lands, or harvested grain, even if they knew a farm's total acreage or the size of the harvest. Urban women frequently did not know their husbands' exact income or the cost of the houses in which they lived. The typical wealthy female was not aware of her husband's net worth because she did not know the amount of his outstanding debts or what was owed to him, and poor women occasionally failed to list any value at all for their meager possessions. Women of all descriptions, moreover, shared an ignorance of legal language and an unfamiliarity with the details of transactions concerning property with which they were not personally acquainted. The sole exceptions to this rule were a few widows who had already served several years as executrices of the family estates; some wives of innkeepers, grocers, or other shopkeepers who had assisted their husbands in business; and a small number of single women who had supported themselves through their own efforts.

Loyalist husbands, then, did not normally discuss economic decisions with their wives. The women lacked exactly that information which their husbands alone could have supplied, for they were able to describe only those parts of the property with which they came into regular contact. That the practice in these loyalist homes was not atypical is shown when one looks at patriot families as well.

American wives and widows alike repeatedly noted their lack of information about their husbands' business dealings. "I don't know anything of his affairs," a Virginian resident in London wrote in 1757; "whether his income will admit of our living in the manner we do, I am a stranger to." Elizabeth Sandwith Drinker, a Philadelphia Quaker, commented years later, "I am not acquainted with the extent of my husband's great variety of engagements," quoting an apposite poem that began, "I stay much at home, and my business I mind." To such married women, their spouses' financial affairs were not of immediate import. But widows, by contrast, had to cope with the consequences of their ignorance. On his deathbed, a New England cleric surprised his wife with the news that she would have "many debts to pay that [she] knew nothing about," and her subsequent experience was replicated many times over—by the Marylander whose husband left no records to guide her administration of his estate, by the Virginian who had to tell her husband's employer that he had evidently neglected to maintain proper rent rolls, by the New Yorker who admitted to her son-in-law that she had known "very little" of her spouse's affairs before his death.

It might seem extraordinary that colonial men failed to recognize the potential benefits—to their children and their estates, if not to themselves—of keeping their wives informed about family finances. Yet the responsibility was not theirs alone. Married women rarely appear to have sought economic information from their husbands, whether in anticipation of eventual widowhood or simply out of a desire to understand the family's financial circumstances. On the contrary, women's statements reveal a complete acceptance of the division of their world into two separate, sexually defined spheres.

"Nature & Custom seems to have destined us for the more endearing & private & the Man for the more active & busy Walks of Life," remarked Elizabeth Willing Powel, a leader of Philadelphia society, in 1784. A similar sense of the character of the difference between male and female realms shone through the 1768 observation of a fellow Philadelphian of Mrs. Powel, the teenager Peggy Emlen, who described the men she saw hurrying about the city streets: they "all seem people of a great deal of business and importance, as for me I am not much of either." Men shared this same notion of the dichotomy between male public activity and female private passivity. In 1745, an essayist warned women that they were best "confined within the narrow Limits of Domestick Offices," for "when they stray beyond them, they move excentrically, and consequently without grace." A New Englander twelve years later worried that women might want "to obtain the other's Sphere of Action, & become Men," but he reassured himself that "they will again return to the wonted Paths of true Politeness, & shine most in the proper Sphere of domestick Life."

If women were accordingly out of place in the world beyond the household, so men were not entirely at home in the female realm of domestic affairs. The family property may have been "his" in wives' terminology, but at the same time the household furnishings were "hers" in the minds of their spouses. Wartime letters from American husbands confirm the separation of male and female spheres, more because of what they do not contain than as a result of what they do. When couples were separated by the Revolutionary War, men for the most part neglected to instruct their wives about the ordinary details of domestic life.

Since they initially sent explicit directions about financial affairs, their failure to concern themselves with household management would seem to indicate that they had been accustomed to leave that realm entirely to their wives. Only if they had not previously issued orders on domestic subjects would they have failed to include such directives in their correspondence.

The evidence, then, suggests that female whites shared a universal domestic experience that differentiated their world from that of men. Their lives were to a large extent defined by their familial responsibilities, but the precise character of those obligations varied according to the nature of the household in which they resided. Although demographic historians have concentrated upon determining the size of colonial households, from the standpoint of an American woman, size— within a normal range—mattered less than composition. It meant a great deal to a housewife whether she had daughters who could assist her, whether her household contained a helpful servant or a demanding elderly relative, or whether she had to contend with a resident mother-in-law for control of her own domestic affairs.

But ultimately of greater significance were differences in the wealth and location of colonial households. The chief factors that defined a white woman's domestic role arose from the family's economic status, which determined whether there would be servants or slaves, and from the household's location in a rural or urban setting. With a similarity of household roles as a basis, one can divide eighteenth-century women into four groups: poor and middling white farm women, north and south; white urban women of all social ranks; wealthy southerners who lived on plantations; and the female blacks held in bondage by those same wealthy southerners.

## II

A majority of white women in eighteenth-century America resided in poor or middling farm households, and so it is reasonable to begin a discussion of female domestic work patterns with an assessment of their experience. Their heavy responsibilities are revealed most vividly in accounts left by two city families who moved to rural areas, for farm women were so accustomed to their burdensome obligations that they rarely remarked upon them.

Christopher Marshall and his wife abandoned Philadelphia when the British occupied the city in the fall of 1777, shifting their large family to Lancaster, Pennsylvania. There Marshall marveled at his wife's accomplishments, at how "from early in the morning till late at night, she is constantly employed in the affairs of the family." She not only did the cooking, baking, washing, and ironing, all of which had been handled by servants in their Philadelphia home, but she also milked cows, made cider and cheese, and dried apples. The members of the Palmer family of Germantown, Massachusetts, had a comparable experience when they moved in 1790 to Framingham, about twenty miles west of Boston. Mary Palmer, who was then fifteen and the oldest daughter in the home, later recalled that her father had had difficulty in adjusting to the change in his womenfolk's roles. "It took years to wean him from the idea that we must be ladies," she wrote, "although he knew that we must give up all such pretensions." Mary herself thrived in the new environment. "Kind neighbors" taught her mother how to make butter and cheese, and the girls "assisted in the laborious part, keeping churn, pans, cheese-hoops and strainers nice and sweet." After she married Royall Tyler and set up housekeeping in Brattleboro, Vermont, Mary continued to practice the skills of rural housewifery she had gained as a teenager. Between managing her dairy in the summer and supervising spinning and weaving in the winter, not to mention raising five children, she observed, "I never realized what it was to have time hang heavy."

Mary Palmer's recollections disclose the seasonal nature of much of farm women's labor. Such annual rhythms and the underlying, invariable weekly routine are revealed in the work records kept by farm wives like Sarah Snell Bryant, of Cummington, Massachusetts, and Mary Cooper, of Oyster Bay, Long Island. Each week Mrs. Bryant devoted one day to washing, another to ironing, and a third at least partly to baking. On the other days she sewed, spun, and wove. In the spring she planted her garden; in the early summer she hived her bees; in the fall she made cider and dried apples; and in mid-December came hog-killing time. Mary Cooper recorded the same seasonal round of work, adding to it spring house-cleaning, a midsummer cherry harvest, and a long stretch of soapmaking, boiling "souse," rendering fat, and making candles that followed the hog butchering in December. In late 1769, after two weeks of such work, she described herself as "full of freting discontent dirty and miserabel both yesterday and today."

Unlike the laconic Mrs. Bryant, who simply noted the work she had completed each day, Mrs. Cooper frequently commented on the fatiguing nature of her life. "It has been a tiresome day it is now Bed time and I have not had won minutts rest," she wrote in November 1768. One Sunday some months later she remarked, "I hoped for some rest but I am forst to get dinner and slave hard all day long." On those rare occasions when everyone else in the household was away, Mary Cooper understandably breathed a sigh of relief. "I have the Blessing to be quite alone without any Body greate or Small," she noted in late October 1768, and five years later another such day brought thanks for "some quiate moments which I have not had in weeks."

Perhaps one of the reasons why Mrs. Cooper seemed so overworked was her obsession with cleanliness. Since travelers in rural America commented frequently upon the dirt they encountered in farmhouses and isolated taverns, it seems clear either that cleanliness was not highly valued or that farm wives, fully occupied with other tasks, simply had no time to worry about sweeping floors, airing bedding, or putting things away. Mary Cooper's experience suggests that the latter explanation

was more likely. Often describing herself as "dirty and distrest," she faithfully recorded her constant battle against filth. "We are cleaning the house and I am tired almost to death," she wrote in December 1768; the following spring, after seven straight days of cleaning, she complained, "O it has been a week of greate toile and no Comfort or piece to Body or mind." Another time she noted with satisfaction, "I have got some clean cloths on thro mercy some little done to clean the house," and again, "Up very late But I have got my Cloths Ironed." Obviously, if a farm woman was not willing to invest almost superhuman effort in the enterprise, keeping her household clean was an impossible task.

Mary Cooper's diary is unique in that it conveys explicitly what is only implicit in other farm wives' journals: a sense of drudgery and boredom. Sarah Snell Bryant would record that she had engaged in the same tasks for days on end, but she never noted her reaction to the repetition. This sameness was the quality that differentiated farm women's work from that performed by their husbands. No less physically demanding or difficult, men's tasks varied considerably from day to day and month to month. At most—during planting or harvest time, for example—men would spend two or three weeks at one job. But then they would move on to another. For a farmer, in other words, the basic cycle was yearly; for his wife, it was daily and weekly, with additional obligations superimposed seasonally. Moreover, men were able to break their work routine by making frequent trips to town or the local mill on business, or by going hunting or fishing, whereas their wives, especially if they had small children, were tied to the home.

Rural youngsters of both sexes were expected to assist their parents. "Their children are all brought up in industry, and have their time fully employed in performing the necessary duties of the house and farm," remarked a foreign visitor to a western Pennsylvania homestead in 1796. His inclusion of both sons and daughters was entirely accurate, for although historians have tended to emphasize the value of boys' labor to their fathers, extensive evidence suggests that girls were just as important as aides to their mothers. The fifteen-year-old Elizabeth Fuller, of Princeton, Massachusetts, for example, recorded occasionally baking pies, making candles, scouring floors, mincing meat for sausages, making cheese, and doing laundry, in addition to her primary assignments, spinning and weaving. Nabby and Betsy Foote, sisters who lived in Colchester, Connecticut, likewise noted helping their mother with housework, again in conjunction with their major chores of sewing, spinning, and weaving. When the parents of Ruth Henshaw, of Leicester, Massachusetts, called her home in mid-July 1789 after she had been visiting a relative for four days, saying, she recounted, that they "could not Subsist with out me any longer," they were only expressing what is evident in all these diaries: the labor of daughters, like that of wives, was crucial to the success of a farm household.

Brissot de Warville, an astute foreign traveler, recognized both the value of women's work and the clearly defined gender role distinctions visible in rural life in his observations upon a fellow Frenchman's Pennsylvania farm in 1788. It is a "great disadvantage," Brissot remarked, that "he does not have any poultry or pigeons and makes no cheese; nor does he have any spinning done or collect goose feathers." The reason: he was a bachelor, and "these domestic farm industries . . . can be carried on well only by women." Brissot's friend had two women indentured servants, so he did not lack female labor as such; what was missing was a wife or daughters to supervise the servants. Significantly, neither he nor Brissot seems to have considered the possibility that he could himself keep poultry or learn enough about cheesemaking to direct the servants. That was clearly "woman's work," and if there was no woman present, such work was not done, no matter how pressing the need or how great the resulting loss of potential income.

Yet in some frontier areas the gender role divisions so apparent in more settled regions did blur, although they did not break down entirely. Farmers' wives and daughters occasionally worked in the fields, especially at harvest time. Travelers from the East were unaccustomed to the sight of white female fieldworkers and wrote about it at length. In 1778, for example, a doctor from Dorchester, Massachusetts, told his wife in some amazement that he had seen Pennsylvania German women "at work abroad on the Farm mowing, Hoeing, Loading Dung into a Cart." A New Hampshire farmer, by contrast, matter-of-factly recorded in his diary his use of female relatives and neighbors for field work. In that same colony in the early 1760s the pendulum swung the other way, and men helped with women's work. In the winters, recalled one woman many years later, "the boys did as much Knitting as the Girls, and the men and boys also did the milking to spare the women."

Backcountry women had to cope with a far more rough-and-ready existence than did their counterparts to the east and south. The log cabins in which many of them lived were crudely built and largely open to the elements. Even the few amenities that brightened the lives of their poor contemporaries in areas of denser settlement were denied them; the Reverend Charles Woodmason, an Anglican missionary in western South Carolina, commented in 1768 that "in many Places they have nought but a Gourd to drink out off Not a Plate Knife or Spoon, a Glass, Cup, or any thing—It is well if they can get some Body Linen, and some have not even that." Later in the century, one woman on the Ohio frontier, lacking a churn, was reduced to making butter by stirring cream with her hand in an ordinary pail. Under such circumstances, simple subsistence would require most of a woman's energies.

How, then, did frontier women react to these primitive conditions? At least one group of pioneer men termed their wives "the greatest of Heroines," suggesting that they bore such hardships without complaint, but other evidence indicates that some women, especially those raised in genteel households, did not adapt readily to their new lives. Many, like a Pennsylvanian, must have vetoed their husbands' plans to move west because of an unwillingness to exchange a civilized life for a residence in "what she deems a Wilderness." Others must have resembled the Shenandoah Valley woman, a mother of eight, who descended into invalidism shortly after her husband moved her and their children to what their son described as a "valuable Farm but with a small indifferent house . . . & almost intirely in woods." Perhaps, like a female traveler in the west, the Virginian "felt oppress'd with so much wood towering above . . . in every direction and such a continuance of it." This was not a unique reaction: a Scottish immigrant, faced with his wife's similar response to the first sight of their new home, comforted her by promising, "[W]e would get all these trees cut down . . . [so] that we would see from house to house."

At least in this case the husband knew of his wife's discontent and reacted to it. In other instances, the lack of communication between spouses resulting from their divergent roles appears to have been heightened on the frontier, as wives deliberately concealed their unhappiness from their husbands, revealing their true feelings only to female relatives. Mary Hooper Spence, who described herself as having been beset by "misfortunes" ever since the day of her marriage, lived with her husband on the "dreary & cold" island of St. Johns (now Prince Edward Island) in the 1770s. In letters to her mother in Boston she repeatedly told of her loneliness and depression, of how she found a primitive, isolated existence "hard to bear." By contrast, her husband characterized their life as "happy" and reported to a relative that they were "comfortably" settled. Likewise, Mrs. Joseph Gilman, said by her husband to be pleased with living in the new settlement of Marietta, Ohio, in 1789, later recounted that on many occasions while milking their cows she would think of her New England home, "sob and cry as loud as a child, and then wipe her tears and appear before her husband as cheerful as if she had nothing to give her pain."

To point out the apparent dissatisfaction of many frontier women with their lives in the wilderness is not to say that they and others did not cope successfully with the trials they encountered. To cite just one example: Mrs. Hutchens, a Mississippi woman whose husband was kidnapped and whose slaves were stolen, pulled her family together in the face of adversity almost by sheer force of will alone. Her son subsequently recalled that she had told her children they could survive if they were willing to work. Accordingly, she and her three sons cultivated the fields while her daughters did the housework, spun cotton, and wove the fabric for their clothing. By the time her husband returned seven years later, she had prospered sufficiently to be able to replace all the slaves taken by the robbers.

The fact that Mrs. Hutchens put her daughters to work spinning and weaving is significant, for no household task was more time-consuming or more symbolic of the female role than spinning. It was, furthermore, a task quintessentially performed by young, single women; hence, the use of the word "spinster" to mean an unmarried female and the phrase "the distaff side" to refer to women in general. Farm wives, and especially their daughters, spent a large proportion of their time, particularly in the winter months, bending over a flax wheel or loom, or walking beside a great wheel, spinning wool. No examination of the domestic sphere can be complete without detailed attention to this aspect of household work.

Before 1765 and the subsequent rise in home manufacturing caused by colonial boycotts of British goods, spinning and weaving as ordinary chores were largely confined to rural areas of the northern and middle colonies and the backcountry South. Planters and even middling farmers who lived along the southeastern coast and city residents throughout America could usually purchase English cloth more cheaply than they could manufacture it at home, and so they bought fabric rather than asking their wives, daughters, or female slaves to spend the requisite amount of time to produce it. But rural women outside the plantation South spent much of their lives spinning. They began as girls, helping their mothers; they continued after their marriages, until their own daughters were old enough to remove most of the burden from their shoulders; and they often returned to it in old age or widowhood, as a means of supporting themselves or making use of their time. Not all farm women learned weaving, a skill open to men as well, but spinning was a nearly universal occupation among them.

Rural girls understood at an early age that spinning was "a very proper accomplishment for a farmers daughter," as the New Jersey Quaker Susanna Dillwyn put it in 1790. Susanna's niece Hannah Cox began trying to spin on an "old wheel which was in the house" when she was only seven, so her mother bought her a little new wheel, upon which Hannah soon learned to spin "very prettily." Similarly, the tutor on Robert Carter's Virginia plantation observed that his small pupils would tie "a String to a Chair & then run buzzing back to imitate the Girls spinning." Such playful fascination with the process of cloth production later turned for many girls into monotonous daily labor at wheels or looms during the months between December and May. The normal output of an experienced spinner who carded the wool herself was four skeins a day, or six if an assistant carded for her. Teenaged girls like Elizabeth Fuller, who were less practiced than their mothers, produced on the average two or three skeins a day. After a long stint of spinning tow (short coarse linen fibers) in January and February 1792, Elizabeth exploded in her diary, "I should think I might have spun up all the Swingling Tow in America by this time." Later that same year, she switched to weaving, at last completing her annual allotment on June 1. In three months she had woven 176 yards of cloth, she recorded, happily inscribing in her journal, "Welcome sweet Liberty, once more to me. How have I longed to meet again with thee."

But clothwork, which could be a lonely and confining occupation, as Elizabeth Fuller learned, could also be an occasion for socializing. Rural girls sometimes attended "spinning frolics" or quilting bees, many of which lasted for several days and ended with dancing. Even more frequently farm women "changed work," trading skills with others experienced in different tasks. Mary Palmer recalled that after her family moved to Framingham her mother would change work with other women in the area, "knitting and sewing for them while they would weave cotton and flax into cloth" for her, since as a city dweller she had never learned that skill. In a similar way Ruth Henshaw and her mother repaid Lydia Hawkins, who warped their loom for them, by helping her quilt or making her a pair of stays. Ruth regularly exchanged chores with girls of her own age as well; in December 1789, for example, she noted, "Sally here Spining Changeing works with Me," while ten days later she was at Sally's house, carding for her.

From such trading of labor farm women could easily move on to work for pay. By 1775 Betsy and Nabby Foote had taken that step. Nabby, like Lydia Hawkins of Leicester, specialized in warping webs and making loom harnesses; her sister Betsy worked in all phases of cloth production, carding wool, hatcheling flax, and spinning, as well as doing sewing and mending for neighbors. In the rural North and South alike white women spun, wove, and sold butter, cheese, and soap to their neighbors, participating on a small scale in the market economy long before the establishment of textile factories in New England and the consequent introduction of widespread wage labor for young northern women.

Given the significance of spinning in women's lives, it is not surprising that American men and women made that occupation the major symbol of femininity. William Livingston had declared that "country girls . . . ought to be at their spinning-wheels," and when Benjamin Franklin sought a wedding present for his sister Jane, he decided on a spinning wheel instead of a tea table, concluding that "the character of a good housewife was far preferable to that of being only a pretty gentlewoman."

Compelling evidence of the link between spinning and the female role in the eighteenth-century American mind comes from the observations of two visitors to Indian villages. Confronted by societies in which women did not spin but instead cultivated crops while their husbands hunted and fished, both the whites perceived Indian sex roles as improper and sought to correct them by introducing the feminine task of spinning. Benjamin Hawkins, United States agent for the Creek tribe, admired the industrious Creek women and encouraged them to learn to spin and weave. This step, he believed, would lead to a realignment of sex roles along proper lines, because the women would be freed from dependence upon their hunter husbands for clothing, and they would also no longer have time to work on the crops. The men in turn would therefore be "obliged to handle the ax & the plough, and assist the women in the laborious task of the fields." A similar scheme was promoted by the Quaker woman Anne Emlen Mifflin, who traveled in the Seneca country as a missionary in 1803. Men should work in agriculture, she told her Indian audience, so that women would be able to learn spinning and dairy management, which were "branches suited to our sex," as opposed to "drudging alone in the labors of the field."

As Mifflin's comment shows, women, too, found spinning a necessary component of femininity, a fact best illustrated by reference to Elizabeth Graeme Fergusson's poem "The Contemplative Spinner." In 1792, Mrs. Fergusson, one of the leaders of intellectual life in republican Philadelphia, composed a poem in which she compared her spinning wheel to a wheel of fortune, leading her to a series of observations on life, death, and religion. But the wheel did more: it also reminded her of other women, linking her inextricably to "a train of Female Hands/Chearful uniting in Industrious Bands." And so, she wrote:

*In such Reflections I oft passed the Night,*
*When by my Papas solitary Light*
*My Wheel I turned, and thought how others*
*   toild*
*To earn a morsel for a famishd Child.*

To Elizabeth Graeme Fergusson, spinning symbolized her tie to the female sisterhood, just as to Benjamin Hawkins and other eighteenth-century men that occupation above all somehow appertained to femininity. It is consequently ironic that the one factor that differentiated the lives of urban women most sharply from those of their rural counterparts was the fact that they did not have to engage in cloth production. Women who had access to stores saw no point in spending hour after tedious hour at the wheel or loom. Not, at least, until doing so came to have political significance in the late 1760s, as Americans increasingly tried to end their dependence on British manufactured goods.

## III

Although urban women did not have to spin and weave, the absence of that time-consuming occupation did not turn their lives into leisured ones. Too often historians have been misled by the lack of lengthy work entries in urban women's diaries, concluding therefrom that city "ladies" contributed little or nothing to the family welfare. Admittedly, white urban women of even moderate means worked shorter hours and at less physically demanding tasks than did their rural counterparts, but this did not mean that their households ran themselves. Women still had the responsibility for food preparation, which often included cultivating a garden and raising poultry. The wives of artisans and shopkeepers also occasionally assisted their husbands in business. Furthermore, their homes were held to higher standards of cleanliness—by themselves and by their female friends—than were the homes of farm women like Mary Cooper. Even if they could afford to hire servants, they frequently complained that supervising their assistants took almost as much time and effort as doing the work themselves.

Middling and well-to-do urban women who described their daily routines in letters or diaries disclosed a uniform pattern of mornings devoted to household work, a late dinner at about two o'clock, and an afternoon of visiting friends, riding, or perhaps reading quietly at home. Although some women arose as late as eight o'clock (which one female Bostonian termed "a lazy hour"), others, including Abigail Adams, recorded that they habitually rose at five. A Pennsylvanian summed up the common practice in a poem:

> *Like a notable house wife* I rise with the sun
> *Then bustle about till the business is done,*
> *Consult with the Cook, and* attend to the
>   spiting [sic]
> *Then quietly seat myself down to my*
>   knitting—
> *Should a neighbour step in we* talk of the
>   weather
> *Retail all the* news *and the* scandle
>   *together, . . .*
> *The* tea things removed *our party disperses,*
> *And of course puts an end to my* very fine
> verses.

The chores that city women performed in the mornings resembled those of farm wives. Their diaries noted hours devoted to washing and ironing, cooking and baking, sewing and knitting. Like that of their rural counterparts, their labor was affected by the seasons, although less consistently so: in the autumn they preserved fruit and stored vegetables, and early in the winter they salted beef and pork and made sausage. Yet there were differences. Most notably, urban dwellers made daily trips to large markets, where they bought most of their meat, vegetables, cheese, and butter. Rebecca Stoddert, a Marylander who had moved to Philadelphia, marveled that her neighbors quickly killed chickens they had purchased without "think[ing] of fattening them up," a practice she deplored as wasteful and short-sighted.

Although urban women were not burdened with the major stock-tending and clothmaking chores that devolved upon farm wives, some of the time thus saved was devoted to cleaning their homes. Many of the travelers in rural areas most horrified by dirty farmhouses and taverns were themselves urban women, who had adopted standards of cleanliness for their homes, clothes, and beds that were utterly alien to farm wives. Certainly no rural woman except Mary Cooper would have written a journal entry resembling that of a Philadelphian in 1781: "As we were whitewashing & cleaning house this day I seemed anxious, I fear over anxious to have every thing clean, & in order." Another Philadelphia resident, the Quaker Sally Logan Fisher, seems to have painted, whitewashed, or wallpapered her house each spring, even though she remarked in April 1785 that it was "troublesome work indeed, the pleasure afterwards of being nice, hardly pays for the trouble." Other wives in smaller towns similarly recorded their commitment to keeping their homes neat and clean.

Cleaning, though, was perhaps the only occupation at which city dwellers of moderate means expended more energy than women living in agricultural regions. One of the benefits of residing in a city or a good-sized town was the availability of a pool of female workers who could be hired at relatively low rates. If a woman decided that she could not afford even a minimal payment, she could take a girl into her home as a sort of apprentice in housewifery, compensating her solely with room, board, and clothes. . . .

The mistresses of such [middling and wealthy] homes felt caught in a dilemma. On the one hand, servants were impertinent, lazy, untrustworthy, careless, and slovenly (to list just a few of their complaints), but on the other hand it was impossible to run a household without some help. The women who offered themselves for hire were usually either single girls or elderly widows; only in rare cases can one identify white females who spent their entire lives as servants. Instead, girls worked as maids, cooks, or laundresses for a few years before marriage, often for a series of employers. From the diaries and letters of mistresses of urban households one gains the impression of a floating population of "young Giddy Headed Girls" who did largely as they pleased, knowing that with the endemic American shortage of labor they could always find another position. Few seem to have stayed in the same household for more than a few months, or a year at most, before moving on to another post. For example, in just the five years from 1794 to 1799, Deborah Norris Logan, Sally Logan Fisher's sister-in-law, employed at least ten different female servants in fairly rapid succession. Among them were two widows, some immigrants from Ireland and Germany, a pair of sisters, and several girls.

Deborah Logan had no daughters to assist her in the home, but even if she had, she, like other urban mothers, would not have expected them to contribute as much work to the household as did their rural counterparts. City daughters from well-to-do homes were the only eighteenth-century American women who can accurately be described as leisured. The causes of their relative lack of employment have already been indicated: first, the work of an urban household was less demanding than that of a farm, so that mothers and perhaps one or two servants could do all that was necessary; and, second, city girls did not have to produce the cloth supply for the family. Accordingly, they could live at a relaxed pace, sleeping late, learning music and dancing, spending hours with male and female friends, and reading the latest novels.

This is not to say, as some historians have argued, that these young women were entirely idle and decorative, for they did extensive amounts of sewing for their families. Girls began to sew at an early age—Hannah, Sally Logan Fisher's daughter, was only eight when she made her first shirt—and they thereafter devoted many hours each day to their needles.

Most of their tasks were mundane: mending and altering clothes; making shirts for their fathers and brothers; and stitching apparently innumerable aprons, caps, and shifts for themselves, their mothers, and their aunts. Such "common sewing" won a girl "no great Credit," the New Englander Pamela Dwight Sedgwick admitted in 1789, but at the same time, she pointed out to her daughter, "[I]t will be thought unpardonable negligence . . . not to doe it very nicely." Sometimes girls would work samplers or make lace, but even the wealthiest among them occasionally felt apologetic for spending a considerable amount of their time on decorative stitchery. Betsy DeLancey, a daughter of the prominent New York family, defended such evidently frivolous employment to her sister Anne in 1768 by referring to Proverbs: "I must be industrious and make myself fine with my own Hands, and who can blame me for spending some of my time in that manner when it is part of the virtuous Womans Character in the Bible."

In poor households, daughters' sewing skills could contribute significantly to family income, as may be demonstrated by reference to the Banckers of New York City. Christopher Bancker was an alcoholic, and his wife Polly tried to support the family by working as a seamstress. Yet she alone could not "du the whole," as she wrote in 1791, and so her two oldest daughters, Peggy and Betsy, also sought employment as seamstresses. Even with the girls' help the family experienced severe economic difficulties, yet the combined income of wife and daughters, coupled with charity proffered by reluctant relatives, kept the Banckers out of the poor house. Peggy and Betsy—and, by implication, other urban girls as well—thus proved to be economic assets to their families in a way that sons were not. The best that could be done with the two oldest Bancker boys was to send them out of the household to learn trades, so that they would no longer be a drag on family resources. Not until they had served apprenticeships of several years, with the expenses being borne by relatives, could they make positive contributions to the support of their parents and siblings. But their sisters had been "apprenticed" to their mother, and so they had developed salable skills at an early age. The other side of the coin was the fact that the Bancker boys' advanced training eventually paid off in higher wages, whereas the girls had little hope of ever improving their position, except through a good marriage.

Because sewing was readily portable, and because they lived so close to each other, well-to-do urban girls frequently gathered to work in sizable groups. While one of their number read, usually from a popular novel, the others would pass the afternoon or evening in sewing. Like farm girls, they created an opportunity for socializing out of the necessity for work, but as a result of their proximity they were able to meet more often, more regularly, and in greater numbers. One sewing group called itself the "Progressive Society" and confined its reading to edifying tracts. "Our design is to ameliorate, by every probable method, the morals, opinions, manners and language of each other," one of the members wrote, explaining why they excluded cardplaying, gossip, and men from their meetings.

In addition to sewing, city girls, like their rural counterparts, were taught what one of them termed "the mysteries of housewifery" by conscientious mothers. Sally Logan Fisher began to instruct her daughter Hannah in "Family affairs" when she was just ten, so that she would become "a good Housewife & an active Mistress of a Family." Daughters did some cooking, baking, and cleaning, helped to care for younger siblings, and on occasion took charge of the household. Sometimes they acquired this responsibility only when their mothers became ill, but in other cases adults deliberately adopted it as a training device. Abigail Adams, who believed it "an indispensable requisite, that every American wife, should herself know, how to order, and regulate her family," commented approvingly in 1788 that her son-in-law William Stephens Smith's four sisters were "well educated for

wives as well as daughters" because "their Mamma had used them to the care of her Family by Turns. Each take it a week at a Time."

The words chosen by Mrs. Adams and Mrs. Fisher revealed a key difference in the domestic roles of urban and rural girls. Farm daughters learned to perform household tasks because their family's current well-being required their active involvement in daily work, whereas city girls acquired domestic skills primarily so that they could eventually become good wives and mothers. The distinction was crucial. Urban daughters participated sporadically in household tasks as a preparation for their own futures, but farm girls worked regularly at such chores as a direct contribution to their family's immediate welfare. The difference points up the overall contrast between the lives of urban and rural white women. In both city and farm, women made vital contributions to the success and survival of the household, but in rural areas those contributions were both more direct and more time-consuming.

## IV

Wealthy southern women were directly responsible for even fewer household tasks than northerners with comparable means. But northerners who moved south soon realized the falsity of an initial impression that "a mrs of a family in Carolina had nothing to doe but be waited on as their was so many negros." Anna Bowen, a young Rhode Island woman who first went to South Carolina to visit a married sister and subsequently married a planter herself, told another sister in 1790 about the problems of running a large household. Required to "think incessantly of a thousand articles of daily supply," she sometimes did not know "which way to turn," Bowen admitted, but, she added confidently, "I shall learn in time."

The daily schedules of mistresses of large plantations resembled those of wealthy urban women in the North, with the exception of the fact that social visits were confined to one or two afternoons a week because of the distance between plantations. The mornings were devoted to household affairs, although white southerners spent their time supervising the work of slaves instead of doing such chores themselves. The day began, sometimes before breakfast, with what one southern man termed "Grand Rounds from the Kitchen to the Larder, then to the Poultry Yard & so on by the Garret & Store Room home to the Parlour." After she had ascertained that the daily tasks were proceeding as planned, the mistress of the household could spend some time reading or playing music before joining her husband for dinner in early to mid-afternoon. Afterward, she would normally turn to needlework until evening, and then again to reading and writing.

The supervision of what were the largest households on the North American continent involved plantation mistresses in varied activities, almost always in the role of director rather than performer. What were small-scale operations on northern farms—running a dairy, raising poultry, tending a garden—were magnified many times on southern plantations, but they remained within the female sphere. Chores that northern women could do in a day, such as laundry, took nearly one week of every two on at least one South Carolina plantation. Food management, easily accomplished in small northern urban families with access to markets, occupied a significant amount of time and required much forethought on large plantations, where each year's harvest had to feed perhaps one hundred or more people for months. White women, it is true, did not usually make the decisions about how many hogs to kill or how many barrels of corn to set aside for food and seed, but they did manage the distribution of food once it had been stored, not to mention the supervision of its initial preservation. Furthermore, they coordinated the manufacture of the slaves' clothing, spending many hours cutting out garments or superintending that work, in addition to making, altering, and mending their families' clothes.

Such women invariably aroused the admiration of observers, who regularly commended their "industry and ingenuity," their "very able and active manner," or their character as "worthy economists" and "good managers." Surviving correspondence indicates that the praise could be completely deserved. A prime example is provided by the Marylander Hannah Buchanan, who in August 1809 returned alone to Woburn plantation while her husband remained in Baltimore on business. She reported to him in anger that the white couple they had left in charge did not have "the smallest idea of the proper economy of a Farm." Among the abuses she discovered were a misassignment of slave women to nonessential tasks, a lack of planning for the slaves' winter clothing, and extremely poor handling of food supplies, including such errors as allowing the slaves to have wheat flour, consuming all the pork, and having no vegetables at all. "This is miserable management," she declared, and set herself to correct the situation. A month later the work on winter clothes was coming along "Wonderfully," and she was filled with ideas on how to prepare and distribute the food more efficiently. Although she expressed a desire to rejoin her husband in the city, she proposed, "[L]et me direct next year and you will spend less believe me and the people will live much better."

Appropriately, then, the primary task of girls from wealthy southern families was to gain expertise in running large estates. Like their northern counterparts, they did some cooking and baking and a fair amount of sewing, but their household roles differed from those of both farm and city girls. Whereas one New England father told his daughter, "[L]earn to work as fast as you can to make Shirts etc & assist your Mother," Thomas Jefferson advised his younger daughter, Maria, who was usually called Polly, that she should know how to "manage the kitchen, the dairy, the garden, and other appendages of the hous[e]hold." Teenaged girls like Eleanor Parke (Nelly) Custis accordingly served as "deputy Housekeeper" to the mistress of the family, who in her case was her grandmother Martha Washington. If this training was successful, parents could look with pleasure upon the accomplishments of such excellent managers as Martha Jefferson Randolph, who assured her father in 1791 that at Monticello under her direction "there is as little wasted as possible," or Harriott Pinckney Horry, whose fond mother, Eliza Lucas Pinckney, had herself managed three South Carolina plantations in the 1740s while she was still a teenager. "I am glad your little wife looks well to the ways of [her] hou[se]," Mrs. Pinckney told her new son-in-law within a month of his marriage, especially remarking upon her daughter's ability to run a "perfectly neat" dairy.

In the end, being a good plantation mistress involved very different skills from those of the usual notable housewife of northern communities. Most importantly, the well-to-do southern white woman had to know how to command and direct the activities of others, often a great many others, not just the one or two servants common to northern households. It was less essential for a wealthy female southerner to know how to accomplish tasks herself than it was for her to know how to order blacks to perform them, and to ensure that her orders were carried out. Thus when the Virginian Elizabeth Foote Washington, who feared that she would not survive until her baby daughter reached maturity, decided to leave her a book of household advice, she devoted most of its pages to hints on the management of slaves. A mistress should behave with "steadiness," she advised; she should show the servants that she would not be "impos'd upon." The most important goal was to maintain "peace & quietness" in the household, and to this end a mistress should be careful not to complain about the slaves to her husband or her friends. Such a practice would make the servants grateful and perhaps encourage their industry, she wrote.

As it happened, both the daughters born to Mrs. Washington died in infancy, and so her detailed delineation of the way to handle house servants was not passed on as she had hoped. But other white southern girls early assumed the habit of command. A telling incident involved Anne, the daughter of James Iredell, the North Carolina attorney and eventual associate justice of the Supreme Court. At the early age of four, she showed how well she had learned her lessons by "strutting about in the yard after Susanna (whom she had ordered to do something) with her work in her hand & an Air of as much importance as if she had been Mistress of the family."

The story of Anne Iredell's behavior inevitably forces one to confront a difficult question: how did Susanna, a mature black woman, react to being ordered about by a white child? Or, to broaden the issue, what sort of lives were led by the black women who, with their husbands and children, constituted the vast majority of the population on southern plantations? Many female slaves resided on small farms and presumably worked in both field and house, but the discussion here will concentrate upon larger plantations, for it was in such households that most black women lived, since the relatively small proportion of white families who possessed slaves tended to own large numbers of them.

Significantly, the size of these plantations allowed the specialization of domestic labor. White northern farm wives had to be, in effect, jills-of-all-trades, whereas planters often assigned slave women more or less permanently to particular tasks. A wide variety of jobs were open to black women, jobs that demanded as much skill as those performed by such male artisans as blacksmiths and carpenters. The slave list prepared by Thomas Middleton for his Goose Creek, South Carolina, plantation in 1784 included a dairymaid, a nurse, two laundresses, two seamstresses, and three general house servants. On other plantations women were also employed as cooks, spinners and weavers (after the mid-1760s), midwives, and tenders of poultry and livestock.

Female blacks frequently worked at the same job for a number of years, but they were not necessarily restricted to it for a lifetime, although practices varied from plantation to plantation. Thomas Jefferson used children of both sexes under ten as infant nurses; from the ages of ten to sixteen he assigned girls to spinning and boys to nailmaking; and then either put them into the fields or had them learn a skilled occupation. Even as adults their jobs might be changed: when Jefferson went to France as ambassador in 1784, his "fine house wench" Dinah, then twenty-three, began to work in the fields, continuing at that assignment at least until 1792. The descriptions of slaves bought or sold on other plantations likewise showed women accustomed to different occupations. Colonel Fitzgerald's Nell, aged thirty-four, was "a stout able field wench & an exceeding good Washer & Ironer"; her daughter Sophy, eighteen, was a "Stout Wench & used to both field & [hou]se Work."

All field work was not the same, of course, and women who labored "in the crop" performed a variety of functions. Evidence of work assignments from both the Jefferson and Washington plantations shows that there were some field jobs reserved for men, most notably cradling wheat and cutting and hauling timber for fences, but that women sometimes built fences. Women plowed, hoed and grubbed the land, spread manure, sowed, harrowed, and at harvest time threshed wheat or husked corn. At Landon Carter's Sabine Hall plantation in Virginia two women, Grace and Maryan, each headed a small gang of female fieldworkers.

On outlying quarters, most women were agricultural laborers, with the occasional exception of a cook or a children's nurse. But female slaves raised at the home plantation could sometimes attain a high level of skill at conventionally "feminine" occupations. White masters and mistresses frequently praised the accomplishments of their cooks, seamstresses, and housekeepers. In a typical passage, Alice DeLancey Izard, a wealthy South Carolinian returning home after a long absence, commended her dairymaid Chloe because she found "the Dairy in excellent order, & plenti-

fully supplied with Milk, & Butter," further observing that Chloe "has made little Chloe very useful in her line."

Mrs. Izard thereby called attention to the transmission of skills among generations of female blacks. Thomas Jefferson's censuses of his plantations demonstrate that women who were house servants tended to have daughters who also worked in the house, and the inventory of a Pinckney family plantation in 1812 similarly included a mother-daughter midwife team. Indeed, midwifery, which was most likely an occupation passed on from woman to woman rather than one taught deliberately by a master, was one of the most essential skills on any plantation. Slave midwives were often called upon to deliver white children as well as black, and masters recognized the special demands of their profession. In 1766, the midwife at Landon Carter's Fork Quarter, who was also the poultry tender, left her post to deliver a baby, an act resulting in the death of four turkeys. Even the petulant Carter realized that her midwifery duties came first, and so he did not punish her.

In this case, a conflict arose between the midwife's divergent duties within her master's household. More commonly, slave women must have had to contend with contradictory demands placed upon them by their plantation tasks and the needs of their own husbands and children. Only a few aspects of the domestic lives led by black women within their own families can be traced in the records of white planters, for masters and mistresses did not, on the whole, concern themselves with the ways in which female slaves organized their homes. Yet occasional comments by slaveowners suggest that black women carefully made the most of what little they had and were even able to exercise some entrepreneurial initiative on occasion. Slave families occasionally maintained their own garden plots and supplemented their meager food and clothing allowances through theft or guile. Further, black women established themselves as the "general Chicken Merchants" in the plantation

South. Whites often bought fowls from their female slaves instead of raising chickens themselves, as a means, Thomas Jefferson once explained, of "drawing a line between what is theirs & mine."

That some black women had a very strong sense indeed of what was "theirs" was demonstrated on Nomini Hall plantation in the summer of 1781. Robert Carter had authorized two white overseers to begin making salt, and in order to accomplish that task they commandeered an iron pot from its two female owners. Joan and Patty, the aggrieved slaves, awaited their chance and then removed the pot from the saltworks. After the whites repossessed it, the women dispatched Patty's husband, Jesse, to complain to Carter about the treatment they had received. Carter sided with the women, agreeing that their pot had been taken in an "arbitrary" manner, and he ordered it returned to them.

One could argue that Joan and Patty were emboldened to act as they did because they anticipated that Carter, a well-meaning master who eventually emancipated his slaves, would sympathize with their position. But bondwomen less favorably circumstanced also repeatedly displayed a desire to control as much of their lives as was possible under the conditions of servitude. Robert Carter's relative Landon was quick to anger, impatient with his servants and children. He frequently had recalcitrant slaves whipped, a tactic to which Robert rarely resorted, yet the women at Sabine Hall were no less insubordinate than those at Nomini. If Robert Carter's "Young & Stout" Jenny deliberately had fits "upon her being reprimanded," Landon Carter's Sarah pretended to be pregnant for a full eleven months so that she could avoid work, and Criss sent her children to milk his cows in the middle of the night in retaliation for a whipping. Similarly ingenious was James Mercer's Sall, who in August 1777 convinced her master that she had consumption and persuaded him to send her to the mountain quarter where her parents lived. That summer he ordered that she should be well fed and allowed to ride six or seven miles on horseback each day until she recovered her health, but by the following year, Mercer had concluded she was faking and directed that "she must turn out at all events unless attended with a fever."

The same willful spirit asserted itself when masters and mistresses attempted to move female slaves from their accustomed homes to other locations. A North Carolina woman who was visiting Boston wanted to have her servant Dorinda sent north to join her, but learned from a relative that Dorinda "would by no means go to Boston or North Carolina, from Cape Fear." Some years later a Pennsylvanian who had sent a slave woman to Cuba to be sold learned that she had managed to convince the white woman accompanying her that she should be returned to her Philadelphia home, because she was "Very Unhappy and always Crying." And "Miss Charlotte," an East Florida black, demonstrated her autonomy by her reaction to a dispute over who owned her. One of the two whites involved reported that she lived with neither of them, but instead "goes about from house to house," saying "now she's a free woman."

Charlotte, Sall, Dorinda, and the others gained at least a little freedom of movement for themselves, but they were still enslaved in the end. All their victories were minor ones, for they could have only limited impact upon the conditions of their bondage. White women were subject to white men, but black women had to subordinate themselves to all whites, men, women, and children alike. The whites demanded always that their needs come first, before those of black women's own families. Female slaves' work lives were thus complicated by conflicting obligations that inflicted burdens upon them far beyond those borne by most whites.

## V

White Americans did not expect their slaves to gain satisfaction from their work, for all that masters and mistresses required of their bond servants was proper behavior and a full day's labor. But white women, as already indicated, were supposed to find "happiness in their chimney corners," to return to William Livingston's striking phrase. Men certainly believed that women should enjoy their domestic role. As a Georgian told his married sister in 1796, "I am sure that those cares which duty requires to your husband, and your child—must fill up every moment of time—and leave you nothing but those sensations of pleasure—which invariably flow—from a consciousness of having left no duty unperformed." Women too anticipated happiness from achieving the goal of notable housewifery. "Domestick oeconomy . . . is the female dignity, & praise," declared Abigail Adams's younger sister, Elizabeth Smith, in the late 1760s, and a Virginian observed to a friend nearly forty years later that she had "always been taught, that within the sphere of domestic life, Woman's chief glory & happiness ought to consist."

The expectation, then, was clear: domesticity was not only a white American woman's inevitable destiny, but it was also supposed to be the source of her sense of pride and satisfaction. Regardless of the exact shape of her household role—whether she was a rural or an urban wife, or the mistress of a southern plantation—she should find fulfillment in it, and she should take pleasure in performing the duties required of her as mistress of the home.

Unsurprisingly, women rarely found the ideal as attractive in reality as it was in theory. But the reasons for their dissatisfaction with the restrictions of notable housewifery, which required them to be consistently self-effacing and constantly employed at domestic tasks, are both illuminating and unanticipated.

First, it must be noted that Mary Cooper was alone among her contemporaries in emphasizing the difficult, fatiguing nature of housework as the primary source of her complaints. Only she wrote of "the continnel cross of my famaly," only she filled her diary with accounts of weariness and endless drudgery. Women's un-

happiness with their domestic lives, in other words, stemmed not from the fact that the work was tiring and demanding. Their husbands' labor was also difficult, and in eighteenth-century America there were few models of a leisured existence for either men or women to emulate. Rather, women's expressed dissatisfaction with their household role derived from its basic nature, and from the way it contrasted with their husbands' work.

As has been seen, farmers' lives were much more varied than those of their wives, not only because they rarely repeated the same chore day after day in immediate succession, but also because they had more breaks from the laboring routine. The same was true of southern planters and of urban husbands, regardless of their occupation. The diaries of planters, professional men, and artisans alike demonstrate that their weeks were punctuated by travel, their days enlivened not only by visits with friends—which their wives also enjoyed—but also by a variety of business activities that took them on numerous errands. It was an unusual week, for example, when Thomas Hazard, a Rhode Island blacksmith, worked in his shop every day without any sort of respite from his labors, or when Ebenezer Parkman, a New England clergyman, did not call on parishioners, confer with neighbors about politics, or meet with other ministers.

Against the backdrop of their husbands' diverse experiences, the invariable daily and weekly routines of housewifery seemed dull and uninteresting to eighteenth-century women, especially those who lived in urban areas, where the housework was less varied and their spouses' opportunities for socializing simultaneously greater. "The same cares and the same wants are constantly returning in domestic Life to take up my Time and attention," Pamela Dwight Sedgwick told her husband, Theodore, the Massachusetts Federalist, in words that reappeared in other women's assessments of their lives. "A continual sameness reigns throughout the Year," wrote Christian Barnes, the wife of a Marlborough, Massachusetts, merchant, and Mary Orne Tucker, a Haverhill lawyer's wife, noted in her diary that she did not record her domestic tasks in detail because "each succeeding day with very little variety would present a compleat history of the last."

New England city dwellers were not the only women who made such observations about the unchanging character of their experiences. The transplanted Rhode Islander Anna Bowen Mitchell reported from her new South Carolina home in 1793, "[T]he detail of one day . . . would be the detail of the last six months of my life," while hastening to add that her days were not "insipid," but rather filled with "heart-soothing tranquility." A Virginia planter's wife was more blunt about her situation in 1785, describing herself and her friends as "almost in a State of vegitation" because of their necessary attention to the "innumerable wants" of their large households.

She thus touched upon yet another source of housewives' discontent with their lot: the fact that their all-encompassing domestic responsibilities left them little time to themselves. In 1755, a New England woman remarked longingly to a correspondent, "[T]he little scraps of time that can be rescued from Business or Company, are the greatest cordials to my tired Spirits that I meet with." Thirty years later Pamela Sedgwick echoed her sentiments, telling her unmarried friend Betsy Mayhew, "[W]e that have connected ourselves in the famely way, find the small circle of domestic concerns engross almost all our attention." Sally Logan Fisher too commented, "[I] find so much to do in the Family that I have not all the time for retirement and improvement of my own mind in the best things that I wish," revealingly referring to her domestic duties as "these hindering things." Again, such complaints were not confined to northerners. A young Virginia wife observed in 1769 that "Domestic Business . . . even deprives thought of its Native freedom" by restricting the mind "to one particular subject without suffering it to enter-

tain itself with the contemplation of any thing New or improving." A wry female poet made the same point in verse: "Ah yes! 'tis true, upon my Life! / No *Muse* was ever yet a *Wife*," she wrote, explaining that "Muses . . . in *poultry yards* were never seen," nor were they required "from Books and Poetry to Turn / To mark *the Labours of the Churn.*"

The point of all these remarks was the same, despite their divergent geographical and chronological origins. White American women recognized not only that their domestic obligations were never-ending, but also that their necessary concentration upon those obligations deprived them of the opportunity to contemplate "any thing New and improving." So Elizabeth Smith Shaw told her oldest sister, Mary Cranch, in 1781, several years after her marriage to the clergyman John Shaw, "[I]f Ideas present themselves to my Mind, it is too much like the good seed sown among Thorns, they are soon erased, & swallowed up by the Cares of the World, the wants, & noise of my Family, & Children." Abigail Adams in particular regretted her beloved younger sister's preoccupation with domestic concerns during her second marriage, to another clergyman, who boarded a number of students. In February 1800 she told Elizabeth (then Mrs. Stephen Peabody) that her "brilliant" talents were "encumbered" and "obstructed" by her household chores, lamenting "that the fire of imagination should be checked, that the effusions of genious should be stifled, through want of leisure to display them." Abigail's characterization of the impact of domestic responsibilities on her sister's life bore little resemblance to William Livingston's glorification of those same activities: "The mind which is necessarily imprisoned in its own little tenement: and fully occupied by keeping it in repair: has no time to rove abroad for improvement," she observed. "The Book of knowledge is closely clasped against those who must fullfil there [*sic*] daily task of manual labour."

Even with their expressed dissatisfaction at the endless, unchanging nature of housework, one might theorize that late eighteenth-century American women could nevertheless have found their domestic lives meaningful if they and their husbands had highly valued their contributions to the family well-being. But such was not the case. Women revealed their assessments of the importance of their work in the adjectives they used to describe it: "my Narrow sphere," my "humble duties," "my little Domestick affairs."

Always the words belittled their domestic role, thereby indicating its low status in contemporary eyes. Modern historians can accurately point to the essential economic function of women within a colonial household, but the facts evident from hindsight bear little relationship to eighteenth-century subjective attitudes. In spite of the paeans to notable womanhood, the role of the household mistress in the family's welfare was understood only on the most basic level. Such minimal recognition did not translate itself into an awareness that women contributed to the wider society. Instead, just as a woman's activities were supposed to be confined to the domestic sphere, so, too, was any judgment of her importance. Americans realized that a successful household needed a competent mistress, but they failed to endow that mistress with an independent social standing or to grant to her domestic work the value it deserved. Notable housewifery was conceived to be an end in itself, rather than as a means to a greater or more meaningful goal. As such, it was an inadequate prop for feminine self-esteem.

Accordingly, it comes as no surprise to learn that women generally wrote of their household work without joy or satisfaction. They spoke only of "the discharge of the necessary duties of life," of "perform[ing] the duties that are annex'd to my Station." Even the South Carolinian Martha Laurens Ramsay, described by her husband, David, as a model wife, regarded her "self denying duties" as "a part of the curse denounced upon Eve," as a penalty to be endured, instead of as a fulfilling experience. The usage was universal and the message unmistakable: their tasks, with rare exceptions, were "duties," not pleasures. The only Americans who wrote consistently of the joys of housewifery and notable womanhood were men like William Livingston. In contrast, Christian Barnes found the household a prison that offered no intellectual stimulation, describing it as a place where women were "Chain'd down to domestic Dutys" that "Stagnate[d] the Blood and Stupefie[d] the Senses."

Yet still women did not question the overall dimensions of the ideal domestic role. Sometimes, to be sure, they inquired about its details, as when Esther Edwards Burr, Jonathan Edwards's daughter, and her close friend Sarah Prince carried on a learned discussion about the precise meaning of the parts of Proverbs 31 that outlined the virtuous woman's daily routine. But ultimately they saw no alternative to domesticity. Many were simply resigned to the inevitable, for they had few options. Certainly some expressed the philosophy that "the height of happiness is Contentment" with one's lot, that although their life had "no great veriety . . . custom has made it agreable . . . and to desire more would be ungreatfull." More probable, though, is the fact that the household duties women found unsatisfying were intertwined in their own minds with responsibilities from which they gained a great deal of pleasure. Their role as mistress of the household, in the end, constituted but a third of their troika of domestic duties. They were wives and mothers as well as housekeepers, and these components of domesticity gave them the emotional and psychological rewards they did not receive from running their households efficiently.

# 7

# WHO WAS BENJAMIN FRANKLIN?

## JOHN WILLIAM WARD

Much like his contemporary George Washington, Benjamin Franklin has become one of the staples of American mythology. As John William Ward makes clear, however, Franklin was in reality no mythological being but a very complex and even contradictory man. The essence of Franklin, according to Ward, was his existence as a symbol of upward mobility. Beginning life as an apprentice printer, Franklin achieved business success before he was 30, earned an international reputation in science through his experiments in electricity, became influential in politics at the state and national levels, and served as one of the new nation's most successful diplomats in the Revolutionary era. The key to Franklin's rise, Ward contends, was his ability to separate appearance and reality: to appear to conform to community norms in public life while following his own desires in private affairs. It was this ability, Ward argues, that accounts for the seeming contradictions in Franklin's character.

Reprinted by permission from Mrs. John William Ward.

Benjamin Franklin bulks large in our national consciousness, sharing room with Washington and Jefferson and Lincoln. Yet it is hard to say precisely what it means to name Franklin one of our cultural heroes. He was, as one book about him has it, "many-sided." The sheer variety of his character has made it possible to praise him and damn him with equal vigor. At home, such dissimilar Yankees as the laconic Calvin Coolidge and the passionate Theodore Parker could each find reason to admire him. Abroad, David Hume could say that he was "the first great man of letters" for whom Europe was "beholden" to America. Yet D. H. Lawrence, brought up, he tells us, in the industrial wastelands of midland England on the pious saws of "Poor Richard," could only "utter a long, loud curse" against "this dry, moral, utilitarian little democrat."

Part of the difficulty in comprehending Franklin's meaning is due to the opposites he seems to have contained with complete serenity within his own personality. He was an eminently reasonable man who maintained a deep skepticism about the power of reason. He was a model of industriousness who, preaching the gospel of hard work, kept his shop only until it kept him and retired at forty-two. He was a cautious and prudent man who was a revolutionist. And, to name only one more seeming contradiction, he was one who had a keen eye for his own advantage and personal advancement who spent nearly all his adult life in the service of others. Small wonder that there have been various interpretations of so various a character.

The problem may seem no problem at all. Today, when we all know that the position of the observer determines the shape of reality, we observe the observer. If Franklin, seeing to it that the streets of Philadelphia are well lit and swept clean at a moderate price, that no fires rage, does not appeal to D. H. Lawrence, we tend not to think of Franklin. We think of Lawrence; we remember his atavistic urge to explore the dark and passionate underside of life and move on. Franklin contained in his own character so many divergent aspects that

each observer can make the mistake of seeing one aspect as all and celebrate or despise Franklin accordingly. Mr. I. Bernard Cohen, who has written so well on so much of Franklin, has remarked that "an account of Franklin . . . is apt to be a personal testament of the commentator concerning the America he most admires." Or contemns.

Yet there still remains the obstinate fact that Franklin could mean so many things to so many men, that he was so many-sided, that he did contain opposites, that he was, in other words, so many different characters. One suspects that here is the single most important thing about Franklin. Rather than spend our energies trying to find some consistency in this protean, many-sided figure, trying to resolve who Franklin truly was, we might perhaps better accept his variety itself as our major problem and try to understand that. To insist on the importance of the question, "Who was Benjamin Franklin?" may finally be more conclusive than to agree upon an answer.

The place to begin to ask the question is with the *Memoirs,* with the *Autobiography* as we have come to call them, and the place to begin there is with the history of the text. Fascinating in and of itself, the history of the text gives us an initial lead into the question of the elusiveness of Franklin's personality.

The *Autobiography* was written in four parts. The first part, addressed by Franklin to his son, William, was begun during some few weeks in July and August, 1771, while Franklin was visiting with his friend, Jonathan Shipley, the Bishop of St. Asaph, in Hampshire, England. Franklin was then sixty-five years old. As he wrote the first part he also carefully made a list of topics he would subsequently treat. Somehow the manuscript and list fell into the hands of one Abel James who eleven years later wrote Franklin, returning to him the list of topics but not the first part of the manuscript, urging him to take up his story once again. This was in 1782, or possibly early in January, 1783. Franklin was in France as one of the peace commissioners. He wrote the second part in France in 1784, after the achievement of peace, indicating the beginning and the ending of this short second part in the manuscript itself.

In 1785, Franklin returned to America, promising to work on the manuscript during the voyage. Instead he wrote three of his utilitarian essays: on navigation, on how to avoid smoky streetlamp chimneys, and on his famous stove. He did not return to his life's story until 1788. Then, after retiring from the presidency of the state of Pennsylvania in the spring, Franklin, quite sick, made his will and put his house in order before turning again to his own history. This was in August, 1788. Franklin was eighty-three years old, in pain, and preparing for death. The third part is the longest part of the autobiography, less interesting than the first two, and for many years was thought to conclude the manuscript.

In 1789, Franklin had his grandson, Benjamin Franklin Bache, make two fair copies of Parts I, II and III in order to send them to friends abroad, Benjamin Vaughan in England and M. le Veillard in France. Then, sometime before his death in April, 1790, Franklin added the last and fourth part, some seven and one-half manuscript pages, which was not included, naturally, in the fair copies sent abroad. For the rest, Mr. Max Farrand, our authority on the history of the text:

> After [Franklin's] death, the publication of the autobiography was eagerly awaited, as its existence was widely known, but for nearly thirty years the reading public had to content itself with French translations of the first and second parts, which were again translated from the French into other languages, and even retranslated into English. When the authorized English publication finally appeared in 1818, it was not taken from the original manuscript but from a copy, as was the preceding French version of the first part. The copy, furthermore, did not include the fourth and last part, which also reached the public in a French translation in 1828.
>
> . . . The complete autobiography was not printed in English from the original manuscript until 1868, nearly eighty years after Franklin's death.

The story is, as I have said, interesting in and of itself. The tangled history of one of our most important texts has its own fascination, but it also provides us the first clue to our question. Surely, it must strike any reader of the *Autobiography* as curious that a character who speaks so openly should at the same time seem so difficult to define. But the history of the text points the way to an answer. All we need do is ask why Franklin wrote his memoirs.

When the Quaker Abel James wrote Franklin, returning his list of topics and asking "kind, humane, and benevolent Ben Franklin" to continue his life's story, "a work which would be useful and entertaining not only to a few but to millions," Franklin sent the letter on to his friend, Benjamin Vaughan, asking for advice. Vaughan concurred. He too urged Franklin to publish the history of his life because he could think of no "more efficacious advertisement" of America than Franklin's history. "All that has happened to you," he reminded Franklin, "is also connected with the detail of the manners and situation of a rising people." Franklin included James's and Vaughan's letters in his manuscript to explain why he resumed his story. What had gone before had been written for his family; "what follows," he said in his "Memo," "was written . . . in compliance with the advice contained in these letters, and accordingly intended for the public. The affairs of the Revolution occasioned the interruption."

The point is obvious enough. When Franklin resumed his story, he did so in full self-consciousness that he was offering himself to the world as a representative type, the American. Intended for the public now, his story was to be an example for young Americans, as Abel James would have it, and an advertisement to the world, as Benjamin Vaughan would have it. We had just concluded a successful revolution; the eyes of all the world were upon us. Just as America had succeeded in creating itself a nation, Franklin set out to show how the American went about creating his own character. As Benjamin Vaughan said, Franklin's life would "give a noble rule and example of self-education" because of Franklin's "discovery that the thing is in many a man's private power." So what follows is no longer the simple annals of Franklin's life for the benefit of his son. Benjamin Franklin plays his proper role. He becomes "The American."

How well he filled the part that his public urged him to play, we can see by observing what he immediately proceeds to provide. In the pages that follow James's and Vaughan's letters, Franklin quickly treats four matters: the establishment of a lending library, that is, the means for satisfying the need for self-education; the importance of frugality and industriousness in one's calling; the social utility of religion; and, of course, the thirteen rules for ordering one's life. Here, in a neat package, were all the materials that went into the making of the self-made man. This is how one goes about making a success of one's self. If the sentiments of our Declaration were to provide prompt notes for European revolutions, then Franklin, as the American Democrat, acted them out. Family, class, religious orthodoxy, higher education: all these were secondary to character and common sense. The thing was in many a man's private power.

If we look back now at the first part, the opening section addressed by Franklin to his son, William, we can see a difference and a similarity. The difference is, of course, in the easy and personal tone, the more familiar manner, appropriate to a communication with one's son. It is in these early pages that Franklin talks more openly about his many *errata,* his "frequent intrigues with low women," and displays that rather cool and calculating attitude toward his wife. Rather plain dealing, one might think, at least one who did not know that William was a bastard son.

But the similarity between the two parts is more important. The message is the same, although addressed to a son, rather than to the world: how to go about making a success. "From the poverty and obscurity in which I was born and in which I passed my earliest years," writes the father to the son, "I have raised myself to a state of affluence and some degree of celebrity in the world." A son, especially, must have found that "some" hard to take. But the career is not simply anecdotal: "my posterity will perhaps be desirous of learning the means, which I employed, and which, thanks to Providence, so well succeeded with me. They may also deem them fit to be imitated." The story is exemplary, although how the example was to affect a son who was, in 1771, about forty years old and already Royal Governor of New Jersey is another matter.

The story has remained exemplary because it is the success story to beat all success stories: the runaway apprentice printer who rose to dine with kings; the penniless boy, walking down Market Street with two large rolls under his arms, who was to sit in Independence Hall and help create a new nation. But notice that the story does not deal with the success itself. That is presumed, of course, but the *Autobiography* never gets to the later and more important years because the *Autobiography* is not about success. It is about the formation of the character that makes success possible. The subject of the *Autobiography* is the making of a character. Having lifted himself by his own bootstraps, Franklin described it that way: "I have raised myself." We were not to find the pat phrase until the early nineteenth century when the age of the common man made the style more common: "the self-made man." The character was for life, of course, and not for fiction where we usually expect to encounter the made-up, but that should not prevent us from looking a little more closely at the act of creation. We can look in two ways: first, by standing outside the *Autobiography* and assessing it by what we know from elsewhere; second, by reading the *Autobiography* itself more closely.

A good place to begin is with those years in France around the end of the Revolution. It is so delicious an episode in plain Ben's life. More importantly—as Franklin said, one can always find a principle to justify one's inclinations—it is in these very years at Passy that Franklin, in response to James's and Vaughan's letters, wrote those self-conscious pages of the second part of the *Autobiography*. Just as he wrote the lines, he played them. As Carl Van Doren has written, "the French were looking for a hero who should combine the reason and wit of Voltaire with the primitive virtues celebrated by Rousseau. . . . [Franklin] denied them nothing." This is the period of the simple Quaker dress, the fur cap and the spectacles. France went wild in its adulation and Franklin knew why. "Think how this must appear," he wrote a friend, "among the powdered heads of Paris."

But he was also moving with equal ease in that world, the world of the powdered heads of Paris, one of the most cosmopolitan, most preciously civilized societies in history. Although he was no Quaker, Franklin was willing to allow the French to think so. They called him *"le bon Quackeur."* The irony was unintentional, a matter of translation. But at the same time that he was filling the role of the simple backwoods democrat, the innocent abroad, he was also playing cavalier in the brilliant salon of Madame Helvétius, the widow of the French philosopher. Madame Helvétius is supposed to have been so beautiful that Fontenelle, the great popularizer of Newton, who lived to be one hundred years old, was said to have paid her the most famous compliment of the age: "Ah, madame, if I were only eighty again!" Madame Helvétius was sixty when Franklin knew her and the classic anecdote of their acquaintance is that Madame Helvétius is said to have reproached him for not coming to see her, for putting off his long anticipated visit. Franklin replied, "Madame, I am waiting until the nights are longer." There was also Madame Brillon, not a widow, who once wrote to Franklin, "People have the audacity to criticize my pleasant habit of sitting on your knee, and yours of always asking me for what I always refuse."

Some, discovering this side of Franklin, have written him off simply as a rather lively

old lecher. Abigail Adams, good New England lady that she was, was thoroughly shocked. She set Madame Helvétius down as a "very bad woman." But Franklin, despite his public style, was not so provincial. He appealed to Madame Brillon that he had spent so many days with her that surely she could spend one night with him. She mockingly called him a sophist. He then appealed to her charity and argued that it was in the design of Providence that she grant him his wish. If somehow a son of the Puritans, Franklin had grown far beyond the reach of their sermonizing. Thomas Hooker had thought, "It's a grievous thing to the loose person, he cannot have his pleasures but he must have his guilt and gall with them." But Franklin wrote Madame Brillon, "Reflect how many of our duties [Providence] has ordained naturally to be pleasures; and that it has had the goodness besides, to give the name of sin to several of them so that we might enjoy them the more."

All this is delightful enough, and for more one need only turn to Carl Van Doren's biography from which I have taken these anecdotes, but what it points to is as important as it is entertaining. It points to Franklin's great capacity to respond to the situation in which he found himself and to play the expected role, to prepare a face to meet the faces that he met. He could, in turn, be the homespun, rustic philosopher or the mocking cavalier, the witty sophist. He knew what was expected of him.

The discovery should not surprise any reader of the *Autobiography*. Throughout it, Franklin insists always on the distinction between appearance and reality, between what he is and what he seems to be.

In order to secure my credit and character as a tradesman, I took care not only to be in *reality* industrious and frugal, but to avoid all *appearances* of the contrary. I dressed plain and was seen at no places of idle diversion. I never went out a fishing or shooting; a book, indeed, sometimes debauched me from my work, but that was seldom, snug, and gave no scandal; and to

show that I was not above my business, I sometimes brought home the paper I purchased at
the stores, thro' the streets on a wheelbarrow.
Thus being esteemed an industrious, thriving
young man, and paying duly for what I bought,
the merchants who imported stationery solic-
ited my custom; others proposed supplying me
with books, and I went on swimmingly.

Now, with this famous passage, one must be
careful. However industrious and frugal Franklin may in fact have been, he knew that for the
business of social success virtue counts for
nothing without its public dress. In Franklin's
world there has to be someone in the woods
to hear the tree fall. Private virtue might bring
one to stand before the King of kings, but if one
wants to sit down and sup with the kings of this
world, then one must help them see one's
merit. There are always in this world, as Franklin pointed out, "a number of rich merchants,
nobility, states, and princes who have need of
honest instruments for the management of
their affairs, and such being so rare [I] have
endeavoured to convince young persons, that
no qualities are so likely to make a poor man's
fortune as those of probity and integrity."

Yet if one wants to secure one's credit in the
world by means of one's character, then the
character must be of a piece. There can be no
false gesture; the part must be played well.
When Franklin drew up his list of virtues they
contained, he tells us, only twelve. But a
Quaker friend "kindly" informed him that he
was generally thought proud and overbearing
and rather insolent; he proved it by examples.
So Franklin added humility to his list; but, having risen in the world and content with the
degree of celebrity he had achieved, he could
not bring himself to be humble. "I cannot boast
of much success in acquiring the *reality* of this
virtue, but I had a good deal with regard to the
*appearance* of it."

He repeats, at this point, what he had already written in the first part of his story. He
forswears all "positive assertion." He drops
from his vocabulary such words as "certainly"

and "undoubtedly" and adopts a tentative
manner. He remembers how he learned to
speak softly, to put forward his opinions, not
dogmatically, but by saying, " 'I imagine' a
thing to be so or so, or 'It so appears to me at
present.' " As he had put it to his son earlier,
he discovered the Socratic method, "was
charmed with it, adopted it, dropped my
abrupt contradiction and positive argumenta-
tion, and put on the humble enquirer." For
good reason, "this habit . . . has been of great
advantage to me."

What saves all this in the *Autobiography*
from being merely repellent is Franklin's self-
awareness, his good humor in telling us about
the part he is playing, the public clothes he is
putting on to hide what his public will not
openly buy. "In reality," he writes, drawing
again the distinction from appearance, "there
is perhaps no one of our natural passions so
hard to subdue as *pride;* disguise it, struggle
with it, beat it down, stifle it, mortify it as much
as one pleases, it is still alive and will every
now and then peep out and show itself. You
will see it perhaps often in this history. For
even if I could conceive that I had completely
overcome it, I should probably be proud of my
humility." Here, despite the difference in tone,
Franklin speaks like that other and contrasting
son of the Puritans, Jonathan Edwards, on the
nature of true virtue. Man, if he could achieve
virtue, would inevitably be proud of the
achievement and so, at the moment of success,
fall back into sin.

The difference is, of course, in the tone. The
insight is the same but Franklin's skeptical and
untroubled self-acceptance is far removed
from Edwards' troubled and searching self-
doubt. Franklin enjoys the game. Mocking himself, he quietly lures us, in his Yankee deadpan
manner, with the very bait he has just described. After having told us that he early
learned to "put on the humble enquirer" and
to affect a self-depreciating pose, he quotes in
his support the line from Alexander Pope, "To
speak, though sure, with seeming diffidence."
Pope, Franklin immediately goes on to say,

"might have joined with this line that which he has coupled with another, I think less properly, 'For want of modesty is want of sense.' "

If you ask why *less properly,* I must repeat the lines,

*Immodest words admit of* no defence,
For *want of modesty is want of sense.*

Now is not the "want of sense" (where a man is so unfortunate as to want it) some apology for his "want of modesty"? and would not the lines stand more justly thus?

*Immodest words admit* but *this defense*
That want of modesty is want of sense.

This, however, I should submit to better judgements.

Having been so bold as to correct a couplet of the literary giant of the age, Franklin quietly retreats and defers to the judgment of those better able to say than he. Having just described the humble part he has decided to play, he immediately acts it out. If we get the point, we chuckle with him; if we miss the point, that only proves its worth.

But one of the functions of laughter is to dispel uneasiness and in Franklin's case the joke is not enough. Our uneasiness comes back when we stop to remember that he is, as his friends asked him to, writing his story as an efficacious advertisement. We must always ask whether Franklin's disarming candor in recounting how things went on so swimmingly may not be yet another role, still another part he is playing. Actually, even with Yale's sumptuous edition of Franklin's papers, we know little about Franklin's personal life in the early years, except through his own account. The little we do know suggests that his way to wealth and success was not the smooth and open path he would have us believe. This leads us, then, if we cannot answer finally the question who Franklin was, to a different question.

What does it mean to say that a character so changeable, so elusive, somehow represents American culture? What is there in Franklin's style that makes him, as we say, characteristic?

At the outset in colonial America, with men like John Winthrop, there was always the assumption that one would be called to one's appropriate station in life and labor in it for one's own good and the good of society. Magistrates would be magistrates and printers would be printers. But in the world in which Franklin moved, the magistrates, like Governor Keith of Pennsylvania who sends Franklin off on a wild-goose chase to England, prove to be frauds while the plain, leather-aproned set went quietly about the work of making society possible at all, creating the institutions—the militia, the fire companies, the libraries, the hospitals, the public utilities—that made society habitable. The notion that underlay an orderly, hierarchical society failed to make sense of such a world. It proved impossible to keep people in their place.

One need only consider in retrospect how swiftly Franklin moved upward through the various levels of society to see the openness, the fluidity of his world. Simply because he is a young man with some books, Governor Burnet of New York asks to see him. While in New Jersey on a job printing money he meets and makes friends with all the leaders of that provincial society. In England, at the coffeehouses, he chats with Mandeville and meets the great Dr. Henry Pemberton who was seeing the third edition of Newton's *Principia* through the press. As Franklin said, diligent in his calling, he raised himself by some degree.

The Protestant doctrine of calling, of industriousness in the world, contained dynamite for the orderly, hierarchical, social structure it was originally meant to support. The unintended consequence showed itself within two generations. Those who were abstemious, frugal and hard-working made a success in the world. They rose. And society, rather than the static and closed order in which, in Winthrop's words, "some must be rich some poor, some high and eminent in power and dignitie; others meane and in subieccion," turned out to be dynamic, fluid and open.

If there is much of our national character implicit in Franklin's career, it is because, early in our history, he represents a response to the rapid social change that has remained about the only constant in American society. He was the self-made man, the jack-of-all-trades. He taught thirteen rules to sure success and purveyed do-it-yourself kits for those who, like himself, constituted a "rising" people. Franklin stands most clearly as an exemplary American because his life's story is a witness to the uncertainties about social status that have characterized our society, a society caught up in the constant process of change. The question, "Who was Benjamin Franklin?" is a critical question to ask of Franklin because it is the question to which Franklin himself is constantly seeking an answer. In a society in which there are no outward, easily discernible marks of social status, the question always is, as we put it in the title of reference works that are supposed to provide the answer, "Who's Who?"

Along with the uncertainties generated by rapid social mobility, there is another aspect to the difficulty we have in placing Franklin, an aspect that is more complex and harder to state, but just as important and equally characteristic. It takes us back again to the Puritans. In Puritan religious thought there was originally a dynamic equipoise between two opposite thrusts, the tension between an inward, mystical, personal experience of God's grace and the demands for an outward, sober, socially responsible ethic, the tension between faith and works, between the essence of religion and its outward show. Tremendous energy went into sustaining these polarities in the early years but, as the original piety waned, itself undermined by the worldly success that benefited from the doctrine of calling, the synthesis split in two and resulted in the eighteenth century in Jonathan Edwards and Ben-

jamin Franklin, similar in so many ways, yet so radically unlike.

Franklin, making his own world as he makes his way through it, pragmatically rejects the old conundrum whether man does good works because he is saved, or is saved because he does good works. "Vicious actions are not hurtful because they are forbidden, but forbidden because they are hurtful," he decides, and then in an added phrase calmly throws out the God-centered universe of his forebears, "the nature of man alone considered."

Content with his success, blandly sure it must be in the design of Providence that printers hobnob with kings, Franklin simply passes by the problem of the relation between reality and appearance. In this world, appearance is sufficient. Humanely skeptical that the essence can ever be caught, Franklin decided to leave the question to be answered in the next world, if there proved to be one. For this world, a "tolerable character" was enough and he "valued it properly." The result was a common sense utilitarianism which sometimes verges toward sheer crassness. But it worked. For this world, what others think of you is what is important. If Franklin, viewed from the perspective of Max Weber and students of the Protestant ethic, can seem to be the representative, *par excellence,* of the character who internalizes the imperatives of his society and steers his own course unaided through the world, from a slightly different perspective he also turns out to be the other-directed character David Riesman has described, constantly attuned to the expectations of those around him, responding swiftly to the changing situations that demand he play different roles.

We admire, I think, the lusty good sense of the man who triumphs in the world that he accepts, yet at the same time we are uneasy with the man who wears so many masks that we are never sure who is there behind them. Yet it is this, this very difficulty of deciding whether we admire Franklin or suspect him, that makes his character an archetype for our national experience. There are great advantages to be had in belonging to a culture without clearly defined classes, without an establishment, but there is, along with the advantages, a certain strain, a necessary uneasiness. In an open and pluralistic society we have difficulty "placing" people, as we say. Think how often in our kind of society when we meet someone for the first time how our second or third question is apt to be, "What do you do?" Never, "Who are you?" The social role is enough, but in our more reflective moments we realize not so, and in our most reflective moments we realize it will never do for our own selves. We may be able to, but we do not want to go through life as a doctor, lawyer or Indian chief. We want to be ourselves, as we say. And at the beginning of our national experience, Benjamin Franklin not only puts the question that still troubles us in our kind of society, "Who's Who?" He also raises the question that lies at the heart of the trouble: "Who am I?"

# PART TWO
# A
# REVOLUTIONARY
# PEOPLE

# 8

# EVANGELICAL REVOLT: THE NATURE OF THE BAPTISTS' CHALLENGE TO THE TRADITIONAL ORDER IN VIRGINIA, 1765–1775

## RHYS ISAAC

By the mid-eighteenth century questions of political and social authority were occupying the minds of all ranks of Americans. While the prosperous governing elites debated the nature of British parliamentary authority in the colonies, those of more humble station discussed the propriety of existing social arrangements. In rural communities where land scarcity meant that fathers could no longer offer the promise of propertied independence to their children, sons and daughters began to question the patriarchal control of their fathers and conceived children to force marriage on their own terms. In towns and cities middling-and laboring-class people joined in questioning the customary authority that the rural gentry and urban merchants had exercised. In the mobilization against Britain these people of lower status demanded a voice in their own affairs, which threatened the system of patronage and deference that had dominated social relations for generations.

In Virginia, as Rhys Issac shows, popular questioning of elite control took a distinctive form. The system of deference in the Chesapeake region was expressed in a gentry-dominated culture of conviviality. Personal events, such as marriages and births, and public affairs, such as quarterly court sessions, were the scenes of drinking, gambling, dancing, horse racing, and general mirth. In the eighteenth century, however, another system of values began to challenge the domination of the elite-directed culture. This alternative culture was based upon a revival of religion among many of Virginia's commoners. Expressed in the growing number of Methodist and Baptist revivals that emphasized strict self-discipline and continence, this emerging culture directly challenged the worldliness of the dominant planter culture. As Isaac suggests, it was this evangelical culture that set the stage for popular support of the anti-British revolutionary movement as well as for a popular challenge to the power and authority of Virginia's planter elite. Finding themselves caught between the intransigence of British imperial policy and growing popular opposition, by the early 1770s most planter elites turned to the patriot cause in an attempt to reassert their leadership over Virginia society.

Reprinted by permission of Rhys Isaac and William and Mary Quarterly.

An intense struggle for allegiance had developed in the Virginia countryside during the decade before the Revolution. Two eye-witness accounts may open to us the nature of the conflict.

First, a scene vividly remembered and described by the Reverend James Ireland etches in sharp profile the postures of the forces in contest. As a young man Ireland, who was a propertyless schoolmaster of genteel origin, had cut a considerable figure in Frederick County society. His success had arisen largely from his prowess at dancing and his gay facility as a satiric wit. Then, like many other young men at this time (ca. 1768), he came deeply "under conviction of sin" and withdrew from the convivialities of gentry society. When an older friend and patron of Ireland heard that his young protégé could not be expected at a forthcoming assembly, this gentleman, a leader in county society, sensed the challenge to his way of life that was implicit in Ireland's withdrawal. He swore instantly that "there could not be a dance in the settlement without [Ireland] being there, and if they would leave it to him, he would convert [him], and that to the dance, on Monday; and they would see [Ireland] lead the ball that day." Frederick County, for all its geographical spread, was a close community. Young James learned that his patron would call, and dreaded the coming test of strength:

> When I viewed him riding up, I never beheld such a display of pride arising from his deportment, attitude and jesture; he rode a lofty elegant horse, . . . his countenance appeared to me as bold and daring as satan himself, and with a commanding authority [he] called upon me, if I were there to come out, which I accordingly did, with a fearful and timorous heart. But O! how quickly can God level pride. . . . For no sooner did he behold my disconsolate looks, emaciated countenance and solemn aspect, than he . . . was riveted to the beast he rode on. . . . As soon as he could articulate a little his eyes fixed upon me, and his first address was

this: "In the name of the Lord, what is the matter with you?"

The evident overdramatization in this account is its most revealing feature for it is eloquent concerning the tormented convert's heightened awareness of the contrast between the social world he was leaving and the one he was entering.

The struggle for allegiance between these social worlds had begun with the Great Awakening in the 1740s, but entered into its most fierce and bitter phase with the incursions of the "New Light" Separate Baptists into the older parts of Virginia in the years after 1765. The social conflict was not over the distribution of political power or of economic wealth, but over the ways of men and the ways of God. By the figures in the encounter described we may begin to know the sides drawn: on the one hand, a mounted gentleman of the world with "commanding authority" responding to challenge; on the other, a guilt-humbled, God-possessed youth with "disconsolate looks . . . and solemn aspect."

A second scene—this time in the Tidewater—reveals through actions some characteristic responses of the forces arrayed. From a diary entry of 1771 we have a description of the disruption of a Baptist meeting by some gentlemen and their followers, intent on upholding the cause of the established Church:

> Brother Waller informed us . . . [that] about two weeks ago on the Sabbath Day down in Caroline County he introduced the worship of God by singing. . . . The Parson of the Parish [who had ridden up with his clerk, the sheriff, and some others] would keep running the end of his horsewhip in [Waller's] mouth, laying his whip across the hymn book, etc. When done singing [Waller] proceeded to prayer. In it he was violently jerked off the stage; they caught him by the back part of his neck, beat his head against the ground, sometimes up, sometimes down, they carried him through a gate that stood some considerable distance, where a gentleman [the sheriff] gave him . . . twenty lashes

with his horsewhip. . . . Then Bro. Waller was released, went back singing praise to God, mounted the stage and preached with a great deal of liberty.

Violence of this kind had become a recurrent feature of social-religious life in Tidewater and Piedmont. We must ask: What kind of conflict was this? What was it that aroused such antagonism? What manner of man, what manner of movement, was it that found liberty in endurance under the lash?

The continuation of the account gives fuller understanding of the meaning of this "liberty" and of the true character of this encounter. Asked "if his nature did not interfere in the time of violent persecution, when whipped, etc.," Waller "answered that the Lord stood by him . . . and poured his love into his soul without measure, and the brethren and sisters about him singing praises . . . so that he could scarcely feel the stripes . . . rejoicing . . . that he was worthy to suffer for his dear Lord and Master."

Again we see contrasted postures: on the one hand, a forceful, indeed brutal, response to the implicit challenge of religious dissidence; on the other, an acceptance of suffering sustained by shared emotions that gave release—"liberty." Both sides were, of course, engaged in combat, yet their modes of conducting themselves were diametrically opposite. If we are to understand the struggle that had developed, we must look as deeply as possible into the divergent styles of life, at the conflicting visions of what life should be like, that are reflected in this episode.

Opposites are intimately linked not only by the societal context in which they occur but also by the very antagonism that orients them to each other. The strength of the fascination that existed in this case is evident from the recurrent accounts of men drawn to Baptist meetings to make violent opposition, who, at the time or later, came "under conviction" and experienced conversion. The study of a polarity such as we find in the Virginia pre-Revolutionary religious scene should illuminate not only the conflict but also some of the fundamental structures of the society in which it occurred. A profile of the style of the gentry, and of those for whom they were a pattern, must be attempted. Their values, and the system by which these values were maintained, must be sketched. A somewhat fuller contrasting picture of the less familiar Virginia Baptist culture must then be offered, so that its character as a radical social movement is indicated.

The gentry style, of which we have seen glimpses in the confrontation with Baptists, is best understood in relation to the concept of honor—the proving of prowess. A formality of manners barely concealed adversary relationships; the essence of social exchange was overt self-assertion.

Display and bearing were important aspects of this system. We can best get a sense of the self-images that underlay it from the symbolic importance of horses. The figure of the gentleman who came to call Ireland back to society was etched on his memory as mounted on a "lofty . . . elegant horse." It was noted repeatedly in the eighteenth century that Virginians would "go five miles to catch a horse, to ride only one mile upon afterwards." This apparent absurdity had its logic in the necessity of being mounted when making an entrance on the social scene. The role of the steed as a valuable part of proud self-presentation is suggested by the intimate identification of the gentry with their horses that was constantly manifested through their conversation. Philip Fithian, the New Jersey tutor, sometimes felt that he heard nothing but "Loud disputes concerning the Excellence of each others Colts . . . their Fathers, Mothers (for so they call the Dams) Brothers, Sisters, Uncles, Aunts, Nephews, Nieces, and Cousins to the fourth Degree!"

Where did the essential display and self-assertion take place? There were few towns in Virginia; the outstanding characteristic of settlement was its diffuseness. Population was rather thinly scattered in very small groupings throughout a forested, river-dissected landscape. If there is to be larger community in such circumstances, there must be centers of action and communication. Insofar as cohesion is important in such an agrarian society, considerable significance must attach to the occasions when, coming together for certain purposes, the community realizes itself. The principal public centers in traditional Virginia were the parish churches and the county courthouses, with lesser foci established in a scatter of inns or "ordinaries." The principal general gatherings apart from these centers were for gala events such as horse race meetings and cockfights. Although lacking a specifically community character, the great estate house was also undoubtedly a very significant locus of action. By the operation of mimetic process and by the reinforcement of expectations concerning conduct and relationships, such centers and occasions were integral parts of the system of social control.

The most frequently held public gatherings at generally distributed centers were those for Sunday worship in the Anglican churches and chapels. An ideal identification of parish and community had been expressed in the law making persistent absence from church punishable. The continuance of this ideal is indicated by the fact that prosecutions under the law occurred right up to the time of the Revolution.

Philip Fithian has left us a number of vivid sketches of the typical Sunday scene at a parish church, sketches that illuminate the social nature and function of this institution. It was an important center of communication, especially among the elite, for it was "a general custom on Sundays here, with Gentlemen to invite one another home to dine, after Church; and to consult about, determine their common business, either before or after Service," when they would engage in discussing "the price of Tobacco, Grain etc. and settling either the lineage, Age, or qualities of favourite Horses." The occasion also served to demonstrate to the community, by visual representation, the rank structure of society. Fithian's further description evokes a dramatic image of haughty squires trampling past seated hoi polloi to their pews in the front. He noted that it was "not the Custom for Gentlemen to go into Church til Service is beginning, when they enter in a Body, in the same manner as they come out."

Similarly, vestry records show that fifty miles to the south of Fithian's Westmoreland County the front pews of a King and Queen County church were allocated to the gentry, but the pressure for place and precedence was such that only the greatest dignitaries (like the Corbins) could be accommodated together with their families; lesser gentlemen represented the honor of their houses in single places while their wives were seated farther back.

The size and composition of the ordinary congregations in the midst of which these representations of social style and status took place is as yet uncertain, but Fithian's description of a high festival is very suggestive on two counts: "This being Easter-Sunday, all the Parish seem'd to meet together High, Low, black, White all come out." We learn both that such general attendance was unusual, and that at least once a year full expression of ritual community was achieved. The whole society was then led to see itself in order.

The county courthouse was a most important center of social action. Monthly court days were attended by great numbers, for these were also the times for markets and fairs. The facts of social dominance were there visibly represented by the bearing of the "gentlemen justices" and the respect they commanded. On court days economic exchange was openly merged with social exchange (both plentifully sealed by the taking of liquor) and also expressed in conventional forms of aggression—in banter, swearing, and fighting.

The ruling gentry, who set the tone in this society, lived scattered across broad counties in the midst of concentrations of slaves that often amounted to black villages. Clearly the great houses that they erected in these settings were important statements: they expressed a style, they asserted a claim to dominance. The lavish entertainments, often lasting days, which were held in these houses performed equally important social functions in maintaining this claim, and in establishing communication and control within the elite itself. Here the convivial contests that were so essential to traditional Virginia social culture would issue in their most elaborate and stylish performances.

The importance of sporting occasions such as horse racing meets and cockfights for the maintenance of the values of self-assertion, in challenge and response, is strongly suggested by the comments of the marquis de Chastellux concerning cockfighting. His observations, dating from 1782, were that "when the principal promoters of this diversion [who were certainly gentry] propose to [match] their champions, they take great care to announce it to the public; and although there are neither posts, nor regular conveyances, this important news spreads with such facility, that the planters for thirty or forty miles round, attend, some with cocks, but all with money for betting, which is sometimes very considerable." An intensely shared interest of this kind, crossing but not leveling social distinctions, has powerful effects in transmitting style and reinforcing the leadership of the elite that controls proceedings and excels in the display.

Discussion so far has focused on the gentry, for *there* was established in dominant form the way of life the Baptists appeared to challenge. Yet this way was diffused throughout the society. All the forms of communication and exchange noted already had their popular acceptances with variations appropriate to the context, as can be seen in the recollections of the young Devereux Jarratt. The son of a middling farmer-artisan, Jarratt grew up totally intimidated by the proximity of gentlemen, yet his marked preference for engagement "in keeping and exercising race-horses for the turf . . . in taking care of and preparing game-cocks for a match and main" served to bind him nonetheless into the gentry social world, and would, had he persisted, have brought him

into contact—gratifying contact—with gentlemen. The remembered images of his upbringing among the small farmers of Tidewater New Kent County are strongly evocative of the cultural continuum between his humble social world and that of the gentry. In addition to the absorbing contest pastimes mentioned, there were the card play, the gathering at farmhouses for drinking (cider not wine), violin playing, and dancing.

The importance of pastime as a channel of communication, and even as a bond, between the ranks of a society such as this can hardly be too much stressed. People were drawn together by occasions such as horse races, cockfights, and dancing as by no other, because here men would become "known" to each other—"known" in the ways which the culture defined as "real." Skill and daring in that violent duel, the "quarter race"; coolness in the "deep play" of the betting that necessarily went with racing, cockfighting, and cards— these were means whereby Virginia males could prove themselves. Conviviality was an essential part of the social exchange, but through its soft coating pressed a harder structure of contest, or "emulation" as the contemporary phrase had it. Even in dancing this was so. Observers noted not only the passion for dancing—*"Virginians are of genuine Blood— They will dance or die!"*—but also the marked preference for the jig—in effect solo performances by partners of each sex, which were closely watched and were evidently competitive. In such activities, in social contexts high or low, enhanced eligibility for marriage was established by young persons who emerged as virtuosos of the dominant style. Situations where so much could happen presented powerful images of the "good life" to traditional Virginians, especially young ones. It was probably true, as alleged, that religious piety was generally considered appropriate only for the aged.

When one turns to the social world of the Baptists, the picture that emerges is so striking a negative of the one that has just been sketched that it must be considered to have been structured to an important extent by processes of reaction to the dominant culture.

Contemporaries were struck by the contrast between the challenging gaiety of traditional Virginia formal exchange and the solemn fellowship of the Baptists, who addressed each other as "Brother" and "Sister" and were perceived as "the most melancholy people in the world"—people who "cannot meet a man upon the road, but they must ram a text of Scripture down his throat." The finery of a gentleman who might ride forth in a gold-laced hat, sporting a gleaming Masonic medal, must be contrasted with the strict dress of the Separate Baptist, his hair "cut off" and such "superfluous forms and Modes of Dressing . . . as cock't hatts" explicitly renounced.

Their appearance was austere, to be sure, but we shall not understand the deep appeal of the evangelical movement, or the nature and full extent of its challenging contrast to the style and vision of the gentry-oriented social world, unless we look into the rich offerings beneath this somber exterior. The converts were proffered some escape from the harsh realities of disease, debt, overindulgence and deprivation, violence and sudden death, which were the common lot of small farmers. They could seek refuge in a close, supportive, orderly community, "a congregation of faithful persons, called out of the world by divine grace, who mutually agree to live together, and execute gospel discipline among them." Entrance into this community was attained by the relation of a personal experience of profound importance to the candidates, who would certainly be heard with respect, however humble their station. There was a community resonance for deep feelings, since, despite their sober face to the outside world, the Baptists encouraged in their religious practice a sharing of emotion to an extent far beyond that which would elicit crushing ridicule in gentry-oriented society. Personal testimonies of the experiences of simple folk have not come

down to us from that time, but the central importance of the ritual of admission and its role in renewing the common experience of ecstatic conversion is powerfully evoked by such recurrent phrases in the church books as "and a dore was opened to experience." This search for deep fellow-feeling must be set in contrast to the formal distance and rivalry in the social exchanges of the traditional system.

The warm supportive relationship that fellowship in faith and experience could engender appears to have played an important part in the spread of the movement. For example, about the year 1760 Peter Cornwell of Fauquier County sought out in the backcountry one Hays of pious repute, and settled him on his own land for the sake of godly companionship. "Interviews between these two families were frequent . . . their conversation religious . . . in so much that it began to be talked of abroad as a very strange thing. Many came to see them, to whom they related what God did for their souls . . . to the spreading of seriousness through the whole neighbourhood."

A concomitant of fellowship in deep emotions was comparative equality. Democracy is an ideal, and there are no indications that the pre-Revolutionary Baptists espoused it as such, yet there can be no doubt that these men, calling each other brothers, who believed that the only authority in their church was the meeting of those in fellowship together, conducted their affairs on a footing of equality in sharp contrast to the explicit preoccupation with rank and precedence that characterized the world from which they had been called. Important Baptist church elections generally required unanimity and might be held up by the doubts of a few. The number of preachers who were raised from obscurity to play an epic role in the Virginia of their day is a clear indication of the opportunities for fulfillment that the movement opened up to men who would have found no other avenue for public achievement. There is no reason to doubt the contemporary reputation of the early Virginia Baptist movement as one of the poor and unlearned.

Only isolated converts were made among the gentry, but many among the slaves.

The tight cohesive brotherhood of the Baptists must be understood as an explicit rejection of the formalism of traditional community organization. The antithesis is apparent in the contrast between Fithian's account of a parish congregation that dispersed without any act of worship when a storm prevented the attendence of both parson and clerk, and the report of the Baptist David Thomas that "when no minister . . . is expected, our people meet notwithstanding; and spend . . . time in praying, singing, reading, and in religious conversation."

The popular style and appeal of the Baptist Church found its most powerful and visible expression in the richness of its rituals, again a total contrast to the "prayrs read over in haste" of the colonial Church of England, where even congregational singing appears to have been a rarity. The most prominent and moving rite practiced by the sect was adult baptism, in which the candidates were publicly sealed into fellowship. A scrap of Daniel Fristoe's journal for June 15–16, 1771, survives as a unique contemporary description by a participant:

> (Being sunday) about 2000 people came together; after preaching [I] heard others that proposed to be baptized. . . . Then went to the water where I preached and baptized 29 persons. . . . When I had finished we went to a field and making a circle in the center, there laid hands on the persons baptized. The multitude stood round weeping, but when we sang *Come we that love the lord* and they were so affected that they lifted up their hands and faces towards heaven and discovered such chearful countenances in the midst of flowing tears as I had never seen before.

The warm emotional appeal at a popular level can even now be felt in that account, but it must be noted that the scene was also a vivid enactment of *a* community within and apart from *the* community. We must try to see that

closed circle for the laying on of hands through the eyes of those who had been raised in Tidewater or Piedmont Virginia with the expectation that they would always have a monistic parish community encompassing all the inhabitants within its measured liturgical celebrations. The antagonism and violence that the Baptists aroused then also become intelligible.

The celebration of the Lord's Supper frequently followed baptism, in which circumstances it was a further open enactment of closed community. We have some idea of the importance attached to this public display from David Thomas's justification:

> . . . should we forbid even the worst of men, from viewing the solemn representation of his [the LORD JESUS CHRIST's] dying agonies? May not the sight of this mournful tragedy, have a tendency to alarm stupid creatures . . . when GOD himself is held forth . . . trembling, falling, bleeding, yea, expiring under the intollerable pressure of that wrath due to [sin]. . . . And therefore, this ordinance should not be put under a bushel, but on a candlestick, that all may enjoy the illumination.

We may see the potency attributed to the ordinances starkly through the eyes of the abashed young John Taylor who, hanging back from baptism, heard the professions of seven candidates surreptitiously, judged them not saved, and then watched them go "into the water, and from thence, as I thought, seal their own damnation at the Lord's table. I left the meeting with awful horror of mind."

More intimate, yet evidently important for the close community, were the rites of fellowship. The forms are elusive, but an abundance of ritual is suggested by the simple entry of Morgan Edwards concerning Falls Creek: "In this church are admitted, Evangelists, Ruling Elders, deaconesses, laying on of hands, feasts of charity, anointing the sick, kiss of charity, washing feet, right hand of fellowship, and devoting children." Far from being mere formal observances, these and other rites, such as the ordaining of "apostles" to "pervade" the churches, were keenly experimented with to determine their efficacy.

Aspects of preaching also ought to be understood as ritual rather than as formal instruction. It was common for persons to come under conviction or to obtain ecstatic release "under preaching," and this established a special relationship between the neophyte and his or her "father in the gospel." Nowhere was the ritual character of the preaching more apparent than in the great meetings of the Virginia Separate Baptist Association. The messengers would preach to the people along the way to the meeting place and back; thousands would gather for the Sunday specially set aside for worship and preaching. There the close independent congregational communities found themselves merged in a great and swelling collective. The varieties of physical manifestations such as crying out and falling down, which were frequently brought on by the ritualized emotionalism of such preaching, are too well known to require description.

Virginia Baptist sermons from the 1770s have not survived, perhaps another indication that their purely verbal content was not considered of the first importance. Ireland's account of his early ministry (he was ordained in 1769) reveals the ritual recurrence of the dominant themes expected to lead into repentance those who were not hardened: "I began first to preach . . . our awful apostacy by the fall; the necessity of repentance unto life, and of faith in the Lord Jesus Christ . . . our helpless incapacity to extricate ourselves therefrom I stated and urged."

As "seriousness" spread, with fear of hell-fire and concern for salvation, it was small wonder that a gentleman of Loudoun County should find to his alarm "that the *Anabaptists* . . . growing very numerous . . . seem to be increasing in afluence [influence?]; and . . . quite destroying pleasure in the Country; for they encourage ardent Pray'r; strong and constant faith, and an intire Banishment of *Gam-*

*ing, Dancing,* and Sabbath-Day Diversions." That the Baptists were drawing away increasing numbers from the dominant to the insurgent culture was radical enough, but the implications of solemnity, austerity, and stern sobriety were more radical still, for they called into question the validity—indeed the propriety—of the occasions and modes of display and association so important in maintaining the bonds of Virginia's geographically diffuse society. Against the system in which proud men were joined in rivalry and convivial excess was set a reproachful model of an order in which God-humbled men would seek a deep sharing of emotion while repudiating indulgence of the flesh. Yet the Baptist movement, although it must be understood as a revolt against the traditional system, was not primarily negative. Behind it can be discerned an impulse toward a tighter, more effective system of values and of exemplary conduct to be established and maintained within the ranks of the common folk.

In this aspect evangelicalism must be seen as a popular response to mounting social disorder. It would be difficult—perhaps even impossible—to establish an objective scale for measuring disorder in Virginia. What can be established is that during the 1760s and 1770s disorder was perceived by many as increasing. This has been argued for the gentry by Jack P. Greene and Gordon S. Wood, and need not be elaborated here. What does need to be reemphasized is that the gentry's growing perception of disorder was focused on those forms of activity which the Baptists denounced and which provided the main arenas for the challenge and response essential to the traditional "good life." It was coming to be felt that horse racing, cockfighting, and card play, with their concomitants of gambling and drinking, rather than serving to maintain the gentry's prowess, were destructive of it and of social order generally. Display might now be negatively perceived as "luxury."

Given the absence of the restraints imposed by tight village community in traditional Virginia, disorder was probably an even more acute problem in the lower than in the upper echelons of society—more acute because it was compounded by the harshness and brutality of everyday life, and most acute in proportion to the social proximity of the lowest stratum, the enslaved. The last named sector of society, lacking sanctioned marriage and legitimated familial authority, was certainly disorderly by English Protestant standards, and must therefore have had a disturbing effect on the consciousness of the whole community.

As the conversion experience was at the heart of the popular evangelical movement, so a sense of a great burden of guilt was at the heart of the conversion experience. An explanation in terms of social process must be sought for the sudden widespread intensification and vocal expression of such feelings, especially when this is found in areas of the Virginia Piedmont and Tidewater where no cultural tradition existed as preconditioning for the communal confession, remorse, and expiation that characterized the spread of the Baptist movement. The hypothesis here advanced is that the social process was one in which popular perceptions of disorder in society—and hence by individuals in themselves—came to be expressed in the metaphor of "sin." It is clear that the movement was largely spread by revolt from within, not by "agitators" from without. Commonly the first visit of itinerant preachers to a neighborhood was made by invitation of a group of penitents already formed and actively meeting together. Thus the "spread of seriousness" and alarm at the sinful disorder of the traditional world tended to precede the creation of an emotional mass movement "under preaching." A further indication of the importance of order-disorder preoccupations for the spread of the new vision with its contrasted life style was the insistence on "works." Conversion could ultimately be validated among church members only by a radical reform of conduct. The Baptist church books reveal the close concern for the disciplinary supervision of such changes.

Drunkenness was a persistent problem in Virginia society. There were frequent cases in the Baptist records where censure, ritual excommunication, and moving penitence were unable to effect a lasting cure. Quarreling, slandering, and disputes over property were other endemic disorders that the churches sought patiently and endlessly to control within their own communities. With its base in slavery, this was a society in which contest readily turned into disorderly violence. Accounts of the occasion, manner, and frequency of wrestling furnish a horrifying testimony to the effects of combining a code of honor with the coarseness of life in the lower echelons of society. Hearing that "by appointment is to be fought this Day . . . two fist Battles between four young Fellows," Fithian noted the common causes of such conflicts, listing numbers of trivial affronts such as that one "has in a merry hour call'd [another] a *Lubber*, . . . or a *Buckskin*, or a *Scotchman*, . . . or offered him a dram without wiping the mouth of the Bottle." He noted also the savagery of the fighting, including "Kicking, Scratching, Biting, . . . Throtling, Gouging [the eyes], Dismembring [the private parts]. . . . This spectacle . . . generally is attended with a crowd of People!" Such practices prevailed throughout the province. An episode in the life of one of the great Baptist preachers, John, formerly "swearing Jack," Waller, illustrates both prevailing violence and something of the relationship between classes. Waller and some gentry companions were riding on the road when a drunken butcher addressed them in a manner they considered insolent. One of the gentlemen had a horse trained to rear and "paw what was before him," which he then had it do to frighten the butcher. The man was struck by the hooves and died soon after. Tried for manslaughter, the company of gentlemen were acquitted on a doubt as to whether the injury had indeed caused the butcher's death. The episode may have helped prepare Waller for conversion into a radically opposed social world.

Nowhere does the radicalism of the evangelical reaction to the dominant values of self-assertion, challenge, and response of the gentry-oriented society reveal itself so clearly as in the treatment of physical aggression. In the Baptist community a man might come forward by way of confession with an accusation against himself for "Getting angry Tho in Just Defence of himself in Despute." The meeting of another church was informed that its clerk, Rawley Hazard, had been approached on his own land and addressed in "Very scurrilous language" and then assaulted, and that he then "did defend himself against this sd Violence, that both the Assailant and Defendent was much hurt." The members voted that the minister "do Admonish Brother Rawley . . . in the presents of the Church . . . saying that his defence was Irregular."

A further mark of their radicalism, and without doubt the most significant aspect of the quest for a system of social control centered in the people, was the inclusion of slaves as "brothers" and "sisters" in their close community. When the Baptists sealed the slaves unto eternal life, leading them in white robes into the water and then back to receive the bread and wine, they were also laying upon them responsibility for godly conduct, demanding an internalization of strict Protestant Christian values and norms. They were seeking to create an orderly moral community where hitherto there had seemed to be none.

The slaves were members and therefore subject to church discipline. The incidence of excommunication of slaves, especially for the sin of adultery, points to the desire of the Baptists to introduce their own standards of conduct, including stable marital relationships, among slaves. A revealing indication of the perception of the problem in this area is found in the recurrent phrase that was sometimes given as the sole reason for excommunication: "walking disorderly." Discipline was also clearly directed toward inculcating a sense of duty in the slaves, who could be excommunicated for "disobedience and Aggrevation to [a] master."

The recurrent use of the words "order," "orderly," "disorderly" in the Baptist records reveals a preoccupation that lends further support to the hypothesis that concern for the establishment of a securer system of social control was a powerful impulse for the movement. "Is it orderly?" is the usual introduction to the queries concerning right conduct that were frequently brought forward for resolution at monthly meetings.

With alarm at perceived disorder must also be associated the deep concern for Sabbath-day observance that is so strongly manifested in autobiographies, apologetics, and church books. It appears that the Virginia method of keeping the Sabbath "with sport, merriment, and dissipation" readily served to symbolize the disorder perceived in society. It was his observation of this that gave Ireland his first recorded shock. Conversely, cosmic order was affirmed and held up as a model for society in the setting aside on the Lord's Day of worldly pursuits, while men expressed their reverence for their Maker and Redeemer.

When the Baptist movement is understood as a rejection of the style of life for which the gentry set the pattern and as a search for more powerful popular models of proper conduct, it can be seen why the ground on which the battle was mainly fought was not the estate or the great house, but the neighborhood, the farmstead, and the slave quarter. This was a contemporary perception, for it was generally charged that the Baptists were "continual fomenters of discord" who "not only divided good neighbours, but slaves and their masters; children and their parents . . . wives and their husbands." The only reported complaint against the first preachers to be imprisoned was of "their running into private houses and making dissensions." The struggle for allegiance in the homesteads between a style of life modeled on that of the leisured gentry and that embodied in evangelicalism was intense. In humbler, more straitened circumstances a popular culture based on the code of honor and almost hedonist values was necessarily less securely established than among the more affluent gentry. Hence the anxious aggressiveness of popular anti-New Light feeling and action.

The Baptists did not make a bid for control of the political system—still less did they seek a leveling or redistribution of worldly wealth. It was clearly a mark of the strength of gentry hegemony and of the rigidities of a social hierarchy with slavery at its base that the evangelical revolt should have been so closely restricted in scope. Yet the Baptists' salvationism and sabbatarianism effectively redefined morality and human relationships; their church leaders and organization established new and more popular foci of authority, and sought to impose a radically different and more inclusive model for the maintenance of order in society. Within the context of the traditional monistic, face-to-face, deferential society such a regrouping necessarily constituted a powerful challenge.

The beginnings of a cultural disjunction between gentry and sections of the lower orders, where hitherto there had been a continuum, posed a serious threat to the traditional leaders of the community; their response was characteristic. The popular emotional style, the encouragement given to men of little learning to "exercise their gifts" in preaching, and the preponderance of humble folk in the movement gave to the proud gentry their readiest defense—contempt and ridicule. The stereotype of the Baptists as "an ignorant . . . set . . . of . . . the contemptible class of the people," a "poor and illiterate sect" which "none of the rich or learned ever join," became generally established. References in the *Virginia Gazette* to "ignorant enthusiasts" were common, and there could appear in its columns without challenge a heartless satire detailing "A Receipt to make an Anabaptist Preacher": "Take the Herbes of Hypocrisy and Ambition, . . . of the Seed of Dissention and Discord one Ounce, . . . one Pint of the Spirit of Self-Conceitedness."

An encounter with some gentlemen at an inn in Goochland County is recorded by Mor-

gan Edwards, a college-educated Pennsylvania Baptist minister. He noted the moderation of the gentry in this area, yet their arrogant scorn for dissenters in general, and for Baptists in particular, is unmistakable from the dialogue reported. Since Edwards had just come from Georgia, they began with ribald jests about "mr Whitefield's children . . . by the squaw" and continued as follows:

> *Esq[uire] U: Pray are you not a*
>     *clergyman? . . .*
> *Capt. L: Of the church of England I presume?*
> *N[orthern] M[inister]: No, Sir; I am a*
>     *clergyman of a*
>     *better church than that; for she is a*
>     *persecutor.*
> *Omnes: Ha! Ha! Ha! . . .*
> *Esq. U: Then you are one of the fleabitten*
>     *clergy?*
> *N. M.: Are there fleas in this bed, Sir?*
> *Esq. U: I ask, if you are a clergyman of the*
>     *itchy true*
>     *blue kirk of Scotland? . . .*
> *Capt. L. (whispers): He is ashamed to own*
>     *her for fear you*
>     *should scratch him 'Squire.' . . .*
> *[When they have discovered that this*
>     *educated man, who shows*
> *such address in fencing with words, is a*
>     *Baptist minister,*
> *they discuss the subject bibulously among*
>     *themselves.]*
> *Esq. U: He is no baptist . . . I take him to be*
>     *one of the*
>     *Georgia law[ye]rs.*
> *Mr. G: For my part I believe him to be a*
>     *baptist minister.*
>     *There are some clever fellows among*
>     *them. . . .*
> *Major W: I confess they have often*
>     *confounded me with their*
>     *arguments and texts of Scripture; and if*
>     *any other people but*
>     *the baptists professed their religion I would*
>     *make it my*
>     *religion before tomorrow.*

The class of folk who filled the Baptist churches were a great obstacle to gentry participation. Behind the ridicule and contempt, of course, lay incomprehension, and behind that, fear of this menacing, unintelligible movement. The only firsthand account we have of a meeting broken up by the arrest of the preachers tells how they "were carried before the magistrate," who had them taken "one by one into a room and examined our pockets and wallets for firearms." He accused them of "carrying on a mutiny against the authority of the land." This sort of dark suspicion impelled David Thomas, in his printed defense of the Baptists, to reiterate several times that "We concern not ourselves with the government . . . we form no intrigues . . . nor make any attempts to alter the constitution of the kingdom to which as men we belong."

Fear breeds fantasy. So it was that alarmed observers put a very crude interpretation on the emotional and even physical intimacy of this intrusive new society. Its members were associated with German Anabaptists, and a "historical" account of the erotic indulgences of that sect was published on the front page of the *Virginia Gazette.*

Driven by uneasiness, although toughened by their instinctive contempt, some members of the establishment made direct moves to assert proper social authority and to outface the upstarts. Denunciations from parish pulpits were frequent. Debates were not uncommon, being sought on both sides. Ireland recalled vividly an encounter that reveals the pride and presumption of the gentlemen who came forward in defense of the Church of England. Captain M'Clanagan's place was thronged with people, some of whom had come forty miles to hear John Pickett, a Baptist preacher of Fauquier County. The rector of a neighboring parish attended with some leading parishioners "who were as much prejudiced . . . as he was." "The parson had a chair brought for himself, which he placed three or four yards in front of Mr. Pickett . . . taking out his pen, ink and paper, to take down notes of what he conceived to be false doctrine." When Pickett had finished, "the Parson called him a schismatick,

a broacher of false doctrines . . . [who] held up damnable errors that day." Pickett answered adequately (it appeared to Ireland), but "when contradicted it would in a measure confuse him." So Ireland, who had been raised a gentleman, took it on himself to sustain the Baptist cause. The parson immediately "wheeled about on his chair . . . and let out a broadside of his eloquence, with an expectation, no doubt, that he would confound me with the first fire." However, Ireland "gently laid hold of a chair, and placed . . . it close by him, determined to argue." The contest was long, and "both gentlemen and ladies," who had evidently seated themselves near the parson, "would repeatedly help him to scripture, in order to support his arguments." When the debate ended (as the narrator recalled) in the refutation of the clergyman, Ireland "addressed one of the gentlemen who had been so officious in helping his teacher; he was a magistrate . . . 'Sir, as the dispute between the Parson and myself is ended, if you are disposed to argue the subject over again, I am willing to enter upon it with you.' He stretched out his arm straight before him, at that instant, and declared that I should not come nigher than that length." Ireland "concluded what the consequence would be, therefore made a peaceable retreat." Such scenes of action are the stuff of social structure, as of social conflict, and require no further comment.

Great popular movements are not quelled, however, by outfacing, nor are they stemmed by the ridicule, scorn, or scurrility of incomprehension. Moreover, they draw into themselves members of all sections of society. Although the social worlds most open to proselytizing by the Baptists were the neighborhoods and the slave quarters, there were converts from the great houses too. Some of the defectors, such as Samuel Harris, played a leading role in the movement. The squirearchy was disturbed by the realization that the contemptible sect was reaching among themselves. The exchanges between Morgan Edwards and the gentlemen in the Goochland inn were confused by the breakdown of the stereotype of ignorance and poverty. Edwards's cultured facility reminded the squires that "there are some clever fellows among [the Baptists]. I heard one Jery Walker support a petition of theirs at the assembly in such a manner as surprised us all, and [made] our witts draw in their horns." The pride and assurance of the gentry could be engaged by awareness that their own members might withdraw from their ranks and choose the other way. The vigorous response of Ireland's patron to the challenge implicit in his defection provides a striking example.

The intensity of the conflict for allegiance among the people and, increasingly, among the gentry, makes intelligible the growing frequency of violent clashes of the kind illustrated at the beginning of this article. The violence was, however, one-sided and self-defeating. The episode of April 1771 in which the parson brutally interfered with the devotions of the preacher, who was then horsewhipped by the sheriff, must have produced a shock of revulsion in many quarters. Those who engaged in such actions were not typical of either the Anglican clergy or the country gentlemen. The extreme responses of some, however, show the anxieties to which all were subject, and the excesses in question could only heighten the tension.

Disquiet was further exacerbated by the fact that the law governing dissent, under which the repressive county benches were intent on acting, was of doubtful validity, and became the subject of public controversy in the fall of 1771. This controversy, combined with the appalling scenes of disorder and the growing numbers of Separate Baptists, led the House of Burgesses to attempt action in its spring 1772 session. The Separates had shown renewed tendencies to intransigence as recently as May 1771, when a move was strongly supported to deny fellowship to all ministers who submitted to the secular authority by applying for permission to preach. The fact that eight months later the House of Burgesses re-

ceived a petition for easier licensing conditions was a sign that a compromise was at last being sought. Nevertheless, prejudices were so strong that the bill that the Burgesses approved was considerably more restrictive than the English act that had hitherto been deemed law in the colony.

The crisis of self-confidence which the evangelical challenges and the failure of forceful responses were inducing in the Virginia gentry was subtly revealed in March 1772 by the unprecedented decision of the House, ordinarily assertive of its authority, not to send the engrossed bill to the Council, but to have it printed and referred to the public for discussion. Nearly two years later, in January 1774, the young James Madison, exultant about the progress of the American cause in the aftermath of the Boston Tea Party, despaired of Virginia on account of religious intolerance. He wrote that he had "nothing to brag of as to the State and Liberty" of his "Country," where "Poverty and Luxury prevail among all sorts" and "that diabolical Hell conceived principle of persecution rages." In April of the same year he still had little hope that a bill would pass to ease the situation of dissenters. In the previous session "such incredible and extravagant stories" had been "told in the House of the monstrous effects of the Enthusiasm prevalent among the Sectaries and so greedily swallowed by their Enemies that . . . they lost footing by it." Burgesses "who pretend too much contempt to examine into their principles . . . and are too much devoted to the ecclesiastical establishment to hear of the Toleration of Dissentients" were likely to prevail once again. Madison's foreboding was correct inasmuch as the old regime in Virginia never accomplished a legal resolution of the toleration problem.

The Revolution ultimately enshrined religious pluralism as a fundamental principle in Virginia. It rendered illegitimate the assumptions concerning the nature of community religious corporateness that underlay aggressive defense against the Baptists. It legitimated new forms of conflict, so that by the end of the century the popular evangelists were able to counterattack and symbolize social revolution in many localities by having the Episcopal Church's lands and even communion plate sold at auction. But to seek the conclusion to this study in such political-constitutional developments would be a deflection, for it has focused on a brief period of intense, yet deadlocked conflict in order to search out the social-cultural configurations of the forces that confronted each other. The diametrical opposition of the swelling Baptist movement to traditional mores shows it to have been indeed a radical social revolt, indicative of real strains within society.

Challenging questions remain. Can some of the appeal of the Revolution's republican ideology be understood in terms of its capacity to command the allegiance of both self-humbled evangelicals and honor-upholding gentry? What different meanings did the republican ideology assume within the mutually opposed systems of values and belief? And, looking forward to the post-Revolutionary period, what was the configuration—what the balance between antagonistic cultural elements—when confrontation within a monistic framework had given way to accommodation in a more pluralist republican society? These questions are closely related to the subject that this study has endeavored to illuminate—the forms and sources of popular culture in Virginia, and the relationship of popular culture to that of the gentry elite.

# 9

# HEARTS AND MINDS IN THE AMERICAN REVOLUTION: THE CASE OF "LONG BILL" SCOTT

## JOHN SHY

All successful revolutions have relied upon the active participation of common people who chose to interrupt the rhythms of their everyday existence in order to risk their lives in the cause of basic social and political transformation. The American Revolution, too, depended on the commitment of farmers, artisans, and laborers to the Revolutionary cause. Yet, though anti-British sentiments were widespread among the common people of the American colonies, the mobilization of such persons required men and women who could focus popular resentments and organize effective resistance to Britain. Without these leaders there would have been no revolution.

In this essay, John Shy traces the career of one of these local leaders, William Scott of Peterborough, New Hampshire. Like his fellow townsmen, Scott was not much inclined toward revolution. Yet in the course of the war he served in four campaigns against the British and escaped capture on three different occasions. What, asks Shy, motivated men like Scott and his townsmen to commit themselves to the revolutionary cause?

The answer, for Shy, resides in the nature of the local militia and the pinched conditions of northern New England life. While the rocky soil, heavily forested terrain, and short growing season of northern New England had never been kind to colonial farmers, early settlers in the region had been able to make an adequate, if not luxurious, life for themselves as tillers of the soil. But by the last quarter of the eighteenth century the grandchildren of the original settlers faced a different prospect. As families increased in size during the eighteenth century and the available land was taken up by succeeding generations of farmers, the rural economy of northern and eastern New England began to stagnate. No longer could a farmer's son depend on an inheritance that would allow him to establish his family's independence. It was the opportunity to escape from these straitened conditions and to achieve some degree of advancement in the world that led men like "Long Bill" Scott to join the Revolutionary cause.

Reprinted by permission of John Shy and University of Minnesota Press.

Armed force, and nothing else, decided the outcome of the American Revolution. Without armed force mobilized on a decisive scale, there would be today no subject for discussion. Deprived even of its name, the "Revolution" would shrink to a mere rebellion—an interesting episode, but like dozens of others in the modern history of Western societies. Crude, obvious, and unappealing as this truism may be, it is still true; without war to sustain it, the Declaration of Independence would be a forgotten, abortive manifesto. Writing about an earlier revolutionary war, Thomas Hobbes rammed home the point when he said that "covenants without swords are but words."

But the cynicism of Hobbes can too easily mask a second, equally important truism, perhaps best expressed a century later by David Hume. "As force is always on the side of the governed," Hume wrote, "the governors have nothing to support them but opinion." For all their peculiar aggressiveness, even human beings do not kill and risk death for no reason. Beneath the raw irrationality of violence lies motive—some psychic web spun from logic, belief, perception, and emotion that draws people to commit terrible acts and to hazard everything they possess. Perhaps Hume's view—that persuasion, not force itself, must ultimately govern, because no ruling minority can control a truly aroused majority—has lost some of its validity in our own time, when technology vastly multiplies the amount of force that a few people can wield, but it certainly held good for the eighteenth century, when even the best weapons were still relatively primitive and widely available. If Hobbes—like all his fellow cynics down through history—is right in believing that public opinion is a fairly fragile flower which can seldom survive the hot wind of violence, Hume reminds us that no one, not even a soldier, uses force without somehow being moved to do so.

John Adams put his finger on this matter of motivation when he said that the real American Revolution, the revolution that estranged American hearts from old British loyalties and readied American minds to use (and to withstand) massive violence, was over before the war began. But Adams also opined that a third of the American people supported the Revolutionary cause, another third remained more or less loyal to Britain, and that the rest were neutral or apathetic. Clearly, Adams conceded that not all hearts and minds had been permanently affected in the same way. Many British observers thought that the real American Revolutionaries were the religious Dissenters, Congregationalists and Presbyterians who had always been secretly disloyal to the Crown because they rejected the whole Anglican Establishment, whose head was the king; and that these Revolutionaries persuaded poor Irishmen, who poured into the American colonies in great numbers during the middle third of the eighteenth century, to do most of the dirty business of actual fighting. American Whigs, on the other hand, generally assumed that all decent, sane people supported the Revolution, and that those who did not could be categorized as timid, vicious, corrupt, or deluded. Each of these opinions contains a measure of truth, but they seem to contradict one another, and they do not carry us very far toward understanding.

Like these stock opinions, we have two standard images of the popular response to the Revolutionary War. One is of whole towns springing to arms as Paul Revere carried his warning to them in the spring of 1775. The other is of a tiny, frozen, naked band of men at Valley Forge, all that are left when everyone else went home in the winter of 1778. Which is the true picture? Both, evidently. But that answer is of no use at all when we ask whether the Revolution succeeded only by the persistence of a very small group of people, the intervention of France, and great good luck; or whether the Revolution was—or became—unbeatable because the mass of the population simply would not give up the struggle, and the British simply could not muster the force and the resolution to kill them all or break their will or sit on all or even any large proportion of them. This problem posed by the motivation for violence breaks down into more specific questions: Who actually took up arms and why? How strong was the motivation to serve, and to keep serving in spite of defeat and other adversities? What was the intricate interplay and feedback between attitude and behavior, events and attitude? Did people get war weary and discouraged, or did they become adamant toward British efforts to coerce them? If we could answer these questions with confidence, not only would we know why the rebels won and the government lost, but we would also know important things about the American society that emerged from seven years of armed conflict. Differing answers to these questions lay at the root of what had divided Charles Lee and George Washington.

The essential difficulty in answering these questions lies less in the lack of evidence than in the nature of the subject. Violence, with all its ramifications, remains a great mystery for students of human life, while the deeper motivational sources of human behavior—particularly collective behavior under conditions of stress—are almost equally mysterious. When these two mysteries come together, as they do in wars and revolutions, then the historian faces a problem full of traps and snares for the unwary, a problem that challenges his ability to know *anything* about the past. A certain humility is obviously in order. If any of us are tempted not to be humble, we might recall how recently intelligent, well-informed American leaders spoke glibly about winning the "hearts and minds" of another few million people caught up by war and revolution [in Vietnam]. That, then, is the subject: the hearts and minds of Americans whose willingness to engage in violence, two centuries ago, fundamentally changed the course of history.

A suitably humble approach to these difficult questions lies at hand in a book written by Peter Oliver, who watched the Revolution explode in Boston. Oliver descended from some of the oldest families of Massachusetts Bay, he was a distinguished merchant and public offi-

cial, and he became a bitter Tory. His book, *The Origin and Progress of the American Rebellion,* . . . is a fascinatingly unsympathetic version of the Revolution, and in it Oliver makes an attempt to answer some of our questions. Using the device, more fully developed by S. L. A. Marshall during the Second World War, of the after-action interview, Oliver asked a wounded American lieutenant, who had been captured at Bunker Hill, how he had come to be a rebel. The American officer allegedly replied as follows:

> The case was this Sir! I lived in a Country Town; I was a Shoemaker, & got my Living by my Labor. When this Rebellion came on, I saw some of my Neighbors get into Commission, who were no better than myself. I was very ambitious, & did not like to see those Men above me. I was asked to enlist, as a private Soldier. My Ambition was too great for so low a Rank; I offered to enlist upon having a Lieutenants Commission; which was granted. I imagined my self now in a way of Promotion: if I was killed in Battle, there would an end of me, but if my Captain was killed, I should rise in Rank, & should still have a Chance to rise higher. These Sir! were the only Motives of my entering into the Service; for as to the Dispute between great Britain & the Colonies, I know nothing of it; neither am I capable of judging whether it is right or wrong.

Those who have read U.S. Government publications of the 1960's will find this POW interrogation familiar; during the Vietnam War, the State and Defense Departments published many like it, and more than one Vietcong or North Vietnamese prisoner is said to have spoken in the accents of the wounded American lieutenant so long ago.

Now the lieutenant was not a figment of Oliver's embittered imagination. His name is given by Oliver as Scott, and American records show that Lieutenant William Scott, of Colonel Paul Sargent's regiment, was indeed wounded and captured at Bunker Hill. Scott turns out, upon investigation, to have been an interesting character. Perhaps the first thing to be said about him is that nothing in the record of his life down to 1775 contradicts anything in Oliver's account of the interview. Scott came from Peterborough, New Hampshire, a town settled in the 1730s by Irish Presbyterians. Scott's father had served in the famous Rogers' Rangers during the French and Indian War. At the news of the outbreak of fighting in 1775, a cousin who kept the store in Peterborough recruited a company of local men to fight the British. Apparently the cousin tried to enlist our William Scott—known to his neighbors as "Long Bill," thus distinguishing him from the cousin, "Short Bill." But "Long Bill"—our Bill—seems to have declined serving as a private, and insisted on being a lieutenant if cousin "Short Bill" was going to be a captain. "Short Bill" agreed. So far the stories as told by Oliver and as revealed in the New Hampshire records check perfectly. Nor is there any reason to think that "Long Bill" had a deeper understanding of the causes of the Revolution than appear in Oliver's version of the interview.

What Peter Oliver never knew was the subsequent life history of this battered yokel, whose view of the American rebellion seemed so pitifully naïve. When the British evacuated Boston, they took Scott and other American prisoners to Halifax, Nova Scotia. There, after more than a year in captivity, Scott somehow managed to escape, to find a boat, and to make his way back to the American army just in time for the fighting around New York City in 1776. Captured again in November, when Fort Washington and its garrison fell to a surprise British assault, Scott escaped almost immediately, this time by swimming the Hudson River at night— according to a newspaper account—with his sword tied around his neck and his watch pinned to his hat. He returned to New Hampshire during the winter of 1777 to recruit a company of his own; there, he enlisted his two eldest sons for three years or the duration of the war. Stationed in the Boston area, he marched against Burgoyne's invading army from Canada, and led a detachment that cut off

the last retreat just before the surrender near Saratoga. Scott later took part in the fighting around Newport, Rhode Island. But when his light infantry company was ordered to Virginia under Lafayette in early 1781, to counter the raiding expedition led by Benedict Arnold, Scott's health broke down; long marches and hot weather would make the old Bunker Hill wounds ache, and he was permitted to resign from the army. After only a few months of recuperation, however, he seems to have grown restless, for we find him during the last year of the war serving as a volunteer on a navy frigate.

What would Scott have said if Oliver had been able to interview him again, after the war? We can only guess. Probably he would have told Oliver that his oldest son had died in the army, not gloriously, but of camp fever, after six years of service. Scott might have said that in 1777 he had sold his Peterborough farm in order to meet expenses, but that the note which he took in exchange turned into a scrap of paper when the dollar of 1777 became worth less than two cents by 1780. He might also have said that another farm, in Groton, Massachusetts, slipped away from him, along with a down payment that he had made on it, when his military pay depreciated rapidly to a fraction of its nominal value. He might not have been willing to admit that when his wife died he simply turned their younger children over to his surviving elder son, and then set off to beg a pension or a job from the government. Almost certainly he would not have told Oliver that when the son—himself sick, his corn crop killed by a late frost, and saddled with three little brothers and sisters—begged his father for help, our hero told him, should all else fail, to hand the children over to the selectmen of Peterborough—in short, to put them on welfare.

In 1792, "Long Bill" Scott once more made the newspapers: he rescued eight people from drowning when their small boat capsized in New York Harbor. But heroism did not pay very well. At last, in 1794, Secretary of War

Henry Knox made Scott deputy storekeeper at West Point; and a year later General Benjamin Lincoln took Scott with him to the Ohio country, where they were to negotiate with the Indians and survey the land opened up by Anthony Wayne's victory at Fallen Timbers. At last he had a respectable job, and even a small pension for his nine wounds; but Lincoln's group caught something called "lake fever" while surveying on the Black River, near Sandusky. Scott, ill himself, guided part of the group back to Fort Stanwix, New York, then returned for the others. It was his last heroic act. A few days after his second trip, he died, on September 16, 1796.

Anecdotes, even good ones like the touching saga of "Long Bill" Scott, do not make history. But neither can a subject like ours be treated in terms of what Jesse Lemisch has referred to as the lives of Great White Men—Washington, Adams, Jefferson, Hamilton, and the handful like them. Scott's life, in itself, may tell us little about how armed force and public opinion were mobilized in the Revolution; yet the story of his life leads us directly—and at the level of ordinary people—toward crucial features of the process.

Peterborough, New Hampshire, in 1775 had a population of 549. Town, state, and federal records show that about 170 men were credited to Peterborough as performing some military service during the Revolution. In other words, almost every adult male, at one time or another, carried a gun in the war. But of these 170 participants, less than a third performed extensive service; that is, service ranging from over a year up to the whole eight years of the war. And only a fraction of these—less than two dozen—served as long as Bill Scott. In Scott we are not seeing a typical participant, but one of a small "hard core" of revolutionary fighters—the men who stayed in the army for more than a few months or a single campaign. As we look down the list of long-service soldiers from Peterborough, they seem indeed to be untypical people. A few, like Scott and his cousin "Short Bill" and James Taggart and Jo-

siah Munroe, became officers or at least sergeants, and thereby acquired status and perhaps some personal satisfaction from their prolonged military service. But most of the hard core remained privates, and they were an unusually poor, obscure group of men, even by the rustic standards of Peterborough. Many—like John Alexander, Robert Cunningham, William Ducannon, Joseph Henderson, Richard Richardson, John Wallace, and Thomas Williamson—were recruited from outside the town, from among men who never really lived in Peterborough. Whether they lived *anywhere*—in the strict legal sense—is a question. Two men—Zaccheus Brooks and John Miller—are simply noted as "transients." At least two—James Hackley and Randall McAllister—were deserters from the British army. At least two others—Samuel Weir and Titus Wilson—were black men, Wilson dying as a prisoner of war. A few, like Michael Silk, simply appear, join the army, then vanish without a documentary trace. Many more reveal themselves as near the bottom of the socioeconomic ladder: Hackley, Benjamin Allds, Isaac Mitchell, Ebenezer Perkins, Amos Spofford, Jonathan Wheelock, and Charles White were legal paupers after the Revolution, Joseph Henderson was a landless day-laborer, Samuel Spear was jailed for debt, and John Miller was mentally deranged.

We can look at the whole Peterborough contingent in another way, in terms of those in it who were, or later became, prominent or at least solid citizens of the town. With a few exceptions, like "Short Bill" Scott and "Long Bill" 's son John, who survived frost-killed corn and a parcel of unwanted siblings to become a selectman and a leader of the town, these prominent men and solid citizens had served in the war for only short periods—a few months in 1775, a month or two in the Burgoyne emergency of 1777, maybe a month in Rhode Island or a month late in the war to bolster the key garrison of West Point. The pattern is clear, and it is a pattern that reappears wherever the surviving evidence has permitted a similar kind of inquiry. Lynn, Massachusetts; Berks County, Pennsylvania; Colonel Smallwood's recruits from Maryland in 1782; several regiments of the Massachusetts Line; a sampling of pension applicants from Virginia—all show that the hard core of Continental soldiers, the Bill Scotts who could not wangle commissions, the soldiers at Valley Forge, the men who shouldered the heaviest military burden, were something *less* than average colonial Americans. As a group, they were poorer, more marginal, less well anchored in the society. Perhaps we should not be surprised; it is easy to imagine men like these actually being attracted by the relative affluence, comfort, security, prestige, and even the chance for satisfying human relationships offered by the Continental army. Revolutionary America may have been a middle-class society, happier and more prosperous than any other in its time, but it contained a large and growing number of fairly poor people, and many of them did much of the actual fighting and suffering between 1775 and 1783: A very old story.

The large proportion of men, from Peterborough and other communities, who served only briefly, might thus seem far less important to our subject than the disadvantaged minority who did such a large part of the heavy work of revolution. This militarily less active majority were of course the militiamen. One could compile a large volume of pithy observations, beginning with a few dozen from Washington himself, in which the military value of the militia was called into question. The nub of the critique was that these part-time soldiers were untrained, undisciplined, undependable, and very expensive, consuming pay, rations, clothing, and weapons at a great rate in return for short periods of active service. By the end of the war, the tendency of many Continental officers, like Colonel Alexander Hamilton, to disparage openly the military performance of the militia was exacerbating already strained relations between State and Continental authorities. And indeed there were a number of cases

in which the failure of militia to arrive in time, to stand under fire, or to remain when they were needed, either contributed to American difficulties or prevented the exploitation of American success. But the Revolutionary role of the men from Peterborough and elsewhere who did *not* serve as did Bill Scott, but whose active military service was rather a sometime thing, is easily misunderstood and underestimated if we look at it only in terms of traditional military strategy and set-piece battles.

To understand the Revolutionary militia and its role, we must go back to the year before the outbreak of fighting at Lexington and Concord. Each colony, except Pennsylvania, had traditionally required every free white adult male, with a few minor occupational exceptions, to be inscribed in a militia unit, and to take part in training several times a year. These militia units seldom achieved any degree of military proficiency, nor were they expected to serve as actual fighting formations. Their real function might be described as a hybrid of draft board and modern reserve unit—a modicum of military training combined with a mechanism to find and enlist individuals when they were needed. But the colonial militia did not simply slide smoothly into the Revolution. Militia officers, even where they were elected, held royal commissions, and a significant number of them were not enthusiastic about rebellion. Purging and restructuring the militia was an important step toward revolution, one that deserves more attention than it has had.

When the news reached America that Parliament would take a very hard line in response to the Boston Tea Party, and in particular had passed a law that could destroy, economically and politically, the town of Boston, the reaction in the colonies was stronger and more nearly unanimous than at any time since the Stamp Act. No one could defend the Boston Port Act; it was an unprecedented, draconian law, the possible consequences of which seemed staggering. Radicals, like Samuel Adams, demanded an immediate and complete break in commercial relations with the rest of the Empire. Boycotts had worked effectively in the past, and they were an obvious response to the British hard line. More moderate leaders, however, dreaded a hasty confrontation that might quickly escalate beyond their control, and they used democratic theory to argue that nothing ought to be done without a full and proper consultation of the popular will. Like the boycott, the consultative congress had a respectable pedigree, and the moderates won the argument. When Congress met in September 1774 there were general expectations in both Britain and America that it would cool and seek to compromise the situation.

Exactly what happened to disappoint those expectations is even now not wholly clear; our own sense that Congress was heading straight toward revolution and independence distorts a complex moment in history, when uncertainty about both ends and means deeply troubled the minds of most decision-makers. Congress had hardly convened when it heard that the British had bombarded Boston. For a few days men from different colonies, normally suspicious of one another, were swept together by a wave of common fear and apprehension. Though the report was quickly proved false, these hours of mutual panic seem to have altered the emotional economy of the Congress. Soon afterward it passed without any serious dissent a resolution in favor of the long-advocated boycott, to be known as the Association. Local committees were to gather signatures for the Association, and were to take necessary steps to enforce its provisions. The Association was the vital link in transforming the colonial militia into a revolutionary organization.

For more than a year, a tenuous line of authority ran directly from the Continental Congress to the grass roots of American society. The traditional, intermediate levels of government, if they did not cooperate fully, were bypassed. Committees formed everywhere to enforce the Association, and sympathetic men volunteered to assist in its enforcement. In some places, like Peterborough, the same men who were enrolled in the militia became the strong right arm of the local committee; reluctant militia officers were ignored because, after all, not the militia as such but a voluntary association of militia members was taking the action. In other places, like parts of the Hudson valley and Long Island, reluctance was so widespread that men opposed to the Association actually tried to take over the committee system in order to kill it; when meetings were called to form the new armed organization of Associators, loyal militiamen packed the meetings and re-elected the old, royally commissioned lieutenants and captains. But even where the Association encountered heavy opposition, it effectively dissolved the old military structure and created a new one based on consent, and whose chief purpose was to engineer consent, by force if necessary. The new Revolutionary militia might look very much like the old colonial militia, but it was, in its origins, less a draft board and a reserve training unit than a police force and an instrument of political surveillance. Although the boycott could be defended to moderate men as a constitutional, non-violent technique, its implementation had radical consequences. Adoption by Congress gave it a legitimacy and a unity that it could have gained in no other way. Ordinary men were forced to make public choices, and thus to identify themselves with one side or the other. Not until the Declaration of Independence clarified the hazy status of the traditional levels of government did the local committees, acting through the new militia, relinquish some of their truly revolutionary power.

It is difficult to overestimate the importance of what happened in 1775 to engage mass participation on the side of the Revolution. The new militia, which repeatedly denied that it was in rebellion and proclaimed its loyalty to the Crown, enforced a boycott intended to make Britain back down; Britain did not back down, but the attempt drew virtually everyone into the realm of politics. Enlistment, training, and occasional emergencies were the means whereby dissenters were identified, isolated, and dealt with. Where the new militia had trouble getting organized, there Revolutionary activists could see that forceful intervention from outside might be needed. Connecticut units moved into the New York City area; Virginia troops moved into the Delmarva Peninsula; in Pennsylvania, men from Reading and Lancaster marched into Bucks County. Once established, the militia became the infrastructure of revolutionary government. It controlled its community, whether through indoctrination or intimidation; it provided on short notice large numbers of armed men for brief periods of emergency service; and it found and persuaded, drafted or bribed, the smaller number of men needed each year to keep the Continental army alive. After the first months of the war, popular enthusiasm and spontaneity could not have sustained the struggle; only a pervasive armed organization, in which almost everyone took some part, kept people constantly, year after year, at the hard task of revolution. While Scott and his sons, the indigent, the blacks, and the otherwise socially expendable men fought the British, James and Samuel Cunningham, Henry Ferguson, John Gray, William McNee, Benjamin Mitchell, Robert Morison, Alexander and William Robbe, Robert Swan, Robert Wilson, and four or five men named Smith—all militiamen, but whose combined active service hardly equalled that of "Long Bill" Scott alone—ran Peterborough, expelling a few Tories, scraping up enough recruits for the Continental army to meet the town's quota every spring, taking time out to help John Stark destroy the Germans at the battle of Bennington.

The mention of Tories brings us, briefly, to the last aspect of our subject . . . Peterborough had little trouble with Tories; the most sensational case occurred when the Presbyterian minister, the Rev. John Morrison, who had been having difficulties with his congregation, deserted his post as chaplain to the Peterborough troops and entered British lines at Boston in June 1775. But an informed estimate is that a half million Americans can be counted as loyal to Britain. Looking at the absence of serious Loyalism in Peterborough, we might conclude that Scotch-Irish Presbyterians almost never were Tories. That, however, would be an error of fact, and we are impelled to seek further for an explanation. What appears as we look at places like Peterborough, where Tories are hardly visible, and at other places where Toryism was rampant, is a pattern—not so much an ethnic, religious, or ideological pattern, but a pattern of raw power. Wherever the British and their allies were strong enough to penetrate in force—along the seacoast, in the Hudson, Mohawk, and lower Delaware valleys, in Georgia, the Carolinas, and the transappalachian West—there Toryism flourished. But geographically less exposed areas, if population density made self-defense feasible—most of New England, the Pennsylvania hinterland, and piedmont Virginia—where the enemy hardly appeared or not at all, there Tories either ran away, kept quiet, even serving in the rebel armies, or occasionally took a brave but hopeless stand against Revolutionary committees and their gunmen. After the war, of course, men remembered their parts in the successful Revolution in ways that make it difficult for the historian to reconstruct accurately the relationship between what they thought and what they did.

The view here presented of how armed force and public opinion were mobilized may seem a bit cynical—a reversion to Thomas Hobbes. True, it gives little weight to ideology, to perceptions and principles, to grievances and aspirations, to the more admirable side of the emergent American character. Perhaps that is a weakness; perhaps I have failed to grasp what really drove Bill Scott. But what strikes me most forcibly in studying this part of the Revolution is how much in essential agreement almost all Americans were in 1774, both in their views of British measures and in their feelings about them. What then is puzzling, and thus needs explaining, is why so many of these people behaved in anomalous and in different ways. Why did so many, who did not intend a civil war or political independence, get so inextricably involved in the organization and use of armed force? Why did relatively few do most of the actual fighting? Why was a dissenting fifth of the population so politically and militarily impotent, so little able to affect the outcome of the struggle? Answers to these questions cannot be found in the life of one obscure man, or in the history of one backwoods town. But microscopic study does emphasize certain features of the American Revolution: the political structuring of resistance to Britain, the play of social and economic factors in carrying on that resistance by armed force, and the brutally direct effects on behavior, if not on opinions, of military power.

# 10

# TWO VISIONS OF THE CONSTITUTION

## DREW MCCOY

The men who met in 1787 to consider how best to reform the national government were of a variety of minds. Northerners, southerners, from cities and the countryside, these men represented the diverging interests that marked early America. Yet, whatever their differences, these men shared a common concern: as leaders of the world's newest republic, how could they prevent the inevitable slide into decline and despotism that marked the history of all previous republics? To these men, schooled in the classical doctrine that republics required a virtuous people who could put self-interest aside, the competing interests of class, region, and party were sure signs of decay and impending doom. How then could they act to prevent these social divisions from developing in America?

As Drew McCoy demonstrates, the men of 1787 offered two answers. Following Benjamin Franklin, many saw the large expanses of land in the West as a safety valve, a way of offering every American a plot of land that would guarantee his family's independence. With every American a small holder of property there would be no large accumulations of wealth to challenge the virtuous government of the republic, and every citizen would have a stake, and thus an interest, in society.

A different and more modern view was offered by Alexander Hamilton, who thought the entire Whig conception of government, upon which so much of contemporary thought rested, misconceived. Instead Hamilton envisioned America as a great commercial and industrial empire on the model of Great Britain. For him the creation of classes and competing interests was both inevitable and ultimately desirable. Much like modern-day conservatives, Hamilton saw capitalists as the creators of national wealth and sought to link the state with these men of wealth, augmenting their power and influence in society and ensuring American economic development. In this way Hamilton hoped to move America away from the agrarian republic of Franklin and Jefferson and make it into a modern industrial state. As McCoy shows, it was ultimately these two notions of national development that competed at the constitutional convention of 1787–1788.

From *The Elusive Republic: Political Economy in Jeffersonian America,* by Drew McCoy. © 1980 by the University of North Carolina Press. Reprinted by permission.

While speaking in January 1811 in defense of the constitutionality of the Bank of the United States, a Virginia congressman rhetorically asked his colleagues if the authors of the Constitution had not wisely anticipated the irrepressible consequences of social development in America:

> Is it in the least probable that the men selected for their wisdom, perfectly acquainted with the progress of man in every age; who foresaw the changes which the state of society must undergo in this country from the increase of population, commerce, and the arts, could act so absurdly, as to prescribe a certain set of means to carry on the operations of a Government intended not only for the present but for future generations?

No doubt the framers would have been pleased with this assessment of their prescience. By the summer of 1787 most of them were acutely aware that America was maturing rapidly and that the future promised the development of an even more complex and sophisticated society. Not all of them found it easy to confront the implications of this promise, but very few refused to accept its inevitability. Even those who had not lost faith in Franklin's original vision of a youthful republic recognized more clearly than ever that they could hope only to forestall for as long as possible the unavoidable ramifications of social development.

"Civilization and corruption have generally been found," noted one of the more pessimistic American observers in 1785, "to advance with equal steps." Ultimately, the United States would become as corrupt as the most advanced areas of Europe; yet it was undoubtedly within the power of its citizens to place this "sad catastrophe at a distance." Perhaps more than any other prominent American of the 1780s, James Madison thought precisely in these terms. Like most supporters of the new Constitution, this astute young Virginian believed that a reorganization of American gov-

ernment was the necessary prerequisite to the establishment of a republican political economy. Madison later discovered, however, that not all of his Federalist colleagues shared his particular conception of a republican America; some of them, he was appalled to learn, even thought in terms of deliberately promoting what he thought necessary to forestall. Different men were developing quite different solutions to the persistent problem of adapting the traditional republican impulse to modern commercial America. Although the ideological flux of the 1780s created the basis for the Federalist consensus of 1787, it also assured future controversy about the precise meaning of American republicanism and the role of the new federal government in securing it.

Madison's initial post-war vision of a republican America was quite similar in its general outline to Franklin's, for above all Madison thought in terms of developing across space rather than through time. Westward expansion was central to Madison's outlook, but equally important were his commitments to the principles of commercial liberalism and to the promise of a new, more open international commercial order. The dynamics of the Virginian's vision were straightforward. If Americans could continue to resort to virgin lands while opening adequate foreign markets for their produce, the United States would remain a nation of industrious farmers who marketed their surpluses abroad and purchased the "finer" manufactures they desired in return. Household industry would be relied upon to supply the coarser manufacturers that were necessary to prevent a dangerously unfavorable balance of trade. Like Adam Smith, Madison believed this brand of social "development" proper because it comported with natural law. America could remain young and virtuous, while offering both a haven for the landless poor of Europe and a bountiful market for the advanced manufacturers that a fully peopled Europe was forced to produce. Indeed, Madison's commitment to westward expansion and "free trade" put him in the mainstream of republican thought at the end of the war.

Like most Americans, however, Madison always realized that the viability of landed expansion in America was contingent on the ability of new settlers to get their surpluses to market. If frontier farmers had no way of marketing what they produced, there was little incentive to emigrate to the West at all. A nonexistent or inaccessible market would turn those who did settle the frontier into lethargic subsistence farmers instead of industrious republicans. This perception of the importance of commerce to the settlement of the frontier had always carried serious implications for the character of American society. If the men and women who emigrated to the West were not properly tied to a commercial nexus, various commentators had long suggested, they would degenerate into a socially and politically dangerous form of savagery. Expressions of this concern often accompanied appeals for the construction of "internal improvements"—roads and canals—that would rescue the fringes of American settlement from this danger by integrating them into a commercial economy. As early as 1770, for example, Pennsylvanians anxious to promote a canal in their state had typically cited the "complicated and numerous" mischiefs that arose from the isolation of their western settlements. "It is from hence," one writer asserted, "that many of the distant back inhabitants are become uncivilized, and little better than barbarians.—They are lazy, licentious, and lawless—and, instead of being useful members of society, are become seditious, and dangerous to the community." Once these settlers were drawn into the civilizing orbit of commerce, however, a dramatic transformation in their character would occur: "The uncivilized will, by a communication with the civilized, lose their ignorance and barbarism. They will learn industry from the industrious, virtue from the virtuous, loyalty from the loyal; and thereby become useful members of society, and good subjects." Most important, they would be molded into productive citizens: "Render it practicable for them to gain by their industry, and they will be industrious, and, by their industry, add to the surplus of our foreign exportation." This matter of civilizing the West had seemed particularly pressing before the Revolution to eastern Pennsylvanians who were disturbed by the chronic political turmoil on their frontier, but the content and wide-ranging implications of their concern were of continuing relevance to all American republicans who worried about the character of their landed expansion.

As America looked westward in the 1780s, control of the Mississippi River to its mouth became an essential goal of national policy, for this river was the necessary avenue to foreign markets for those who were settling the immediate frontier. This concern drew the United States into an inevitable confrontation with the Spanish, who in early 1784 formally denied Americans the right to navigate the Mississippi and to deposit their goods at New Orleans. The problem of gaining uncontested American control of the Mississippi River arose from disputes over the boundary settlements of the peace treaties that ended the Revolution and would not be fully resolved until the Louisiana Purchase of 1803. During the initial decade of independence, control of the Mississippi posed an especially disturbing dilemma for Madison and other American republicans.

Madison was both outraged and perplexed by the unexpected display of Spanish arrogance, and he insisted that it was not in the interests of either Spain or the United States to deny Americans use of the Mississippi. Writing to Jefferson in the summer of 1784, Madison argued that American settlement of the backcountry, which only a free use of the Mississippi could promote, would benefit all European nations who traded with the United States by delaying the establishment of competitive American manufactures for many years and by increasing the consumption of foreign manufactures. If Americans were kept profitably occupied in agriculture, in other words, there would be no "supernumerary hands" to produce manufactures who might compete with foreign producers for the American market. In a passage that reflected many of the traditional assumptions of eighteenth-century political economy, Madison sketched two possible scenarios for American development:

> The vacant land of the U.S. lying on the waters of the Mississippi is perhaps equal in extent to the land actually settled. If no check be given to emigrations from the latter to the former, they will probably keep pace at least with the increase of people, till the population of both become nearly equal. For 20 or 25 years we shall consequently have few internal manufactures in proportion to our numbers as at present, and at the end of that period our imported manufactures will be doubled. . . . Reverse the case and suppose the use of the Miss. denied to us, and the consequence is that many of our supernumerary hands who in the former case would [be] husbandmen on the waters of the Missipi will on this other supposition be manufacturers on this [side] of the Atlantic: and even those who may not be discouraged from seating the vacant lands will be obliged by the want of vent for the produce of the soil and of the means of purchasing foreign manufactures, to manufacture in a great measure for themselves.

The thrust of Madison's analysis was clear; in order to remain predominantly agricultural, America needed to combine landed and commercial expansion. If, on the contrary, Americans were denied access to export markets for their produce, a fundamental reorientation of their political economy in the direction of increased manufacturing was inevitable.

The diplomatic crisis in the West neatly fused the issues of western expansion and foreign trade, but Madison's concern with the latter issue extended far beyond the question of the Mississippi River. By the mid-1780s the commercial crisis afflicting the United States was wreaking havoc in virtually all areas of the country. This commercial problem, according

to Madison, spawned the political and moral chaos that threatened the republican character of America. "Most of our political evils," he wrote in March 1786, "may be traced up to our commercial ones, as most of our moral may to our political." Like most Americans, Madison was particularly concerned with the restrictions Britain placed on American trade with its West Indian islands. Many Americans argued that the interest of every state was involved with this trade and, in a broader sense, that American commerce as a whole was dependent on it, since without a prosperous intercourse with these islands the balance of American trade with Great Britain would inevitably be unfavorable. "Access to the West Indies," as Jefferson put it in 1785, "is indispensably necessary to us." Several ways existed to improve the unfavorable balance of American trade, including the exercise of self-restraint on the part of those citizens who overindulged in their consumption of foreign luxuries. The key for Madison, however, was to liberate American trade from the shackles of British mercantilism. Above all, the United States had to break down the barriers that confined its commerce to "artificial" channels and denied it full access to "natural" markets like those in the West Indies.

By 1786 many Americans had decided that a policy of commercial retaliation against restrictions on their trade was mandatory. Few of them, however, could match Madison's faith in the efficacy of such a policy. His confidence in the ability of the United States to coerce Britain and other foreign countries into lowering barriers to American commerce was predicated on several key assumptions, the primary belief being that a young, virile society had natural advantages in its intercourse with older, fully peopled, more complex societies. Due to its highly advanced, luxury-ridden condition, for instance, Britain depended on foreign demand to employ its surplus inhabitants. "It is universally agreed," wrote one American of England, "that no country is more dependent on foreign demand, for the superfluous produce of art and industry;—and that the luxury and extravagance of her inhabitants, have already advanced to the ultimate point of abuse, and cannot be so increased, as to augment the home consumption, in proportion to the decrease that will take place on a diminution of foreign trade." The prosperity of the British economy was thus contingent on access to the rich American market. Should the United States ever restrict this market for British manufactures in retaliation for restraints on its export trade, the "manufacturing poor" in England would be thrown out of work and perhaps even starve. Such were the pitfalls, Franklin and Madison would have reminded the British, of a mercantilist political economy geared to the exportation of finer manufactures and luxuries.

By 1786 Madison thought it obvious that the implementation of an effective commercial policy, as well as the resolution of the crisis in the West, required a national government stronger than the Continental Congress. In a broader sense, this reorganization of the American political system was necessary to create the basis for a republican political economy. Madison feared, as did many other members of the American elite, that the disorder and unrest of the 1780s signified the decay of industry, diligence, frugality, and other republican character traits among the American people. The task at hand was to form a national political economy capable of permitting and encouraging Americans to engage industriously in virtue-sustaining occupations. To Madison this task entailed the creation of a central political authority able to reverse the dangerous trends of the decade and to stave off, for as long as possible, the advance of America into a more complicated and dangerous stage of social development. Because social conditions in the United States encouraged such reflection, Madison entered the constitutional convention in the spring of 1787 having already given much serious thought to the problems of poverty and unemployment in advanced, densely populated societies.

Of particular interest in this regard is an exchange of letters between Madison and Jefferson in late 1785 and early 1786. Writing from France, Jefferson pondered the plight of the laboring and idle poor of Europe. He blamed their wretchedness on an unequal division of property and entrenched feudal privilege, then further observed that "whenever there is in any country, uncultivated lands and unemployed poor, it is clear that the laws of property have been so far extended as to violate natural right." The earth had been given as a common stock for all men to labor and live on, and "if, for the encouragement of industry we allow it to be appropriated, we must take care that other employment be furnished to those excluded from the appropriation." Jefferson extended this analysis of the situation in France to his native land. Although it was "too soon yet in our country to say that every man who cannot find employment but who can find uncultivated land, shall be at liberty to cultivate it, paying a moderate rent," it was "not too soon to provide by every possible means that as few as possible shall be without a little portion of land." Indeed, Jefferson's sobering contact with the landless poor in Europe made him all the more anxious to prevent the development of a similar class in America.

Madison agreed that Jefferson's reflections formed "a valuable lesson to the Legislators of every Country, and particularly of a new one." However, in assessing the causes of the comparative comfort of the people in the United States, at least for the present, he asserted that more was involved than the absence of entrenched feudal privileges. "Our limited population," Madison argued, "has probably as large a share in producing this effect as the political advantages which distinguish us." "A certain degree of misery," he stated, as a general rule "seems inseparable from a high degree of populousness." This rule had profoundly disturbing implications for Madison, because it meant that even if a nation's land was equitably distributed and its laws thoroughly liberal and republican, a large population in itself might still create dangerous social problems. "No problem in political economy has appeared to me more puzzling," he wrote,

> than that which relates to the most proper distribution of the inhabitants of a Country fully peopled. Let the lands be shared among them ever so wisely, and let them be supplied with labourers ever so plentifully; as there must be a great surplus of subsistence, there will also remain a great surplus of inhabitants, a greater by far than will be employed in cloathing both themselves and those who feed them, and in administering to both, every other necessary and even comfort of life. What is to be done with this surplus? Hitherto we have seen them distributed into manufacturers of superfluities, idle proprietors of productive funds, domestics, soldiers, merchants, mariners, and a few other less numerous classes. All these classes not withstanding have been found insufficient to absorb the redundant members of a populous society.

Madison thus wrestled with the familiar problem of securing viable and sufficient sources of employment for the landless human surplus characteristic of the highly developed, old countries of Europe. He was struck, furthermore, by a depressing irony. Referring to the "manufacturers of superfluities, idle proprietors of productive funds, domestics, soldiers, merchants, mariners," and the like, he observed that "a reduction of most of those classes enters into the very reform which appears so necessary and desirable." The equal, more republican division of landed property that Jefferson espoused, he explained, would inevitably lead to "a greater simplicity of manners, consequently a less consumption of manufactured superfluities, and a less proportion of idle proprietors and domestics," while a "juster government" would also occasion "less need of soldiers either for defence against dangers from without, or disturbances from within." Republican reforms thus eventually compounded rather than ameliorated the problem, since they closed off the customary

avenues of escape for an idle, surplus population. For this reason, Madison implied, the dilemma in a "fully-peopled" republic would ironically be even worse than in a corrupt, luxury-ridden society.

As always, Madison had one eye on the American future. During the constitutional convention, Charles Pinckney of South Carolina chastised his countrymen for considering themselves "the inhabitants of an old instead of a new country," and Madison's response to this charge is revealing. Pinckney made the traditional argument for America's youthfulness by pointing to the West: "In a new Country, possessing immense tracts of uncultivated lands, where every temptation is offered to emigration and where industry must be rewarded with competency, there will be few poor, and few dependent." Indeed, Pinckney concluded, "that vast extent of unpeopled territory which opens to the frugal and industrious a sure road to competency and independence will effectually prevent for a considerable time the increase of the poor or discontented, and be the means of preserving that equality of condition which so eminently distinguishes us."

Madison was not convinced by Pinckney's analysis of American society. "In all civilized Countries," he observed, "the people fall into different classes havg. a real or supposed difference of interests." In addition to creditors and debtors, farmers, merchants, and manufacturers, there "will be particularly the distinction of rich and poor." Madison agreed with Pinckney that America had neither the hereditary distinctions of rank nor the horrendous extremes of wealth and poverty that characterized Europe, but he quickly added that "we cannot however be regarded even at this time, as one homogeneous mass, in which every thing that affects a part will affect in the same manner the whole." Indeed, America was already a fairly complex, stratified society. "The man who is possessed of wealth, who lolls on his sofa or rolls in his carriage," Madison was reported to have argued, "cannot judge of the wants or feelings of the day laborer." And when Madison looked at the inevitable ramifications of continued population growth in America, he became even more pessimistic. "In framing a system which we wish to last for ages, we shd. not lose sight of the changes which ages will produce. An increase of population will of necessity increase the proportion of those who will labour under all the hardships of life, and secretly sigh for a more equal distribution of its blessings." When in time such men would outnumber "those who are placed above the feelings of indigence," there would be a serious danger of social upheaval and of radical attacks on property. Referring to the Shays uprising in Massachusetts, Madison remarked that although "no agrarian attempts have yet been made in this Country, . . . symptoms of a leveling spirit . . . have sufficiently appeared in a certain quarters to give notice of the future danger."

Madison returned to this general theme again and again during the course of the convention. "In future times," he predicted of the United States, "a great majority of the people will not only be without landed, but any other sort of property." As the population of America increased, its political economy would inevitably become more complex. Although the relative proportion between the commercial and manufacturing classes and the agricultural was yet small, Madison contended that it would daily increase. "We see in the populous Countries in Europe now," he declared, "what we shall be hereafter." And in the Virginia ratifying convention of 1788, Madison hinted strongly that the day when "population becomes so great as to compel us to recur to manufactures" lay not very far in the future: "At the expiration of twenty-five years hence, I conceive that in every part of the United States, there will be as great a population as there is now in the settled parts. We see already, that in the most populous parts of the Union, and where there is but a medium, manufactures are beginning to be established."

The profound impact of the economic and social dislocations of the 1780s on Madison's vision of America is perhaps best revealed in his correspondence with John Brown in 1788 concerning a constitution for the prospective state of Kentucky. Madison argued strongly that property be made a qualification for suffrage, and that there be a dual suffrage for the upper and lower houses of the legislature in order to protect both "the rights of persons" and "the rights of property." His reasoning here was that both the indigent and the rich, who invariably formed classes in any civilized society, had each to be given its proper share in government. Madison reminded Brown that although the specific need to protect property rights had not been given much attention at the commencement of the Revolution, subsequent experience had demonstrated the naïveté of the assumption that the United States was a peculiarly undifferentiated society in which "the rights of property" and "the rights of persons" were synonymous.

> In the existing state of American population, and American property[,] the two classes of rights were so little discriminated [at the commencement of the Revolution] that a provision for the rights of persons was supposed to include of itself those of property, and it was natural to infer from the tendency of republican laws, that these different interests would be more and more identified. Experience and investigation have however produced more correct ideas on this subject. It is now observed that in all populous countries, the smaller part only can be interested in preserving the rights of property. It must be foreseen that America, and Kentucky itself will by degrees arrive at this state of Society; that in some parts of the Union a very great advance is already made towards it.

Prudence thus demanded that the Kentucky constitution, as well as the United States Constitution, allow for the changes that the future would inevitably bring.

While Madison always worried about the political implications of these future developments, he never really resolved his underlying dilemma: once the inevitable pressure of population increase had created large numbers of propertyless indigents in America, what would sustain the republican character of the United States? At the core of republicanism was an intense concern with the autonomy or "independence" of the individual, and particularly with the material or economic basis for that autonomy. Since the abject dependence of the landless or laboring poor rendered them vulnerable to bribery, corruption, and factious dissension, a society with large numbers of these dependents was hardly suited to the republican form. Although Madison evinced a fatalistic acceptance of the future as he envisioned it, always urging that the new Constitution be so drawn that it could accommodate these social changes, he seemed unable to escape the traditional fear that all republics, including the one in America, were necessarily short-lived. It was wise to anticipate and provide for future changes; it was even wiser to forestall their development for as long as possible. Madison's republic was in a race against time.

The new Constitution promised to create a government equal to the task of forestalling, if not of preventing, these adverse developments. A stronger national government with the power to raise revenue and regulate commerce would ideally be capable of resolving the foreign policy problems that threatened to prematurely age the country. Such a government could pave the way for westward expansion by dealing forcefully with threatening foreign powers like Spain, but even more important, it could fulfill the commercial promise of the Revolution by forcing the dismantling of the restrictive mercantilist systems that obstructed the marketing of American agricultural surpluses. As Oliver Ellsworth of Connecticut argued in defense of the Constitution, American farmers suffered because American merchants were "shut out from nine-tenths of the ports in the world" and forced to sell at low prices in the "few foreign ports" that were open to them. Addressing the farmers of America, he asserted that "you are oppressed for the want of power which can protect commerce, encourage business, and create a ready demand for the productions of your farms." Thomas Jefferson, writing in early 1789, agreed that the American system should be to "pursue agriculture, and open all the foreign markets possible to our produce."

Continued westward expansion would ease the impact of a rapidly increasing population in the United States, and the opening of foreign markets for American produce would further ensure that Americans not be forced into occupations detrimental to the republican character of their society. It could be hoped, then, that Madison's human "surplus" in America might continue to produce "necessaries" required by foreigners for as long as possible rather than be forced by adverse circumstances like those of the 1780s to become manufacturers of superfluities, idle proprietors of productive funds, soldiers, or the like. In short, the exportation of American agricultural surpluses appeared to offer a tentative republican solution to the "problem in political economy" that had so puzzled the young Virginian. America needed open markets as well as open space to make republicanism work. Perhaps a government strong enough to encourage the proper form of westward expansion and to force free trade could answer the dilemma of population growth in an agricultural and republican nation—at least for the foreseeable future.

One of Madison's closest allies in the struggle to ratify the Constitution was a brilliant lawyer from New York, Alexander Hamilton, who several years earlier in *The Continentalist* had warned his countrymen against their obsession with classical republicanism. In many respects Hamilton was an anomaly; perhaps more than any of his countrymen, he had succeeded in discarding the traditional republican heritage that had so heavily influenced the Revolutionary mind. He was particularly receptive in this regard to the writings of David

Hume as they applied both to political economy and to constitutional thought. Indeed, it seems clear that Hamilton's introduction to many of Hume's works during the course of the Revolution had greatly influenced the development of his social and political outlook. He came to accept the commercialization of society as not only inevitable but fundamentally salutary as well, and he never doubted that the real disposition of human nature was toward luxury and away from classical virtue. Such a condition, he concluded, made traditional or classical republicanism hopelessly irrelevant to the American experience. Any talk either of Spartan equality and virtuous agrarianism, or of fear of commercial corruption, was nothing more than sententious cant that evaded the necessary realities of life in modern commercial society. In this connection, his reaction to Pinckney's speech in the constitutional convention was even more incisive than Madison's. "It was certainly true," Hamilton remarked, "that nothing like an equality of property existed: that an inequality would exist as long as liberty existed, and that it would unavoidably result from that very liberty itself." The "difference of property" in America was already great, and "commerce and industry" would inevitably increase it still further.

Hamilton's commitment to constitutional revision long predated the convention of 1787. He subscribed to the formula for reform that Robert Morris and other nationalists had established at the end of the war, a formula that integrated constitutional change with the funding of the Revolutionary debt and a vigorous program of economic expansion tied to the consolidation and mobilization of mercantile capital. Hamilton envisioned America not as a virtuous agrarian republic, but as a powerful, economically advanced modern state much like Great Britain—a state that would stand squarely on the worldly foundations of "corruption" that Bernard Mandeville had spoken of in *The Fable of the Bees*. Thus Hamilton's vision of the future was not clouded by the traditional republican fears that continued to

plague Madison and much of agrarian America. He simply accepted social inequality, propertyless dependence, and virtually unbridled avarice as the necessary and inevitable concomitants of a powerful and prosperous modern society. In one sense, Madison was still caught between the conflicting claims of classical republicanism and modern commercial society, struggling to define and implement a viable synthesis that was relevant to the American experience. Hamilton had stepped confidently and unequivocally into modernity.

On a very general but significant level, therefore, Hamilton supported the new Constitution for reasons quite different from Madison's. He did not intend to use the new government as a means of promoting the conditions that would stabilize America at a predominantly agricultural state of development; he wanted instead to use that new government to push the United States as rapidly as possible into a higher stage of development, for he interpreted this change as progress, not decay. Unlike Madison, in other words, Hamilton had an unabashedly positive sense of development through time. As his famous economic reports of the next decade revealed, he looked forward to the establishment of advanced, highly capitalized manufacturers in the United States and did everything he could within the constraints of his fiscal system to promote them. An anonymous pamphleteer caught the spirit of Hamilton's vision in 1789 when, after praising England as "the most opulent and powerful nation in Europe," he urged the new national government to give every possible encouragement to large-scale manufactures, the hallmark of British greatness. To men of this stripe, England offered a positive rather than a negative model for American development. Both Madison and Hamilton had abandoned the idea of perpetual youth for the republic; both accepted the inevitability of social complexity and the futility of the purely classical vision. Nevertheless, they brought very different attitudes and expectations to bear on their incipient careers as national political leaders.

The new American government thus began its operations in April 1789 in an ideological environment that can best be described as confused and transitional. The dislocations of the 1780s had raised complex questions and problems about the nature of American society and its republican potential. Caught between ancient and modern ways of thinking, most Americans came to realize that there could be no simple formula for a republican America. Perhaps no better evidence of the recognition of this new complexity can be found than in two premiums offered by the *American Museum* in 1789. The first was for "the best essay on the proper policy to be pursued in America, with respect to manufactures—and on the extent to which they may be carried, so as to avoid, on the one hand, the poverty attendant on an injurious balance of trade—and, on the other, the vices—the misery—and the obstruction of population, arising from assembling multitudes of workmen together in large cities or towns." The second premium was for "the best essay on the influence of luxury upon morals—and the most proper mode, consistent with republican freedom, to restrain the pomp and extravagance of ambitious or vain individuals."

These premiums reflected an ideological universe in flux. No single individual, however, could possibly have done more to draw and harden the lines of ideological combat among Americans than Alexander Hamilton who, as the first secretary of the Treasury, quickly seized the policymaking initiative in the new federal government.

# 11

## THE FARM AND THE MARKETPLACE: THE SPRINGER HOUSEHOLD OF MILL CREEK, DELAWARE

### BARBARA CLARK SMITH

For the first three hundred years of its history, America was predominantly a land of farmers. As late as the turn of the nineteenth century more than nine out of ten people lived in agrarian settings, most of them members of small, independent farming families. Regulated by the yearly cycle of the seasons and the daily rhythms of the field and barnyard, life on these farms changed little between the seventeenth and early nineteenth centuries. Life in these pastoral communities centered around land and family, and even such apparently economic transactions as the purchase of land or the borrowing of money were family affairs undertaken in the spirit of neighborliness. But as regional and international commerce expanded after the Revolution and new markets in the trans-Appalachian South and West fostered the beginnings of industrialization, farmers found themselves dealing with a rapidly changing world where contracts and money were valued more than neighborliness and community.

In this essay, Barbara Clark Smith reconstructs the fortunes of one of these farming families in the post-Revolutionary era. More than most independent farm families, the Springer clan had prospered and had successfully passed land down from generation to generation since the late seventeenth century. But in the years after the Revolution opportunities beyond their Delaware locale beckoned with increasing urgency, and the Springer family began to disperse. By 1805 Springer land had passed into stranger's hands.

If it were not for a band of English kidnappers, people named Springer might never have lived in Delaware. Born into a prominent Swedish family in 1658, Carl Springer was an unwilling immigrant to the New World. He grew up in Stockholm, studied in Riga, then traveled to London to further his education under the guidance of the Swedish minister. He had nearly completed his work in English and arithmetic when, late in the 1670s, he was abducted and shipped to Virginia. As he later remembered the experience: "I was kidnapped and, against my will, taken aboard an English ship. And against my will I was carried to America, in the West Indies, to Virginia. And when I got there I was sold off like a farm animal that is driven to market. Thus I was sold, to labor, and held in very slavery. . . ."

The temporary "slavery" that Virginia imposed on Swedes and other Europeans differed markedly from the lifelong slavery the colony imposed on Africans, but for Carl Springer, a five-year term as an indentured servant still proved hard to bear. The work, he later said, was "unspeakable" and the Virginia climate devastating. "In summer it was *Extra Ordinary* hot during the day, and my work was mostly in the winter, clearing land and cutting down the forest and making it ready for planting *Tobacco* and the Indian grain in the summer. I had a very hard master. . . ." When he gained his freedom in 1683, he heard rumor of a settlement of Swedes living along the Delaware River in the English colony of "Pensellvenia." With little in his pockets but anxious to put Virginia behind him, Springer set out on foot to travel four hundred miles to the north.

The community that welcomed him had been established for forty years. In the 1630s, investors in the "New Sweden Company" had built a fur trading outpost called Fort Christina a few miles from the Delaware River. Swedish settlers followed in the 1640s. Within a generation, both the fur trade and the colony had been taken over twice—first by the Dutch in the 1650s, then by the English a decade later. Despite their changing fortunes, the Swedes

had cut away the forests and planted farms along the riverbanks. They chose farming rather than "traffick," according to William Penn, and preferred to make "enough rather than plenty." When Springer arrived in 1684 there were roughly a thousand people of Swedish descent living in fewer than two hundred households in the Delaware valley.

Carl Springer quickly put down roots in the community. He became a founder, warden, and vestryman of its central institution, Holy Trinity (Old Swedes') Church. He took up land in the area, married a local woman, and established himself as a yeoman farmer. He wrote to his mother describing his success: "I have two plantations that I have bought, and on one of them I live, and plough and plant, sowing all kinds of seed during the year. I also have livestock for the needs of my household, and so live, thank God, that I and mine suffer no want."

Not every Swede did so well on the Delaware: if Carl Springer owned two plantations, someone else unable to afford land probably lived as a tenant on one of them. Yet Springer did not define success solely in terms of the economic well-being of his own household. He also cared about the spiritual life of his family and his countrypeople. He devoted time, money, and labor to the construction and welfare of Old Swedes' Church. For five years after the colonists' minister died, Springer read sermons to his brethren and led in singing psalms. In 1693 he wrote to Sweden asking for Bibles, catechisms, and other Swedish readers, and stressing the colonists' desire for a Swedish pastor. He described both the bounty of the American land and the colonists' fidelity to Swedish ways:

Wee are for the most part husbandmen, and plow and sowe and Till th[e] ground, and wee use yet the good ould fashions in meate and drink; this Land is a mighty fruitful good and plentiful Contry and here doth growe all sorts of grains in great plenty; and this River, out of it is sent and shipt away all sorts of grains every yeare . . . , and heare is also great plenty of all sorts, beasts, fowls and fishes; and our wives and daughters follow spinning of flax and wool, some with weaving, so that we have great occasion to thanck the Almighty God for his manyfold mercies and benefits. . . . We also live in peace, friendship, and amity with one an other. . . ."

Amity was no easy accomplishment. Governed by the English proprietor William Penn, and living alongside Dutch and English settlers, the Swedes struggled to maintain a distinct identity and way of life. No one was more fervent in that struggle than Carl Springer. Despite his cosmopolitan background he held fast to parochial values. When one Swedish minister spent too much of his time preaching in the English churches nearby, Springer registered his objections. Like a great many other settlers in America, he deeply valued ties of common language, background, and culture. Like many others, he sought both material security—the chance to work for himself and his household—and a wider network of social relations to give meaning to his life.

Over the next century, generations of Springers continued in Carl Springer's footsteps, tilling the strong clay soil of New Castle County, tending livestock, and raising families of their own. In many regards, Thomas Springer, who farmed the Mill Creek tract after the Revolution, followed the same way of life that his great-grandfather Carl had established. He too planted "all kinds of seed" and raised animals on a family farm. He too enjoyed material success; by his late thirties, in 1798, he stood in the top 10 percent of all taxpayers who lived in his section of the county. Yet by Thomas's day, the "lower counties" of Pennsylvania Colony had become Delaware State, and society in the river valley community had changed. Swedes no longer formed a tight-knit, separate culture; neither ethnic nor religious ties bound the Springers to many of their neighbors, and forces from an increasingly wider social and economic world shaped the everyday life of Thomas and his household. The Springers' story is the story of a family farm in the midst of change, commerce, and the early stirrings of industrialization.

From his childhood, Thomas Springer's future as a farmer was planned. His father, Charles, already had three sons and a daughter in 1762 when he learned that his wife, Ann, was expecting another child. Charles took his responsibilities as a father seriously: he worked to provide his sons with the skills and the wherewithal to support households of their own, and to provide for his daughter "as girls ought to be reasonably done by," with a dowry in expectation of marriage or a sufficiency to survive in the household of a relative while single. Parents passed on property in a number of forms: linen, furniture, and other household goods, livestock, tools, and black slaves. Yet above all else, the property that mattered in Delaware was land. Accordingly, Charles laid his plans for his fourth son, Thomas, even before the child was born. In 1762, he purchased 170 acres of farmland along the "westerly bank" of Mill Creek and a "parcel of Marsh land" nearby. When Ann delivered a baby boy, Charles set the Mill Creek tract aside for his son's future use.

Thomas learned from his father the skills he would eventually need to run his own farm. He learned about the needs of the land, the care of horses, sheep, and cows, and the growing cycles of different crops. Thomas watched his father deal with millers, artisans, and storekeepers. As he developed specific skills, he also began to form expectations for his own future life. Someday he would be working his own land, building his own household, and establishing his own independence.

Gaining that independence took a little time. Thomas was the fourth in line and had to wait for his three brothers to be "settled off" on their own land. Each brother's departure left more work on the farm to those who remained. Dependent on his children's labor, Charles, now in his fifties, might have been somewhat reluctant to let his last son leave the family farm. When Thomas reached the age of twenty-one, in 1785, he was still living in his parents' house. For the next several years he worked on his father's farm but probably claimed part of his time to devote to improvements on the Mill Creek tract. He may have cleared and even planted some land on the tract. Sometime in the 1780s he built a simple log building (or "tenement") there, and perhaps a small log barn to house a few animals.

We don't know if Thomas begrudged the time he spent working for his parents, but it was normal for rural people to start out working for family or for someone else. Fathers with land routinely kept title to much of their property until death, making sure they would be secure in old age. Other fathers lacked the resources to provide for all their offspring. So, most rural children expected to spend their twenties working at home, as tenants on another's land, or as paid laborers in the household of an established farmer, trying to accumulate enough money to buy land of their own. Knowing that his father's prosperity secured his future, Thomas Springer probably took his obligations to his parents in stride.

The death of Thomas's mother hastened her youngest son's move toward independence. Charles remarried in 1787. His new wife, Elizabeth Graham Rice, was a moderately wealthy widow with children of her own—seven of them under the age of seventeen. By marrying Charles Springer she gained a father for them as well as a companion for herself. Charles too gained more than companionship, for his new wife's wealth solidified his financial position, and her children would contribute labor in the household and on the farm for many years. His father's remarriage may have deepened Thomas's desire to get out of his father's house. More to the point, it gave Charles the security to let his youngest son go.

In 1788, Thomas bought two small parcels of land that abutted the Mill Creek tract, and soon he was living there on his own. He built a proper log house, about 19 by 23 feet in size,

with a single room on each floor. About the same time, he got married. His wife was named Elizabeth—the records do not tell us her last name. She moved into the log house sometime about 1790 and had two baby daughters shortly thereafter. Finally, in 1792, Thomas was able to buy 104 acres of the Mill Creek tract from his father. Charles charged him less than the market price for the land, and he allowed his son to owe him part of the price. With his father's help, then, by age twenty-nine, Thomas was settled on 129 acres of his own land as the head of his own small family. He was an independent householder, listed alongside his father and brothers as a "yeoman" in the records of New Castle County and Delaware State.

From those records—land deeds, tax lists, probate inventories, the federal census—emerges a picture of the Springers' daily life during the 1790s. The scene includes many patterns common to pre-industrial communities. In the eighteenth century, as before, households were the site of production of foodstuffs and goods. It followed that many households contained laborers as well as immediate family members. In 1798, a tax assessor listed Thomas as the owner of four slaves—an uncommonly large number for the northern part of Delaware, where most white families owned no slaves at all. Ace, a young adult, was probably the Springers' most valuable laborer. In addition there were Sara and Amelia, one a young girl between the ages of eight and fourteen, the other slightly older. There was also Will, about sixty years old, perhaps the same "Will" who had appeared in the estate of Even Rice, the first husband of Thomas's stepmother, a few years earlier. But no evidence has survived to tell us how the Springers' slaves were acquired, how they were related to one another, or how they experienced life on the Springer farm. They probably lived together in the log tenement.

The 1800 census reported three young white people—a female and two males, aged sixteen to twenty five—in the Springer household too. These might have been servants, or perhaps Thomas's stepbrothers and stepsister—children of Evan and Elizabeth Rice—or possibly relatives of Elizabeth Springer. We do not know their relationship to Elizabeth and Thomas, or whether they lived in the log house with the Springers or shared the tenement with the African-American slaves. For an "independent" yeoman, though, Thomas Springer clearly depended heavily on the labor of many others.

Not least, he counted on the labor of his wife. From their youth Thomas and Elizabeth had learned separate skills, and with adulthood they assumed responsibility for different domains. White women were less likely than men to travel far from the homestead visiting artisans' shops and stores, and they rarely worked in the fields. Elizabeth might do men's work at harvest, at apple-picking time, or whenever her husband's absence required her to act in his place, but most of the time her realm was the house, the kitchen, the yard and its animals, and the garden she probably planted nearby. White people commonly assigned jobs more flexibly to their African-American slaves; black women probably performed "men's work" more often than white women. But over all the division of labor by gender applied to blacks as well as whites.

These social and economic arrangements were far from egalitarian. Household members—bound and free, young and old, male and female—stood unequal to one another in legal status and more: they enjoyed different amounts of control over their everyday labor; they made different contributions to the household and benefitted from its prosperity in different degrees. As yet only African-American slavery—perhaps the most glaring and recent of these inequalities—had come under attack in Delaware. Ace appeared on the Springer inventory in 1804 as having "nine years left to serve"; apparently he had made some arrangement to buy his freedom. For the most part, however, the Springers remained untouched by the antislavery fervor that swept much of the state in the 1770s and 1780s. And few people in the Springers' day questioned the right of age to rule youth or male to rule female.

Under Thomas's direction, the household practiced a brand of diversified farming. Like most other farmers in New Castle County, Thomas produced a variety of crops: oats, hay, and Indian corn to feed livestock, vegetables to feed the household and exchange with neighbors, and wheat both for home consumption and for distant markets. But Thomas differed from the majority of nearby farmers in his dependence on livestock. In 1798, farmers in the Springers' section of the county owned, on average, $132 worth of animals—a sum that might represent a half-dozen cows, a dozen sheep, and one or two horses, along with poultry and hogs. By contrast, Thomas's holdings were worth $644. Only one other landholder in the area possessed more valuable livestock than Thomas, and the vast majority owned animals valued at less than half as much. To a degree, then, the Springers specialized in raising livestock. Thomas's choice of crops reflected the importance of animals to the household's economic success: in the one year we know about, he devoted the most acreage on his farm to oats, slightly less to corn, then wheat, rye, potatoes, clover, and timothy, in that order.

Some thirty acres of the Springers' land remained unimproved—probably woodland, forested with oak, hickory, poplar, walnut, maple, and ash, and providing forage for farm animals. From the forest the Springers could gather firewood for cooking their meals and heating their home, lumber for building, and in season, berries, nuts, and maybe mushrooms. Another ten acres was grassy marsh, yielding a grass particularly fine for cattle. There was also an apple orchard and outbuildings, yard, and—almost certainly—a vegetable garden near the log house, leaving in all roughly ninety acres for cultivation.

In one year, the records show, Thomas

planted about half of those ninety acres. Like other farmers throughout the East, he probably found the "freshness and richness of the soil" declining and adopted techniques for saving the soil and its nutrients. Few Delaware farmers practiced a systematic rotation, but they knew that fields could not support the same crop for many years running and that the land needed years of rest. It was approved practice to leave about half of the acreage used for cultivation fallow in any one year.

Some of the Springers' unplanted acres might have been pasture. Thomas grew timothy and clover, perhaps to replenish his arable land, though his workers cut and stacked some for fodder as well. His large holdings of livestock made it possible to manure tired soil and to impose stricter crop-rotation schemes. His choice of crops, numerous animals, and command over the labor of others all suggest that Thomas might have followed the lead of English farmers who sought a balance among animals, fodder crops, and grain to increase their land's productivity. He might have been a rather progressive farmer; his father's wealth gave him that choice.

Relying as they did on the land and its products, the Springers' lives followed a seasonal pattern. Winter was a slow time for farmers, when the most pressing tasks were cutting firewood, keeping animals fed, clean, and warm and doing small chores like mending tools and harnesses. Delaware's cold winters kept the Springers inside the house as much as possible during December, January, and February. Someone had to venture out of doors to tend the cattle and horses in the log barn and the sheep in the fields, but it seems likely that Thomas often delegated those tasks. He could use the slack season to travel to nearby towns—New Castle to register a deed or settle other legal affairs, Wilmington for commercial dealings with storekeepers, visits to artisans' shops, and socializing at Francis Dunlap's tavern. In the winter months, Thomas had time to walk his fields, surveying the acres planted with wheat and rye the previous fall and figur-

ing how to use the rest of his land in the year to come.

In March, when Mill Creek had thawed and buds and blossoms began to appear on the trees, it was time for spring planting to begin. The first crops were oats for feeding livestock and flax for making linen. If he was dissatisfied with his last year's crop, or if he wanted to experiment, Thomas might trade with neighbors for a new batch of seed. Most often, however, farmers simply used the seed saved from their previous season's harvest. Thomas, Ace, and Will sowed the seed broadcast over the plowed ground. Agricultural experts recommended plowing again to cover the seed over with fresh soil and fresh nutriments. But it was easier to attach a harrow, an A-shaped frame fitted with spikes, to a draft animal and lead the animal up and down the fields, cutting more shallowly into the earth but raking soil over the seeds in wide swathes at a time. Most Delaware farmers preferred the latter method.

As soon as oats and flax were in the ground, May brought the job of planting Indian corn. Once they were planted, Thomas could leave his oat and flax fields alone, but cornfields required weeding through the spring and summer months. Thomas might choose a new and grassy field for planting corn; it would require frequent plowing between the corn rows that year, but he had the labor—slave and free—to do it, and then the field would be clear and ready for wheat in the fall.

In June and July came the heaviest labor of the year. It was harvest, time to bring in the ripened wheat, barley, and rye planted the fall before. Using a sickle, one man could cut about an acre of wheat a day. All male hands were called on to work the fields in the long days of midsummer, and perhaps some female hands as well. Amelia and Sara most often helped Elizabeth with household work and manufacturing, but they might be pressed into service in the rush of harvest. When weather made speed essential, white women worked in the fields as well, but the Springers' wheat harvest was not extensive enough to make that a frequent occurrence. To prevent infestation by flies, the harvested grains had to be threshed as soon as possible. It was common practice to "tread out" wheat with horses, whose heavy hooves broke the fibrous chaff away from the grain. The men of the Springer household probably used the same method to thresh barley. They flailed oats and rye by hand, or left these crops to straw for the cattle.

Interspersed with other summer labor was mowing in the meadows. From late June through early autumn, rural men used scythes to cut grass, timothy, and clover. The common practice was to pile both hay and grain in tall stacks or long ricks, housing only oats and clover in the barn. The most well-to-do farmers could afford to hold their wheat for a good market price, but most could not risk spoilage nor delay sale to millers and grain merchants. We do not know if the Springers waited for the market or, like the majority, sold their surplus in late summer.

Finally, with fall came new tasks. In September the men sowed wheat and rye fields. The household harvested apples in the orchard for Elizabeth to use in baking and making conserves and for Thomas to use in making cider. There might be second and third cuttings of meadow grass to store as winter fodder for cattle. In the years he kept sheep, Thomas had to make special preparations for their winter comfort. Dr. James Tilton described one method: some farmers took mown grass from the marshland and laid it out on horizontal poles set about four feet from the ground, creating a shelter for sheep to eat away by spring.

In different years, Thomas Springer owned various numbers of sheep, cows, and horses. In 1796, he bought nine sheep from a relative's estate to provide both mutton and wool. Two years later, local tax assessors listed his holdings at $644 worth of livestock—a sum that must have included at least a few horses for pulling the plow and for driving the "chaise" later listed among Thomas's possessions. Yet his holdings reflect more than the ordinary

needs of farming. One rough indication of the extent of Thomas's holdings comes from the enumerated holdings of his neighbor John Ball. In 1804, Ball's estate inventory listed the following livestock:

| | |
|---|---:|
| 16 sheep | 22.00 |
| 2 calves | 6.00 |
| 8 milch cows | 96.00 |
| 2 Bulls | 18.00 |
| 3 2-yr. old calves | 18.00 |
| 1 bay horse | 45.00 |
| 1 old black horse | 4.50 |
| 1 3-yr old colt | 35.50 |
| 1 old mare | 2.00 |
| 7 shoats | 7.00 |
| poultry | 8.00 |

In all, Ball owned $262 worth of animals—only 40 percent of the value of Thomas Springer's holdings.

Unfortunately, when appraisers listed Thomas Springer's estate, in December of 1804, it included only seven horses (most of them old) and "1 red cow," worth $182 all together. Thomas had sold off his nine sheep and a great many other animals. Luckily, other evidence suggests what sort of animals Thomas owned. A "Barrel churn," pails, and milk pans listed among the Springers' possessions indicate dairying; two spinning wheels suggest that the household processed wool. In addition, the low valuation of livestock in the winter of 1804 might have reflected seasonal variations in the number of animals Thomas owned. There was good reason not to keep large numbers of cattle on hand in the winter. A single cow ate about forty pounds of hay a day, and a good farmer added vegetables and grains to the feed—boiled potatoes, turnips, bran, buckwheat, lentils, carrots, corn. Therefore, *Poor Richard's Almanac* told farmers, "If you live within thirty miles of a good market, you will find it much cheaper to sell all your calves for veal and keep up your stock of milch cows by purchasing such as are brought from distant parts at a low price."

The Springers lived only six miles from Wilmington, and they may have taken Poor Richard's advice. Farmers in the southern two counties of Delaware bred cattle in the forests and marshes, then drove them north to be fattened for marketing in Wilmington and Philadelphia. Moreover, ships outbound from Philadelphia often stopped at the town of New Castle, near the Mill Creek farm, to take on livestock for export. The Springers might have taken advantage of the rich meadows along the creek and their proximity to town to specialize in fattening cattle from the south.

Sketching Elizabeth Springer's everyday life and work is a little bit harder than piecing together Thomas's. Eighteenth-century women appear less often than men in the official records that historians rely on. Even "free" women like Elizabeth enjoyed few political and legal rights; they could not vote, sue in court, or, when married, possess real estate of their own. Unfortunately, we have no letters or diaries that tell us about Elizabeth Springer's early life, her decision to marry Thomas, or her personal experience of marriage and motherhood. But we do know that her life was shaped by her role as the wife of a yeoman farmer. In the eighteenth century, a woman's status depended on the men to whom she was legally attached. Contemporary women knew that their husband's situation determined their own: as one woman put it, marriage was *"the important Crisis, upon which our Fate depends."* From her husband's position, then, we can try to draw the outlines of Elizabeth's everyday experience. On the basis of Sara and Amelia's position as slaves, we can try to imagine the nature of their daily labors.

Women's work in the Delaware countryside had seasonal rhythms and variations much like men's. In the spring, most women planted a garden near the house, where they grew peas, cabbage, and other vegetables through the summer for family use in the fall. Dairying was another seasonal job for women. It began after calves were born in the spring and continued through the hot months of the year. Milking took place twice a day, in the early morning and again in the evening.

Some women saved the "strippings"—the milk that came last from the udder and that contained the most butterfat—in a separate pail. The next step was to pour the milk into wooden or ceramic pans to separate, and put the pans aside. The Springers may have used shelves in the log kitchen for the purpose, but since the milk had to cool it would have made more sense for them to build a small springhouse by the creek. Depending on the temperature, it took from eight to twenty hours for the cream to rise. With the cream skimmed off, there was milk to use in baking, to feed the pigs, and for the family to drink. The cream went into the barrel churn, often mixed with salt, saltpeter, sal ammoniac, or a mixture of sugar and water to keep it fresh-tasting. When enough cream had accumulated, it was time for churning.

One contemporary writer counseled that dairying was "too ticklish a business to be trusted to servants," but in practice women followed their own ideas and experience about that. It seems likely that Elizabeth left much of the tedious work to Sara and Amelia. The barrel churn represented a distinct improvement on the older plunger type, producing more butter in less time, but bringing the cream to butter still took hours. After churning, butter needed to be pressed, either by hand or with a wooden utensil, to remove the remaining liquid. Dairywomen added salt to preserve the butter, put it in a pot, and stored it in some cool place in the summer and in the flour bin in winter. From a good dairy cow, a woman could get about two gallons of milk a day, with enough cream for one pound of butter.

Even in urban areas of Delaware many families kept cows and produced milk and butter of their own, so that large-scale dairying ventures were few. Yet it does not seem likely that the Springers' dairying was just for family consumption. With their location near markets, their valuable livestock, their barrel churn, and their female labor force, it seems probable that the Springers sometimes marketed butter. Perhaps Elizabeth could exchange some butter locally, although the Balls nearby owned "milch cows" and other families in the neighborhood owned livestock too. Wilmington and New Castle provided larger markets, and merchants operating in the port cities of the region exported some butter as well. We can only speculate about the scale of the venture, but—especially if Thomas fattened livestock for sale—marketing butter would have been easy enough for the Springers to do.

Dairying often tailed off in the fall, but then other work took its place. Rural women helped in the slaughter of small animals, then salted pork and bacon for use in winter and early spring. They preserved fruits and vegetables, often in wide-mouthed stoneware jars sealed with animal bladders or skins and stored on kitchen shelves. In all these jobs, Elizabeth Springer could call on the help of Amelia, Sara, and her young daughters as they grew. Here, as in other tasks, it was in Elizabeth's interest to train the young women to take over the jobs she found most difficult or boring.

The women of the household worked with one another and with local artisans to produce cloth. Imported cloth was available; Wilmington merchants stocked English broadcloth, shalloon, and other fabrics, which the Springers could get in exchange for farm surplus. But store-bought cloth could be expensive, and Thomas owned his own sheep. The animals were washed and sheared during the summer. To make woolen cloth, women first had to clean and card the fibers. Then they spun the wool into yarn, feeding the short fibers into a spinning wheel, twisting them and holding them taut and steady enough to produce yarn of an even gauge. The Springer women passed on the yarn to a professional weaver—possibly John Robinson, a close neighbor—who possessed the loom and the skills to transform it into cloth. From the weaver the cloth went to Robert Johnson's fulling mill, where it was soaked in water and pounded with heavy hammers powered by a water wheel. Fulling tightened the weave of the cloth and softened the finish. When it was returned from the mill, the cloth was almost done. There was probably a professional dyer in Wilmington, but if Elizabeth preferred she could make her own dyes by gathering, pounding, and then boiling roots, bark, berries, or flowers in her large kettle. It was arduous work, but, like Thomas, Elizabeth had help and she may have felt the results worth it, either because she preferred the colors produced by her own recipes or because she saved the cost of a dyer.

In some years the Springer women probably made linen rather than wool. Household spinning of flax took place "in almost every private family" in the state of Delaware. Like producing woolen cloth, producing linen was a cooperative project between private home and skilled craftsmen in the neighborhood. Women processed the flax plant by removing the seed pods, breaking off the outer stalk, beating the flax to remove the chaff, and finally spinning and reeling the fiber itself. The yarn went to the weaver and dyer from there.

From homespun wool and linen or imported materials, rural women cut and sewed clothing for the household. They also produced textiles for household use—curtains for the windows, linen towels, and bed hangings. There was everyday mending too. Elizabeth must have welcomed the chance to delegate much of this labor to Sara and Amelia, working herself on the parts of the process about which she was particular or in which she could show skill and taste. From a very young age, her two daughters, Mary and Ann, could help by taking on some of the spinning. Elizabeth might have taught her girls quilting and a little fancy needlework as well.

As with dairy products, it is hard to judge how much of the Springers' wool, yarn, or cloth reached the wider marketplace. They could trade wool to neighbors who owned no sheep or else sell it in town. According to James Tilton, in 1788, a fleece would sell for six to eighteen shillings; that it had a common price indicated that fleece was commonly exchanged. The Springers could also market yarn. When Thomas Springer died in 1803, his largest debtor was Mordecai McKinney, an entrepreneur who opened a complete water-powered woolen manufactory in nearby Stanton in 1809. There were no woolen manufactories in the area in the late 1790s, but McKinney and other men may already have been engaged in processing cloth, putting out wool to rural women, who would clean, card, and spin the fibers, then return them to the wool merchant for weaving, finishing, and sale. Some fullers in the 1790s began to add dyeing, napping, and shearing to their services, and merchants became increasingly involved in coordinating the process of cloth production. At least one farmer in northern Delaware owned "a spinning house" on his property a few years before factories were built. Elizabeth, Amelia, and Sara may have spun yarn for wool dealers too.

Cooking's daily routine cut across the changing work of the seasons. Like many Delaware farm families, the Springers had an outside kitchen, a small log building that removed heat and servants from the log house. Here the Springer women tended fires and cooked three meals a day. Meat was central to the household diet. As James Tilton wrote in 1788: "Few men breakfast without a portion of meat, and it is an universal practice to dine in the middle of the day, upon a full meal of meat, with bread & vegetables. The meanest slaves have this indulgence." Rural women roasted fresh mutton, poultry, and fish in the summer and fall and boiled salted meats the rest of the year. They often used vegetables from the garden to make a sauce for the meat. Households frequently baked bread; there was wheat bread for the family, and possibly cornbread for the slaves.

One other life pattern cut across all other women's work in the eighteenth century. Married women could expect to become pregnant about once every two years. If all went well during her pregnancy, a woman kept working at household tasks until very close to her lying-in time. If she had servants, slaves, or older daughters, she might be able to afford a few weeks of recovery after childbirth before returning to work. Most women breastfed their infants for a year or so. Then, soon after the baby was weaned, another pregnancy became likely. In all, eighteenth-century women were likely to spend some twenty years in a cycle of bearing, nursing, and raising children. In fact, Elizabeth Springer bore her two daughters, Mary and Ann, in quick succession shortly after her marriage. If she had other pregnancies in the late 1790s, either she did not carry to term or the children died in infancy. Both were common tragedies for women of the day, though no records survive to tell us more about Elizabeth's experience. Motherhood meant nursing, teaching, and loving her daughters, and passing on the household skills that would enable them to run homes of their own in the future.

Mary and Ann learned a variety of skills proven by time and many traditional attitudes toward household life. Work on the Springer farm varied in pace and intensity from season to season and from day to day. Some days Thomas, Will, and Ace probably labored until nightfall; on others they probably finished at midday. In some seasons women pitched into the rush of harvest; in other seasons there was time for a slower pace. This was a fundamental characteristic of preindustrial living, when people worked to finish the task before them rather than punching a time clock. Moreover, like farmers from time immemorial, Thomas had to worry about early frosts and late rains. But to a traditional anxiety over the weather he added a concern for the market price of wheat and livestock. In subtle ways, engagement with the marketplace altered the meaning of Elizabeth's work as well. She tended to traditionally female tasks, but like her husband, she produced in part for a new and growing market. In some regards the Springer household was "self-sufficient"—they grew much of the food they ate and produced many of the goods they used. Yet they relied on neighbors to grind grain and process cloth, and on the wider Atlantic marketplace as well. If Mary and Ann learned traditional ways, they also grew up in a household adapting to change. To understand those adaptations, we have to look more closely at the world surrounding the Mill Creek farm.

The Springers lived in a section of the county called Mill Creek Hundred. In 1798, tax assessors there counted 455 taxpayers—free males aged twenty-one or older and women who headed households of their own. Of that number, 255, or 56 percent, owned neither land nor houses. Some of the landless were in the same position that Thomas Springer had been in a decade before: they were the sons of landed farmers but not yet established on their own. Thomas's young friend Joshua Johnson, for example, had only fifty-two dollars' worth of livestock to his name in 1798, but the tax assessors listed him next to his very successful father, Robert, owner of a brick house, sawmill, gristmill, fulling mill, and 111 acres of land. Joshua might be impatient to have property of his own, but owning land was just a matter of time.

Others among the landless were artisans, such as carpenter Joseph Robinson, tailor Thomas Dixson, and wheelwright David Parker, men more likely to invest in the tools of their trade or a few head of livestock than in land. Yet many apparently had neither artisans' skills and tools nor landowning fathers. Some men without land worked as tenants on other men's farms, paying an annual rent by handing over a share of their harvest or a portion of their livestock. Many must have been laborers, living in the households of others.

Some people owned almost nothing. A handful of women owned substantial farms, like Mary Beason and widow Hannah Moore, but most widows lived closer to Pheby Hughes's standard of living: she had a house, a barn, twenty acres of land, and only eight dollars' worth of livestock. Among the most impoverished men were free blacks—"Black Sam" and "Black Frank" owned virtually noth-

ing—and there were white men on the bottom too. In 1798, the bottom half of the taxable population controlled only 16 percent of the hundred's taxable wealth. The fact that he owned land at all set Thomas Springer apart from many others of his generation. It made him more successful than most other free men in the hundred in 1798, and more successful than some of them would ever be.

Thomas's 129-acre farm put him in the top 35 percent of all those with land in the category of total acreage. Not quite 40 percent of the landowners had less than 100 acres, and another 25 percent owned between 100 and 129 acres. On the other side, many landowners held substantially more land than the Springers did: about 16 percent of the landed had between 130 and 199 acres, and another 17 percent owned between 200 and 400 acres. A few—just seven taxpayers—owned more than 400 acres.

In total wealth, Thomas Springer stood better than the great majority. His land, his slaves, and his livestock holdings put him in the upper 10 percent of all taxables in 1798. Moreover, his land was valued more highly per acre than the average land in Mill Creek Hundred, reflecting its location along a waterway, its proximity to Wilmington market, and the improvements that Thomas, Will, and Ace had made on the farm.

With the Mill Creek farm, the Springers acquired neighbors. As the deed to the land put it, the farm began at "a marked corner Maple near to Mill Creek being a corner of this and Land of the Reverend William McCannon and the Land of Captain Montgomery." From there the Springers' holding ran down the creek "to a Gum on the corner of this and Land of Andrew Reynolds." The boundary ran south and west after that, to "a corner for land belonging to the heirs of Simon Paulson Deed . . . to a Whiteoak tree . . . in the line of land of John Ball." The deed defined a neighborhood as well as a plot of land.

In addition to the McKennons, Montgomerys, Reynoldses, and Balls, there were other close neighbors. In 1790 Samuel Stroud, an established mill owner, had bought thirty-three acres of the original Mill Creek tract from Charles Springer. The purchase included a narrow strip of land that cut from the creek through the farm—then being worked by Thomas—to act as a millrace, conveying water to power a mill. In the nineties the Strouds constructed a three-story mill, 35 feet by 47 feet in size. By 1798 it was owned and operated by Joshua Stroud. On the other side of the Springer homestead was Milltown, a crossroads village consisting of a sawmill, a gristmill, a few houses, and a small store. During Thomas Springer's lifetime, most of these buildings belonged to Caleb Harlan and his family.

Members of the neighborhood did not all share a common background or a common faith. Swedish, English, Scots, and increasing numbers of Irish lived in the area. The Reverend William McKennon, next-door to the Springers, served as minister at Red Clay Presbyterian Church. The Harlans were Quakers, while the Springers maintained ties with Immanuel (Episcopalian) Church. Neighborhood households were not knit together by the bonds of common worship, but there were many other social ties. Close neighbors might also be relatives by blood or by marriage. Thomas Springer's brother Jeremiah and his second cousin Charles lived nearby, and Elizabeth Springer may have had kin in the neighborhood too. The Balls, Giffins, Strouds, and Springers all had ties by marriage as well, so that many neighbors were also in-laws at one remove or another.

Rural life created other connections. Women in the eighteenth century formed deep bonds by helping each other through the difficult hours of childbirth. Except in the few urban centers, doctors rarely supervised women's labor. Most women depended on neighbors to bring herbs and medicines, their own experience, and emotional support to ease the ordeal of giving birth. Catherine, Ann, and Sarah Harlan, Nancy Ball, Elizabeth

McKennon and her two daughters, and Mary Reece Springer, wife of Jeremiah, made up part of the female community who might have attended Elizabeth Springer in childbirth—and whom she might have attended in turn.

Women also visited one another's homes on more ordinary occasions, taking sewing and young children with them in order to work in company and talk together. There were more formal occasions for visiting as well. One contemporary observer reported that in Delaware, "the genteel people generally indulge in the parade of tea, in the afternoon." The Springers' teacups and sugar dishes suggest that from time to time Elizabeth emulated the genteel. On such occasions she could serve her guests her fanciest baked goods or perhaps imported nuts or other delicacies.

Much of Thomas Springer's socializing probably took place in public settings. Francis Dunlap's tavern in Wilmington drew many of the men from the Springer neighborhood, and many also patronized Wilmington stores. Caleb Harlan, Jr.'s store in nearby Milltown was small—it recorded "no neet profit" in 1798—but it must have been a handy place for Thomas to pick up a few necessities and talk with the Harlans. From time to time, Thomas had to travel to nearby mills to have wheat and corn ground into meal for the family's use. At mills and artisans' shops, men gathered and shared news and information.

On many occasions when men or women met together, social exchange and economic exchange were combined. Early in the 1800s, many of the Springers' immediate neighbors had occasion to describe some of their ordinary economic dealings. When Andrew Giffen sued John Ball's estate, the neighborhood testified about the two parties' transactions. Their testimony affords us a glimpse of neighborhood exchange in the Springers' area, and offers one insight into the ways the Springer household's daily activities connected them with people outside.

The dispute arose following John Ball, Sr.'s death, when his nephew and executor, John

Ball, Jr., pressed Giffin to repay a longstanding debt of over two hundred dollars. Giffin admitted that he had borrowed money long ago, but thought he had paid off the debt over the years by delivering "divers sums of money" and "divers Articles of property," and by performing "work and labour" for Ball. As Giffin saw it, his payments more than satisfied the original debt. He thought that the Ball estate owed him for "a Beef Cow, Half a Stack of Hay, 13 bushels and a half of corn, 600 pounds weight of Hay, 3 bushels wheat, a Cart Saddle, a Barrel of Cyder, 2 days work drawing logs, 3 yards of linen, 2 items of Cash—1 dollar and 10 dollars."

To settle the matter, Giffin entered an "Amicable Action" in the New Castle court. A justice of the peace referred the dispute to three local referees: Caleb Harlan, Jr., John Hall, and James Stroud. The investigators listened to the other side of the case too. John Ball, Jr., who had lived a decade in his uncle's house, testified that Giffin had already received remuneration for all the items he had listed. Ball said his uncle had paid for Giffin's apples and cider by pruning Giffin's orchard. Moreover, "the three yards of shirting linen were given to the sd Testator [Ball] in consideration of a hieffer calf" that Ball gave Giffin's daughter. Finally, "the drawing of logs charged" by Giffin had only constituted payment for the use of three of Ball's horses "for two days treading out wheat."

The referees found Ball's account the more convincing one and decided that Giffin still owed the Ball estate $209.85. As interesting as the outcome of the dispute, however, is what it tells us about relationships in the Springers' immediate neighborhood. To begin with, those relationships were of many years' standing. Most witnesses in the Giffin-Ball case testified that they had known Giffin for twenty or twenty-five years ("since he came into the country"), and most had known John Ball, Jr., for the ten years since he had joined his uncle's household. Joseph Ball, age sixty-seven, said he had known Giffin for almost a quarter of a century, and John Ball, Sr., for at

least half a century. Neighborhood exchange took place between acquaintances if not always between friends. Giffin and Ball had traded cows, linen, labor, and money over the course of many years.

Second, other members of the household were involved in the two men's longstanding economic dealings. Ball gave a calf to Giffin's daughter in exchange for three yards of shirting linen; women as well as men engaged in local exchange. Finally, only a few of these local transactions involved cash or immediate payment. People exchanged hours of work, the products of their labor, the use of tools or animals, and money. The result was a complicated relationship between Giffin and Ball. When we add in the trading that took place among all the families of the neighborhood, we see an intricate network of economic exchange. How common and accepted these practices were appears in the testimony of another witness in the case: James Ball told the court that he knew none of the particulars of the dealings between Giffin and John Ball, Sr. He knew only that they "did neighbor with each other, by borrowing & lending, etc." Economic exchange was so common a part of local life that it made sense to call it "neighboring."

The "borrowing and lending" of the Springers' neighborhood was neither casual nor unimportant: Giffin's dealings with just one of his neighbors amounted to several hundred dollars' value—well worth a lawsuit. But neighboring apparently was something different from simple buying and selling. Borrowing and lending was a sort of economic exchange in a social context. It was economics mixed with kinship, friendship, or longstanding social relationships between households.

The Springers took an active part in this local network. When Thomas died in the early nineteenth century, his executors had to settle forty-seven small accounts—debts owed and credits due to near neighbors like Andrew Reynolds, the Strouds, Samuel Paulson, and Charles Springer and to many others in the hundred. The Springers must have produced some of their surplus crops and manufactures with their Mill Creek neighbors in mind. At least two neighbors specialized in milling and probably welcomed farm produce from nearby. In turn, Elizabeth could get honey from Nancy Ball's bees; like Andrew Giffin, Thomas might have called on John Ball's skills at pruning apple trees.

The Ball-Giffin dispute underscores one other aspect of life in rural Delaware. Witnesses in the case were very familiar with the details of their neighbors' transactions. Day-to-day deals were often struck in public, so members of different households were often privy to one another's business. It made sense for neighbors to referee each other's disputes, not because they were impartial, but because they commonly had informed opinions about the neighborhood already. Local men could be expected to know what was going on or else whose word to trust about it.

It was an attitude toward neighbors reflected in the Springers' two-room house. Judging from the inventory, Thomas and Elizabeth slept upstairs, as did at least one of their daughters. They also used the space for storing clothing and extra bedding, and perhaps for spooling yarn. Another bed sat in the common room downstairs, along with the family's best chairs and tables, a looking glass, a linen chest, and a corner cupboard filled with queen's ware, teacups, and wine glasses. How the Springers arranged these furnishings is hard to say. Some of the items they owned had quite specific uses: a dining table, a breakfast table, and a tea table. People whose houses had several first-floor rooms commonly set such specialized items in different rooms. By contrast, the Springers lived more of their lives in a single setting. By building a separate log kitchen, they removed some work (cooking) and some people (slaves) from that setting. By building a second-floor space for sleeping, they claimed some privacy. Still, for the most part visitors to the Springers could step right into the midst of household life.

The Springers' experience "buying and selling" took them out of their own neighborhood and into an expanding Atlantic market. They dealt directly with mere acquaintances in nearby towns, and indirectly with people in distant cities and countries. The products of their farm might travel to Europe, the West Indies, South America, or even China. Household members stayed closer to home, of course, but though their lives were rural, they were not necessarily isolated. The Limestone Road passed right by the Springer homestead and was a major route from Stanton, Delaware to the Pennsylvania state line. It was a short journey for Thomas into two nearby towns.

One of the towns was New Castle, dismissed in 1760 by an English traveler as "a place of very little consideration." Twenty years later, the town consisted of "a Parish Church, a Presbyterian Meeting-House, a Court House, a Gaol, a Pillory, a Pair of Stocks, one old Cannon for Signals or rejoicing Days and a Pound for Hogs." Nor was the village likely to grow very rapidly, for there was "no Wharf or Dock, where ships can ride out of the strong Current." Yet New Castle was the city where growing numbers of Irish immigrants entered the country to settle farms in the region. Forty miles below Philadelphia, it was a stopping place for overland travelers between that city and Baltimore, and a port where outbound Philadelphia ships stopped to take on livestock and inbound ships stopped to pick up pilots. Equally important, it was the political capital of the county, the seat of courts of justice, and a center for legal affairs. Thomas Springer had to travel there to register his will, record land deeds, and cast his vote for local officials like the county sheriff or for president of the United States.

There were shops in New Castle, but the most important economic center of the region was Wilmington, six miles east of the Springer farm. Originally founded—as "Fort Christina"—by the New Sweden Company in the 1630s, the town remained small for a century's time. In the 1730s Wilmington took on a new name and new life. Its growth depended in part on its location. Settlers began pouring into Lancaster and Chester counties in Pennsylvania, pushing the farming frontier to the west. Soon farmers in the region began producing surplus wheat. Many found the shortest route to market was to send it overland in wagons to the Christiana River near Wilmington, where it was loaded into shallops, twin-masted freighters that sailed east to the Delaware River and then north to Philadelphia. Wilmington's location made it a center for the transhipment of grain.

By the 1770s, Wilmington merchants dealt with many parts of the Atlantic market. For the most part they carried staples: bread, flour, beef, pork, and lumber for the West Indies; potash and flaxseed for Ireland; and a variety of goods (including rice and indigo acquired through trade with the southern colonies) for England. They brought in rum, molasses, sugar, and coffee from the West Indies, linens and glass from Ireland, china and tinware from Britain, as well as Indian cottons, Chinese tea and silk, Eastern spices, and European wines. They distributed these foreign goods, English manufactures, and items produced locally or by Philadelphia artisans to the inland farmers of Delaware and Pennsylvania. Around this commerce developed a community of local artisans, including shipbuilders, coopers, and others closely tied to commerce, and "hatters, coppersmiths, Booksellers, &c."

Around midcentury, another element contributed to Wilmington's growth: millers began using the powerful waters of the Brandywine River to grind grain on a large scale. Early in the 1780s, there were seven mills within 150 yards of one another along the river. In most mills, two pairs of grindstones were connected to a single set of gears, so that one pair could cool while the other ran. Wagons brought in Pennsylvania wheat, and ships could anchor right off the banks of the city's merchant mills. Millers reached out for supplies from farms in New Jersey, Maryland, Virginia, and New York. By 1788, said James Tilton, it was "a prevailing opinion in Delaware that we have the largest

and most perfect manufacture of flour, within a like space of ground known in the world."

The output of the mills was indeed prodigious. By the 1790s, mills along the Brandywine were grinding 300,000 to 500,000 bushels of wheat every year, and entrepreneurs were still buying up expensive millsites and building more mills. Wilmington merchants expanded their trade accordingly, shipping more and more grain to the West Indies and sending both flour and wheat to Philadelphia for local consumption, for export, and for making ship's biscuit and bread. In the last decade of the century, the French Revolution increased the demand for wheat and other grains in both Europe and the West Indies. Thomas Springer's surplus wheat eventually reached distant consumers.

The expansion of their operations changed the millers' relationship with farmers in the area. Milling had always been a part of life in rural Delaware, but it had been a part-time occupation of farmers with lands located on the riverbanks. The men who established mills along the Brandywine in the late eighteenth century were rarely farmers too. Increasingly they specialized, and when they branched out into new ventures their pursuits were seldom agricultural. Many millers took over much of their own shipping, so that they became flour merchants as well as mill owners. Moreover, by 1785, the Brandywine millers were getting to be quite well-to-do; said one traveler, "these mills belong to 11 people and bring them an immense income." Although the cold of winter sometimes froze millraces in Wilmington, otherwise the mills operated all year long. And "in active or busy times," wrote James Tilton, "the mill grinds perpetually night and day." Late in the 1790s a French traveler remarked upon the novel principles by which one family ran their milling business: "Their Mill is not employed for the public but solely for their own private service. It is called a flour Manufactory."

Such changes made a difference in the lives of Delaware farmers. In 1783, complaints about the behavior of Brandywine millers reached the ears of the state government. Over forty farmers from the Brandywine and Christiana hundreds petitioned the legislature. In the past, the farmers said, they had customarily taken wheat and corn to the mills "to be ground into Meal for the use of their families, paying therefor a stated Toll." Yet recently mill owners had come to prefer the "very great advantage arising to themselves by purchasing large quantities of Wheat and Manufacturing the same into Flour for distant Markets." As a result, the farmers charged, mill owners had "neglected and even refused grinding the Corn belonging to the adjoining Inhabitants for the supply of their respective Familys—by which means the Inhabitants are subjected to great inconvenience and often distress."

The farmers considered it a "Matter of Right" to have access to local mills. Mills, they thought, had been built "as well for the ease and convenience of the Neighbouring People and the private emolument of the particular Owners," so millers should work both for their own self-interest and for the welfare of their neighbors and neighborhood. Milling represented a sort of quasi-public venture to Delaware farmers; a mill was not quite a private business. Apparently the state agreed with that assessment, for the legislature set fines for millers who refused to grind grain for local use at least one day out of every week. Farmers expected millers to continue neighboring, to keep borrowing and lending in the local market as well as buying and selling in the wider world. There is evidence, however, that many Brandywine millers preferred profit to neighborliness; within a very few years the legislature had to increase the fine for turning away local customers.

No similar complaints survive from farmers in the Springers' part of the county. Perhaps millers in the area did not withdraw so fully from neighboring. Yet they did withdraw from agriculture; many of the millers in Mill Creek Hundred owned too little land to be farmers as well. Some branched out into other pursuits. A few took advantage of their location along the

water to run a sawmill, paper mill, or fulling mill too. At least one put capital into livestock and owned a springhouse for butter making. Moreover, like Brandywine millers, Mill Creek millers developed connections outside the immediate neighborhood. The Harlans' son William carried on the family's dealings in Philadelphia; Joshua Stroud acquired another mill in New London, Pennsylvania. The Stroud mill next to Thomas Springer's land boasted the latest technological improvements: a grain elevator to take wheat to the mill's top floor, and a "hopper boy," a revolving rake to spread the meal out to cool and then gather it up again. These devices increased the volume of flour produced and reduced the labor needed. In Mill Creek as in neighboring hundreds, the world of selling and buying threatened to change relationships in the community.

Not surprisingly, millers in the hundred could be distinguished from farmers around them by their wealth. In 1798 there were seventeen men in the area who owned a mill or held an interest in one. Nine of them were assessed in the top 5 percent of all taxables. Most of the rest fell into the top 15 percent. Moreover, millers acted increasingly to make their wealth visible. To the eye, Mill Creek Hundred presented a landscape of houses made of logs and houses made of stone. Yet many country millers built themselves houses like those in Wilmington: houses made of brick. Late in the century, millers were three times more likely than farmers to live in brick houses. Building these substantial homes, millers marked their distance from their neighbors, expressing both material prosperity and cosmopolitan taste.

Thomas Springer did not live to build a house of brick—and maybe he would have chosen not to build one, anyway. Yet in some measure he and Elizabeth oriented their lives toward the city of Wilmington and beyond. The Springers seem to have found opportunities in many of the changes that threatened other farmers. Thomas could accept the growing power of millers with equanimity because his household was relatively independent of them. The Springers did grow some grain, but they concentrated on raising livestock. The household found several ways to gain from the market: fattening animals, producing butter, selling wool, yarn, and meat. They could live with one foot in a local network of exchange, the other in a wider market. In large part, what made this strategy possible were the inherited advantages that gave Thomas land, livestock, and control of others' labor. He had managed to gain "independence" in the first place only with the help of his successful father, and he prospered only by depending on the work of Elizabeth, some white servants or relatives, and four African-American slaves. Such affluence was out of the reach of many young men in the Springers' neighborhood. In material terms, Thomas and Elizabeth Springer were among the lucky ones.

Just after the turn of the century, Elizabeth Springer died. We do not know the cause. Left with two young daughters and a household to run, Thomas decided to remarry. He chose twenty-two-year-old Margaret Wells. Margaret's father had died five years earlier, and her mother passed away in 1801. Marriage to Thomas Springer made sense to her. They were wed in 1802. Margaret brought her share of the family inheritance into the marriage. There is some evidence that she brought an eight-day clock—listed as the Springers' most expensive possession a few years later—into the household, where it was prominently displayed in the downstairs room. Margaret took over Elizabeth's duties as household manager and mother of Ann and Mary. In 1804, Thomas fell ill. He died in the fall of that year, having lived forty years. He provided as best he could for his family. He left Margaret "the white-face cow" and the proper legal settlement for widows: a one-third interest in his estate for life. He appointed Joshua Johnson as a guardian for Ann and Mary during their minority, and

instructed his executors, Joshua Stroud and Jeremiah Springer, to sell the farm for his children's support.

The household broke up quickly. The slaves Will and Ace were sold away from the family. They probably joined the stream of unfree labor moving to the south and west, eventually to grow cotton to supply textile mills along the Brandywine and elsewhere. Amelia and Sara were left to the Springer girls by Thomas's will. Margaret must have gone to live with relatives for a few years. Mary and Ann may have joined their stepmother, but it seems more likely that they settled in with closer relatives in the Mill Creek area. In 1806 Margaret married again and moved into New Castle as Mrs. George Peirce, Esq., leaving many rural routines behind.

Mary Springer remained closer to the land. In 1808, when she was still in her teens, she married Robert McMurphy, son of a farmer and gristmiller. She and her husband ran a farm and a tavern "on the State road leading from New Castle to Dover on the North side of Black Bird Creek." The growth of cloth manufacture freed Mary from the spinning wheel, but she must have used most of the other skills she had learned growing up on the Mill Creek farm. Ann Springer was to experience town living like her step-mother. She moved to Middletown, Delaware, and married Richard Craddock in 1814. The two sisters remained close: when Mary's husband wrote his will, he appointed Ann's husband as his executor. By 1820, Robert McMurphy had died, and Mary McMurphy and Ann and Richard Craddock had all left the state. It is nice to speculate that they moved south and west, perhaps following growing numbers into Kentucky and beyond. A man named David Eastburn bought the Mill Creek farm at auction in 1805. Within a few years he rented it out to a tenant farmer.

# 12

# ABSALOM JONES: FREE BLACK LEADER

## GARY B. NASH

The American Revolution wrought profound changes in the lives of the nation's African-American peoples. In the North, the new state governments passed gradual emancipation laws that set slavery on the road to extinction for the thousands of blacks held in bondage above the Mason-Dixon line. In the South, where the continuation of slavery was ensured by the rapid expansion of cotton production after the 1790s, masters found their bondspeople increasingly emboldened by the rhetoric of the Revolution and by the successful desertion of thousands of slaves to the British ranks during the war. While much has been written about post-Revolutionary slavery, until recently historians have paid relatively little attention to the the free blacks who resided in the North. Yet recent scholarship has revealed that the end of slavery in the northern states prompted one of the most dramatic migrations in American history. Fleeing from rural isolation and the legacy of bondage, newly freed blacks flocked to northern cities in search of jobs, community, and family life.

Of all the northern cities, Philadelphia exerted the greatest magnetic attraction for free blacks. At the center of Philadelphia's free black community stood the religiously oriented Free African Society and the African Church. More than any other institution, independent black churches symbolized and reinforced the African-American quest for racial parity following the Revolution. In this essay, Gary B. Nash tells the story of Absalom Jones, an ex-slave who became one of the central leaders of Philadelphia's free black community. By setting Jones's life in the context of the city's developing black religious institutions, Nash reveals the difficulties and prejudice faced by free blacks as well as their steadfast desire to become free and equal citizens of the new republic.

From the Spanish-language edition of David G. Sweet and Gary B. Nash, eds., *Struggle and Survival in Colonial America* (Berkeley, Calif.: University of California Press, 1987). Reprinted by permission of Gary B. Nash and University of California Press.

"I, Absalom Jones, was born [a slave] in Sussex [Delaware] on the 6th of November, 1746." So he wrote nearly half a century later when he was a free man, a leader of the free black community in Philadelphia, and the first licensed black minister in the United States. Though hardly noticed in traditional history books, nor even in the recent wave of writing on Afro-American history, the story of Absalom Jones encapsulates much of the experience of the first generation of freed slaves in America. Moreover, his accomplishments, especially his role in establishing the first separate black church in America, entitle him to a place among the "men of mark"—the early black leaders who laid the foundations of modern Afro-American life by fashioning social and religious institutions that carried forward the black quest for freedom and equality after the American Revolution.

His master, Benjamin Wynkoop, took him from the fields, Absalom remembered, when "I was small . . . to wait and attend on him in the house." Removed from the world of field labor, he developed a desire for learning. With pennies given to him from time to time, he recalled, "I soon bought myself a primer and begged to be taught by any body that I found able and willing to give me the least instruction. Soon after this, I was able to purchase a spelling book . . . and a Testament." Literacy could only have increased the distance between him and those of his age who did not live in the big house; and hence Absalom—who had only this slave name—became introspective, or "singular," as he termed it. Then, in 1762, at age 16, his master sold his mother, five brothers, and a sister after deciding to move north to Philadelphia, the Quaker capital of Pennsylvania.

The breaking up of his family, though doubtless traumatic, proved to be a turning point in his life. While bereft of his kin, he was taken to the earliest center of abolitionism in America and to the city where humanitarian reformers had created an atmosphere conducive to education and family formation among slaves.

Thus, while he had to work in his master's shop from dawn to dark, Absalom soon prevailed upon Wynkoop to allow him to attend a night school for blacks.

In 1770 Absalom married the slave of his master's neighbor, taking vows in the Anglican church where the Wynkoop family worshiped. Soon after this, encouraged by the abolitionist sentiment that Quakers and others had spread through Philadelphia, he put the tool of literacy to work. Drawing up an appeal for his wife's release, he carried it, with his wife's father at his side, to "some of the principal Friends [Quakers] of this city," asking for their support. "From some we borrowed, and from others we received donations," he recounted. Thereafter, Absalom "made it my business to work until twelve or one o'clock at night, to assist my wife in obtaining a livelihood," and to pay the money that was borrowed to purchase her freedom. It took years to repay the debt. But by 1778, while the American Revolution was occurring, Absalom had apparently discharged his obligations because he was then pleading with his master to allow him to purchase his own freedom. Wynkoop would not consent to this until October 1, 1784—six years after the first of what Absalom remembered as a series of humble requests.

It was probably in 1784, upon gaining his release, that Absalom authenticated his freedom to the world around him by taking the surname Jones. It was a common English name but nonetheless one that *he* had chosen and one that could not be mistaken for the Dutch name of his master whom he had served until the age of 38. But he acted as if he bore his master no grudges. Forbearing and even tempered, he continued to work in Wynkoop's shop. Years later, in an obituary for Jones, it was said that his master "always gave him the character of having been a faithful and exemplary servant, remarkable for many good qualities; especially for his being not only of a peaceable demeanour, but for being possessed of the talent for inducing a disposition to it in others."

Two years after gaining his freedom in Philadelphia, Absalom Jones met another recently freed slave from Delaware named Richard Allen. Allen was much Jones's junior in years but much his senior in his commitment to leading out of physical bondage fellow Africans still enslaved and out of psychological bondage those who had been recently freed. While still a slave, Allen had been converted to Methodism by itinerant preachers during the revolutionary years in Kent County, Delaware. After gaining his freedom in 1780 he spent six years interspersing work as a sawyer and wagon driver with months of riding the Methodist circuits from South Carolina to New York. He learned to preach with great effect to black and white audiences and traveled with some of the leading Methodist sojourners. By the time he arrived in Philadelphia in 1786, full of Methodist zeal and convinced that God had appointed him to special tasks, Allen seems to have completed the crucial psychological middle passage by which those who gained freedom in a legal sense procured as well the emotional autonomy that came only when they overcame servility to whites and dependence upon them.

Invited to preach in the white Methodist church in Philadelphia, Allen soon "raised a Society . . . of forty-two members." Among them was Absalom Jones, who had abandoned Christ Church where his former master worshiped in favor of St. George's Methodist Church. Like taking a surname, this was a step in the forging of a new self-identity, a part of the difficult throwing off of dependency that was indispensable in learning how to live as a fully free person.

Within months of Allen's arrival in Philadelphia Absalom Jones and several other recently freed slaves joined the Methodist preacher to discuss forming an independent black religious society. Religion and education had been the mainsprings of freedom and achievement for all these men. So it was natural that when they looked around them to find the majority of former slaves illiterate and unchurched, they "often communed together

upon this painful and important subject" and determined "to form some kind of religious society." Shortly thereafter, Allen proposed this "to the most respectable people of color in this city," only to be "met with opposition." Leading white Methodists objected even more strenuously, using "very degrading and insulting language to try to prevent us from going on." Nevertheless, out of these deliberations came the Free African Society of Philadelphia, which Jones and Allen founded in April 1787. Though mutual aid was its purported goal, the Society was quasi-religious in character and, beyond that, was an organization for building black strength and pride through collective and independent action. Before we can examine how the Free African Society midwived the birth of the first black churches in North America we must form a mental picture of the world these former bondspersons found themselves in and explore their understanding of the possible strategies that they might adopt in hammering out a postslavery existence that went beyond mere legal release from thralldom.

Black Philadelphians, like former slaves in other parts of America, had to rethink their relationship to white society in the early days of the Republic. Were they Africans in America who might now return to their homelands? Were they Afro-Americans whose future was bound up in creating a new existence on soil where they had toiled most of their lives but whose cultural heritage was African? Or were they simply Americans with dark skin, who in seeking places as free men and women had to assimilate as quickly as possible to the cultural norms and social institutions of white society?

Outwardly, Philadelphia represented a haven from persecution and an arena of opportunity for manumitted blacks. It was the center of Quaker abolitionism, the location of the national government that had issued ringing phrases about freedom and equality for all, and the capital of the state that in 1780 had passed the first abolition act in America. It was also a bustling maritime center that held out the promise of employment for migrating Afro-

Americans. For all these reasons Philadelphia became a magnet for those released from bondage during the 1780s, and this drawing power also owed something to the considerable sympathy among some of its white inhabitants for freed blacks setting out on the road to freedom. Hence, from a city with about 450 slaves and an equal number of free blacks at the end of the American Revolution Philadelphia grew to contain 2,100 blacks, all but 273 of them free, in 1790, and more than 6,500 blacks, of whom only 55 remained in bondage, in 1800.

In its internal workings, however, Philadelphia was far from ideal for former slaves. The illiterate and often unskilled men and women who trekked there after the Revolution had to compete for jobs with lower-class Irish and German immigrants and did not always find work. Though not disenfranchised by law, free blacks were prohibited by white social pressure from voting. Also, virtually every institution and social mechanism in the city—religious or secular, economic and social—engaged in discriminatory practices which flowed like a natural force from the pervasive belief in black inferiority. The common assumption was that blacks were either innately handicapped or had been irreparably degraded by the experience of slavery.

For black wayfarers who found their way to Philadelphia after the Revolution overcoming patterns of behavior peculiar to slavery became a crucial matter. By its nature, slavery assumed the superiority of the white master class, and even the most benevolent master occupied a power relationship vis-à-vis his slaves that daily reminded blacks of their lowly position and condition. Probably few American slaves believed they were inferior human beings, but slavery required them to act so, and daily behavior became so patterned that dependency and servility developed as a way of life among many of them. Newly freed, they had to face the dominant culture, which was far from ready to treat them as equals and continued to demand deferential comportment from them. We can infer from the fact

that almost all the early black institutions in the North used the adjective "African" in their titles—the Free African Society, the African School, the African Church of Philadelphia—that these ex-slaves identified positively with their ancestral homelands and did not subscribe to the common white characterizations of Africa as a dismal, cultureless environment. Nonetheless, white racism impinged on their lives at every turn and, although not of the virulent form it would assume early in the nineteenth century, it tended to keep cowed the poorest and weakest members of the emerging black communities.

Recognizing the hidebound nature of white attitudes and the psychic scars inflicted by slavery, a few former slaves in the North attempted to solve the problem simply by opting out of American society and returning to Africa. But the small colonization movement of the 1780s that was centered in New England made virtually no impact on black Philadelphians, who overwhelmingly cast their lot with America. Nonetheless, the will to plan rationally, to strive for an independent and dignified existence, and to work for the future of their children depended upon throwing off the incubus of slavery, an institution which had perpetuated itself by exacting a terrible price for black attempts at independent or self-reliant behavior. Some freedmen in Philadelphia believed that in this work of emotional self-reconstruction their future lay not in trying to pry open the doors of white institutions but in building autonomous black organizations where the people emerging from the house of bondage could gather strength, develop their own leaders, and socialize and worship in their own ways.

In the post-Revolutionary era free blacks also had to confront the role that benevolence played in perpetuating feelings of servility and in shaping black-white relations. "There can be no greater disparity of power," writes David Brion Davis, "than that between a man convinced of his own disinterested service and another man who is defined as a helpless object." Thus, white benevolence perpetuated black dependence, often stood in the way of mutual respect, and impeded the growth of positive self-images among freedmen and freedwomen, who could not feel truly free so long as they had to rely on white help in creating a new life for themselves.

Only a few years out of bondage in the 1780s, Philadelphia's free blacks thus lived in a highly fluid situation full of dangers and full of opportunities. Their lowly position and circumscribed means made it imperative to accept the support of benevolent whites who offered education, sometimes jobs, and almost always moral guidance. Likewise, they could hardly hope to obtain the release of their racial brethren still in bondage without white leadership and support. Yet many of them understood that while short-term circumstances required white patronage, the long-term goal must be to stand independent of white largesse.

It is within this ideological context that we can see the Free African Society of Philadelphia as much more than a black mutual aid society. Beginning as an organization in which free blacks were taking the first halting steps toward developing their own leaders and solving their own problems, it became a society which founded churches, assumed a supervisory role over the moral life of the black community, and worked to create a visionary black consciousness out of the disparate human material that had found its way to Philadelphia in this period. But this took time.

While the Free African Society got underway, Richard Allen's preaching and Absalom Jones's quiet aid to those he found in need increased the black congregants at St. George's. Philadelphia's blacks, both slave and free, had married, baptized their children, and attended religious services at most of the city's churches since before the Revolution and had particularly flocked to the Anglican churches, which encouraged them with religious and secular instruction. Now they began transferring their allegiance to the Methodist church, an offshoot of the Anglican church which had declared itself independent only in 1784. This transfer of allegiance is not difficult to understand, for the new Methodist ministers "made no pretensions to literary qualifications," as the first black historian of the African Church of Philadelphia wrote in the 1850s, "and being despised and persecuted as religious enthusiasts, their sympathies naturally turned towards the lowly, who like themselves, were of small estimate in the sight of worldly greatness." Also commending Methodism to former slaves were the well-known antislavery views of founder John Wesley and the Methodist discipline and polity formulated in 1784, which attacked slave trading and slaveholding and barred persons engaged in these practices from holding church offices.

Meanwhile, Jones and Allen enlarged the activities of the Free African Society. In early 1790 the Society attempted to lease the Stranger's Burial ground in order to turn it into a black cemetery under black control. In the next month the Society instituted "a regular mode of procedure with respect to . . . marriages" and began keeping a book of marriage records. Having assumed quasi-ecclesiastical functions, the Society took the final step in September 1790 when a special committee led by Jones recommended the initiation of formal religious services.

All of these enlarged functions bore a decidedly Quakerly stamp, reflecting the strong influence of the Society of Friends on many of the leading members. More particularly, this influence came through the work of Anthony Benezet, the wizened, saintly little Huguenot immigrant who dedicated so much of his life to the Negro's cause. Benezet wrote half a dozen pamphlets against slavery and the slave trade between 1759 and 1784, founded a school for blacks in 1770, and tirelessly devoted himself to it for the rest of his life. In 1780 he personally lobbied with every member of the Pennsylvania legislature to pass a gradual abolition act. When Benezet died in 1784, slaves and free blacks alike turned out en masse to follow his funeral procession to the graveyard and testify to his work on their behalf.

While Quaker support was indispensable to the African Society at first, it also caused difficulties and eventually a deep rift in the black ranks. Quaker humanitarianism was never of the sort that was based on a deep sense of the "likeness among all persons." Quakers held themselves apart from other people, white and black, and in fact the Society of Friends was the only religious group in Philadelphia that refused to accept blacks as members in the 1780s. Theirs was more a policy "of stewardship than a true humanitarianism," and their efforts on behalf of blacks "partook more of condescension than humanitarianism."

The Quakerly leanings of many Free African Society members caused Richard Allen great pain. He made no objections when the African Society adopted Quaker-like visiting committees in early 1788 to call on black families or when they instituted the disownment practices of Quakers in September of that year, to disenroll wayward members. But two months later, when the Society adopted the Friendly practice of beginning meetings with fifteen minutes of silence, Allen led the withdrawal of "a large number" of dissenters whose adherence to Methodism had accustomed them to "an unconstrained outburst of their feelings in religious worship." Allen came no more to meetings of the African Society but privately began convening some of its members in an attempt to stop the drift of the organization toward the practices of the Quakers.

Jones and others made repeated efforts to bring Allen back into the bosom of the group and censured him "for attempting to sow division among us." When their efforts failed, they followed the Quaker procedure of declaring that "he has disunited himself from membership with us." This was in June 1789. Nineteen months later, following four months of deliberations, they began holding formal religious meetings in the Quaker African Schoolhouse.

After Allen's disownment from the Free African Society, the leadership role fell primarily to Absalom Jones. It was the mild-mannered and conciliatory Jones who made the crucial connections in the white community that launched plans for building a black church. The ties with the Society of Friends were wearing thin by the summer of 1791 because many Quakers objected to the Sunday psalm singing by blacks in the Quaker schoolhouse. But Jones had been forging new patronage lines to one of Philadelphia's most influential citizens—the powerful, opinionated doctor, Benjamin Rush. Over the next four years it was Rush who became the Anthony Benezet of the 1790s so far as Philadelphia's free blacks were concerned.

As a young physician before the American Revolution, Rush had written a passionate antislavery pamphlet. But this ardor for the cause had cooled during the war, and he had played no role in the work of the Pennsylvania Abolition Society when it was reestablished in 1784. Then, in a poignant example of trans-Atlantic abolitionist influence, Rush threw himself into the fray in 1787 after reading Thomas Clarkson's recently published *Essay on the Slavery and Commerce of the Human Species,* which in turn had been inspired by Clarkson's reading of Anthony Benezet's *Historical Account of Guinea,* one reading of which convinced him to devote his life to abolitionism. So thoroughly was Rush converted to the free blacks' cause that he immediately joined the Pennsylvania Abolition Society, freed his slave, William Gruber, and shortly thereafter wrote to a friend that "I love even the name of Africa, and never see a Negro slave or freeman without emotions which I seldom feel in the same degree towards my unfortunate fellow creatures of a fairer complexion."

During the summer of 1791 plans went forward for promoting the black church, although white opposition among those who had claimed to be friends of the free blacks surfaced quickly. Working with Absalom Jones, and perhaps with Richard Allen, who had reconciled his differences with members of the African Society, Rush drew up a plan of church government and articles of faith. A white merchant, Robert Ralston, joined Rush in composing subscription papers to be carried about the city to solicit building funds. Aware that many Philadelphians regarded him as impetuous and idiosyncratic, Rush tried to stay in the background, convinced that "the work will prosper the better for my keeping myself out of sight." Rush was hardly capable of self-effacement, however, and word of his role in the plans circulated through the city. Within days of composing the plan of government Rush found himself accosted in the street by William White, rector of Christ Church and recently appointed bishop of the Episcopal Church in Pennsylvania. White "expressed his disapprobation to the proposed African church" because "it originated in pride." Leading Quakers also conveyed their displeasure to Absalom Jones, and the Methodists threatened disownment of any black Methodist who participated in the undertaking. Paternalistic Philadelphians discovered that helping their black brothers gave greater satisfaction than seeing them help themselves.

Such criticism from Anglicans, Quakers, and Methodists, many of whom had been active in the Abolition Society, drove home the lesson that benevolent whites regarded freedmen as deeply inferior and could not abide independent action—pride, Bishop White called it—that challenged that characterization. An early historian of black Methodism, reflecting in 1867 on the final separation of Richard Allen from the white Methodist church, dwelt on precisely this point. "The giant crime committed by the Founders of the African Methodist Episcopal Church," wrote Benjamin Tanner, "was that they dared to organize a Church of men, men to think for themselves, men to talk for themselves, men to act for themselves: A Church of men who support from their own substance, however scanty, the ministration of the Word which they receive; men who spurn to have their churches built for them, and their pastors supported from the coffers of some charitable organization; men who prefer to live

by the sweat of their own brow and be free."

No chance yet existed in 1791 for Philadelphia's free blacks to gain the full meaning of freedom through completely independent action. Half of them still lived in the households of whites as domestic servants and hired hands; many had to indenture out their children through the good offices of the Abolition Society; and, as a group, they still were obliged to rely heavily on benevolent white Philadelphians for organizing schools and, in the present case, the African Church. Hence, Absalom Jones and the other black leaders worked closely with Benjamin Rush, Robert Ralston, and other whites in the summer of 1791 to raise subscriptions for their own place of worship. The work went on "swimmingly," Rush reported in August. An "Address of the Representatives of the African Church," an appeal for building funds, was carried to prominent men in the city. This succeeded in garnering some modest contributions, including donations from George Washington and Thomas Jefferson. Attempting to appeal as widely as possible to both blacks and whites, Jones and the other leaders adopted articles of association and a plan of church government "so general as to embrace all, and yet so orthodox in cardinal points as to offend none." But the flow of money soon stopped, perhaps because of the opposition to the church expressed by leading white churchmen. So Jones and Allen decided to broaden their appeal. Believing "that if we put our trust in the Lord, he would stand by us," Allen recounted, they took to the streets in March 1792. "We went out with our subscription paper," recalled Allen, "and met with great success," collecting $360 on the first day.

But thereafter the going got harder and some of the early optimism began to fade. The early subscriptions proved sufficient to buy two adjacent lots on Fifth Street, only a block from the Statehouse, for $450. But most blacks had little to contribute from their meager resources, and most whites seem to have snapped their pocketbooks shut at the thought of a black church. Whereas they had initially responded to the idea of an "African" church as a piece of arrogance on the part of a people so recently released from slavery, they now began calculating the effect on their own churches. "The old and established [religious] societies," wrote Rush, "look shy at them, each having lost some of its members by the new association." Still, Rush did not waver in his conviction that "the poor blacks will succeed in forming themselves into a distinct independent church."

Despite these early difficulties, the resolve of black Philadelphians to form a separate church grew mightily in the fall of 1792 after one of the most dramatic confrontations in early American church history. A number of black leaders were still attending services at St. George's Methodist Church, where the congregation had outgrown the seating capacity. When the white elders decided to expand their house of worship, black Methodists contributed money and labor to the effort. But on the first Sunday after the renovations were completed the elders informed the black worshipers who filed into the church that they must sit in a segregated section of the new gallery rather than along the walls, as had been their custom before. Richard Allen later recounted:

We expected to take the seats over the ones we formerly occupied below, not knowing any better. We took those seats; meeting had begun, and they were nearly done singing, and just as we got to the seats, the Elder said, "Let us pray." We had not been long upon our knees before I heard considerable scuffling and loud talking. I raised my head up and saw one of the trustees, H——— M———, having hold of the Rev. Absalom Jones, pulling him off his knees, and saying, "You must get up, you must not kneel here." Mr. Jones replied, "Wait until prayer is over, and I will get up, and trouble you no more." With that he beckoned to one of the trustees, Mr. L——— S———, to come to his assistance. He came and went over to William White to pull him up. By this time prayer was over, and we all went out of the church in a

body, and they were no more plagued by us in the church.

The St. George's incident confirmed what many blacks had already suspected—that there would be no truly biracial Christian community in the white churches of the city. If they were to worship with dignity, it must be in churches of their own. The first black historian of the black church movement described this striving for dignity in the black exodus from St. George's that followed the discriminatory treatment. It was an "age of general and searching inquiry," wrote William Douglass, "into the equity of old and established customs," a time when "a moral earthquake had awakened the slumber of ages" and caused "these humble men, just emerged from the house of bondage . . . to rise above those servile feelings which all their antecedents were calculated to cherish and to assume, as they did, an attitude of becoming men conscious of invaded rights. . . ." They were determined, wrote Allen, "to worship God under our own vine and fig tree" and "were filled with fresh vigor to get a house erected to worship God in."

Despite such renewed commitment Jones, Allen, and the other black leaders reluctantly concluded by late 1792 that they could not raise sufficient money to build their African church on the lots they had purchased. To their rescue came the unlikeliest of figures— the Welsh immigrant John Nicholson, who had blazed meteorically onto the Philadelphia scene after the war as state comptroller and high flying speculator in western lands and revolutionary loan certificates. Barely accepted in polite Philadelphia circles, not attached to any church, and uninvolved in the work of the Abolition Society, Nicholson provided what none of the Philadelphia elite would offer—a large loan of $1,000 with which to begin construction. "Humanity, charity, and patriotism never united their claims in a petition with more force than in the present instance," wrote Rush to Nicholson in a letter hand carried by William Gray and Absalom Jones. "You *will* not—you *cannot* refuse their request." Five days later Jones and Gray wrote Nicholson suggesting a 10-year mortgage with "Lawful interest to be paid Quarterly" and pressed their request "for the sake of Religion & Christianity and as this is the first Institution of the kind. . . ."

It took another two months to execute the mortgage and another to draw up building contracts. Finally, in March 1793, as reports of black rebellion in the French West Indies filtered into Philadelphia, the city's free blacks and some of their white benefactors gathered to see earth turned for the church. Richard Allen remembered the day vividly a quarter of a century later. "As I was the first proposer of the African Church, I put the first spade into the ground to dig the cellar for the same. This was the first African Church or meeting house to be erected in the United States of America."

Before the two-story brick building on Fifth Street could be completed its humble founders had to endure additional difficulties. Like most visionaries, Jones and his cohorts had planned expansively, designing a church capacious enough to seat 800. The cost estimates for the building ran to $3,560. Even with the $1,000 loan from Nicholson, more money had to be raised. Ironically, black revolt in the Caribbean undermined this attempt. With hundreds of French planters fleeing the black rebellion in Saint Domingue and streaming into Philadelphia with French-speaking slaves at their sides, many white city dwellers reneged on their pledges to the African Church in order to help the destitute white slaveholders taking refuge in their city. Philadelphia's free blacks learned that even the most sympathetic whites placed the distress of white slaveowners ahead of the aspirations of those who had been slaves.

John Nicholson again came to the rescue, loaning another $1,000 in mid-August. Ten days later the black leaders staged a roof-raising banquet in an open field on the edge of the city. About 100 whites, most of them construc-

tion artisans, sat down at long tables "under the shade of several large trees" and consumed a bounteous dinner complete with excellent liqueurs and melons for dessert. They were served by a company of free blacks. Then, in a display of racial reciprocity, the whites arose, about fifty blacks took their places, and were waited on at a second sitting of the banquet by "six of the most respectable of the white company." Benjamin Rush toasted "Peace on earth and goodwill to men" and "May African churches everywhere soon succeed to African bondage." Describing to his wife the outpouring of emotion on that hot afternoon, he wrote: "Never did I witness such a scene of innocent—nay more—such virtuous and philanthropic joy. After dinner all the blacks converged on Nicholson and clasped the hand of the city's entrepreneur who had loaned $2,000 for the building of the church. One old man "addressed him in the following striking language: 'May you live long, sir, and when you die, may you not die eternally.' " Rush concluded: "To me it will be a day to be remembered with pleasure as long as I live."

But even as glasses were raised in toast on that August afternoon ill fortune struck again, and this time it delayed the completion of the church for nearly a year. It came in the form of the worst epidemic of yellow fever in the history of North America. The first victims succumbed late in July 1793, but another month passed before the fever reached epidemic proportions. By late August twenty Philadelphians were dying every day of the putrid fever, shopkeepers were closing their doors, and all who could afford it were commandeering horses, wagons, and carriages to carry their families out of the city. Hardest hit were the laboring poor. Living in crowded alleys and courts, where the fever spread fastest, they were too poor to flee, too poor even to pay a doctor.

By early September the social fabric of the city was falling to pieces. The work of tending the sick and burying the dead proved beyond the capacity of the doctors and city authorities because most nurses, carters, and gravediggers, fearing for their own lives, refused to go near the sick, dying, and dead. Husbands fled wives of many years in the throes of death, parents abandoned sick children, masters thrust servants into the streets. Mathew Carey, the main chronicler of the catastrophe, wrote that "less concern was felt for the loss of a parent, a husband, a wife or an only child than, on other occasions, would have been caused by the death of a servant, or even a favorite lap-dog." Hundreds perished for lack of treatment, "without a human being to hand them a drink of water, to administer medicines, or to perform any charitable office for them." By mid-September the poor were starving and the dead were lying everywhere in the streets, while thousands of middle- and upper-class Philadelphians fled to the country.

Into this calamitous breach stepped Philadelphia's free blacks. Benjamin Rush, who played generalissimo of the relief forces, implored Absalom Jones and Richard Allen in early September to lead their people forward as nurses, gravediggers, and drivers of the death carts. Assuring the black leaders that the malignant fever "passes by persons of your color," he suggested that this God-bestowed exemption from the disease laid blacks "under an obligation to offer your services to attend the sick."

The Free African Society met on September 5 to consider Rush's request. Much of what had transpired in the last six years might have inclined them to spurn the requests for aid—the humiliating incident at St. George's, the opposition to establishing a church of their own, and the readiness of even those who had signed their subscription lists to beg off in order to aid slave-owning French planters who arrived with their chattel property in tow and then attempted to evade the state law which required the manumission of any slave brought into the state within six months. But much had also transpired that argued for contributing themselves to the white community's desperate plight—the encouragement they had received in planning their church, the dedicated work of the Abolition Society, and the personal solicitation of Rush, their closest advisor. Indeed, their explanation of how they decided to come forward suggests that they saw this as a God-sent opportunity to prove their courage and worth, to show they could drive anger and bitterness from their hearts, to dissolve white racism by demonstrating that in virtue and civic-mindedness they were not inferior, but in fact superior, to those who regarded former slaves as a degraded, hopelessly backward people. The "god who knows the hearts of all men, and the propensity of a slave to hate his oppressor," wrote Jones and Allen "hath strictly forbidden it in his chosen people." They would succor those who despised and opposed them because "the meek and humble Jesus, the great pattern of humanity, and every other virtue that can adorn and dignify men hath commanded to love our enemies, to do good to them that hate and despitefully use us."

On September 6, 1793, Jones and Allen offered their services to the mayor, who immediately placed notices in the newspapers notifying citizens that they could apply to Jones or Allen for aid. "The African Society, intended for the relief of destitute Negroes," writes the best authority on the epidemic, "suddenly assumed the most onerous, the most disgusting burdens of demoralized whites." They nursed the sick, carried away the dead, dug graves, and transported the afflicted to an emergency lazaretto set up outside the city. Jones, Allen, and William Gray, under instructions from Rush, acted as auxiliary doctors, bleeding patients and administering purges. By September 7, wrote Rush, Jones and Gray "furnish nurses to most of my patients." Before the epidemic ran its course they had bled more than 800 persons, making notes on each case for Rush as they worked through the day. Then at night they drove the death carts to the cemeteries.

Within two weeks, Rush's claims that Negroes were immune to the infectious fever transmitted by the *Aedes aegypti* mosquito had proven a ghastly error. Seventy Philadelphians were dying each day and now blacks were numerous among them. "The Negroes are everywhere submitting to the disorder," Rush wrote disconsolately on September 26, "and Richard Allen who has led their van is very ill." In the first weeks of October the mortality raged through the half-abandoned city like a brushfire. On October 11 alone 119 died. Still convinced "that it was our duty to do all the good we could to our suffering fellow mortals," Allen, Jones, and the other blacks carried out their gruesome tasks. By the end of the month nearly 12,000 whites, along with most of the national government, had fled the city, and nearly 4,000 persons, including about 300 blacks, had succumbed to the fever. Not until early November did the epidemic pass.

Work on the African Church, suspended for nearly three months during the yellow fever crisis, resumed in December 1793. By the end of the year workmen had covered in the building and completed the exterior work. It took further fundraising and another six months to complete the interior work. In soliciting support in the white community the black leaders may have expected to draw on the credit they had accumulated through their heroic efforts during the terrible days of autumn. But even this altruism had to be defended, for Mathew Carey, the Irish immigrant publisher in the city, publicly vilified the free blacks for opportunistically charging exorbitant fees to nurse the sick and remove the dead.

Carey's pamphlet, *A Short Account of the Malignant Fever,* was itself a lesson in deriving profit from mass misery. Selling briskly, it went through four editions between November 14 and December 20. Carey provided a narrative account of the holocaust, lists of the dead, and a discussion of the origins of the epidemic. But the saviors of the city in Carey's account were the rising immigrant merchant Stephen Girard and other whites who organized an emergency hospital just outside the city, where they self-

lessly tended the sick and dying. For the black Philadelphians who drove the death carts, buried the dead, and nursed the sick in the back streets and alleys of the city Carey had mostly words of denigration.

Carey's *Short Account* drew a shocked response from Jones and Allen. The black leaders did not deny that some persons "in low circumstances," both white and black, charged extravagant prices to nurse the infected. They argued that this was to be expected, "especially under the loathsomeness of many of the sick, when nature shuddered at the thoughts of the infection, and the task was aggravated by lunacy, and being left much alone" with the sick. But Philadelphians should balance such stories, they argued, alongside those of the many blacks who asked no recompense at all and were content to take whatever the patient thought proper to give. One old black woman, when asked her fee, answered "A dinner, master, on a cold winter's day." Ceasar Cranchell, a founding member of the African Society, swore he would not "sell his life for money, even though he should die," which he did in the process of tending sick whites. Jones, Allen, Gray, and most other blacks had remained in the city throughout the biological terror, while nearly 20,000 whites, including Carey, had fled in fear of their lives. Widely assured that blacks were immune from the disease, they had learned otherwise, so that before cold weather ended the scourge nearly one-tenth of the black population died, nearly as great a mortality rate as among whites. "Was not this in a great degree the effects of the services of the unjustly vilified black people?" asked Jones and Allen.

As the workmen completed the African Church in the spring of 1794, Philadelphia's blacks gathered to make a momentous decision about denominational affiliation. Absalom Jones and Allen still favored uniting with the Methodists, even though the white elder stationed in the city remained opposed to a separate black church and "would neither be for us nor have anything to do with us." But the "large majority" favored uniting with the Anglicans (now called Episcopalians), which is understandable in light of the fact that so many of them, both as slaves and free persons, had married, worshiped, and christened their children in the city's three Anglican churches. Steadfast in his conviction that "there was no religious sect or denomination that would suit the capacity of the colored people as well as the Methodist," Allen quietly withdrew again. Nor could he accept the invitation of the majority to be their minister. "I informed them," he wrote later, "that I could not be anything but a Methodist, as I was born and awakened under them, and I could go no further with them, for I was a Methodist, and would leave them in peace and love.

With Allen declining to lead them, the deacons and elders turned to Absalom Jones. He lacked Allen's exhortatory gifts, but his balance, tenacity, education, and dignified leadership all commended him. In July steps were taken to formalize the decision to unite with the Episcopal Church. The black Philadelphians pragmatically agreed to "commit all the ecclesiastical affairs of our church to the government of the Protestant Episcopal Church of North America," while at the same time securing internal control of their church through a constitution that gave them and their successors "the power of choosing our minister and assistant minister," provided that members were to be admitted only by the minister and churchwardens, and specified that the officers of the church—the vestrymen and deacons—were to be chosen by ballot from among members of at least twelve months standing. Finally, only "men of color, who are Africans, or the descendants of the African race," could elect or be elected into any church office except that of minister and assistant minister. With the help of Benjamin Rush, they had contrived a formula for maintaining black control of the church, while allowing for the absence of trained blacks to fill the ministry.

On July 17, 1794 the African Church of Philadelphia opened its doors for worship. The published account of the dedication ceremony indicates that much of the white ministerial opposition had melted. "The venerable Clergy of almost every denomination, and a number of other very respectable citizens were present," it was noted. Samuel Magaw, rector of St. Paul's Church, gave the sermon from the text "Ethiopia shall soon stretch out her hands unto God." The discourse was from Isaiah: "The people that walked in darkness have seen a great light"—the same epigram that was etched in marble above the church doors.

Magaw's sermon provides a window into the attitudes of Philadelphia's benevolent white leadership at this time. Reconciled to the idea of a black church, they still remained convinced of the free blacks' inferiority and consequently focused on the overriding importance of moral management and social control. Showing his ignorance of the mainsprings of action in the black community, Magaw stressed the need for gratitude and deference on the part of the blacks who crowded the church. They or their fathers, he preached, had come from the heathenish lands of Senegal, Gambia, Benin, Angola, and Congo, and that burden of birth had been increased by the dismal effects of slavery, which "sinks the mind, no less than the body, . . . destroys all principle; corrupts the feelings; prevents man from either discerning, or choosing aright in anything." Having been brought from "a land of Pagan darkness, to a land of Gospel light" by white Christian goodness, these former slaves must now maintain their gratitude to those who freed them and donated or loaned money to build the church. They must pray—but not take action—for their brethren still in bondage.

The emphasis in Magaw's sermon was on black passivity and moderation in all things. He warned the black congregation to suppress pride, which he claimed was on the rise among them. Rather they should cultivate "an obliging, friendly, meek conversation." Their church, he counseled them in a perfect display of white paternalism, owed its existence to the benevolent action of whites. That it had been born in strife and had arisen only when free blacks defied the passive roles assigned them escaped his notice. But if we set alongside Magaw's dedication sermon the "Causes and Motives" for establishing the African Church, written by Absalom Jones just a month later, we can better comprehend the dialectical struggle that free blacks were engaged in. It is this document, which also announced the decision to name the church St. Thomas's African Episcopal Church of Philadelphia, in honor of the apostle, that indicates the quest for a black ideology and for strategies that would promote strength, security, and meaning in the lives of the first generation of ex-slaves in America. They had been encouraged, Jones wrote, "to arise out of the dust and shake ourselves, and throw off that servile fear, that the habit of oppression and bondage trained us up in." This statement can be taken as almost directly evidence of the influence of Anthony Benezet, under whom Jones and many of the other blacks active in the African Society had been schooled. The Quaker teacher had frontally challenged the deeply rooted doctrine of black inferiority, urged his pupils to regard themselves as "citizens of the world," argued doggedly as early as 1762 that the African environment had produced notable cultures and must not be considered as a place of jungle barbarism, and thus taught his black students that it was the environment of slavery, not innate condition, that turned Africans in America into degraded and defective human beings.

Inspired by Benezet's theories of human brotherhood and the environmentalist argument that it was slavery that had incapacitated Africans in America, Absalom Jones, Richard Allen, and others received further encouragement to strike out on their own from Benjamin Rush and others. An equally important factor in the shedding of the debilitating fear "that the habit of oppression and bondage trained

us up in" was the day-to-day accomplishments of Philadelphia's blacks during the decade that followed the Revolution. Through their ability to establish families and residences, by their demonstrated capacity to sustain themselves as free laborers and artisans, and in their success at conducting themselves morally, soberly, and civilly they had proved to themselves the groundless character of the prevalent white view that former slaves were permanently corrupted and unassimilable people.

The reports of the Pennsylvania Abolition Society, which conducted house-to-house surveys of black families in the mid-1780s, and the observations of other Philadelphians bear out the successful transition to freedom that blacks made in the city after the war. In 1785 Benjamin Rush reported that "the slaves who have been emancipated among us are in general more industrious and orderly than the lowest class of white people." Two years later the Abolition Society reiterated this observation. In 1790 the first federal census takers found only three blacks among the 273 inmates of the almshouse and five black prisoners among the 191 felons in the Walnut Street Prison, indicating a much lower incidence of poverty and criminality among a people only a few years out of bondage than among the free white population. Five years later, after conducting a census of black households, the Abolition Society noted that more than one-fourth of the free blacks owned houses, most "live comfortably," and their behavior, "in point of morality, is equal to those whites who are similarly situated as to employment and means for improvement."

This is not to argue that the transition from slavery to freedom was easy. Philadelphia was full of struggling black migrants in the 1790s—poor and often unskilled sojourners who arrived by water and land from every direction. Hundreds of them could not establish independent black households at first, many had to bind out their children, and most lived in pinched and precarious circumstances. But their general ability to fashion a respectable life for themselves must have given credence to the arguments of Benezet and others. Hence, it was a fusion of ideas inculcated by white tutors and ideas derived from daily experience that galvanized black leaders and convinced them of the need—and of their capacity—to establish a separate church.

In drawing up their "Articles of Association" with the Protestant Episcopal Church, Absalom Jones and his cohorts indicated their understanding that, while they had made progress, the road ahead was strewn with barriers that could be surmounted only with the support of white patrons. The Articles announced, in a direct reference to the charges of Bishop White about black "pride," that they wished "to avoid all appearance of evil, by self-conceitedness, or an intent to promote or establish any new human device among us," and hence they had decided to "resign and conform ourselves" to the Episcopal Church of North America. Nonetheless, this was to be a black church, as their constitution spelled out.

In September 1794, one month after the constitution for their church had been accepted by the Convention of the Episcopal Church in Pennsylvania, the trustees and "representatives of the congregation" moved to solidify the racial character of their church by requesting Bishop White to qualify Absalom Jones "to act as our minister." Many years later it was recorded that Jones's "devotion to the sick and dying" during the yellow fever epidemic of 1793 had brought him wide recognition in the black community. "Administering to the bodily as well as spiritual wants of many poor sufferers, and soothing the last moments of many departing souls among his people, he became greatly endeared to the colored race." The Episcopal Convention took nearly a year before approving Jones as the minister of St. Thomas's, and it did so only after arranging a *quid pro quo* whereby they waived the Greek and Latin requirement for the ministry in exchange for the stipulation that the African church forego the right to send a representative to the yearly convention where denominational policy was set.

As St. Thomas's African Episcopal Church was being completed and its affiliation with the white Episcopal church formalized, Richard Allen pursued his vision of black Methodism. Successful as a carter, master chimney sweep, and trader, he used his own money to purchase a lot at Sixth and Lombard streets and to purchase a blacksmith's shop, which he hauled to the site and renovated as a house of worship. Seventeen days before the dedication of St. Thomas's Bishop Francis Asbury officiated at the first service and Reverend John Dickens, the white Methodist elder in Philadelphia, prayed "that it might be a 'Bethel' to the gathering of thousands of souls." This marked the birth of "Mother Bethel," the first congregation of what would become 22 years later the independent African Methodist Episcopal Church, the largest black Christian movement in the United States.

The separate black churches led by Absalom Jones and Richard Allen became the first major expression of racial pride and a major instrument for furthering the social and economic liberation of recently freed slaves. Bishop White had been correct, though in ways he knew not, when he reacted in anger in 1791 to word that the free blacks were planning a church of their own by charging that their plan "originated in pride." The pride was really a growing feeling of strength and a conviction that black identity, black self-sufficiency, black self-determination, and the black search for freedom and equality in the early years of the republic could best be nurtured through the black church.

Absalom Jones spent nearly a quarter of a century ministering to his flock at St. Thomas's before he died in 1818 at the age of 72. In this role he was far more than a religious leader, for the black church was the center of social, educational, and political life as well. As W. E. B. Du Bois observed, it "is the world in which the Negro moves and acts." Jones's church launched a school for young black children in the late 1790s. It organized several mutual assistance and moral reform societies. Its members stood prominently among petitioners to the state and national legislatures who over the years called for ending the slave trade, abolishing slavery, and repealing discriminatory laws.

Both a place of refuge in a hostile white world and a site from which to attack discrimination and exploitation, the church built by the humble slave from Delaware stood at the center of the black struggle for dignity, freedom, and social justice in the new American nation.

# 13

## THE TAX MAN COMETH: IDEOLOGICAL OPPOSITION TO INTERNAL TAXES, 1760–1790

### THOMAS P. SLAUGHTER

One of the most controversial issues of the Revolutionary era was that of taxation. Beginning with colonial opposition to the Stamp Act of 1765, ordinary Americans and their leaders questioned the authority of any central legislative or executive body to tax the people directly. Instead, most Americans thought that the authority to tax their property, income, and possessions directly lay solely with their locally controlled provincial and state legislatures. National governments, they argued, properly derived their incomes from external taxes, such as commercial imposts. Even in times of emergency such as the Revolutionary War, the American people were generally content to allow the national government, embodied in the Continental Congress, no more direct fiscal power than to request funds from their state legislatures.

Thus, as Thomas P. Slaughter argues in this essay, the question of internal taxation played an important role in the ideological struggles of the Revolution. First between 1765 and 1776, as colonial resistance to direct taxation by Parliament grew into revolution, and again in the late 1780s and early 1790s, as the Federalists attempted to enlarge the powers of the national government through a program of direct taxation, ordinary Americans raised the cry of "no taxation without representation" in an attempt to retain local control of the power of the purse. Although the Federalists secured the national government's authority to tax with the ratification of the Constitution in 1788, the issue of direct taxation continued to animate American politics well into the next century.

From *William and Mary Quarterly,* 3rd ser., 41:566–91 (1984). Reprinted by permission of Thomas P. Slaughter and William and Mary Quarterly.

Opponents of the proposed national Constitution in 1786 and 1787 were appalled by its surrender of the very principles for which they had fought the Revolution. "In this new Constitution," a South Carolinian wrote, "every thing is transferred, not so much power being left us as Lord North offered to guaranty to us in his conciliatory plan." Antifederalists were especially shocked by the Constitution's taxation clause. "By sect. 8 of article I," a Massachusetts Antifederalist argued, "Congress are to have the unlimited right to regulate commerce, external and *internal*. . . . They have also the unlimited right to imposts and all kinds of taxes, as well to levy as to collect them. They have indeed very nearly the same powers claimed formerly by the British parliament. Can we have so soon forgot our glorious struggle with that power, as to think a moment of surrendering it now?"

Antifederalist pamphleteers despised far more than the Constitution's taxation clause. Theirs was a broad attack on the document's philosophy and the entire system of government designed to implement its principles. They saw themselves as defending the ideal of local rule against potential encroachments of an ambitious central government, just as, they believed, Revolutionaries had defended America against Great Britain. In this light, Antifederalists were especially enraged by the proposal to entrust a national congress "with every species of *internal* taxation." They could not comprehend how men who so recently had shed blood to secure individual liberty and local control over taxation could turn around and give both away. "When I recollect," one lamented, "how lately congress, conventions, legislatures, and people contended in the cause of liberty, and carefully weighed the importance of taxation, I can scarcely believe we are serious in proposing to vest the powers of laying and collecting internal taxes in a government so imperfectly organized for such purposes."

This article focuses on the ideological concept of "internal taxes." It relates part, but only part, of the story of ideological conflict in late eighteenth-century America. For those Americans who divided the world of taxes into internal and external spheres, the distinction was only one of many principles that shaped their views of the political world. Their arguments about the justice and constitutionality of these two sorts of taxes were intimately tied to beliefs about representation, sovereignty, and the relationship between local and central governments. Nonetheless, for reasons of clarity and coherence, this article must eschew the temptation to try to weave the entire fabric of this ideology as well as refrain from devoting much space to others. As a first step toward these grander goals, however, it isolates this one central thread of "localist" ideology. It attempts to define the meanings of the internal-external distinction at two points in time—the 1760s and 1780s—and to suggest, though not to trace, the role of the distinction in the conflicts that racked America after the Revolution.

The article does not offer a continuous history of opposition to centrally imposed internal taxes between 1766 and 1786, when the controversy was not a lively one at the intercolonial or national level. Localist sentiment persisted during those years. Opposition to internal taxes was deep and unappeased but dormant. During the two decades after repeal of the Stamp Act, few Americans articulated this fear. Other menaces occupied their energy. . . .

When Parliament met in the early months of 1766 to discuss the Stamp Act rebellion, its members focused on the argument used by Americans to contest the act's constitutionality. A year earlier, M.P.s had dismissed the "strange language" of colonists who did "not think an internal and external duty the same." Now, in the face of unprecedented colonial resistance to a law of Parliament, its members were more inquisitive about what North Americans were saying.

William Pitt tried to explain. According to Pitt, the colonists believed that *"the House had no right to lay an internal tax upon America, that country not being represented"* in Parliament. Barlow Trecothick made essentially the same point to his peers when he observed that "the Americans think that the imposition of internal taxes ought to be confined to their own assembly." The North Americans thought "this law unjust in its original," Richard Hussey told the Commons, because it was constitutionally novel. No previous act of Parliament had "laid an internal tax, at least no internal tax which can so fairly be called so as this Act." Colonists, according to their British interpreters, maintained that sovereignty was constitutionally divided between Parliament and their local assemblies. They held that internal taxes could be levied justly only by local, representative institutions—not by a remote Parliament in which they were not represented.

Some members of Parliament were still not sure they comprehended the American position or that it made any sense. "I cannot understand the difference between external and internal taxes," George Grenville asserted in response to Pitt's explanation. William Blackstone and Lord Mansfield, the two reigning experts on such matters, could find no such distinction in law, either common or statute. Blackstone also denied that under British law "the right of imposing taxes arises from representation." Lord North, perhaps most subtly of all, later argued that "in point of right there is no difference [between internal and external taxes]; in point of operation there certainly is: external might not go further, internal might."

North's comment is most helpful for understanding Parliament's confusion. It seems odd to find Grenville, for example, claiming not to comprehend the distinction between internal and external taxes since he had used the adjectives himself for years prior to this confrontation. North, Townshend, and other M.P.s also commonly distinguished between internal or interior taxes on the one hand and external

taxes or customs duties on the other. But North's distinction between "right" and "operation" helps clarify how Grenville and other British politicians could use the internal-external configuration at one moment and then deny understanding it the next. They apparently perceived the difference between the two types of taxes in operation but were surprised and honestly befuddled by the argument against Parliament's constitutional right to lay internal taxes. Americans had apparently taken a commonplace operational description, invested it with ideological significance, and turned it into a constitutional argument.

The ideological distinction that Parliament was hearing for the first time in the mid-1760s was made frequently by theorists of American rights. In 1764, before the Stamp Act rebellion, Massachusetts Lt. Gov. Thomas Hutchinson informed a Connecticut correspondent that "your distinction between duties upon trade and internal taxes agrees with . . . the opinion of most People here." There is no reason to question his assessment. American witnesses called before Parliament in 1766 told its members the same thing. Testimony from residents of Massachusetts, Rhode Island, New York, Pennsylvania, and Virginia agreed; Parliament heard that crowds, newspapers, pamphlets, politicians, and private citizens in each of these colonies "make the distinction between internal and external duties." It was the understanding of most American witnesses, even those who did not share the sentiment, that colonists opposed the Stamp Act because it was an internal tax, that they would predictably resist any other internal tax, but that there was less danger of violent protest against external taxes, at least on ideological grounds.

In America, the distinction had reached the level of popular song by 1765. On August 29, a crowd paraded through the streets of Newport, Rhode Island, and constructed a gallows for the effigy of a "Stampman." On one of the gallows posts they hung a copy of a ditty heard on the streets of American towns that summer. The pertinent stanza read as follows:

> *Those Blessings our Fathers obtain'd by their*
> *blood,*
> *We are justly oblig'd as their Sons to make*
> *good;*
> *All internal Taxes let us then nobly spurn,*
> *These Effigies first—next the Stamp Paper*
> *burn.*

The language of the ideological distinction between internal and external taxes had penetrated beyond the intellectually rarefied world of pamphlet literature. We might even surmise, as Hutchinson and others did, that crowds mouthing such words had some understanding of their meaning. Those who sang this song apparently shared a hatred of the stamp tax. They expressed a disdain for internal taxes of all sorts and saw this internal tax as a threat to the liberties hard-won by their ancestors. They were also, it appears, distinguishing between two types of taxes and making an ideological argument against only one.

Such popular expressions of ideology tell us little more about the particulars of this distinction. Other sources are needed to define the terms of debate and to isolate the fears shared by Americans. Pamphlets, newspaper articles, private correspondence, and resolutions of legislative assemblies are all helpful for understanding ideological conflict and agreement among the colonists.

The 1760s can be considered as a unit for discussing internal taxes. All the ingredients of the distinction were present before the Stamp Act rebellion. All remained potent spices in America's ideological stew thereafter. What changes occurred were those of precision and definition. Under the pressure of conflict in 1765, proponents of the distinction were forced to articulate previously unexamined beliefs more clearly and perhaps more consistently. They did not, however, modify or retract any significant component of their ideology.

At the heart of the distinction were theories about the relationship between representation and freedom, about the constitutional necessity for dividing sovereignty between Parliament and colonial assemblies, and about the role played by taxes in all of these theories. In each case the distinction between internal and external taxes seemed crucial to some Americans.

Definition of terms, although not always the prime concern of colonial theorists, must be the next step for us. It is not always as clear as it might be—in the case of the song posted by the Newport crowd, for example—exactly what colonists meant when they attached the limiting modifier "internal" to "taxes." Few bothered to explain so familiar a term. Several contemporary definitions do survive, however, that help to translate the shorthand language of popular protest. Charles Carroll of Carrollton, for one, explained the distinction between internal and external taxes to a British correspondent in September 1765. "England restrains our trade," Carroll wrote, "she appoints our Governors, lays duties on our exports and imports, and the exertion of this power or right, as a necessary consequence of our dependence on the mother country, has all along been admitted and acquiesced in by the colonies. It was in this sense I admitted the propriety of her taxing us." Carroll clearly and forthrightly conceded Parliament's right to tax the colonies, but not in the form of internal taxes. When he denied Parliament's right to tax the colonies, according to Carroll, what he meant was Parliament's authority to tax the colonies internally. For him, sovereignty was necessarily divided between Parliament and colonial assemblies; only the assemblies could constitutionally assess internal taxes on their constituents.

Representation was the key. As Benjamin Franklin defined the terms for Parliament, an American theory of representation lay at the heart of the distinction colonists were making. "I think the difference [between internal and external taxation] is very great," Franklin testified. "An external tax is a duty laid on commodities imported; that duty is added to the first cost, and other charges on the commodity, and when it is offered to sale, makes a part of the price. If the people do not like it at that price, they refuse it; they are not obliged to pay it. But an internal tax is forced from the people without their consent, if not laid by their own representatives." A majority of the Massachusetts assembly had advanced this same theory of representation in a November 1764 petition to Parliament. The assemblymen pointed out in this official communication that the colonies "have always judged by their representatives both of the way and manner, in which internal taxes should be raised within their respective governments." According to this argument, garnering the consent of the people through their chosen representatives was a necessary precondition for the just exaction of internal taxes. Colonists differed about what it would take to represent them adequately, but Stamp Act resisters, with few exceptions, could agree that Americans were not represented in Parliament. In other words, they did not accept the notion of virtual representation.

While American opponents of the Stamp Act concurred that there was a necessary link between representation and authority to assess internal taxes, they disagreed profoundly about what constituted adequate representation for the task. Some maintained that tensions between the colonies and Britain would be eased by acceptance of M.P.s elected by colonists. "If you chuse to tax us," Franklin wrote to Richard Jackson, "give us Members in your Legislature, and let us be one People." Other Americans were not so sanguine: the geographical remoteness of Parliament would always, under any conceivable electoral arrangement, deny them adequate representation in Parliament for the purpose of assessing internal taxes. Thomas Fitch, for example, thought the colonies were "subordinate jurisdictions or governments which by distance are so separated from Great Britain that they are not and cannot be represented in Parliament."

According to Stephen Hopkins, the colonies were "at so great a distance from England" that Parliament could never truly know American conditions and could not become sufficiently representative to levy internal taxes. During the 1760s this ideological quarrel among Americans had little impact on the organization of intercolonial opposition to Great Britain. It was not the sort of issue that would prevent Fitch and Franklin—or others who had different standards of representation—from uniting against Parliament and its internal stamp tax. By either standard, colonists were not represented in Parliament.

The terms of another potential ideological clash were also defined during the 1760s but submerged on an intercolonial or national level beneath other concerns until the 1780s. Some Americans contended during the 1760s that sovereignty could be divided between Parliament and colonial assemblies but not shared—that divided sovereignty in fact described traditional relationships within the empire. Those who embraced this critical distinction separated authority over internal taxes from authority over external taxes. Writing before the Stamp Act revolt, Richard Bland pointed out that Virginians were "in every instance . . . of our EXTERNAL government . . . subject to the authority of the British Parliament, but in no others." Since Bland maintained that colonial legislatures had exclusive right to legislate matters relating to their "INTERNAL government," it seemed to him that "any tax respecting our INTERNAL polity which may hereafter be imposed on us by act of Parliament is arbitrary . . . and may be opposed." The Connecticut legislature drew the line dividing sovereignty in the same place, as revealed in the title to its 1764 pamphlet: *Reasons Why the British Colonies in America Should Not Be Charged with Internal Taxes.* Thomas Hutchinson expressed to one of its authors his estimate that most people in his acquaintance agreed.

Even before the Stamp Act it seemed clear to Franklin that "two distinct Jurisdictions or

Powers of Taxing cannot well subsist together in the same Country. They will confound and obstruct each other." He reasoned that sovereignty could be divided between different levels of government, but that authority over internal and external taxes, for example, could not be shared. In the case of the North American colonies, which were an ocean away from Parliament, the division of authority over taxation was traditional, practical, and necessary. "When any Tax for America is propos'd in your Parliament," Franklin wrote, "how are you to know that we are not already tax'd as much as we can bear? If a Tax is propos'd with us, how dare we venture to lay it, as the next Ship perhaps may bring us an Account of some heavy Tax impos'd by you." Franklin, Bland, and the Massachusetts assembly in its 1764 petition to Parliament all argued that this traditional arrangement of divided sovereignty should continue as long as the colonies were not represented in Parliament.

Some Americans rejected this vision of divided sovereignty in 1765, as others would during the 1780s. James Otis, for one, denied any limitation on Parliament's authority. He believed that "the Parliament of Great Britain has a just and equitable right, power, and authority *to impose taxes on the colonies, internal and external, on lands as well as on trade."* Even in dissent, however, Otis communicated in the language of America's popular protest. Even those who denied the validity of the ideological distinction in 1765 recognized its vitality and thus legitimized the terms of its argument. Rhode Island physician Thomas Moffatt did not like it, but he read the distinction "in the newspapers." William Kelly, of New York, did not understand it, but he knew colonists made "a distinction between internal taxes and some others which I did not quite comprehend." Virginia merchant James Balfour reported that "the distinction between internal and external duties" was common in his colony, and his fellow Virginian Col. George Mercer agreed that "the Stamp Act being an internal tax was one of the great objections to it."

Understandably, given the plethora of contradictory information before it, Parliament remained confused about what colonists thought. American witnesses testified to the ideological force of the internal-external distinction throughout the colonies. Private correspondence, newspaper excerpts, and pamphlets reaching London all provided supporting evidence. But the official protests of several colonial assemblies made no explicit distinction of that kind, while the resolutions of other assemblies seemed to deny Parliament's authority to levy taxes of any sort for America.

The colonists interrogated before Parliament were put on the spot to explain this apparent discrepancy in the "American" position. They clearly felt obliged to paper over some of the disagreements among colonists on the issue of taxation. They were also trying to minimize American claims in order to placate Parliament and assure repeal of the Stamp Act. Nonetheless, the official resolutions of the assemblies and Franklin's testimony explaining them help us to understand better some of the difficulty historians have had in interpreting the colonial positions—usually depending upon which sources they credit—and some of the problems associated with translating the language of two hundred years ago.

The position of Rhode Island's legislature was the clearest. This assembly's official protest against the Stamp Act forthrightly limited its own claim to authority over internal taxes. The "Rhode Island Resolves" stated plainly that "his Majesty's liege People, the Inhabitants of this Colony, are not bound to yield Obedience to any Law or Ordinance, designed to impose any internal Taxation whatsoever upon them, other than the Laws or Ordinances of the General Assembly aforesaid."

The case for other colonies—Connecticut, Maryland, and Virginia—is more complex. It is a matter of interpretation over which historians may reasonably disagree. The official Maryland and Virginia Stamp Act protests referred respectively to "Taxes and internal Polity" and "internal Polity and Taxation."

Connecticut's assembly asserted exclusive jurisdiction over "taxing and internal Police." Each of these phrases explicitly made the "internal" distinction. None specifically attached the adjective to taxes. The drafters certainly understood and accepted the common belief in an exclusive authority over "internal" affairs for their bodies. They all said that sovereignty was divisible but could not be shared by two distinct legislative bodies—that one assembly could legislate externally and another internally but that two legislatures could not share power over either category of taxes, and each writer remained vague about where (in which category) to place import duties. The authors of all three protests believed that Parliament acted constitutionally only in the "external" sphere. And, finally, all three saw the Stamp Act as a novel and insidious type of legislation. It was the first time Parliament had ever "taxed" them.

To these legislatures, "taxation" was apparently synonymous with the "internal taxation" of Rhode Island's assembly and of other Americans during the 1760s. To embrace their position, the drafters of the resolves must either have seen previous customs duties as "external" taxes or not as taxes at all but perhaps only as regulations of trade. In either case they came close to making the same distinction and endorsing the same constitutional relationship as those who specifically used "internal" and "external" to describe two types of taxation and two legislative sovereigns. Possibly because the Chesapeake colonies and Connecticut had no major molasses trade, they were better able to concentrate their fury against the Stamp Act while overlooking the Sugar Act. But this explanation can hardly apply to Rhode Island.

The intercolonial Stamp Act Congress also chose to imply rather than assert the distinction between types of taxes, as Carl Becker pointed out over sixty years ago. This assembly described the Stamp Act as "imposing Taxes" having "a manifest tendency to subvert the rights and liberties of the colonies," while it referred to the Sugar Act only vaguely as one of "several late acts" imposing "duties" that "will be extremely burthensome and grievous." The Congress thus implied, without ever using the words "internal" and "external," that there was a distinction to be made between the ideologically invidious (internal) Stamp Act and the economically odious (external) Sugar Act.

The assemblies of Connecticut, Maryland, and Virginia were not alone in using "taxation" and "internal taxation" synonymously. Charles Carroll of Carrollton, Daniel Dulany, Thomas Fitch, Benjamin Franklin, and Stephen Hopkins also employed the terms interchangeably. And, according to Franklin, so did other Americans. During his examination it was pointed out to Franklin that the resolutions of several assemblies, including that of his own colony of Pennsylvania, said that "all taxes," not just "internal" taxes, lay outside the bounds of Parliament's authority over America. "If they do," Franklin replied, "they mean only internal taxes; the same words have not always the same meaning here and in the Colonies. By taxes they mean internal taxes; by duties they mean customs; these are their ideas of the language."

Thus we must be careful not to dismiss the internal-external distinction even in those cases where it does not explicitly appear. The difference was apparently so common that it was assumed by many of its users. At least two witnesses to William Pitt's pleas for repeal of the Stamp Act, for example, heard him make the distinction. At least one witness, on the other hand, neglected to record it in his notes on Pitt's speech. All three notices appeared in the *Virginia Gazette* without comment, raising the possibility that the differences in the language used to report the speech may not even have struck some Americans, because they used "taxation" and "internal taxation" interchangeably. This understanding of internal taxes may have been so common among the colonists that we anachronistically impose precision on their words by demanding the appearance of the distinction before we recognize its validity. By focusing only on the presence or the absence of a word we may misconstrue their meaning.

There can be no confusion, however, about the range of fears shared by Americans who embraced an ideology imbued with the distinction between internal and external taxes. Theirs were embellishments of radical whig horrors conjured for the education of a public at risk of losing its liberty. "It is seldom," wrote a contributor to the *Boston Evening-Post* in February 1765, "indeed very seldom, that any people have had more at stake than we at Present have." "The parliament of Great Britain have no right to level an internal tax upon the colonies," another writer stormed.

What were these rights at stake in 1765? Stephen Hopkins thought that when Parliament sought "to establish stamp duties and other internal taxes" for the colonies, it threatened to reduce Americans to "the miserable condition of slaves." Linking the issue of representation to his fears, Hopkins argued that a legislature too remote to appreciate American conditions and interests could not possibly "determine with confidence on matters far above their reach." In all likelihood, such policy would compel Americans "to go naked in this cold country" or else clothe themselves in animal skins. Property, civilization, even the physical survival of the colonists seemed at risk. Expanded jurisdiction for admiralty courts to enforce the new tax would inflict cruel punishments—in costs, time, and anxiety—even on those found innocent of charges. Remote, unrepresentative legislatures and remote, inaccessible courts of law threatened colonial prosperity, according to Hopkins. Local legislative bodies and local courts knew local conditions. They could, therefore, better dispense justice and more equitably assess internal taxes.

The British justification of the Stamp Act as necessary to raise funds for American defense seemed to Hopkins similarly fallacious: "To take the money of the Americans . . . and lay it up for their defense a thousand leagues distance from them when the enemies they have to fear are in their own neighborhood, hath not the greatest probability of friendship or prudence." Again Hopkins was expressing a localist argument and fears. He would leave laws, justice, and even defense (despite its external connotations) to those who knew local conditions from experience. Since circumstances varied widely among the colonies, each, according to Hopkins, should administer its own affairs; otherwise, central authority would threaten the property, the lives, and hence the freedom of colonists. "They who have no property," Hopkins concluded, "can have no freedom, but indeed are reduced to the most abject slavery." Here was a classic summary of localist logic and fears for any decade in the second half of the eighteenth century.

Some Americans did not endorse the concept of divided sovereignty in the 1760s. They disagreed about the meaning of "representation," and the disagreement was already an important ideological quarrel. Other Americans demanded division of authority over internal and external taxes between local and central governments and denied in principle the right of a central government to tax their property. By "taxes" they may have meant "internal taxes," but by "representation" American localists did not mean sending several delegates hundreds of miles to be outvoted by politicians with interests alien from theirs.

The riots stopped with repeal of the Stamp Act. There were few protests against the Revenue Act of 1766, a blatant revenue-raising measure but an external one. Efforts to organize intercolonial resistance to the Townshend duties after 1767 were divisive and far less successful than the Stamp Act protests. Never again before the Revolutionary War would Americans—outside of Boston—achieve the same sort of unanimity against British taxes that they enjoyed during Stamp Act resistance. And that was due at least in part to Parliament's de facto respect for the constitutional distinction Americans had made during the 1760s. In the absence of the ideological dimension of internal taxation, it was clearly difficult to unite Americans of diverse economic interests against British external taxes. It would take the presence of British soldiers in Boston after 1768, "customs racketeering," and the Coercive Acts to ignite again the localist fires fueled by the Stamp Act.

The principle of divided sovereignty—of divided authority over internal and external taxes—was not abandoned by localists during the 1770s. Since the concept was never challenged, there was no perceived need to articulate or defend it. Americans did not reach a consensus about this principle during those years. They still disagreed about the validity of divided sovereignty as a description of the British constitution and as an eternal verity for political society. When the issue of Parliament's authority emerged in the first Continental Congress, according to John Adams, "some were for a flat denial of all authority; others for denying the power of taxation only; some for denying internal, but admitting external, taxation." In other words, Americans still differed about the ideological significance of internal taxes and about the localist description of divided sovereignty within the empire. But this dispute was a secondary issue of intercolonial affairs in 1774, one that could again be ignored as Americans united to confront more pressing threats to their liberties.

For over twenty years after the Stamp Act controversy few Americans ever explicitly mentioned internal taxes as an immediate threat to liberty. Those who did were usually only explaining to foreigners or to posterity—or reminding themselves—what had happened in 1765 and why. Financier Robert Morris, for one, certainly would have liked to invest the Continental Congress with the sovereign power to exact internal taxes. Nonetheless, Congress posed no widely perceived threat to those who believed in divided sovereignty or to those who denied any remote central government's authority to levy internal taxes.

This ideological fissure among Americans continued to exert a subterranean influence on American politics; it was a component of political conflict, and one that probably reflected social-structural and interregional strains. Conflicting views of representation would become even more critical on a national level, though, when Americans organized their own central government and considered levying internal taxes in a national legislature some still considered remote and inadequately representative. This then became one key place to draw the defining line between localists or provincials and those who shared a more national or cosmopolitan ideology.

As we have seen, Americans who challenged Parliament's authority to impose internal taxes based their claims on a localist theory of representation and an ideology that assumed the impossibility of assigning concurrent jurisdiction to two independent governments. Since colonists were not represented in Parliament—and some believed they never could be—British politicians had no right to tax them. Since the colonies taxed themselves internally, Parliament could not possibly share that right.

When they established their own central government under the Articles of Confederation, Americans reserved all tax-making authority to the states. Because the Continental Congress possessed no independent power over taxes, the latent disagreement over divided sovereignty never became a divisive issue within that body, at least from a localist perspective. Granted, when the impost seemed a genuine possibility, some in Congress insisted that the states retain control over collectors. This certainly was a variant of localist fears of tax collectors appointed by remote central governments. Congress, however, with its circumscribed powers, never posed the same sort of threat as Parliament. The danger of this central government enacting internal taxes never materialized, but a public outcry would certainly have met an amendment to the Articles vesting the Congress with such authority. Given the fate of the much less ideologically controversial impost, it is unimaginable that the states would have approved any internal tax.

When delegates gathered to reorganize the central government in 1787, the voices of Americans who cared deeply about divided sovereignty and the ideological distinction between internal and external taxes were not heard. The Constitution proposed by the Philadelphia convention granted a national congress the unlimited "power to lay and collect taxes, duties, imposts, and excises." The document thus gave the central government taxing authority in both internal and external realms as defined during the 1760s. The Constitution also denied the states power to act independently in the external sphere; it reserved for the central government exclusive control over customs duties, regulation of interstate trade, international treaties, and other portions of the parliamentary sovereignty that localists acknowledged in the 1760s. The taxing authority of the proposed national government would be no less, and was certainly designed to be even greater, than anything attempted by the British government during the 1760s and 1770s.

Localists—now pejoratively termed Antifederalists by proponents of the Constitution—discovered and passionately denounced parallels between British claims in the 1760s and powers granted by the document to the central government. Most shocking of all was the renunciation of local control over internal taxes so soon after the war to secure such rights from Britain. A Pennsylvania writer had not forgotten the "glorious struggle" with Great Britain; he was appalled that the proposed national congress would be "vested with every species of *internal* taxation," and he feared that the collection of such taxes would be enforced by that bane of all radical whigs, "the standing army."

This anonymous author and others believed, as some colonists had in the 1760s, that "there is a strong distinction between external and internal taxes." William Goudy of North Carolina feared that the taxation clause of the proposed constitution "will totally destroy our liberties." He and the majority of North Carolina's ratifying convention thought Article I, section 8 should be amended to substitute a quota system for authority to lay internal taxes. Only if the quota remained unfilled by the states should the national congress be permitted to enact excises and other internal taxes.

Localists in 1787 shared a more precise understanding of what they meant by external and internal taxes than colonists had displayed during the 1760s. The "Federal Farmer" saw clear differences between the two sorts of taxes. "External taxes," he wrote, "are import duties, which are laid on imported goods; they may usually be collected in a few seaport towns, and of a few individuals, though ultimately paid by the consumer; a few officers can collect them, and they can be carried no higher than trade will bear, or smuggling permit—that in the very nature of commerce, bounds are set to them." For these reasons—the natural and fixed limitations on the amounts assessed, the few places where the taxes could be collected, the few officers employed in collection, and the limitation of taxes to items produced by foreigners—localists believed that external taxes might be assessed legitimately and collected by a republican central government.

Taxes laid on property, produce, manufactures, and commerce were different matters. The "Federal Farmer" thought that only the states should act in these realms. "Internal taxes," he wrote, "as poll and land taxes, excises, duties on all written instruments, &c. may fix themselves on every person and species of property in the community; they may be carried to any lengths, and in proportion as they are extended, numerous officers must be employed to assess them, and to enforce the collection of them." Localists agreed that the result must be a proliferation of taxes on every species of property in order to keep the collectors engaged, and that the resulting "disorder and general dissatisfaction" with the national government would ultimately provoke violent suppression by a national army.

Others foresaw a similar result for the system proposed in the Constitution. The new government would immediately lay excise and other "internal taxes upon your lands, your goods, your chattels, as well as your persons at their sovereign pleasure," and "the produce of these several funds shall be appropriated to the use of the United States, and collected by their own officers, armed with a military force, if a civil aid should not prove sufficient." First would come a raft of internal tax laws; then tax collectors would follow shortly behind. "The tax-gatherers will be sent," warned Joseph M'Dowall of North Carolina, "and our property will be wrested out of our hands." "If the tax-gatherers come upon us," he predicted, "they will, like the locusts of old, destroy us." But not all Americans would simply roll over and submit to such oppression. In some regions, at least, the locusts M'Dowall warned of would be met by armed men determined to defend their hard-won liberties. Robert Livingston of New York thought the result must be either abdication of duties and office by the tax collectors or "an internal war."

This civil war was perhaps what localists feared most from the internal taxing power of the proposed central government. Patrick Henry warned: "Look at the part which speaks of excises, and you will recollect that those who are to collect excises and duties are to be aided by military force. . . . Suppose an excise-man will demand leave to enter your cellar, or house, by virtue of his office; perhaps he may call on the militia to enable him to go." Americans had not submitted to such intrusions in the past, and they would not do so now. Blood would flow.

Lack of knowledge of and sympathy for, the conditions and views of many regions would make the national legislature the wrong institution to enact internal tax laws. As in 1765, it was hardly certain that the whole people could ever be represented in a national legislature. Since only experience would tell, localists be-

lieved that powers of internal taxation must be reserved to the states, at least for the time being. "If a proper representation be impracticable," reasoned the "Federal Farmer," "then we shall see this power resting in the states, where it at present ought to be, and not inconsiderately given up." For now, it was at least certain that the legislative branch of the central government would have "but very little democracy in it." Compared to the states, then, the central government would be freer to ignore the desires of a large portion of the citizenry and would possess the financial and military might to enforce its will—to the possible extinction of the states and individual liberty.

Pennsylvania localists not only decried the weakness of the democratic element in the Constitution, but in their ratifying convention they even doubted the goodwill and intentions of those who would represent them in the national legislature. Not just lack of knowledge about many constituents, but an actual contempt for some citizens, would lead the national representatives to enact oppressive taxes *deliberately.* Thus "that strongest of all checks upon the conduct of administration, *responsibility to the people,* will not exist in this government." Because of the imprecise election methods and the length of terms served by representatives under the proposed system, "they will consist of the lordly and high minded; of men who will have no congenial feelings with the people, but a perfect indifference for, and contempt of them; they will consist of those harpies of power that prey upon the very vitals, that riot on the miseries of the community."

Pennsylvania localists could not trust the system embodied in the Constitution, or the sort of men who would run it, with internal taxing power under any circumstances. The Constitution seemed almost to ensure a wave of economic repression and political violence. To them it appeared certain that the "same force that may be employed to compel obedience to good laws, might and probably would be used to wrest from the people their constitutional liberties." They foresaw use of state militias "to enforce the collection of the most oppressive taxes"; they predicted the marching of Pennsylvania militiamen to New England or Virginia to "quell an insurrection occasioned by the most galling oppression." Ultimately, they believed, the death of state governments would certainly follow adoption of this constitution with its authority to levy internal taxes and raise armies to enforce the laws.

Localists contended in 1787, as colonists had in 1765, that to assign concurrent taxing powers to both local and central governments was to assure the demise of local political institutions. It was a hard-and-fast rule of the political world, they maintained, that the strong devour the weak—as power consumes liberty—if wealth and might are not isolated and caged. According to William Findley of Pennsylvania, "the powers given to the federal body for imposing internal taxation will necessarily destroy the state sovereignties for there cannot exist two independent sovereign taxing powers in the same community, and the strongest will, of course, annihilate the weaker." Some foresaw the state governments gliding "imperceptibly and gradually out of existence." Others anticipated the end coming quickly and violently with the state governments being "totally annihilated." But all localists agreed that it was fanciful to trust that the state and national governments would cooperate in the collection of internal taxes.

Some localists portrayed the Constitution's advocates as well intentioned but misguided. Others were more suspicious and saw in the taxation clause an active conspiracy to destroy the states and create a consolidated government. The minority at the Pennsylvania ratifying convention predicted that the national government would "monopolize every source of revenue [and] indirectly demolish the State governments." Were the states "to impose taxes, duties or excises on the same articles with Congress," the Pennsylvania localists believed that the national government would "abrogate and repeal the laws whereby they are imposed." In Virginia, Patrick Henry was

also quick to discover conspiracy afoot. "Your rich, snug, fine, fat, Federal offices—The number of collectors of taxes and excises will outnumber any thing from the States," Henry prophesied. These excise men would graze the states clean, leaving nothing but a consolidated national government behind. Henry had no doubt who would win the inevitable battle between the state and national authorities. "If we are to ask which will last the longest," he argued, "the State or the General Government, you must take an army and a navy into the account." Clearly, the central government would triumph. "Can, then, the State Governments look it in the face?" he queried. "You dare not look it in the face now, when it is but an *embryo.*" Indeed, a New York delegate believed that this talk of concurrent jurisdiction over taxation was ludicrous in the light of claims for the supremacy of laws adopted by the proposed national congress. He argued that if state and national taxes conflicted, Congress would simply "abolish the state governments."

For Antifederal localists, then, the issues and the stakes had changed little from the 1760s. The constitutional conflict over internal and external taxation had at least as much meaning for Americans in 1787 as in 1765. In both cases some saw the reservation of internal taxation to the colonies/states as crucial to the survival of liberty. In each case they predicted violent conflict and consequent loss of liberty as the likely results of granting the central government authority to assess internal taxes. It made little difference that the central government after 1787 would be managed by elected Americans rather than British politicians over whom they had virtually no influence. The problems of representation remained largely the same. Whether elected or not, men who shared no sympathy for the needs of some regions could not represent all their constituents' interests adequately to tax them. In 1787 as in 1765, localists believed that internal taxing authority must be left to local representatives who lived among their constituents and knew their wants and needs. Under the proposed system this would not be possible. Each congressman would represent as many as 30,000 people, and districts would grow even larger. A senator from Philadelphia, Boston, or Charleston, for example, could never truly appreciate or represent the unique problems and needs of frontiersmen.

Furthermore, as a matter of logic and political theory, localists strongly resisted the idea that two sovereign governmental bodies could coexist, share concurrent jurisdiction, cooperate, and survive. They believed that sovereignty could be divided but not shared. To give both the central government and the states authority to lay internal taxes was to decree the virtual death of the states. The larger and stronger government would inevitably overwhelm the states with taxes, tax collectors, and, if necessary, soldiers to enforce its laws. In the face of such might, state governments would be compelled to repeal tax laws or simply leave an overburdened populace alone and not collect taxes at all. In the end, the states would either fade to shadows or be violently annihilated by a national army. However the end came, the fate of the citizen, the state, and the nation would ultimately be the same. Discontent, resistance, repression, violence, tyranny, and death would be the short and brutal history of the American republic.

As subsequent events showed, the localists of 1787 were only partially correct in their predictions. The state governments were not annihilated, nor did they glide out of existence. The national government did not dissolve in a cauldron of tyranny and anarchy. On the other hand, the nationalists' assurances—which localists interpreted as promises—that a direct excise would only be a tax of last resort proved false. One of the earliest fiscal measures of the new Congress was the whiskey excise of 1791. Localists were also correct in predicting that passage of internal taxes by a remote central government would bring the nation to the brink of "internal war." The Pennsylvania milita would not march to New England or Virginia to "quell an insurrection occasioned by

the most galling oppression." The militias of Pennsylvania, New Jersey, Maryland, and Virginia would march west, however, to suppress an excise-tax revolt on the other side of the Appalachian Mountains in 1794. The Whiskey Rebellion would result from precisely the sorts of tensions foreseen by localists in 1765 and 1787–1788.

Localists of the 1780s and 1790s were also heirs to a consistent pattern of beliefs. There was more continuity than change in the ideology that had the internal-external distinction at its heart. The theories of constitutionalism, sovereignty, representation, and taxation embraced by some Americans altered little, except in achieving greater clarity and precision, from 1765 though 1787 and beyond. And the Antifederalists' defense of this ideology in 1787 is one clear case where their claims to recognition as true defenders of the principles of the 1760s and 1770s can be vindicated.

Looking forward in time, we can define America's "court" and "country" political factions in part by their respective stands on the ideological distinction between internal and external taxes. Federalist or "court" administrations during the 1790s would propose and enforce the internal taxes that provoked the Whiskey Rebellion and Fries's Rebellion. The Washington administration's justification for its proposed excise tax on whiskey would bear a remarkable resemblance to the Grenville ministry's rationale for the Stamp Act. George Washington's armed enforcement of the law at the head of a 15,000-man army—a force comparable in size to the one he led against Great Britain in the Revolution—was a militant defense of law and order equal in spirit to Great Britain's attempts in Boston after 1768 and throughout America beginning in 1775. And it was more successful.

"Country" opponents of the whiskey excise began in 1790 to articulate the same ideology, in the same language, as anti-Stamp Act pamphleteers. They explicitly resurrected the Stamp Act as symbol and example of their cause. They defined their philosophy of divided sovereignty between central and local governments in the same way as Stamp Act rebels and Antifederalists had done; they shared the same attitudes toward representation; and they divided the world of taxes into internal and external spheres. Localist fears had not changed, but the threat to liberty once perceived to emanate from London now seemed to localists to reside in the national capital of Philadelphia. The Washington administration's militant enforcement of the excise and the resulting bloodshed seemed to localists of 1794 horrific vindication of their ideology.

When the Jeffersonian Republicans emerged victorious in 1800, one widely celebrated consequence was repeal of the whiskey excise. The "country" party of America's first party system remained loyal to its ideological roots and never adopted a peacetime internal tax. Only in war—James Madison's excise during the War of 1812—would the Republicans invoke what they saw as the emergency taxing power of the Constitution. Only for the duration of an extraordinary threat, localists agreed, might an exception be made to their ideological demand that remote central governments refrain from intrusion on local control over internal taxes.

# 14

# TECUMSEH, THE SHAWNEE PROPHET, AND AMERICAN HISTORY

## R. DAVID EDMUNDS

The close of the Revolutionary War meant many things to the American people. To some it conferred a guarantee of freedom, to others a return to the peacefulness of everyday life, and to yet others an opportunity to establish a life of independence beyond the Appalachian Mountains. But for Native Americans the defeat of the British meant the removal of their last defense against expanding American settlements full of farmers hungry for their land. Even before the war ended in 1783, settlers poured onto Indian land in the middle South and the Ohio River valley. There they met tribes that, cut off from a reliable supply of arms and trade goods, had difficulty preventing these incursions on their ancestral land. Moreover, in the eyes of these advancing Americans, who had gained vast military experience during the Revolution, Indians were enemies, having sided with the British during the Revolution in hope of receiving royal protection for their lands.

As tribes were pushed west, small pockets of resistance began to develop. Settler outposts were raided, outlying settlements attacked, farmers and livestock killed. But these remained isolated incidents and offered little prospect for sustained resistance to white incursions. It was against this background that two extraordinary Indian leaders emerged. Tenskwatawa and Tecumseh, Shawnee brothers, learned of the rapacity of American land hunger at an early age and from the dishonor of displacement dreamed of an Indian nation as strong and vigorous as the thirteen colonies that had just won their independence. In different ways they both worked for the revitalization of Native American culture and the securing of an independent nation for all Native Americans. Their quest is the subject of this essay by R. David Edmunds, who offers a different view of the better-known Tecumseh than is generally found in history books.

High upon a granite pedestal overlooking "the Yard" at the United States Naval Academy at Annapolis stands a bronze statue of an Indian warrior. Midshipmen passing in and out of Bancroft Hall traditionally salute the statue before taking examinations in the hope that the renowned warrior's medicine will assist them during their tests. Most midshipmen, if asked whom the statue represents, will reply that it is a replica of Tecumseh, the famous war chief of the Shawnees. In reality, however, the statue was never intended to be Tecumseh. It represents Tamenend, a chief among the Delawares.

The midshipmen's incorrect identification of the bronze figure is not surprising, for Americans have long regarded Tecumseh as one of their foremost Indian heroes. He is one of the few militant Indian leaders who was almost universally praised by his white contemporaries. During the War of 1812 both British and American officers spoke highly of the Shawnee, and since his death his image has grown accordingly. Eulogized by historians, Tecumseh has achieved an almost legendary status. His biographers have presented an Indian of superhuman qualities; and Alvin M. Josephy, in his volume *The Patriot Chiefs,* entitles his chapter on the Shawnee as "Tecumseh: The Greatest Indian."

If the white observers and historians have been laudatory in their description of Tecumseh, they have been universal in their condemnation of his brother, Tenskwatawa, the Shawnee Prophet. Both British and American leaders denounced the holy man as a "pretender" and a "coward," and historians have enlarged upon such qualities to present an image of a charlatan who manipulated the tribesmen for his own purposes. While Tecumseh's political and military movement is pictured as logical and praiseworthy, the Prophet represents the darker side of Indian life. A religious fanatic, Tenskwatawa is presented as riding his brother's coattails to a position of minor prominence.

Unquestionably, the Shawnee brothers emerged to positions of leadership during a period of great stress for Native Americans. Although the Treaty of Greenville supposedly had drawn a line between Indian and American lands in Ohio, the treaty was ignored. Frontier settlement continued to advance north from the Ohio valley, threatening the remaining Indian land base in the region. Meanwhile, white hunters repeatedly trespassed onto Indian lands to hunt game needed by the tribesmen, and by the first decade of the nineteenth century game was becoming scarce. The fur trade declined in a similar manner, and after 1800 many warriors were hard pressed to provide for their families. Not surprisingly, the Indians retaliated by stealing settlers' livestock, and the resulting clashes produced casualties on both sides. Obviously, both Indians and whites suffered, but losses were much larger among the natives. Governor William Henry Harrison of Indiana admitted that "a great many of the Inhabitants of the Fronteers *(sic)* consider the murdering of the Indians in the highest degree meritorious," while Governor Arthur St. Clair of the Northwest Territory reported that "the number of those unhappy people (the Indians) who have been killed since the peace at Greenville . . . is great enough to give serious alarm for the consequences."

Much of the Indian-white conflict was triggered by alcohol. Frustrated over their declining political and economic status, beleaguered tribesmen drowned their sorrows in frontier whiskey. Although illegal, alcohol was in plentiful supply, and brawls resulting from the Bacchanalia spread social chaos throughout the Indian villages. Once-proud warriors quarreled among themselves or abused their kinsmen, while others retreated into drunken stupors. Some Shawnees, weakened by their dissipation, fell victims to influenza, smallpox, and other diseases. Others sat passively in their lodges, bewildered by the changes swirling around them. Meanwhile, the clans—traditional kinship systems designed to regulate and provide cohesiveness among the separate

Shawnee villages—were unable to cope with the multitude of problems besetting the tribe.

Overwhelmed by the chaos within their villages, the Shawnees pondered the causes. Although many tribesmen realized that the majority of their problems emanated from outside sources such as loss of lands, economic deterioration, injustice, and alcohol, others suspected darker elements and probed inward, examining the fabric of tribal society. Predictably, traditional Shawnees concluded that much of their trouble resulted from witchcraft, for the fear of witches and their evil power permeated Shawnee culture, and neighboring tribes believed the Shawnees to have a particular affinity for sorcery and the supernatural.

The basis for such fear lay deep in tribal tradition. The Shawnees believed that in the dim past, when they first crossed the Great Water in search of their homeland, they had been opposed by a huge water serpent who represented the evil powers in the universe. Although their warriors had killed the serpent, witches had saved part of its body, which still held a potent and malevolent power. Contained in medicine bundles, this evil had been passed down through the ages and was used by witches to spread disorder throughout the tribe.

The balance between order and chaos formed a focal point for Shawnee cosmology. The Shawnees believed they were a people chosen by the great power in the universe— "the Master of Life"—to occupy the center of the earth and bring harmony to the world. For their assistance, the Master of Life provided the Shawnees with a sacred bundle possessing powerful medicine that could be used for good. He also gave the tribe a series of laws regulating their personal conduct. If the Shawnees cherished the bundle, and used its medicine properly, and if they followed the sacred laws, they would prosper and their world would be orderly. But if witches gained the ascendancy, or if the Shawnees relinquished the ways of their fathers, their lives would be full of turmoil. In the years following the Treaty of Greenville, many traditional Shawnees believed that the witches had gained the upper hand.

Not surprisingly, many associated the Americans with these forces of evil. The Shawnees believed that the sea was the home of the Great Serpent—the embodiment of disorder. Their forefathers had always warned that pale-skinned invaders might emerge from the water to disrupt the harmony of the Shawnee homeland. Since the Americans had first appeared on the eastern seashore, many tribesmen were certain the invaders were the children of the Serpent, intent upon the Indians' downfall. In 1803 Shawnees at Fort Wayne informed Indian agents that their ancestors had stood on the eastern seashore, watching as a strange ship came over the horizon.

> At first they took it to be a great bird, but they soon found it to be a monstrous canoe filled with the very people who had got the knowledge which belonged to the Shawnees. After these white people had landed, they were not content with having the knowledge which belonged to the Shawnees, but they usurped their lands also.—But these things will soon end. The Master of Life is about to restore to the Shawnees their knowledge and their rights and he will trample the Long Knives under his feet.

And even Black Hoof, a government chief committed to the American cause, admitted, "The white people has spoiled us. They have been our ruin."

Yet the same chaos that threatened the tribesmen also produced a man who promised them deliverance. Known as Lalawethika ("The Noisemaker" or "Loud Mouth"), the man had been born in 1775 on the Mad River in eastern Ohio. Prior to Lalawethika's birth, his father had been killed by the Americans and his mother had abandoned him when he was only four years old. Raised by a sister, his childhood had been overshadowed by two older brothers, Chiksika and Tecumseh.

Lalawethika never excelled as a hunter or a warrior, and during his adolescence he became an alcoholic. Following the Treaty of Greenville he lived in a small village headed by Tecumseh, where he unsuccessfully aspired to the status of shaman. But in April 1805 this alcoholic ne'er-do-well experienced a vision that changed his life and propelled him to the forefront of Indian leadership.

While lighting his pipe from the fire in his lodge, Lalawethika collapsed, falling into a coma so deep his wife and neighbors believed him to be dead. As his wife began her mourning song he astonished his family by first stirring, then regaining consciousness. Visibly shaken, he informed the gathered onlookers that indeed he had died and had visited heaven, where the Master of Life had shown him both an Indian paradise and a hell where eternal fires lay in wait for sinful tribesmen. Alcoholics like himself suffered the most, for molten lead was poured down their throats until flames shot out their nostrils. Amidst much trembling, Lalawethika vowed to renounce his former ways and never again drink the white man's whiskey. No longer would he be known as Lalawethika. Henceforward he would be called Tenskwatawa—"The Open Door"—a name symbolizing his new role as a holy man destined to lead his people down the narrow road to paradise.

In the following months Tenskwatawa experienced other visions and enlarged upon his doctrine of Indian deliverance. Much of his teachings addressed the decline of traditional moral values among the Shawnees and other tribes. Tenskwatawa claimed he "was particularly appointed to that office by the Great Spirit" and that his "sole object was to reclaim the Indians from bad habits and to cause them to live in peace with all mankind." While he continued to denounce whiskey as "poison and accursed," he also condemned the violence that permeated tribal society. He urged warriors to treat each other as brothers, to stop their quarreling, and to refrain from striking their wives and children. Husbands and wives should remain faithful to each other, and marriages should be monogamous. Shawnee warriors currently married to more than one woman "might keep them," but such marriages displeased the Master of Life.

Convinced that his forefathers had enjoyed a happier existence, the new Shawnee Prophet attempted to revitalize some facets of traditional tribal culture. Indeed, much of Tenskwatawa's teaching was nativistic in both tone and content. He asked his followers to return to the communal life of the past and to renounce all desire to accumulate property as individuals. Those tribesmen who hoarded their possessions were doomed, but others who shared with their kinsmen, "when they die are happy; and when they arrive in the land of the dead, will find their wigwams furnished with everything they had on earth." He also instructed them to use only the food, implements, and dress of their fathers. Pork, beef, and mutton were unclean, and the tribesmen were instructed to eat only the game they killed in the forests. Neither were the Indians to eat bread, but only corn, beans, and other crops raised by their ancestors. Stone or wood implements should replace metal tools, and although guns could be used for self-defense, the warriors were to hunt with bows and arrows. With the exception of weapons, all items of American manufacture were to be discarded. In a similar manner, the Indians were to dress in skin or leather clothing and were ordered to shave their heads, leaving only the scalp lock of their forefathers. False gods should be forgotten, but the tribesmen should pray to the Master of Life, asking that he return fish to the streams and game to the forest. To assist his disciples, Tenskwatawa provided them with sacred "prayer sticks." The sticks were inscribed with pictographs illustrating certain spirits who would help the tribesmen in their supplications. If the Shawnees were faithful and their hearts pure, the Master of Life would restore order, the earth would be fruitful, and they would prosper.

While Tenskwatawa attempted to revitalize

some part of Shawnee culture, he condemned others. He warned that many of the traditional dances and ceremonies no longer had any meaning and offered new ones in their place. He also instructed his followers to throw away their personal medicine bundles, which he claimed had been powerful in the past, but no longer possessed the potency needed to protect the Shawnees from the new dangers that threatened them. Tenskwatawa alone spoke for the Master of Life, and only those tribesmen who subscribed to the new faith would ever know happiness. But his disciples would be rewarded above all men, for they alone would eventually "find your children or your friends that have long been dead restored to life."

If the Prophet condemned some of the old religious practices, he was particularly suspicious of those tribesmen who held religious beliefs differing from his own. At best those shamans or medicine men who opposed his doctrine were misguided fools. At worst they were witches, in league with the Great Serpent to spread disorder among the tribes. And the Prophet did not limit his accusations to religious leaders. For the holy man, religion and politics were the same. He had been chosen by the Master of Life to end the chaos in the Shawnee world. All those who opposed him also opposed the Master of Life. Therefore, he was particularly suspicious of tribesmen who were becoming acculturated or who had been converted to Christianity. Such men also were suspect of witchcraft. Unless they repented, they too should be destroyed.

Tenskwatawa's distrust of those Indians who adhered to American values reflected his general condemnation of the Long Knives. He informed his followers that the Master of Life had made the British, French, and Spanish, but the Americans were the children of the Great Serpent. In his visions Tenskwatawa had seen the Americans take the form of a great crab that crawled from the sea, and the Master of Life had told him, "They grew from the scum of the great water when it was troubled by the

Evil Spirit. And the froth was driven into the woods by a strong east wind. They are numerous, but I hate them. They are unjust. They have taken away your lands, which were not made for them." Only if the Indians rejected the Americans would order ever be restored to the Shawnee world. The Prophet instructed his people to cease all contact with the Long Knives. If they met an American in the forest, they might speak to him from a distance, but they should avoid touching him or shaking his hand. They were also forbidden to trade Indian foods to their white neighbors, for these provisions were the special gifts of the Master of Life, to be used by his children, not the spawn of the Serpent. Tenskwatawa instructed his disciples to cut their ties with frontier merchants, and "because they (the Americans) have cheated you," the Indians were to pay "no more than half their credits." Moreover, Indian women married to American men should return to their tribes, and the children of such unions were to be left with their fathers.

The new faith soon spread to other tribes, who like the Shawnees were unable to adjust to the great changes sweeping around them. By the autumn of 1805 warriors from the Delawares and Wyandots were traveling to Greenville, Ohio, where the Prophet had established a new village. There Tenskwatawa converted the visitors, then sent them back to proselytize their home villages. The Delawares proved particularly susceptible to the new religion, and during the late winter of 1806 they accused about one dozen of their tribesmen of witchcraft. In March 1806 the Prophet journeyed to the Delaware villages, where he examined the captives, exonerating some, but condemning others. The Delawares eventually burned four of their kinsmen before the witch-hunt terminated. Predictably, all those burned were converted Christians whose acculturation made them more suspicious.

The witch-hunt among the Delawares frightened Moravian missionaries associated with the tribe and brought a storm of protest from government officials. During the spring of 1806 Harrison wrote to the Delawares denouncing the Prophet and asking, "If he is really a prophet, ask him to cause the sun to stand still—the moon to alter its course—the rivers to cease to flow—or the dead to rise from their graves. If he does these things, you may believe that he has been sent from God."

Ironically, Harrison's challenge played into Tenskwatawa's hands. In the spring of 1806 several astronomers had traveled through Indiana and Illinois locating observation stations to study an eclipse of the sun scheduled to occur on June 16. Although Harrison either ignored or forgot about the event, the Prophet remembered. Among the Shawnees such an eclipse was known as a "Black Sun," an event surrounded with dread and portending future warfare. Accepting Harrison's challenge, in early June Tenskwatawa surprised even his closest followers by promising to darken the sun. On June 16, while his disciples and skeptics both assembled in his village, the Prophet remained secluded in his lodge throughout most of the morning, but as the noon sun faded into an eerie twilight he stepped forth exclaiming, "Did I not speak the truth? See the sun is dark!" He then assured his audience that he would restore the sun's former radiance, and as the eclipse ended even those tribesmen who still remembered him as Lalawethika, the drunken loudmouth, now were convinced of his medicine.

Following the eclipse, the Prophet's influence spread rapidly. During the summer of 1806 Kickapoos from the Wabash visited his village, were converted, and by the following summer their towns in eastern and central Illinois had become seedbeds for the new religion. Early in 1807 large numbers of Potawatomis and Ottawas from the Lake Michigan region traveled to Greenville and then carried the new faith back to the western Great Lakes. One of the Ottawas, Le Magouis, or "the Trout," became a special envoy for Tenskwatawa and journeyed into upper Michigan where he taught the Prophet's doctrines to the Chippewas. The results were phenomenal. At Chequamegon Bay hundreds of Chippewas gathered opposite Madeline Island to "dance the dances and sing the songs" of the new deliverance. Subscribing to the Prophet's instructions, they threw their medicine bags into Lake Superior and made plans to visit the holy man in Ohio. In the following months so many tribesmen were enroute to the Prophet's village that white traders found most of the Chippewa towns along the southern shores of Lake Michigan deserted. The Menominees, Sacs, and Winnebagos also were swept up in the religious frenzy, and during the summer of 1807 they trekked to Greenville in large numbers.

Unable to comprehend the religious nature of the movement, American officials at first believed that Tenskwatawa was only a figurehead controlled by more traditional chiefs among the Shawnees. During 1807 several groups of American agents arrived at the Prophet's village to investigate the character of the new movement. After meeting with Tenskwatawa, most of the envoys agreed that the holy man was the dominant Indian leader in the village. Moreover, the Prophet was able to persuade them that his religion posed no threat to the government. But Harrison and other officials refused to admit that the movement was an indigenous uprising, resulting from desperate conditions among the Indians. Instead, they charged that the Prophet was actually a British agent, intent upon raising the tribes against the United States.

Yet the British were as mystified about Tenskwatawa as were the Americans. During the summer of 1807 British agents were active among the Indians of Michigan and Wisconsin, but they remained suspicious of the Prophet. Although they invited the Shawnee to visit them in Canada, he refused. In response, William Clause, Deputy Superintendent of Indian Affairs for Upper Canada, warned other Indians to avoid him, speculating that the holy man might be working for the French.

The large numbers of Indians who journeyed to Tenskwatawa's village enhanced his prestige, but they also alarmed white settlers in Ohio. Moreover, the influx of tribesmen exhausted Tenskwatawa's food supply, and he was hard pressed to feed his followers. In November 1807 the Potawatomis suggested that he withdraw from Greenville and establish a new village on the Tippecanoe River in Indiana. The new site would be much less exposed to white influence and was located in a region where game was more plentiful. Therefore, in April 1808 the Prophet and his followers abandoned Ohio and moved to Prophetstown.

The withdrawal to Indiana temporarily removed Tenskwatawa from white scrutiny, but his logistical problems continued. Since Prophetstown was located further west, it was more accessible to potential converts, and during 1808 and 1809 Indians flocked to the new village in numbers surpassing those who had visited him at Greenville. Although the villagers planted fields of corn and scoured the surrounding countryside for game, they could not feed the multitude. To obtain additional food, the Prophet brazenly turned to the Americans. In June 1808 he sent a delegation of warriors to Harrison assuring the governor of his peaceful intentions and asking for provisions. The Indians were so persuasive that Harrison sent food to Prophetstown and invited Tenskwatawa to meet with him in Vincennes. Two months later, in August 1808, the Prophet and his retinue arrived at Vincennes and spent two weeks conferring with Harrison. The governor was astonished at "the considerable talent of art and address" with which Tenskwatawa mesmerized his followers. Moreover, the holy man's pleas of friendship toward the United States were so convincing that Harrison provided him with additional stores of food and gunpowder and reported to his superiors that his earlier assessments of the Shawnee were in error, for "the influence which the Prophet has acquired will prove advantageous rather than otherwise to the United States."

Tenskwatawa was also able to hoodwink John Johnston, the Indian agent at Fort Wayne. In May 1809 he met with Johnston, and although the agent previously had expressed misgivings about the Prophet's motives, Tenskwatawa assured him of his friendship. The Shawnee spent four days, denying "in the most solemn manner, having any views inimical to (the Americans') peace and welfare." Indeed, when the conference ended, Johnston, like Harrison, exonerated the holy man from all charges and reported, "I have taken much pains and have not been able to find that there existed any grounds for the alarm."

But the facade of friendship was too fragile to last. Although the Prophet feigned goodwill toward the government, he could not control his followers, many of whom were less devious in their relations with the United States. As Indian depredations spread along the Wabash Valley, Harrison became convinced of the Shawnee's duplicity. During the summer of 1809 Tenskwatawa again visited with the governor in Vincennes, but this time Harrison was less hospitable. Tenskwatawa's protestations of friendship had little impact, and Harrison informed the War Department that his suspicions of the Prophet "have been strengthened rather than diminished in every interview I have had with him since his arrival." Moreover, by the summer of 1809 Harrison was making preparations for the Treaty of Fort Wayne, and he assumed that such a transaction would terminate any pretense of amity between the government and the holy man.

Harrison was correct. The Treaty of Fort Wayne, signed in September 1809, ceded over three million acres in Indiana and Illinois to the United States. Negotiated by friendly chiefs among the Miamis, Delawares, and Potawatomis, the treaty was adamantly opposed by Tenskwatawa. In response, he redoubled his efforts to win new disciples. Messengers were sent to the Ottawas and Potawatomis, and many Wyandots who earlier had shunned the new faith now were converted to the Prophet's teachings. Once again Harrison received reports that the Indians were burning witches, and friendly chiefs among the Miamis and Piankashaws complained that warriors long faithful to the government now were flocking to Prophetstown.

Concerned over the new upsurge in the Prophet's influence, Harrison sent informers to the Tippecanoe and invited Tenskwatawa to again meet with him in Vincennes, but the holy man refused. He also ignored an invitation by the governor to travel to Washington and meet with the president. Instead, he informed Harrison that the recent treaty was illegal and threatened to kill all those chiefs who had signed it. He also vowed that the lands would never be settled by white men and warned Harrison to keep American settlement south of the mouth of the Vermillion River.

The Treaty of Fort Wayne ended any pretense of cooperation between Tenskwatawa and the government. By 1810 the lines were drawn. Tenskwatawa and his movement were unequivocally opposed to American expansion, and in the years following the treaty the anti-American sentiment was both transformed and intensified.

Tecumseh's role in the formation of this movement was entirely a secondary one. He subscribed to the new faith and lived with the Prophet at Greenville, where he assisted his brother in meeting the delegations of both Indian and white visitors. Tecumseh sometimes spoke in council upon such occasions, but no more so than Blue Jacket, Roundhead, or other Indians prominent in the village. In 1807 he accompanied a group of tribesmen who met with Governor Thomas Kirker of Ohio, but in this instance he spoke in defense of his brother, convincing the governor that the Prophet and his movement were no threat to peace. Although primary materials from this period are full of references to the Prophet, almost none mention Tecumseh. Most accounts of Tecumseh's activities during these years are from the "reminiscences" of American observers recorded decades later.

Indeed, Tecumseh did not challenge the Prophet's position of leadership until 1810, two years after the move to Prophetstown and five years after the religious movement's beginnings. During 1808 Indians continued to flock to Prophetstown to see the holy man, not his brother; and in that year it was the Prophet, not Tecumseh, who met with Harrison at Vincennes. In the summer of 1808 Tecumseh did visit Malden seeking supplies for the Indians at Prophetstown, but he made no claims to leadership; and British accounts of the visit, which are quite specific in listing other Indians' names, refer to him only as "the Prophet's brother," not as Tecumseh, a chief among the Shawnees.

The springboard to Tecumseh's emergence was the Treaty of Fort Wayne. From Tecumseh's perspective it was obvious that the religious emphasis of his brother could no longer protect the remaining Indian land base. During the summer of 1809 he visited a few Indian villages in Illinois, but after the treaty Tecumseh took a new initiative and began to travel widely, emphasizing a political and military solution to the Indians' problems. The tribesmen should still adhere to the new religion, but they should abandon their old chiefs who remained friendly to the Americans. Instead, all warriors should politically unite under Tecumseh, for in his own words, "I am the head of them all. . . . I am alone the acknowledged chief of all the Indians."

Therefore, for two years—in 1810 and 1811—Tecumseh traveled extensively among the Indians of the West. During these years he met twice with Harrison, who reported to his superiors that Tecumseh now had emerged as "really the efficient man—the Moses of the family." In this period Tecumseh slowly eclipsed the Prophet's position of leadership, but ironically as the character of the Indian movement changed, its appeal to the tribesmen declined. In 1810 and 1811 parties of warriors recruited by Tecumseh temporarily joined the village at Prophetstown, but their numbers never approached the multitude of Indians who earlier had flocked to the Prophet.

And although the Prophet no longer dominated the movement, he continued to exercise considerable influence. For example, his ability to convince his followers that they could easily obtain a victory over the Americans contributed to their ill-fated attack upon Harrison's forces at the Battle of the Tippecanoe in 1811. Obviously, after the battle the Prophet's influence was broken, and Tecumseh remained the dominant leader of the battered movement. But Tecumseh's preeminence was of short duration, for he was killed less than two years later, on October 5, 1813, at the Battle of the Thames.

It is evident, therefore, that the Prophet, not Tecumseh, was the most important figure in the emergence of the Indian movement prior to the War of 1812. Tecumseh used the widespread religious base earlier established by his brother as the foundation for his unsuccessful attempt to unite the tribes politically and militarily. Although the Prophet has been pictured as either a charlatan or a religious fanatic whose teachings seem quite bizarre, such an appraisal reflects an ethnocentric bias. He certainly seemed logical to the Indians, and for several years he exercised a widespread influence throughout the Old Northwest. In retrospect, such a phenomenon is not surprising. In times of oppression native American peoples have often turned to a religious deliverance. The Shawnee Prophet fits into a historical pattern exemplified by the Delaware Prophet, Handsome Lake, Wovoka and the Ghost Dance, and many others. Indeed, Tecumseh's emphasis upon political and military unification was much less typical than the Prophet's messianic nativism.

Why then has Tecumseh emerged as "the Greatest Indian"? The answer is obvious. If white Americans could design an "ideal Indian," they would have designed Tecumseh. His concepts of political and military unification under a centralized leadership appealed to whites because it was what *they* would have done. His solution had much less appeal to native Americans who had little tradition of either centralized leadership or of pan-Indian confederacies in response to American expansion. White Americans also praised Tecumseh's intervention in behalf of prisoners, but such intervention reflected European concepts of warfare more than those practiced by native Americans. Much of traditional Indian warfare was based upon vendetta, and prisoners expected the worst. Indeed, captured warriors took pride in their ability to withstand torture and laugh in the faces of their captors.

White Americans have championed Tecumseh because he, more than any other Indian, exemplifies the American or European concept of the "noble savage": brave, honest, a true "prince of the forest"—natural man at his best. Since his death, his American and British contemporaries and later historians have continued to embellish his memory with qualities and exploits that have added to his image. Many of the attributes and incidents were apocryphal (for example, his reputed love affair with the white woman, Rebecca Galloway, or the assertion that his skin was of a lighter hue than other Indians), but they only strengthened what Americans wanted to believe and have been incorporated into his biographies. Even his death added to the romantic appeal of the man. He fell, fighting to the last, in the Battle of the Thames—the red Armageddon. And his body was not among the dead on the field, but buried mysteriously by his followers in the forest. In contrast, the poor Prophet survived the war, was exiled in Canada, returned to the United States, was removed to the West, and in 1836 died an inglorious death in Kansas.

This reassessment does not mean that Tecumseh was not a remarkable man. Indeed, he was a brave and farsighted leader who sacrificed his life for his people. But the real Tecumseh stands on his own merits. He does not need the romantic embellishments of ethnocentric historians. Tragically, the Tecumseh who has emerged from the pages of history is, in many respects, a "white man's Indian."

# PART THREE

# AN
# EXPANDING
# PEOPLE

# 15

# "NOTHING ON COMPULSION": THE LIFE STYLES OF PHILADELPHIA ARTISANS, 1820–1850

## BRUCE LAURIE

The growth of factories in the first half of the nineteenth century was the most visible aspect of American industrialization. The creation of large three- and four-story buildings housing hundreds of operatives who worked to the rhythm of steam- or water-driven machinery presented a striking contrast to the predominantly rural scale and pace of American life.

But while the factory system has long been the hallmark of America's transformation from an agrarian to an industrial nation, the most important industrial changes took place, not in the factory, but in the small artisan shops that dominated the American economy. As late as 1850, for example, Philadelphia, one of America's industrial centers, counted fewer than a third of its work force employed in shops with more than 20 workers.

In these shops skilled craftsmen, who had learned their trades through long years of apprenticeship and journeyman training, controlled the shop's daily output, product quality, and the rhythm of work itself following long-established craft rules and customs. Beginning early in the nineteenth century, however, growing numbers of merchants and master craftsmen began to view the slow pace of craft production as a hindrance in their quest to supply large quantities of cheap manufactured goods to the rapidly expanding West and South. Breaking craft skills into simple, easily learned tasks and hiring unskilled workers to perform them, these early manufacturers undercut the craft system and placed all aspects of production under their control.

The demise of the craft system meant more than changes in work regimes, however; it announced the end of an ancient culture and way of life as well. In this study of Philadelphia artisans at the cusp of industrialization, Bruce Laurie explores the variety of life styles exhibited by craftsmen and the challenges they faced in attempting to maintain their own unique way of life.

Reprinted from *Labor History* 15:337–66 (1974).

Labor historians are only beginning to appreciate the cultural dimensions of working-class life. Progress has been slow principally because students of working people find it difficult to transcend the legacy left by John R. Commons and his associates. Commons and company were institutional economists who focused on the position of wage earners in the marketplace and the adjustments they made to new modes of distribution and production. Workers, to them, were members of trade unions who did little else than defend their immediate and long-range interests by striking or by voting for third parties when the opportunity presented itself. They ignored working-class attitudes toward the market itself, or toward work for that matter, and consequently left the impression that workers are mono-dimensional men obsessed with economic matters of one sort or another and condemned to a life of incessant toil. This essay attempts to go beyond the narrow constraints of institutional history in order to explore preindustrial working-class culture and to examine how and why that culture changed between 1820 and 1850 in the city of Philadelphia.

Philadelphians saw their world dramatically altered by wholesale changes in transportation between 1820 and 1850. Private promoters and the state legislature invested heavily in transportation, developing in the process a network of canals and railroads which linked Philadelphia with New York and Baltimore, the coal region of northeastern Pennsylvania, and interior towns and cities in the west. Seagoing transportation developed and boomed as Philadelphians, following their more innovative rivals in New York, introduced packets in the coastal and transatlantic trade in the 1820s. More reliable than regular traders or transients, packets made scheduled runs and merchants quickly took advantage of them. By 1827 they carried more than half of the city's coastal trade, delivering agricultural products and manufactured goods to southern and Caribbean ports in return for cotton, hides, and other vital raw materials.

Improvements in transportation paved the way for mass production by reducing shipping costs and penetrating new markets. Manufacturers of textiles, shoes, clothing, and other commodities gained access to the rich markets in Pennsylvania's back country as well as in the Ohio Valley and also strengthened traditional ties with the South. The textile industry, in turn, spurred the city's small but innovative machine tool industry, which was the envy of many foreign observers. By the Civil War, Philadelphia was surpassed only by New York as a manufacturing center.

Rapid population increases and ethnic diversification went hand in hand with economic change. The population of Philadelphia County tripled between 1820 and 1850, increasing from about 136,000 to just over 408,-000. The factors which contributed to such impressive growth are not yet known, but it is probable that natural increase and in-migration from nearby farm areas gave way to immigration from western Europe. Ireland and Germany sent the bulk of the immigrants, and the greatest inflows probably occurred in the late 1820s–early 1830s and the mid 1840s. By 1850, the first year for which we have accurate data on nationality, the Irish comprised 27 percent of the population and the Germans accounted for 11.4 percent.

Immigrants and native-born Americans clustered in select tiers of Philadelphia's highly diversified occupational hierarchy by 1850 but also overlapped at certain points. The Irish, who arrived in America without benefit of skills, concentrated at the bottom, performing the most menial tasks. Over 42 percent of them toiled as day laborers, carters, teamsters, and the like. An equal proportion reported skilled trades at mid-century, but they were chiefly confined to the most "dishonorable" trades. Many of them had manned hand looms in Ireland and England and dominated this easily learned trade in Philadelphia. Others moved into trades which were undergoing segmentation of labor and dilution of skill, such as tailoring and shoemaking. By 1850 they comprised nearly 25 percent of the city's tailors and shoemakers. Germans practiced skilled trades in the Old World and readily assumed the role of craftsmen in America. Slightly more than two-thirds of them plied skilled trades in Philadelphia by 1850. They had a special affinity for woodworking, tailoring, and shoemaking, which together accounted for nearly 20 percent of their number. Native-born Americans could be found in the most prestigious occupations. About a third of them worked at non-manual jobs, while only 10 percent, the smallest proportion of all groups, were unskilled laborers. They supplied a smaller proportion of their number to the crafts (57 percent) than did the Germans, but dominated the most honorable trades, such as printing, the building trades, and the metal trades.

Most working people resided in the county's industrial suburbs, which formed a semi-circular ring around the old port city. They clustered according to occupation, ethnicity, or both, and lived in close proximity to their place of employment. Indeed, dwelling and shop were one for hand loom weavers as well as for many tailors and shoemakers who worked at home under the putting-out system. For the great majority of the labor force, the shop was not the mill or factory which we commonly associate with the "take-off stage" of economic growth. The average shop size in 1850 hovered around ten workers; the median was slightly less than four. Most of these workers, moreover, did not operate power-driven machinery. Three-quarters of them were handicraftsmen employed by bosses whose sole source of power was the journeyman himself.

Even without the aid of mechanization this emerging capitalist order bore down heavily on the wage earner. Merchant capitalists captured mass markets by contracting with buyers in distant markets and with producers in Philadelphia. Most of these producers were small employers who increased productivity by closely supervising teams of highly specialized workers and by slashing piece rates at every opportunity. Master shoemakers cut the rates on first-rate boots from $2.75 to $1.12 a pair, and reduced the scale on "cheap work" 30 percent in the late 1820s and early 1830s, which compelled journeymen to turn out "triple the quantity . . . to obtain a living. . . ." Some employers compounded this insult by demanding better craftsmanship without additional compensation, which moved one journeyman to protest that the "improvement in the finish of every article produced by the Mechanic, requiring thereby more time in its production, and the improvement bringing with it no extra remuneration, was in fact a reduction of . . . wages. . . ." Carpet weavers lodged a similar protest in 1836, staging a strike when offered an advance in rates to weave a new design. The new pattern required "extra work," and the "extra labor required reduced the quantity each could turn out," which cancelled the advance.

The response of these wage earners to such exploitation in the 1830s has been well charted. It is now common knowledge that between 1834 and 1839 all manner of wage earner—skilled and unskilled, native-born and foreign-born—formed trade unions and joined together under the aegis of the General Trades' Union of the City and County of Philadelphia in protest against low wages and excessive toil. The Trades' Union reached its membership peak in 1836 when it represented over fifty unions and 10,000 workers, but it is best remembered for the general strike of the previous summer. In early June carpenters and shoemakers affiliated with the Trades' Union dropped their tools and joined day laborers on strike for a ten-hour day. Bearing signs with the slogan "6 to 6," they paraded through Philadelphia, attracting supporters along the way. Within a week the cause spread to every conceivable trade, including factory hands, and thereby produced the first general strike in our history. Such unprecedented solidarity convinced most employers and the city council to concede.

For most workers, however, the general

strike proved to be a pyrrhic victory. The devastating depression of 1837 depleted the ranks of many trade unions and destroyed others, leaving workers defenseless against employers determined to restore the long work day. Mill owners imposed longer hours when prosperity resumed, and those who did not do so accomplished the same result by cutting piece rates. One of their victims complained in 1849 that "almost every pursuit of labor, has within ten or fifteen years . . . been shorn of from one-third to one-half of its former gains; or where the rates remain nominally the same, instability of employment . . . has produced the same effect; though in a majority of cases, an actual reduction of rates is the active cause." Numerous artisans pointed out the obvious consequence of plummeting piece rates, namely a longer workday to compensate for their loss and more intensive pace of work.

Yet these same wage earners complained about unemployment as bitterly as they complained about overwork. They repeatedly lamented the days, weeks, and even months spent jobless or in search of work, though historians have been more attentive when they protested against excessive toil, perhaps because such protests normally precede or accompany dramatic events which make for exciting reading. This oversight is unfortunate, since it has encouraged a narrow view of working-class experience.

A number of factors contributed to sporadic employment, one of which was the nature of the transportation system. The very system which made mass production and its consequences possible also contributed to slack times. The "Transportation Revolution" may have penetrated new markets, but it did not reduce irregularities and discontinuities in supply and demand. Delays, spoilage, and loss of goods plagued Pennsylvania's canals. The Main Line, which connected Philadelphia with Pittsburgh by a series of canals, railroads, and a motorized inclined plane, angered merchants and manufacturers because of high costs and delays caused by bottlenecks at

transshipment points as well as by excessive lockage on waterways. Some of them grew so frustrated that they preferred to use the Erie Canal, despite the inconvenience of shipping through New York City. Others gave up on the Main Line and moved to New York to take even greater advantage of the Erie.

Railroads conquered the weather but little else. Lines that employed steam engines were so beset by breakdowns that they kept teams of horses in reserve. Service improved with advances in steam engines, but many problems remained. Faulty track, poor scheduling, and plain carelessness caused repeated wrecks and derailments, giving antebellum railroads a "nightmarish quality." Connections between different lines were lacking because competitors refused to adopt a standard gauge. The Pennsylvania and Ohio lines had seven distinct gauges, which inspired contemporaries to dub their rivalry the "war of gauges."

Coastal packets offered the most dependable mode of shipment, but they had their own drawbacks. They made scheduled sailings only during the "season," which stretched from early fall to late spring. Shippers cut back in summer, transferring some craft to the transatlantic run and sending others northward or southward only when guaranteed adequate cargo. Coastal packets therefore resembled ordinary traders in the warm months when they were governed by profits rather than schedules. Merchants and manufacturers sometimes waited months for an arrival.

The capriciousness of these transportation facilities may well have aggravated the nagging problem of erratic deliveries of goods. Such unpredictable deliveries inevitably made work itself unpredictable and helped shape the work habits of artisans. Wage earners could expect fairly steady employment when markets were good and raw materials available, but faced frequent layoffs when raw materials failed to arrive on time, if at all. This was the assessment of an Englishman who spent part of a tour of America toiling in a hatter's shop. He reported that journeymen anticipated being laid off when they exhausted the supply of fur and leather. Rather than spread the work by slowing down, however, the more experienced hands made hats as quickly as possible in order to garner enough money to tide them through the impending layoff. In slack times hatters and other journeymen either left the city to search for work elsewhere or took whatever employment they could find. Many shoemakers and tailors found temporary employment in repair work or day labor; some hand-loom weavers were so accustomed to shifting into casual labor during periodic downturns that they considered themselves weavers/laborers.

Winter months were unusually trying. Frozen waterways curtailed trade and brought on the slack season, throwing journeymen out of work for long periods and forcing them to seek relief from Philadelphia philanthropists who distributed soup, bread, and fuel. Seasonal fluctuations in trade also determined wage rates. Journeymen, aware that the warm months normally ushered in brisk business, negotiated differential wage scales, demanding higher rates in spring and summer. Carpenters, for example, earned about 10 percent more per day in spring and summer than in fall and winter. Hand-loom weavers negotiated contracts twice yearly—in early spring and late fall—and exacted higher rates in the warm season.

The shape of Philadelphia's industrial plant also determined the quantity and quality of employment. The dominant form of business organization, the small shop, was extremely fragile. Owners operated on hopelessly thin profit margins and were so anxious to reduce fixed costs that they slashed employment rolls at the "slightest hint" of a downturn in trade. They kept the best workers, leaving slower, less experienced hands to forage for work or wait until business improved.

Incessant toil, in a word, was not the bane of Philadelphia's antebellum artisan. What really gnawed at him was the combination of plummeting wage rates and the fitful pace of work, the syncopated rhythm of the economy with its alternating periods of feverish activity broken by slack spells. In slow months, the dull season, or periods with "broken days," he was on his own, without work or the ability to meet day-to-day costs of running the household. Such times could be extremely demoralizing and may be a factor in the frequency of working-class suicides reported in local newspapers. In the case of shoemaker William Reed there is no question about the cause. January 2, 1845, marked his sixth week without work: "The prospective appeared gloomy, and starvation apparently surrounding him, caused him to seek repose in death" by slitting his throat with his shoemaker's knife.

Fluctuations in trade were not the only determinants of employment. Popular attitudes toward work also figured prominently in the equation, for many artisans who lived in the transitional period between the preindustrial and industrial age adhered to values, customs, and traditions that went against the grain of early industrial discipline. Prizing leisure as well as work, they engaged in a wide spectrum of leisure-time activities, ranging from competitive sport to lounging on street corners. Many of them also belonged to volunteer organizations, which successfully competed with their places of employment for their attention and devotion.

Traditions die hard, and perhaps none died harder than drinking habits. Advances in science and medicine, early industrial change and, as we shall see, the advent of revivalism, eroded customary drinking habits among some sectors of the medical profession, the clergy, and the emerging industrial elite. But the old commercial classes and most artisans still clung tenaciously to older ways. They valued alcohol for its own sake and used it as a stimulant or as medicine to combat fatigue, to cool the body in summer or warm it in winter, and to treat common illness.

Numerous contemporaries report that artisans were not particular about where they imbibed. Presbyterian minister Sylvester Graham found them drinking in workshops as well as at home in the early 1830s and, he lamented, they especially enjoyed a drink in the late afternoon when "treating" time arrived and journeymen took turns sipping from a jug. Graham's observations are supported by Benjamin T. Sewell, a tanner and vice president of the Trades' Union in 1834 and 1836 who became a Methodist minister in the 1850s. Looking back on his days as a journeyman, Sewell recalled that young apprentices learned to drink while they learned a trade. Journeymen arrived at work with flasks and appointed an apprentice to make periodic trips to the local pub in order to have them filled, "for which service" he "robs the mail . . . takes a drink before he gets back. . . ." This training ground turned many young wage earners into hardened drinkers, inclined to go on an occasional binge. Such workers, said another observer, toil "soberly and industriously for a season, and then, by way of relaxation, indulge in a carouse, often of some day's continuance. The saturnalia, and its effects being terminated, they again return to their former occupations and habits of very moderate drinking."

Employers winced at such behavior, but one ought not assume that all of them were martinets who enforced regulations against drink. Owners of textile mills could afford to do so because they relied upon a semi-skilled labor force which could be replaced with relative ease. The concentration required by operators of power-driven machinery, moreover, caused some to relinquish drink without much prompting from employers. The millhands of Manayunk, for example, boasted in 1835 that they formed a temperance society "without the aid or countenance of the influential or talented members of the community," for experience taught them that drinking was a liability which tended to "confuse the brain, cloud the mind, and warp the judgment, thereby rendering the person who indulges in them [textile mills] totally unfit to superintend the movements of complicated machinery." Smaller

employers, on the other hand, were more tolerant of workers who drank. Reverend Thomas P. Hunt went so far as to claim that masters also enjoyed an occasional dram or two. He knew a young man who was fired on account of "idleness and neglect of business but not for drinking; for they all [including the employer] drank themselves." We should allow for some exaggeration on Hunt's part, but there is truth in his assessment. Many, if not most, small employers were former journeymen themselves steeped in pre-industrial culture, and those who did custom work anticipated fluctuations in trade and therefore tolerated irregular work habits. These employers "expected" journeymen to shun the shop on holidays—official as well as self-proclaimed—and they endured drinking, as long as their journeymen worked "tolerably regularly" and managed to avoid getting "absolutely drunk."

Most artisans did their drinking in pubs, and pubs probably assumed greater importance in their lives after some employers began to prohibit drinking in the shop. Working-class pubs had a style all their own. Signs with piquant inscriptions hung above entranceways and stood in bold contrast to the sedate placards which graced the vestibules of middle-class establishments. "The Four Alls," a public house in Moyamensing, owed its namesake to the following apothegm.

1. *King*—I govern all.
2. *General*—I fight for all.
3. *Minister*—I pray for all.
4. *Laborer*—I pay for all.

Immigrant taverns sometimes advertised popular political causes. An Irish tavern in Kensington, for example, sported a placard with a bust of Daniel O'Connell and the slogan:

*'Hereditary bondsmen! who would be free,*
*Themselves must strike the blow.'*

These taverns offered a wide variety of entertainment, illicit and otherwise. Cockfighting, a popular spectator sport in colonial times but eschewed by people of social standing thereafter, prospered in the working-class pubs of antebellum Philadelphia. Cockfights drew either handfuls of fans or large crowds, depending upon the size of the facility. One of the larger and more popular cockpits could be found in William Cook's pub in Moyamensing. Cook constructed an amphitheater around the pit, which comfortably seated seventy-five enthusiasts. He also concealed it in the tavern loft, since cockfighting invited betting, which was illegal.

Working-class gamblers not excited by cockfights could try their hand at games in the gambling halls or the taverns. Policy houses, which operated lotteries, dotted Philadelphia and concentrated in the suburbs. Furtively located on side streets and in back alleys, they lured workers who wagered from "3¢ to 50¢ with the sanguine hope of having this money returned fourfold. . . ." Taverns sponsored games that probably resembled "menagerie," in which participants sat around a circular board divided into pie-shaped units, each of which bore the picture of an animal. Each player placed a coin on his choice and waited breathlessly while a pinwheel whirled and designated the winner upon coming to a stop.

Despite these attractions most workers, we may believe, visited pubs for the sake of camaraderie. At the end of the workday homebound artisans, made detours to their favorite taverns, where they exchanged stories or discussed politics over drams or mugs of a variety of malt liquor. Outworkers broke the boredom of toiling alone by visiting the local pub during the day, and shopworkers probably went there to celebrate the completion of a task or an order. Most observers agree that tavern traffic increased dramatically on Sunday night and in winter when trade slowed.

Circuses and road shows also captured the fancy of workingmen. Heavily publicized in newspapers and in broadsides posted on fences, such entertainments rarely respected the industrial time clock. Occurring on week-

days as well as on weekends, they dazzled throngs of onlookers with bizarre acts and feats. One of the most prestigious companies that thrilled Philadelphians was the internationally acclaimed team of Messrs. LaConta and Gonzalo and Master Minich of exotic Spain. LaConta captured the limelight in the Pennsylvania Museum when he danced the popular "fisherman's hornpipe on the tightrope, and performed the much more difficult exercise of saltation on the same rope with a living boy tied to each foot." Less elaborate but equally exciting fare took place in the streets when daredevils or athletes visited Philadelphia. Sizable crowds gathered to watch balloonists ascend or to witness competition staged by tramping athletes. Long-distance runner William Jackson, affectionately known as the "American Deer," attracted a crowd upon challenging all bettors that he could run eleven miles in less than an hour. The outcome of this race against time is unknown, but those who gathered at the finish line had quite a time "gambling, fighting, drinking, etc."

Though fascinated by these events, artisans especially enjoyed pastimes in which they could participate. They simply loved shooting matches and hunting small game, according to an observer who bemoaned that "every fair day" yielded a "temptation to forsake the shop for the field." The most avid hunters, he contended, were artisans who toiled indoors, for they found a jaunt in the fields especially relaxing. Artisans who resided in the same neighborhood sometimes set aside time for exercise by declaring holidays and staging competitive games; hand-loom weavers, for instance, often did so. In August 1828, those living near Third and Beaver streets laid down their shuttles and passed the day—a classic "Blue Monday"— footracing and merrymaking.

Sport, merrymaking, and drinking were also staples at ethnic gatherings. English, German, and Irish immigrants honored Old World customs and traditions, celebrated weddings and holidays, or gathered simply in order to socialize regardless of the time of day or day of the week. Germans, for instance, set aside Monday as their "principal day for pleasure," and festivities could spill into the middle of the week. Würtemburgers once journeyed to Philadelphia's rural suburbs for a *Volksfest* which stretched from Sunday to Tuesday, ample time for them to consume untold kegs of beer, participate in games, and dance at weddings. The Irish were also known to set aside Monday for outings in the suburbs. Their national games, the Donneybrook Fair, traditionally attracted hundreds of enthusiasts and no self-respecting Irish Protestant missed the annual July 12 parade commemorating the glorious victory on the banks of the Boyne in 1690. On July 12, 1831, Orangemen marched through Philadelphia and taunted angry Catholic bystanders with offensive songs such as "Kick the Pope" and "Croppies Go Home." Tensions built steadily until the Catholics, unable to restrain themselves any longer, attacked the paraders, touching off a melee which led to many arrests. Witnesses from both sides appeared in court, including journeyman James Mitchell, a perky young artisan who, speaking in behalf of his class, testified that he joined the procession because "all work and no play makes Jack a dull boy. . . ."

An elderly tailor elaborated upon this point. Reclining in a field with a companion, he met James W. Alexander, a Presbyterian minister from nearby Princeton, who sought their reaction to the 1837 depression. Alexander assumed that hard times kept both men from their workplace. "Not at all," snapped the quick-witted old man, "we are only enjoying the *Tailor's Vacation. Pressure* is well enough, to be sure," he went on, "as I can testify when the last dollar is about to be pressed out of me; but *Vacation* is capital. It tickles one's fancy with the notion of choice. 'Nothing on compulsion' is my motto."

Membership in voluntary fire companies also interrupted the daily work routines of Philadelphia artisans. Indeed, the city fire department enjoyed its greatest growth between 1826 and 1852, when sixty-eight new companies appeared. The department was nearly equally divided between hose companies, which connected lengths of hose to fire plugs and to pumps, and engine companies, which transported mobile pumps. City law limited engine companies to fifty members and hose companies to 25, but the ordinance was a dead letter. Memberships swelled and sometimes reached two or three hundred to the company.

Firemen were fierce competitors. Hose companies fought for the fire plugs nearest a blaze, and engine companies did battle for rights to the prime hose locations. Firemen loved racing their gaudy tenders and hose carriages through the city streets and went to extraordinary lengths to preserve their pride, shoving wrenches into the spokes of a rival rig, cutting its tow ropes, or assaulting its towers. Races usually ended in brief scuffles, but competition reached fever pitch in the 1840s when ethnic tensions polarized Philadelphians and artisans formed fire companies along ethnic lines. Irish Catholic, Irish Protestant, and nativist companies emerged and allured gangs of intensely loyal young toughs so that, when rivals crossed paths, riots ensued which caused enormous property damage and some loss of life.

As competition increased, so did the devotion of firemen. An observer knew a volunteer who "work[ed] better after a long sun and race with the P—— and had beaten her, but if his company was waxed, he could'[nt] (sic) work at all and had to lose a day." The most devoted firemen earned the title of "bunkers." Spending the night in the firehouse, they took turns watching for fires from the house tower in the hope of getting the jump on rivals and arriving first at the scene of a blaze. Some of them even "delighted in a day watch."

These pursuits and activities—drinking and gaming, participating in popular sports and in fire companies—characterized a vibrant, preindustrial style of life. A number of factors underpinned this style, the most significant of which were demographic and material. First, as Herbert Gutman notes, it was repeatedly replenished by waves of immigrants and rural-urban migrants, who came from widely divergent sub-cultures but whose values and behavior collided with the imperatives of early industrial discipline. Second, and perhaps more important, at mid-century many wage earners worked in traditional (as against modern) settings which, together with the boom-bust quality of the economy, supported sporadic work habits. Those who know this environment best were outworkers—especially hand-loom weavers, shoemakers, and tailors—who toiled at home without direct supervision of employers and custom workers, who fashioned consumer goods to the taste of individuals and who thereby evaded the more vigorous regimen of workers producing for the mass market.

Outworkers and custom workers displayed traditional forms of behavior in that they made no sharp distinction between work and leisure. Blending leisure with work, they puncutated workdays with the activities sketched above. Nor did they respect the specialization of role and function which normally accompanies modernization. Instead they persisted in assuming the dual role of artisans and firemen in the face of strong opposition from urban reformers who wished to relegate firefighting to paid professionals. It is probable, moreover, that the values, activities, and organizations of this style of life filled the basic needs of its adherents by sanctioning and supplying vehicles for recreation, neighborhood cohesion, ethnic identity, and camaraderie.

At the same time, however, there emerged a competing culture with its own organizations and institutions. Unlike preindustrial culture, it made a sharp distinction between work and leisure and regarded preindustrial culture as wasteful, frivolous and, above all, sinful. Sanctioning a more modern style of life, it originated not among the working class but with the emerging industrial elite and the Presbyterian clergy. This elite was in the process of displacing the old Quaker oligarchy and included manufacturers who represented the most advanced industries, such as locomotive builder

Matthias W. Baldwin, as well as merchants and professionals with investments in industry and transportation, such as Thomas Newkirk, a dry goods merchant, banker and railroad promoter, and the merchant-investor Alexander Henry. Nearly all of them shifted their political loyalty from the Federalists to the Whigs. They filled the first pews of the fashionable Presbyterian churches of the center city, and some were attentive to evangelical ministers like Albert Barnes. Adapting Protestantism to industrial capitalism, Barnes assaulted the embattled ramparts of orthodoxy (paving the way of the 1837 schism), and preached a brand of Protestantism that bordered on arminianism. Such ministers did not proselytize for the vindictive, arbitrary God of John Calvin, but a benevolent deity who promised salvation to all who willed it, rewarded worldly success with grace, and exhorted His people to do good in the world. God thus freed man to accumulate wealth without the pangs of guilt that had tortured the orthodox conscience and He inspired them to launch a moral crusade against sin.

These ministers and their lay advocates did not regard sin as doctrinal error but as moral laxity of the sort displayed by Philadelphia's working class. Such behavior threatened the material progress sanctioned by God himself, and those who crusaded against preindustrial behavior did God's work and their own at the same time. The elite pursued its God-given commission with staggering energy, forming and funding a spate of moral reform organizations, beneficial societies, and lobbies designed to proscribe working-class pastimes and to teach working-class children the value of deference and self-discipline.

It is difficult to assess the extent to which reformers succeeded in some of these efforts, but it is doubtful that they enjoyed much success prior to the Civil War. While they convinced the state to establish a system of free public schools in 1834, working-class parents did not immediately take advantage of it. They appear to have more interest in teaching a trade to their children than in schooling them, which may account for low, erratic attendance in antebellum classrooms. The elite found it difficult to regulate working-class pastimes because it did not have authority over the police, the principal agent of social control. Each suburban district raised its own police force prior to 1854 from the very population the elite wished to control, and voluntary policemen were notoriously lax in their day-to-day duties. They exerted authority only in cases of emergency.

Temperance may have been another matter entirely. The elite, and large factory owners in particular, found working-class drinkers quite troublesome and equated them with gremlins whose behavior interrupted operations in mills and factories. The "steady arm of industry," went one bizarre metaphor, "withers" from drink. And so the elite channeled its energies into changing the drinking habits of wage earners.

Philadelphia's temperance movement formally began in 1827 when parishioners in the stylish Second Presbyterian church joined likeminded ministers, physicians, and industrialists and formed the Pennsylvania Society for Discouraging the Use of Ardent Spirits. The Society's name belied its intentions, however, since it soon advocated the extreme position of total abstinence from all intoxicants, as did the Pennsylvania Temperance Society, which succeeded it in 1834. These organizations supported lectures and distributed polemics which linked intemperance to poverty and economic ruin and marshalled the latest medical opinion about drinking on their side. They relied heavily on Presbyterian ministers, some of whom, like evangelists Thomas P. Hunt and C. C. Cuyler, rejected arminianism but endorsed revivalism and preached temperance in the late 1820s and early 1830s. Their efforts swelled the rolls of Presbyterian churches, filling the pews with thousands of converts, who formed local temperance societies and affiliated with the Pennsylvania Society. By 1834 the Pennsylvania Society boasted a following of 4,300.

Membership lists of these affiliates do not survive, which makes it difficult to assess their class composition. But it appears that the movement did not reach very deeply into the social structure, except perhaps in Southwark and Northern Liberties where aggressive ministers converted some artisans. The typical temperance advocate of the 1830s is best described, however, as a church-going member of the middle and upper-middle classes.

The temperance crusade of the late 1820s and 1830s aroused the suspicion of most wage earners because it was so closely identified with the Presbyterians and advocated total abstinence. Presbyterian domination of the temperance movement did not sit well with most workers whose religious interests ranged from the popular sects to Free Thought and skepticism, and who looked upon the crusade as a subterfuge for Presbyterian influence or for creeping priestcraft. Some workers were offended by the Presbyterian's upper-class pretentiousness; so was Thomas P. Hunt, a Presbyterian minister himself, who accused his colleagues of being "too conservative" and prone to "cast a look of suspicion upon all workingmen." Wage earners, moreover, endorsed temperance, if anything, in the 1830s and equated partisans of total abstinence with "fanatics." Holding this opinion, Benjamin Sewell recalls having had "no objection" to moderate drinking in that decade. "My company all drank, a little," he recalled, " 'but nothing to hurt' we used to say." Men like Sewell and his friends were so accustomed to drinking, so convinced of its value, that they could not break the habit—even if so inclined—simply by signing their names to a total abstinence pledge, which the Pennsylvania Temperance Society naively considered "essential to the support and prosperity" of the cause. They needed the encouragement and understanding of peers, but most workers were not yet prepared to lend such support. Sewell, for example, recalls the tragedy of a young friend who signed a total abstinence pledge against the advice of his comrades, who suggested that he simply "cut down." Stigmatized as a teetotaler and chided by his friends, he relapsed into heavy drinking and lost his job. So he left for a suburb in west Philadelphia in order to "hunt work and reform," but was told by an employer acquainted with his drinking problem "we have no work for *you.*" Distraught and demoralized, he wandered aimlessly for a few days and then hanged himself.

Between 1837 and 1843, however, a new temperance crusade suddenly developed, which bore little resemblance to the older movement in terms of organizations, constituency, and tactics. It appeared in the form of temperance-beneficial societies which were located in the industrial suburbs. The membership lists of these organizations indicate they were dominated by skilled journeymen and master craftsmen with small numbers of small shopkeepers, clerks, and unskilled workers as well. Their supporters were critical of the older societies, which had "no provision by which all members may be brought together at short intervals" so as to exert their "united influence." Temperance-beneficial societies remedied this glaring shortcoming by holding frequent meetings, sometimes nightly gatherings, not just in churches but in the streets and public squares—or anywhere they could attract a crowd. In anticipation of the Washingtonians, they appealed to hardened drinkers and drunkards, whom the older societies had studiously ignored and would become featured speakers at temperance rallies, visible examples of the possibility of self reform. Such tactics yielded striking results. Temperance-beneficial societies mushroomed between 1837 and 1841, when the *Public Ledger* counted 17,000 teetotalers in the country and exulted that, in two months of 1841 alone, 4,300 formerly wayward souls enlisted in the crusade. These organizations did not necessarily turn drinkers into teetotalers overnight. Apostasy continued to plague them, but they did establish a significant foothold among the lower middle class and working class by employing peer-group pressure, eternal vigilance, and the power of example.

To what can we attribute the sudden emergence of this temperance movement? We ought to extend credit to those who pioneered the crusade, since some of their converts emerged in the temperance-beneficial societies. But the movement would not have enjoyed such a mass following without the economic turmoil of the late 1830s and early 1840s. The new movement flourished in the wake of the 1837 panic, the most devastating and prolonged economic downturn in Philadelphia's experience. Press and pulpit concurred in attributing hard times to God's wrath visited upon people fallen from grace and, it is hardly surprising, the depression triggered a new wave of revivals. Revivalists were especially active in the industrial suburbs, where their protracted meetings made thousands of conversions and brought hundreds into the churches. There was unprecedented growth for Methodists, though it is difficult to determine the precise rate because they suffered defections in 1828 and 1843 which tend to skew the figures before and during the depression. Even with these losses, however, they made impressive gains. Between 1815 and 1836, for example, Methodists enjoyed fairly steady growth, attracting about 240 members per year, while they lost about 140 members yearly between 1844 and 1850. But during the depression years (1837–1843), they more than doubled their previous rate of growth, taking in slightly less than 540 new members a year. This accretion is probably several times greater than it appears because hundreds who experienced conversion attended church but did not become members.

The depression not only swelled the membership of the Methodist Church (and other denominations as well), it also altered the message its ministers conveyed to communicants. Methodists lagged behind the Presbyterian vanguard in adjusting their discipline to the exigencies of industrial capitalism. The General Conference, for instance, did not restore Wesley's ban on buying and selling liquor, repealed in 1791, until 1848. The reasons for this lag are not entirely clear, though we might consider the fact that the Methodist ministry was recruited from the lower classes and less influenced by the industrial elite than were Presbyterian clergymen. Whatever the reason, the Methodists did not wax enthusiastic over the prospect of a prosperous, industrial America until the 1830s. Some of them then hailed the rise of railroads and steam power as evidence of God's blessing and "man's elevation" and began to attack behavioral patterns that impeded such progress, emphasizing instead "habits of industry." Most Philadelphia ministers, however, showed precious little enthusiasm for temperance or total abstinence until the depression, which they interpreted as God's punishment for man's depravity. Hard times strengthened the resolve of some clergyman to tighten morality and converted others to the cause, for when the Philadelphia Conference met in 1841, it suspended a rule permitting the use of alcohol for medicinal purposes, resolved to recommend "total abstinence from all intoxicating liquors as a beverage" to "all our people," and applauded the "triumphs" in the crusade against liquor "during the past year."

These ministers had every reason to be pleased. They played a key role in delivering messages of total abstinence to the working class by joining together with other revivalists as well as laymen to form the temperance-beneficial societies. Working people who flocked to these societies in the late 1830s formed their own temperance societies, often along craft lines, in the early 1840s.

The revived temperance crusade turned into the first of a series of events which pitted middle-class and working-class Protestants against the city's growing Catholic minority. Catholics perceived a threat to their culture in the evangelical zeal of the movement and began to disrupt temperance rallies. Their activity aroused the anger of Protestant workingmen chastened by hard times and disposed to look for scapegoats. Catholics were the most convenient targets, and they became even more vulnerable when their leaders protested against Protestant domination of the public schools. They objected to the use of anti-Catholic texts and to the reading of the King James Bible during opening exercises and requested that the school board permit their children to hold separate religious exercises. This emotionally charged issue incited revivalist ministers (who were also involved in the temperance crusade) to form the American Protestant Association in the winter of 1842–43, which interpreted the Catholic request as a veiled threat to "kick" the King James Bible out of the public schools and to undermine American institutions. The convergence of the school controversy and the temperance crusade breathed life in nativist American Republican Associations which had been operating since 1837 without much success. Middle-class temperance advocates led by Lewis Levin, editor of the *Temperance Advocate and Literary Repository,* fused their cause with the nativists, drawing thousands of working-class teetotalers with them. American Republicans scored a landslide victory in the 1844 municipal election which proved to be ephemeral in the center city as voters returned to the Whig fold the following year. But in most formerly Democratic suburbs the American Republicans showed more staying power and tallied solid majorities at the polls in the 1840s.

American Republicans did not enlist all working-class temperance advocates. Some of them remained loyal Democrats, but the temperance movement of the depression and American Republicanism shared much the same constituency. American Republicanism, repellent to the Presbyterian and Quaker elite, drew its strength from the native-born Protestant middle class and working class. Such people fancied themselves the solid "middle" of society, bone and sinew of Protestant Republicanism. Their leaders continually stressed the connection between temperance and prosperity. Total abstinence, one of them was convinced, "restores the drunkard to his prosperity, and makes him secure. . . ." Another gave assurance that the cause inspired people to "maintain their *glorious independence,* which has contributed so essentially to their health, happiness, respectability and worldly prosperity." Such claims were clearly those of ambitious people, but American Republicanism was not simply the mother's milk of *parvenus* or of paranoids suffering from fear of domination by immigrants. It was more complex and more subtle than that. It conveyed a strong sense of class identity and what might be called a modern work ethic.

American Republicans cut their teeth on the labor theory of value. This doctrine, which had informed the General Trades' Union and which existed in the popular mind well into the 1890s, held that labor is the source of all wealth. People created wealth by blending their labor with the soil or with raw materials, and those who did so were considered to be "producers," chiefly mechanics, farmers, or anyone who produced commodities by working with his hands. Those who did not—doctors, lawyers, merchants, bankers, landlords, and the like— but who amassed wealth by selling commodities made by producers, by performing services, or by investing capital, were stigmatized as "accumulators." They were drones and parasites, but nonetheless powerful people who exacted special privileges from legislators in the form of bank and corporate charters, land grants, and the like. They were responsible for the enormous maldistribution of wealth and for the misery of the majority.

This analysis of American Republicans allowed for only two classes, and middle-class nativists differed over where employers fit in. A minority, comprised of former journeymen, considered small, traditional masters to be "producers" and, defending them, contrasted these small masters with the ambitious, innovative bosses who squeezed workingmen. One of them contended that a "conscientious man in these times, can scarcely expect to earn more than a *competency*. If more than this is aimed at, man is apt to become the oppressor of his fellows—taking advantage of their necessities and obtaining the fruits of their labor without rendering them a just recompense." On another occasion he admonished, "National prosperity, as it is generally described, (that is, the prosperity of the wealthy classes, or capitalists,) is perfectly reconcilable with a

prostrate and miserable condition of the laboring people." Oliver P. Cornman, who rose from journeyman house painter to editor of the principal organ of the American Republican Party, the *Daily Sun,* aped the leaders of the General Trades' Union when, in the late 1840s, he drew a distinction between masters and employers. As a former workingman he was well acquainted with the "soulless men who would grind down the journeyman to the point of starvation and drive his family to the point of desperation." Such men were " 'masters' in name (only). . . ." Honorable masters respected the maxim that the journeyman was worthy of his hire and of being paid a just wage.

Most middle-class nativists, however, found fault only with the crudest, most grasping employers such as those who exploited women and children. They normally praised entrepreneurs and endorsed those who accumulated wealth. Commending employers, master printer H. H. K. Elliott exhorted an audience of mechanics to "Look around . . . and . . . discover in your own city, among those who now have high places, great wealth and much respect, very many who started in life as, and who continue to be mechanics." Master craftsmen, after all, were producers whose honest labor had created capital and "capital acquired by labor," claimed a nativist editor, "is a friend of labor . . ."

Middle-class American Republicans in fact had nothing but disdain for detractors of employers. They looked upon the class warfare of the previous decade with some regret and imagined their cause as a bridge between employer and employee. Levin, for example, considered temperance the "most effectual means of closing this fatal chasm in our social system, of knitting up those sympathies again. . . ." And while Levin and his middle-class colleagues recognized working-class poverty, they sought to convince workers that their immiseration had less to do with the advance of industrial capitalism than with the crimes perpetrated by accumulators and immigrants.

These American Republicans pronounced accumulators guilty of cultural and economic crimes, each of which caused poverty in its own way. These accumulators had a style of life which bred intemperance and disrespect for hard work and honest toil. Levin thus traced the "rise and prevalence of intemperance" to the "mushroom aristocracy" who "rioted on the wealth bequeathed to them by their fathers, affected to despise the honest industry by which it had been acquired, and by their upstart and debauched habits set a pernicious example. . . ." The same people who led others to ruin by spreading depravity also controlled the vital purse strings of the economy and exploited masters and journeymen alike. Employers were simply the *"agent[s]* of capital," beholden to the iron laws of supply and demand. When capital was plentiful, wages were high and everyone benefitted. But when the money market contracted, masters had to slash wages or lay off workers. The real culprits were monied aristocrats, bankers, and speculators who had the "leisure to combine . . . scheme and make enormous profits, sometimes without investing a cent. . . ." They also had the "power to elevate or depress the market . . . make money plenty [sic] or scarce . . . gamble with impunity, and even control, by combination and monopoly, the very circulating medium. While they lounge at ease in their palatial mansions, or roll about in their carriages, in elegant indolence and luxury. . . ."

Catholics, on the other hand, threatened native-born workers from the bottom of society. They depressed the wages of honest workers because they flooded the labor market and because they were accustomed to "liv[ing] on less than the Native" and more than willing to work for pittance. Unchecked immigration promised to "reduce" American workers to the level of Irish peasants. American Republican politicians rarely missed an opportunity to raise this specter, but did not object to the Irish simply because they competed with native-born workers in the labor market.

Middle-class American Republicans har-bored an image of a Catholic life style at variance with the new virtues of sobriety, respectability, and self-control. And since they measured Catholics by the same standards they applied to accumulators, they employed common metaphors to describe both groups and held strikingly similar images of them. Both groups loved to drink, and "riotous," wreckless accumulators had counterparts among Catholics who engaged in "disgusting debauchery" and "rioted" in the city streets as every observer of the 1844 riots was aware. At least one nativist conceded that all Catholics were not necessarily lower class. Some were aristocrats, others mobocrats. "If the former class, they are generally the profligate gambler, spendthrift or worse. If the latter, they are either lazy, drunken paupers, or transported felons. . . ." The aristocrats, like their American counterparts, spent their life in "riotous living"; the others were a "riotous, drunken set. . . ."

Nor did the Irish qualify as producers in the opinion of nativists. "Three-forths of the grocery stores, and nine-tenths of the liquor stores, in this country," one of them declared, "seem to be kept by Irishmen." These stores, he emphasized, "are not *productive* occupations. . . ." Irishmen who did find honorable employment did not linger there very long, because "as soon as they get five or ten dollars 'ahead,' we find them opening grog shops, peddling lemons, or . . . in some other occupation which is little better than idleness, or perhaps a little *worse.* ". . . That some Irish did accumulate property did not surprise another nativist. They saved enough money to purchase property by "living in mean, squalid, filth and degradation . . . and harder landlords than these are seldom to be found."

American Republicanism, then, can be viewed as the amalgam of the labor theory of value and the revivalism of the depression years. This merger provided native-born, middle-class Protestants with their own sense of identity, a means of distinguishing themselves from the mercantile and financial upper class and the foreign-born lower class. And while it is difficult to distinguish the contributions each of these forces made to the American Republican synthesis, it may be said that revivalism imbued Party members with faith in industrial capitalism, intolerance of immigrants, and a moral code which deprecated moral laxity and stressed sobriety, diligence, and respectability. The labor theory of value imparted a peculiar class analysis of society which located exploitation not in the relationship between employer and employee but in the relationship between producers and accumulators. The synthesis of these forces, in turn, offered a multi-causal analysis of the plight of producers. That is, workers were impoverished because they did not work hard enough and because immigrants depressed wages. And all producers—journeymen and masters—were not justly rewarded because of the machinations of accumulators.

At first glance it appears that native-born wage earners accepted this analysis. In 1845, for example, a handful of skilled workers and master mechanics met at the Jefferson Temperance Hall and formed the Order of United American Mechanics (U.A.M.), which quickly established branches throughout the country. Membership was limited to native-born producers—masters and journeymen—who upheld the new respectability by pledging to honor "Honesty, Industry, and Sobriety," and by listening attentively to lectures on how to save money and to accumulate property. Ostensibly a fraternal-beneficial organization, the U.A.M. sponsored a funeral fund and paid benefits to members too ill to work. It also vowed to employ "every honorable means to obtain a 'fair day's wage for a fair day's work' " so that workers could "support themselves and their families in comfort and respectability . . ." and "accumulate a sufficient sum, during many months of toil, to support and sustain them through the mischances and mishaps of a 'rainy day'. . . ." These means included pressure upon employers to hire only native-born Americans. It also included encouraging con-

sumers to patronize American craftsmen and to boycott business owned by foreigners in the hope that employers would increase their businesses and then pay better wages. But higher wages alone did not guarantee that journeymen would live a respectable life. So members policed one another's morality to guarantee that they did not engage in dissipation, reporting cases of intemperance and frivolity and visiting those who claimed eligibility for welfare payments—in order to make sure that they did not feign illness. Members found guilty of immoral conduct were either reprimanded or expelled.

Like most nativist organizations, the U.A.M. assumed that employers and employees had common interests, that journeymen did not have interests peculiar to them as a class. But the model nativist worker who joined a temperance society, belonged to the U.A.M., and voted for or held membership in the American Republican party was also likely to be a militant working-class spokesman. Leaders of unions of house carpenters, printers, shoemakers, saddlers, and other trades belonged to both organizations. They firmly believed the labor theory, but unlike their middle-class coreligionists, they endorsed the corollary that the wage earner was entitled to the full product of his labor. Precisely what they meant by this remains somewhat of a mystery. But it clearly implied that wage earners had rights to what *they* produced and were entitled to wages sufficient to support themselves and their families in dignity and respectability. This theory, moreover, armed workers with a principle that distinguished their interests from those of employers.

American Republican wage earners, consequently, found themselves pursuing the illusory goal of aspiring to a respectable life style on subsistence wages. One such American Republican was George F. Turner, a founding member of the United American Mechanics and President of the Association of Journeymen House Carpenters in 1850–51. Like most unions led by nativists, the carpenters refused to organize the foreign-born members of their trade until they learned that this strategy was counterproductive. But it invited immigrants to undermine the bill of prices which the union had sacrificed so much to establish, and by the late 1840s and early 1850s the carpenters dispatched organizers to Irish districts during "standouts," as their walkouts were called. One of these strikes was particularly bitter and protracted. It began in the fall 1850, collapsed, and then recommenced the following spring. It elicited numerous letters from strikers to local newspapers, one of which was by Turner. Describing the dilemma of the respectable artisan, he asserted that the "worthy mechanic" was entitled to "a house . . . on a front street, three stories high, bath room, hydrant, good yard, cellar . . . house furniture, bedding, clothing, amusements. . . ." But the cost of these "necessities" left him without sufficient income to feed his family adequately. The only course of action bringing respectability to the journeymen was pursuit of their class interests: "Unite to work fewer hours, and organize and inquire into that system of acquisition and distribution of the products of their own industry. . . ." Carpenters who had failed to obtain the rate advance followed Turner's advice and formed their own producers' cooperative.

Printers behaved in much the same manner. American Republicans who belonged to temperance societies or the U.A.M. occupied nearly every elective office in the printers' union, the Franklin Typographical Society. They steadfastly declined to cooperate with a union of German printers until 1850, when they launched a work stoppage for a series of non-wage demands and a rate advance. Those who failed to convince employers of the justice of their cause also formed a cooperative. Their leader, George W. Heilig, revealed the mentality of the newly evangelized workingman when he explained that man was no longer content simply to "eat and clothe himself," because science and art "have at this day disclosed an *artificial, intellectual, moral, and social life,* which . . . is as essential to maintain

as the merely natural; and, as it is more refined and exalted, so also does it require a freer and more liberal nourishment." Printers who worked for Philadelphia's large book houses did not earn enough money "to meet the demands of this more elevated life, which . . . is the religious as well as the political duty of every American to seek and maintain. The *true light* now lighteth every man that cometh into the world, and *it will be received.* We must, therefore, also be in a condition that will enable us to contribute to the support of churches and other associations that will afford us the opportunity of engaging in such religious exercises and social duties as may tend to bring into genial activity our religious feelings and moral affections."

Not all native-born Protestant workers who enrolled in the American Republican Party and its auxiliary organizations necessarily subscribed to these values. A sizable sector of the Party, which appears to have been comprised of young, unmarried men, embraced nativism simply because they hated Catholics. They adhered to older values and forms of behavior, shunning the church, frequenting pubs, taverns, and gaming houses, joining fire companies, and engaging in the rough-and-tumble life of the streets. On the other hand, some nativist workers endorsed the middle-class version of American Republicanism and became obsequious employees, repelled by trade unionism and radicalism alike. There is no way of knowing the origins of these people, though it is probable that they were recent rural-urban migrants who lacked the laboring traditions of Philadelphia's more experienced workers and, perhaps, most upwardly mobile artisans.

The more vocal working-class partisans of American Republicanism, however, did not fulfill the expectations of their middle-class exponents by acting the part of submissive workers wedded to employers by common economic and cultural interests. Day-to-day experience with entrepreneurs who refused to recognize their rights to what they produced made a compelling case that "wage slavery" was more responsible for poverty than intemperance, a glutted labor market, or the exploitation of accumulators. But while they rejected the American Republican analysis of immiseration, they did not cast off the new morality imparted by it. The irony is that this morality of sobriety, self-control, and respectability emphasized the grim reality; namely, that workers could not support a respectable style of life on wage labor alone. It is also ironic, as Paul Faler suggests, that this morality fortified workers in their struggle against competitive capitalism by arming them with a sense of self-discipline and commitment to purpose. The final irony may be that in employing the new morality in their own interests, they followed the advice of a middle-class nativist who described the ideal society as one which recognized the maxim: *"Act well thy part—there all the honor lies."*

One can safely equate nativist morality with the "cult of respectability," which British labor historians associate with the Victorian middle class and the "aristocracy of labor." The nature of this morality is not in dispute. Most writers agree that it rejected the spontaneity and moral laxity of preindustrial culture for a morality that valued sobriety, hard work, and respectability. Instead, what appears to be at issue is the means by which wage earners became exponents of it.

Implicity or explicitly, most American writers argue that the new morality was foisted upon workers by Whig industrialists and Presbyterian clergymen who operated through the government and private organizations. While it is clear that these reformers erected the organizational apparatus with which they could manipulate or control their social inferiors, it is improbable that they experienced much success in the period under discussion. The evidence presented here suggests an alternative explanation.

There is little doubt that early industrialization gave rise to a new form of evangelical Protestantism which emphasized the morality of self-control. Nor is there much doubt that workers engaged in those modern industries which required the most discipline—textile mills for example—endorsed evangelical Protestantism and the new morality in the late 1820s and early 1830s. But these workers were a decided minority both in terms of their work environment and religious convictions. Most artisans worked either in traditional or transitional settings at midcentury, laboring at home or in small shops without power-driven machinery. Those who produced for mass markets were forced to toil more intensively as time wore on, and some of them may have been inspired to adopt the new morality. But trade was also rather erratic. Consequently, the work environment of most artisans encouraged sporadic work habits, not steady application to work. And precious few artisans, or Methodist clergymen, found the new morality appealing prior to the depression of 1837.

The chilling effect of hard times appears to have changed their attitudes dramatically. The depression expedited the conversion of Methodist divines to the new morality and made the lower middle class as well as the upper echelon of the working class receptive to it. Methodists and New School Presbyterians in the industrial suburbs struck a resonant chord among these elements in the social strata when they claimed that the depression was inflicted by a God of wrath, angered over the moral depravity of man. They converted thousands of Philadelphians to the new morality, which gained political salience in the American Republican party and its auxiliary organizations. Nativism, then, was the means by which many artisans registered their commitment to a more modern work ethic, and those who converted them were not the elite and its clergy but their own clergy and that of the lower middle class.

Just as preindustrial culture filled the needs of its adherents, so nativism catered to the needs of its followers. It offered both the lower middle class and the upper level of the working class a coherent and seemingly credible explanation for their plight, which the rigors of hard times and the strain of industrial change had brought. It enabled them to assert their dignity and sense of self-worth. It held out prospect of prosperity and worldly success to those who would shun drink, the gaming room, and moral laxity in favor of sobriety and self-discipline. It promised to eliminate class conflict by uniting employers and employees on cultural issues.

Yet nativism fell short of being this cement for masters, and journeymen. Those who were native born were, to be sure, united at the polls and in various nativist organizations, but parted ways over divisive class issues in the workshop. Journeymen mediated nativism through values which proclaimed their right to the full product of their labor. Grafting nativist morality onto this formula they emerged as militant spokesmen for their class.

# 16

## "TRUE EARNEST WORKERS": REFORMING SISTERS

### JOAN M. JENSEN

The years between 1820 and 1860 witnessed the development of an intensive campaign to redefine the proper place of women in American society. Sponsored initially by established male religious leaders, the impulse to create a distinctively American conception of womenhood spread rapidly throughout America. Depicting the home as a realm of special virtue and a domestic haven in an increasingly competitive and commercial world, the "Cult of True Womanhood" attributed to women a vital function in maintaining republican virtue during the threatening period of industrialization and urbanization. This "Cult of True Womanhood" prescribed a series of characteristics that women, as guardians of national virtue, must cultivate. Of these, the most important were religious piety, moral purity, submissiveness to men, and the maintenance of the home as place of comfort and moral education.

While many women embraced the virtues of true womanhood, a life of domesticity did not appeal to all women. Feeling confined by their domestic roles, many middle- and upper-class women moved from the private world of their homes into the public world of antebellum reform. Beginning with the organization of Sunday schools and ladies benevolent societies designed to assist the poor, by the 1830s many of these reforming women took up the cause of temperance, abolition, and, eventually, woman suffrage. In this essay, Joan M. Jensen follows the development of the woman suffrage movement in rural Pennsylvania, where she finds that the success of the movement relied on women's personal bonds as much as reform ideology.

From Joan M. Jensen, *Loosening the Bonds: Mid-Atlantic Farm Women, 1750–1850* (New Haven, Conn.: Yale University Press, 1986). Reprinted by permission of Joan M. Jensen and Yale University Press.

On February 6, 1852, Hannah M. Darlington sat down in her Kennett farmhouse to write a letter to Jacob Painter, a wealthy Middletown acquaintance, about holding a women's rights conference. "The interest I feel in the cause impells me to it," she wrote, "yet in truth I scarce know what to say—if we could get up such a convention as we *ought* to have great good would result from it, but if we get up a *failure* it will be a misfortune to the cause, and tho I have unwaivering confidence in the eternity of truth and the certain advancement of great principles, that advancement may be retarded for a time by imprudent action on the part of its advocates. It is a considerable labor to get up a convention. This must be done by a few *true earnest* workers."

With this discussion of ideology and practice, Darlington opened the planning phase of what was to be the first Pennsylvania conference on the rights of women. She was forty-two at the time and had no children. She and her husband Chandler shared their farmhouse with a female relative and her seven-year-old daughter. The Darlingtons' small farm was worth thirty-seven hundred dollars, according to the census taker who visited them two years earlier. Jacob Painter, the thirty-eight-year-old bachelor to whom she wrote, was the youngest son of Enos Painter, a farmer in neighboring Middletown Township, whose estate the census taker had valued at seventy-five thousand dollars in 1850. Although separated economically, Darlington and Painter shared a progressive Quaker persuasion, an interest in social reform, and a latter-day Enlightenment culture that joined them in a common concern about women's status in society.

Since the original women's rights conference in Seneca Falls in 1848, Lucretia Mott had been trying without success to get the Philadelphia women to sponsor a state convention. Elizabeth Cady Stanton was not free to visit in the fall of 1848, cholera raged the following summer and fall, and even an eloquent defense of women's rights by Mott in December 1849 failed to rouse the Philadelphia women to organize. Mott attended the regional conference in Salem, Ohio, in April 1850 and the First National Women's Rights Conference in Worcester, Massachusetts, the following year. Lucretia Mott and twenty-nine men and women from Pennsylvania signed the call for the Worcester conference. Hannah Darlington was one of them.

Even the exciting Worcester conference failed to move the Philadelphia reformers on the question of a women's conference. In fall 1851, Mott wrote to Stanton that only a few Hicksites were interested. Nowhere was the failure of urban women to support the fledgling feminist movement more clear than in Philadelphia. It remained for the rural families of Kennett and a few surrounding townships finally to plan the conference. Bayard Taylor later described these men and women of Kennett in his *Pastoral Sketches* as "zealous for temperance, peace, and the right of suffrage for women." But that was after the Civil War. Before the war, antislavery was more prominent than peace, women's rights in general more important than suffrage. But Kennett was the center and women of the little community could date their reform tradition from the early eighteenth-century New Warke meeting.

Traditional histories of the nineteenth-century women's rights movement gave it a particular heritage. Suffragist authors linked it to the meeting of Lucretia Mott and Elizabeth Cady Stanton at the London antislavery conference, the exclusion of Mott and other Pennsylvania women elected as representatives from their antislavery societies, Mott and Stanton's subsequent meeting near Seneca Falls eight years later, and the calling of the first conference there in 1848. More recently, some historians have wondered about the eight-year lapse between the London and Seneca Falls meetings. Judy Wellman and Gerda Lerner have shown from their examination of petitions to the U.S. Congress that antislavery petition activity by women reached its peak in 1838, two years before the London meeting. Thereafter, petitions show a marked decline as a focus for women's political activity. So there is an unexplained gap not only in the activities of leaders Stanton and Mott but also in the activities of the masses of women who rallied to the antislavery standard.

Peggy A. Rabkin recently argued in *Fathers to Daughters* that the base from which the feminist movement sprang was not antislavery at all but the interest of New York women in the married women's property rights law. She makes the point that fathers were increasingly interested in passing on family property to daughters as well as to sons and that the impetus for Seneca Falls was not moral but legal. The women's property rights movement, according to this argument, is the key to understanding the convention of 1848 because it undeniably preceded that event. The antislavery gap, in this interpretation, is closed by legal reform efforts.

Even if this interpretation explained the women's movement in New York—and there are scholars who question the Rabkin thesis—it would not necessarily explain the motivation of the Pennsylvania movement. To understand it, one must examine the history of reform there, particularly the types of reform in which the people of Chester County engaged. Many documents remain from these struggles—petitions, memorials, tracts, and the rich collection of diaries and letters of Esther Lewis who lived in Vincent but was part of the wider circle of Kennett reformers. Temperance, antislavery, and women's rights were three great antebellum reforms, but the context within which each evolved was broader and more encompassing than any or all three.

Chester County women had long been concerned about the effects of intemperance in the eighteenth century. As early as 1761, a tract by minister Elizabeth Levis, written at Kennett, laid out the arguments against the "too frequent use of spiritous liquors." Although Quakers John Churchman and John Woolman were also condemning the use of alcohol for harvest workers, there was a feeling in Chester County that this was a women's issue, for a friend had written to Levis, "What can we women do? The men uphold it." Levis wrote her tract in reply. The main occasion for excess seemed to Levis to be harvest time with its tradition of drinking in the fields. Although she did not mention how this affected women directly, she saw drinking as an occasion for both self-destruction and oppression of others. Masters, she argued, could no longer guide their workers in right conduct.

If temperance surfaced in mid-eighteenth-century rural Chester County as a concern of at least some women, so too did concern about abolition, but only after women had helped introduce slavery into Pennsylvania. No antislavery tracts by women remain. What influence women had in the late eighteenth century seem to have been exerted within their monthly meetings between 1755 and 1774, when Chester County Monthly Meeting urged the Philadelphia Yearly Meeting to move from a policy of admonishing against owning slaves to one of disownment for selling or transferring slaves except to set them free. The statements by male Quakers during this period are eloquent in their determination to liberate both blacks and whites from the system. Wilmington minister David Ferris, for example, wrote in 1766 that "negro captives" must be delivered from their captivity and Quakers freed from slaveholding. Blacks, he said, were "fellow creatures." Although they left no ideological statements, women did participate actively in the Quaker manumission movement of the late eighteenth century. In 1806, Quaker minister Alice Jackson first proposed a boycott of the products of slave labor.

During the first three decades of the nineteenth century, Chester County males moved into associations to work together toward abolition of slavery. Some twenty joined the Pennsylvania Abolition Society, and others formed the Chester County Abolition Society in 1820 to provide education for black children, establish a fund for refugees, and oppose the kidnapping of blacks. Most Chester County activists advocated legal reform and gradual abolition, but by the early 1830s a group of Hicksite families in the county were forming antislavery societies in support of immediate national abolition. The slavery issue did not move women into public until after the Hicksite split of 1829. The newly organized antislavery associations petitioned both state and federal governments for abolition, but women confined their efforts to the support they could offer from their homes. They did not ask to mingle in the groups publicly nor did they create their own groups.

The 1830s changed all that. The movement to organize women into antislavery associations was not confined to Quakers or to Pennsylvania women, but in areas of Hicksite influence these women quickly assumed leadership in the growing movement. That leadership emerged from a broad-based mass movement that linked country and city together in Pennsylvania.

In that state, the growing black population was the most important influence in the movement. During the 1820s, freed and escaping blacks settled in Chester County in large numbers, especially in New Garden Township. Migration from Delaware was particularly heavy, with settlement across the state lines facilitated by the demand for black labor in the rural areas of Chester. By 1830, black communities existed in West Chester and Wilmington and in rural townships, but precariously. . . .

The formation of separate black churches was the first evidence of their presence. Few blacks followed Abigail Franks into the Quakers after the 1780s. From the comments of Quaker women ministers who conducted services for blacks in the eighteenth century, it is clear that the style of Quaker services—increasingly controlled and silent—was not popular with blacks who felt the spirit manifested itself in movement and sound. Most blacks first joined Methodist congregations, but as black communities grew in the late eighteenth century and expressed an interest in establishing separate black congregations, first Philadelphia and then Wilmington Methodist whites moved to spatially segregate the large minority of black parishioners in their churches. Segregation extended even to communion, the symbol of Christian unity. In protest, blacks withdrew and founded all-black congregations. These churches soon created their own powerful institutions, which developed a style of African Methodism suited to their spiritual and cultural needs. In 1814, the Wilmington congregation began a yearly meeting that came to be called "Big Quarterly" and drew both free and unfree blacks from Delaware and Pennsylvania into spiritual and cultural unity. In 1816, West Chester blacks formed a Bethel African Methodist Episcopal church there. By 1837, almost nine hundred black churches existed in Delaware and Pennsylvania to serve many thousands of members.

Wilmington had the most members and the most hearers. Philadelphia had fewer, but New Garden and New Brittain townships and New Castle, Delaware City, and Christiana had sizable churches. These had become centers of anticolonization thought by 1820, and although blacks did not join Quaker meetings, they saw them as allies in their struggle for freedom. At the same time, in Wilmington and West Chester, a group of secular black leaders also began to emerge. They worked with Quaker ministers in organizing politically to oppose slavery ideologically and to help refugees escape from captivity and settle in southeastern rural Pennsylvania.

Historian Larry Gara has argued that the emergence of this first black liberation movement was essential to the success of the underground railroad and rightly pointed out that only small groups of Quakers supported this movement. But Quaker assistance was not as unorganized as he indicates. In Chester County, the movement was especially well organized among rural Hicksites. The growing consciousness of blacks in northern Delaware and southern Pennsylvania of their need to oppose slavery, colonization, gradual emancipation, and the enforcement of the Fugitive Slave Act was a major element in the changing attitude of the more liberal Hicksite Quakers toward their role in that struggle. But the organized collaboration of that small group of rural Quakers in Pennsylvania and the large number of blacks they assisted in the struggle is well documented and real.

Quaker activity depended on and drew upon the collaboration of a specific network of women and men to aid refugees as well as to change the climate of opinion among the Hicksite Quakers and within their neighborhoods. Most of these people did not believe during the 1830s and 1840s that electoral politics could change the institution of slavery. They did, however, believe that they had a mission to collaborate with the black free population in assisting refugees and to lobby in nonelectoral ways to change the sentiment of their communities. Quaker women in rural Pennsylvania played a crucial role in both these activities between 1830 and 1850.

The underground railroad took form during the early 1830s, which were days of high mobility and immigration into Pennsylvania. By this time, blacks were asking for and obtaining help from Quakers in the effort to move refugees north in violation of federal fugitive slave law. After making contact with Thomas Garrett in Wilmington, refugees would go to Quaker farms across the border in Kennett, then up to northern Chester County, and on to Philadelphia or directly north to Canada. Garrett, who kept careful track of the numbers of assisted refugees, started fourteen hundred along their way before 1848. Esther Lewis kept no accounts, but her diary records taking "blacks to the railroad." Her tenant Maris Norris often carried them by wagon as he moved back and forth to the Philadelphia market with country produce.

One of the best-known escapees assisted by Hicksites was Rachel Harris. Harris had worked at Kimberton School before marrying and settling with her husband in West Chester. Her earlier owner swore out a complaint, and West Chester officials took her into custody and incarcerated her at a judge's house, plan-

ning to return her south. The alert woman managed by a stratagem (she probably got permission to go to the privy) to go out to the backyard of the place of her confinement at Church and Miner streets, where she scaled a seven-foot fence and made a dash for freedom down the back alleys to the home of a trusted woman Quaker friend. By evening, she was at Esther Lewis's home. Lewis wrote in indignation to her daughter: "She will stay here to day, and go further this evening. Poor wretch she is hunted like a partridge on a mountain. She has been a resident of W.C. five or six years, thought herself secure, and with her husband had acquired considerable property." Harris apparently left for Bucks County that evening dressed as a male and from there made her way to Canada.

The work of clothing in northern dress, feeding, and nursing refugees went on at the Lewis home for over two decades. Graceanna Lewis later recalled, "There was never a time when our house was not a shelter for the escaping slave."

The passage of a new, more stringent fugitive slave law in 1850, together with hardening resistance by the blacks in Chester and Lancaster counties led to open conflict. In 1851, when a group of blacks resisted reenslavement with arms in Christiana, just across the Chester County line in Lancaster, Quakers helped care for the dead and wounded southerners but also sent black resisters along the same network through Chester County and on to Canada. Black women who stayed behind later joined the men there. Thus the illegal underground activity in Chester County went on for twenty years.

At first, it seemed as though the legal antislavery movement of the 1830s would follow the same course as the abolitionist movement of the 1820s. Males would organize public groups, petition for changes in state and federal laws limiting the civil rights of blacks, and attempt to change the attitudes among their white neighbors and in the country at large. In fact, the second phase of the nineteenth-century movement began in just this way. Dr. Bartholomew Fussell, Esther Lewis's brother, was one of the early signers of the Declaration of Sentiments of the first Philadelphia Anti-Slavery Society formed in 1833, but neither Lucretia Mott nor her other female relatives who attended this meeting signed the document. Instead, the women formed their own Philadelphia Female Anti-Slavery Society. The same year, local Chester County organizations began to take form. The Clarkson Anti-Slavery Society in the southwest and then societies in Bradford, East Fallowfield, Uwchlan, Willistown, and other townships formed, and in November 1837 these organizations sent delegates to organize a Chester County Anti-Slavery Society.

From the beginning, these organizations encountered stiff resistance from the general public, so strong, in fact, that organizers found few allies even among the Hicksite Quakers. At a meeting in the Willistown schoolhouse, opponents threw a hornet's nest through an open window. At a meeting in 1837, a mob surrounded the courthouse where one group was holding a meeting and threw cayenne pepper into the stove and rotten eggs through the window. Local organizers brought suit against the leaders of the mob in an effort to halt the violence and to defend their right to assemble peaceably.

The Lewis daughters attended that 1837 meeting, but they were still a part of the small minority of women who believed it was acceptable to attend mixed meetings. The sentiment of those few had been fueled by the writings of Elizabeth Chandler, a Quaker born just across the border on a Centre, Delaware, farm. Chandler had not taken part in earlier organizing, but through her antislavery writings of 1825 to 1834, she helped change women's perceptions of what they could do publicly to bring an end to slavery. She had only written, but in those writings she urged women to action.

Blanch Hersch has called attention to the extraordinary role played by Chandler, a little-known writer who began publishing her anti-

slavery work at nineteen. She stressed in her romantic rhetoric that women had a responsibility to their black sisters in bondage. In her early poems like "The Kneeling Slave," she exhorted her readers to "Pity the negro, lady! her's is not,/like thine, a blessed and most happy lot/Thou, shelter'd 'neath a parent's tireless care,/ . . . But her—the outcast of a frowning fate." Later she wrote "Letters on Slavery: To the Ladies of Baltimore," where she urged women to unite to carry emancipation plans into effect. Chandler continually sounded the theme of responsibility, association, and immediate action. After Benjamin Lundy published her collected works in 1836, Esther Lewis and other backcountry Hicksites bought her books in lots and circulated them to neighbors and friends. Soon after publication of Chandler's works, stationery began to appear in Chester County, bearing the picture of a shackled black woman and the logo "Am I not a Woman and a Sister," the same that had appeared in Garrison's *Liberator* in 1832. Chester women did not take an active part in the first Philadelphia Female Anti-Slavery Society in 1833, but by 1837, they were distributing antislavery tracts, arranging for male advocates to speak in local churches, and campaigning to win the support of neighbors to the antislavery cause.

Some sense of the new political awareness of the young countrywomen is conveyed in letters of Rebecca Lewis, a daughter of Esther Lewis, who moved to Kennett to teach in late 1837. She attended the meeting broken up by the mob with cayenne pepper and rotten eggs and tried to shield the male speakers by sitting in the window, assuming the mob would not attack her. She was right; they did not. Rebecca had as her bedfellow in Kennett a good abolitionist woman who belonged to the Anti-Slavery Society and subscribed to Garrison's *Liberator*. Rebecca wrote to Esther, "It does me so much good to have *one* think just as I do." Later they were the only two women to attend a public meeting to discuss what could be done to counter mob action against antislavery advocates in other parts of the country. Quakers at Kennett seemed to be reluctant to take action after meeting, however. Some even refused to open the meetinghouse to abolitionist lecturers. "It makes me feel very unpleasant to be in such a place—and feel there are those around me who have not hearts to feel for the oppressed in our land," Rebecca wrote.

In the Lewis family, both mother and daughters worked to spread the ideology of abolitionism. While Rebecca taught antislavery attitudes in her classes and attended public meetings, Esther preached more quietly at home. She related stories of outrages to visiting friends, giving them copies of Theodore Weld's *Slavery As It Is.* She wrote after one such visitor had left that she had not continued the conversation too long so as not to pour "water too fast into a narrow necked bottle." Thus conversation went on at home and abroad.

Out of this grass-roots activity came the petition movement. This movement began early in 1836 with the publication by the Philadelphia Anti-Slavery Society of an address to the women of Pennsylvania, asking their support for a petition campaign. Eventually, thirty-three hundred women of Philadelphia and its vicinity signed petitions. Undoubtedly, they were circulated at the Philadelphia Yearly Meeting, for the name of a Quaker woman headed the first petition, and the signatures of Lucretia Mott and Sarah Grimké both appear on it. The women asked that slavery be abolished in the District of Columbia and the territories and that the slave trade between the states be ended.

Women took the movement back to their communities, where they carried petitions from neighbor to neighbor. After the May 1837 women's antislavery convention in New York City, the women's campaign increased in the hinterland. During that fall and winter, thousands more women signed their names to petitions, asking Congress to abolish the slave trade in the District of Columbia, among the states, and in territories. Philadelphia women climaxed the campaign with a long petition bearing almost five thousand names early in 1838.

This massive campaign was the first time in American history that women collaborated to exercise one of their political rights as citizens, the right to petition. The insecurity about their political status is evident from the variety of ways in which they addressed the petitions. The longest ones were printed memorials by "undersigned Female citizens of Pennsylvania, and parts adjacent." Smaller hand-written petitions showed important variations in how women described themselves. Some used the title "ladies" and the word "inhabitants" instead of "citizens." One Chester County petition proclaimed its signers "women." A Westmoreland petition had two neatly divided columns with "single ladies" in one, "married ladies" in the other. An Erie County petition with both men's and women's names had three sections, one male "voters," a second male "citizens," and a third "ladies." A petition from Allegheny bore a number of names in the same handwriting with Xs after them, apparently indicating that the women who were not able to write signed with a mark. The petition campaign did not penetrate far into the illiterate ranks of society, however, for almost all the women not only signed but signed with a firm clear hand. The row on row of names is eloquent testimony to a people newly awakened to their political rights.

Antislavery petitions reflect a geographical pattern of abolitionist sentiment in the hinterland. Out of thirty-three counties submitting petitions, Chester, Washington, and Allegheny counties sent in those with the largest number of women's names. Most petitions were gender segregated, with more males than females signing. When petitions were mixed, more males than females signed, and the names were usually segregated. On only a few were the names mixed together.

This outpouring of female political action was greeted in Congress by a move to restrict the newly used political right by refusing to consider the petitions. Historians are still debating other results of the campaign. Many of the petitions were destroyed, which makes the evidence uncertain, but as both Judy Wellman and Gerda Lerner point out, there seems to have been a drastic decline in petitioning activity at the national level by women after 1840. Petitions from Pennsylvania in 1854 protesting the repeal of the Missouri Compromise are almost entirely male.

What happened to the women? Lerner suggests that in Massachusetts the antislavery campaign shifted to a state civil rights campaign. Because Congress excluded abolition petitions from 1836 to 1844, it seemed more practical to petition the state. In Pennsylvania, violence intensified the crisis in the antislavery ranks, leading many of the more conservative urban Quaker women and men to abandon public activities. In May 1838, four thousand women and men met in the new Pennsylvania Hall to hold the second annual women's antislavery convention. A mob of ten thousand with another ten thousand spectators thronged the streets around the hall, burned it to the ground, and attacked a black church and an orphanage.

Chester County women attended that spectacular meeting. Later they circulated reports about the burning in periodicals and by word of mouth. They did not cease their activity but continued to circulate antislavery petitions through August 1838. By the following year, however, women had difficulty in finding a place to hold their annual conference in Philadelphia. A study of women's antislavery activity in Rochester, New York, by Nancy Hewitt points to a defection of evangelical women from the antislavery ranks in the 1840s because of dissension over women's role in the movement. In Pennsylvania, a similar crisis occurred. When Chester radicals wanted to hold an abolitionist meeting in West Chester in May 1842, not a single church or public building was open to them, so they resolved to hold the meeting in the street.

Although rural lectures continued, the em-phasis shifted to state legislation for civil rights. In 1848, for example, hundreds of Chester County women signed petitions asking for state enfranchisement of colored citizens. Only 290 women signed federal antislavery petitions that year, and long petitions from Delaware County carried only men's names. Chester County activists continued to gather signatures of both male and females and the radical Hicksites continued to sign. A memorial from the antislavery society of eastern Pennsylvania bore the names of Lucretia Mott, Mary Grew, and Sarah Pugh. But the petitions seem to have represented only a hard core of committed female activists. These were the women who were emerging as the first Pennsylvania feminists.

The progress of women within antislavery societies and the decline of those societies is reflected in the minutes of one group organized in northeast Chester County. Organized first in early 1837 as the Schuylkill Township Anti-Slavery Society, members changed the name to the Franklin Anti-Slavery Society in 1839, and then merged with the nearby Kimberton Society in 1840 to form the Lundy Union Auxiliary to the Chester County Anti-Slavery Society. It met in schoolhouses and in Friends, Presbyterian, and Baptist meetinghouses, for the last time in June 1847. Its fate seems to have been typical of many township antislavery groups formed by Hicksite Quakers in the late 1830s.

From the beginning, the new organization admitted women to membership. Although no total membership roster survives, one has the impression that women soon outnumbered men as members. Lists of new members show that almost twice as many women as men joined during the first years. Esther Lewis and her daughter Graceanna, as well as Abby Kimbert, belonged. A resolution signed by members in 1840 contained the names of seventeen females and thirteen males. Men held all the offices at first and represented the group at general county conventions. In April 1838, however, the group authorized all women members to attend the women's conference to be held in Philadelphia in May (the one that was burned out by the mob), and in August of that year one woman was elected secretary-treasurer and another to the executive committee. Committees usually comprised nearly equal numbers of men and women from that time on. In October, the members nominated seven women and eight men to represent them at a state antislavery conference, and in November, when the male officers did not show up, Sarah Coates chaired the meeting and signed the minutes as president. Members elected a new male president to the faltering leadership at the next meeting, but when the organization revived and changed its name early in 1840, members elected Benjamin Fussell, brother of Esther and a strong women's rights advocate, as president. Sarah Coates then became vice president. Women thereafter appear in minutes as active discussants, proposers of resolutions, and even as the majority of delegates to a Philadelphia conference in May 1840.

During its decade of existence, the society reflected the grass-roots antislavery movement and the issues that gave birth to the organization and eventually caused its death. The political philosophy, as recorded in its discussions, reflected a deep commitment to Enlightenment thought. In discussing antislavery issues, members asserted their belief in the right to petition as being an inalienable right that Congress could not take away, however much it wished to avoid the controversy engendered by antislavery petitions. Members also talked of the American Revolution being unfinished "until we pass through a blodless & peaceful revolution" and all people including blacks were free. They opposed the use of force to free blacks but also opposed any assistance in reenslaving refugees. The right of black people to assemble peaceably and participate in political groups became an issue when the head of the local natural history museum refused to allow the county antislavery group to meet there because it included representatives from black antislavery groups. The society opposed a state law penalizing racial intermarriage as increasing "a feeling which gives rise to injustice & an interference with individual freedom." The society upheld the right of persons regardless of sex or race to belong to the American Anti-Slavery Association and opposed both colonization and paid emancipation. It denounced paid emancipation in the British West Indies as a great burden imposed by the wealthy on the laborers of Britain. The group continued through its short life to oppose organizing a separate antislavery party and urged male voters to oppose candidates who did not support human rights. It gradually moved toward supporting for Congress men who promised not to "give votes for slaveholders." The last entry in July 1847 indicated there were few remaining members and recorded the feeling that it was "not thought necessary to organize." Politics at the polls had replaced associationalism. Women were now isolated from men.

Dissension within Chester County Quaker meetings on antislavery questions continued through the 1840s. Progressive Hicksites were forcibly ejected from the Kennett Meeting for their antislavery stance. A Quaker wrote in 1845 that one member in ejecting another who refused to be silenced "gave his pantaloons a kick just as he was going out the door." Supporters refused to attend further Kennett Meetings and in East Fallowfield another fifteen resigned. Mobs continued to harass those who persisted in their antislavery activity. Electoral politics seemed not to be a major issue because antislavery militants had little chance of election to office and, in fact, opposed the formation of a separate anti-slavery party. Throughout the 1840s, those candidates who did run as abolitionists received few votes in Chester County. The formation of the Liberty party brought little change. As late as 1852, an abolitionist candidate won only 338 of 1,100 Chester County votes. Fusion of abolitionists with a major party would not take place until the late 1850s. Then, of course, it would be part of the monumental shift that fueled the election of Abraham Lincoln to the presidency in 1860.

The most militant antislavery advocates of the Hicksite Quakers were not in a majority either in meeting or in their communities through the 1840s. Although their work continued, it was not popular. As the progressive Hicksites moved out ahead of public opinion on antislavery and as members quarreled within as to whether or not to form a political party, support dwindled. If political activity were to be the direction of the antislavery advocates, as it seemed increasingly to be, then women in their present disfranchised state would be unable to follow. They needed enfranchisement, but it could not be obtained on the basis of antislavery advocacy. Women needed a more popular cause.

Pennsylvania women did not fill the gap left by the declining antislavery movement with activity on behalf of the married women's property rights as did reformers in New York. The movement to obtain legislation guaranteeing property rights for women previously excluded from holding property after marriage flourished in New York during the 1840s. In Pennsylvania, however, this movement was not widespread, although Mott, Grew, and a few other women did gather signatures. Ten petitions, signed only with the names of men, were sent to Harrisburg in 1848, the year the legislature considered this most important act. The movement for married women's property rights did not involve women at the grass roots as had the antislavery movement. Women's political consciousness was not expanded by this legal battle but by the revival of an older concern—temperance.

After Elizabeth Levis published her temperance tract in 1761, public discussion in Chester County merged into a general concern over harvest intemperance. According to one oral tradition, the Gibbons family of Westtown refused one summer to furnish rum and found no workers. Neighbors then pitched in to help with the harvest and decided not to provide rum to their workers either. This incident apparently occurred sometime in the late eighteenth century. Marietta cites Joshua Evans as also refusing to keep his agricultural workers in rum and paying them higher wages instead. The reform measure of providing nonalcoholic beverages to farm workers was probably complete among Quakers by the early nineteenth century, before the public phase of the campaign opened. Tavern licenses were issued in Chester County without much concern and certainly without public complaint by women until the 1810s. Women's names begin to appear on petitions in 1818 against issuance of tavern licenses. The first temperance societies were formed in Pennsylvania soon after, but not until the 1830s and 1840s did Hicksite women and men begin to move their concerns about intemperance outside their society.

Males formed the first temperance societies. In 1832, for example, the Union Temperance Society in Chester County reported fifteen to twenty farmers had discontinued the use of ardent spirits in their agricultural concerns. Drinking, proclaimed the officers, led to murder, pauperism, and crime. By the 1830s, then, the workers were being transformed into a modern agricultural work force, expected to remain sober on the job. At least, the employers were establishing a policy of not providing liquor to their employees.

There was no highly visible public temperance activity by women before the 1840s, when the abolitionist and antislavery movements had moved women first to public protest and then to dissension over the public forms of that protest. In Rochester, New York, public advocacy of temperance reform by women emerged immediately following the withdrawal of evangelical women from the public antislavery campaign. These groups now saw intemperance as the primary source of all vice, so threatening to society that women must publicly organize against it. Between 1840 and 1850, hundreds of rural women in western New York took up the new cause, forming societies and joining in petition campaigns. Chester County women followed a similar pattern of involvement in temperance. In 1842, Esther Lewis noted that in her neighborhood 130 people signed pledges not to drink within a few weeks. Large meetings were held in the Vincent area the following year. By 1846, there was enough state-wide support for temperance to enable the legislature to pass a local option law. Temperance crusaders mobilized in hundreds of small rural towns throughout Pennsylvania to pass local ordinances prohibiting the sale of liquor. In Chester County, the law passed by a large plurality. Then, two years later, the state supreme court held the law unconstitutional, invalidating the local laws in operation under its provisions.

The antitemperance backlash in Pennsylvania was typical of trends in other states. In New York, temperance advocates like Susan B. Anthony were remarking about the "retrograde march of the temperance cause," as state legislatures began to respond to antitemperance pressure. The response of temperance women everywhere was a new militance and political activism. The emerging feminist leaders had found a grass-roots cause that touched large numbers of white women as slavery never had.

The outburst that followed resulted in hundreds of petitions inundating the Pennsylvania capital asking for state prohibition. Almost one hundred petitions from eighteen counties remain in the legislative files in Harrisburg. Chester, along with Allegheny, Washington, and Delaware counties, sent over two-thirds of the petitions, with women being the most active in Cambria and Chester counties. . . . Over 150 Chester County women signed. In addition, they organized a public meeting at Kennett in February 1848 under the leadership of Hicksite women and then carried a long memorial to the legislature at Harrisburg recording their support for prohibition, which Sidney Pierce read before a legislative committee.

In the memorial, the women wrote consciously as women "debarred from voting in public matters," as citizens who bore the consequences of the system that licensed the sale of liquor. While couched in terms of the "sanctuary of our homes," and men made "maniacs and monsters," the argument also cited practical reasons, such as secular law, natural law, and political rights. Intemperance was expensive, and it caused taxation without protection, it abolished the natural right of self-defense, and it violated the political rights of the majority who voted for prohibition. "Had our sex been permitted to vote on this particular question," the memorial concluded, "the majority would have been greatly increased." The address was sent to Harrisburg proudly as an address from a "Meeting of Women" in the name of womanhood.

In the months following, Hannah M. Darlington, Sidney Pierce, and Ann Preston went from place to place in Chester County spreading the message. Hannah's husband Chandler drove them around. Hannah later recalled in a letter to Elizabeth Cady Stanton, "We addressed many large audiences, some in the day-time and some in the evening; scattered appeals and tracts, and collected names to petitions asking for a law against licensing liquor-stands."

In December 1848, the women held an even larger temperance convention at Marlborough Friends Meeting Hall, this time addressing the men and women of Chester County. At this meeting the ideology of sisterhood became more pronounced, for the address to women began "Dear Sisters." The supreme court had held the local option law unconstitutional and the women began by asking "What must now be done?" The answer to this rhetorical question was to call women to the cause. "By meeting together and taking counsel one with another," the call urged, "we will become more alive to our duty in relation to this momentous subject." Here was a clear call to one gender with a separate interest: "If *men* will remain comparatively supine we must the more energetically sound the alarm, and point them to the danger." Although the women also made a call to the men, to "fathers and brothers," they saw a special role for women.

Again the women appointed committees to obtain petitions in their respective neighborhoods and to call meetings to read the addresses. Women met twice more, in February and December of 1849. These meetings provide a vital link to the later women's rights convention, for the women active in the later convention were also active in the temperance meetings, speaking, organizing, and collecting petitions.

Much has been written of temperance as a response to immigration, one aimed at social control. Immigration of the Irish into southeastern Pennsylvania may have accelerated support, but Irish working-class immigration into that area was not new, and had been fairly constant during the early century. It is possible that middle-class men became more active during the early nineteenth century with the goal of social control. In the 1854 Pennsylvania plebiscite, Philadelphia and Delaware County males voted heavily for prohibition. But so too did males in western rural areas, the very areas that had staged the Whiskey Rebellion in the 1790s in support of free distilling.

Rural women might have been responding to increased migration, but their public pronouncements and private letters do not single out Irish immigrants. Rather they explain their concern in the gender-specific terms of physical abuse of women and the disruption of their lives by male intemperance. Battering of women seems to occur most frequently where women are isolated from relatives and social institutions, and rural women for centuries had to deal with physical abuse as best they could, often without the support of local officials. Esther Lewis referred in her diary several times to husbands beating wives. In an era when the physical abuse of women was seldom discussed publicly, temperance rhetoric may have been a proxy for that discussion. At any rate, the consciousness of prohibition as a

women's issue was an important link in the chain of reform moving women from private to public politics in the 1840s.

Consciousness of women's rights had, however, formed part of the motivation for women's involvement in both the antislavery and the temperance drives. That consciousness began to surface in the Lewis correspondence in 1837. When a lyceum lecturer advertised in December of that year that women and boys would be admitted for half price, a group of young women at Kennett protested. The lecturer then reduced the price for men so that it would be equal for all. Private jokes went back and forth in the Lewis correspondence that indicate family conversations on the subject. Women's rights, joked Edwin, the husband of Rebecca Lewis Fussell, "are just what is Convenient to *men* you know!" To which Rebecca added: "If *you* do *know* that women's rights are just what is convenient to men *I* have yet to learn it." Graceanna Lewis reported with interest in 1838 an address by Abby Kelly in New England. After ministers had interrupted her defense of women's rights, wrote Graceanna, Kelly had finished with a "short but pithy and pertinent speech."

Yet such private consciousness and support did not result in public meetings such as those held earlier by women for antislavery and temperance. The 1850 Worcester Convention in Massachusetts became a link joining Chester County organizers, and especially Hannah Darlington, to the emerging women's rights movement. She signed her name along with Lucretia Mott and twenty-eight other men and women from Pennsylvania for the call to the first national convention. She also attended the conference along with representatives from Chester and Delaware counties. Jacob Painter was one of the seven delegates from Delaware County. It was through the network of people who had attended the conference that Hannah heard Jacob might be interested in working on a conference and wrote of the need for "true earnest workers."

In her first letter, Darlington sketched her idea for a women's rights conference for the eastern part of Pennsylvania, to be held for two days in late May or early June in the new Horticultural Hall in West Chester. She planned that a "few certain friends" would issue a call; a committee of correspondence would write inviting people to attend and would select officers and "drill" them to act with "propriety and grace." She stressed the solidarity of the sexes to elevate both men and women: "they must rise and fall together." It was clear from this first letter that Darlington had already contacted a number of women.

In the next two weeks, Darlington contacted many more about the possibility of the conference. "Everybody says *have one*," she reported to Painter. The Kennett supporters and Lucretia Mott soon approved the time and place. All this preliminary organizing was done, as Darlington later wrote, "helter skelter, almost anytime & almost anyhow." As to rights to be discussed, Darlington listed legal, educational, and industrial rights. Social relations, she concluded, "come more under the *spheres* and are more matters of compromise than positive rights." She wanted to keep women's rights distinct from antislavery, to keep it "womanly," but strong of purpose and upon the "leveling up principle."

The call, issued in April, reflected the influence of Darlington. Addressed to the "friends of Justice and Equal Rights," forty-seven people signed the call to discuss the position of woman in society, her natural rights, and her relative duties. As Darlington had advised, the call stressed the need to discuss ways to remove legal, educational, and vocational disabilities and proclaimed: "The Elevation of Woman is the Elevation of the Human Race." It did not mention the spheres.

Both city papers reported the resolutions of the conference, including the slogan, "Equality before the law, without distinction of sex." They reprinted resolutions proclaiming that natural rights entitled women to an equal part with men in political institutions, that participa-

tion in government did not involve "sacrifice of refinement or sensibility of true womanhood," and that women should be represented in government. One West Chester paper attacked the men who attended the conference as "old women in pantaloons" and the women as old maids, amazons, and infidels. Still there was ample publicity for women who did not attend to learn about what had been advocated.

The conference passed fourteen resolutions. Of these, a number were concerned with arguing what equal rights would *not* do—they would not sacrifice "the refinement and sensibilities of true womanhood," they did not reflect "conflicting interests between the sexes," they would not obliterate "distinctive traits of female character" but would make more apparent the "sensibilities and graces which are considered its peculiar charm," and they would leave the question of spheres, "the differences in the male and female contributions to take care of themselves." Two more resolutions simply expressed satisfaction at recent changes—that the exposure of the "wrongs of women" was being met by a kind spirit and redress of these wrongs, that the passage of the married women's property rights bill was evidence of the equity of their demands.

Seven other resolutions asserted more positive demands. The first was that anyone claiming to represent humanity, civilization, or progress must subscribe to equality before the law, that women must be allowed to study the physical, mental, and moral sciences with men, that tax-supported colleges and universities should not exclude women, that women should inherit the property of the husband exactly as he did hers (in effect, a call for community property), that women should also have custody of children if they were qualified, and that women should be paid equally for equal work. The last two resolutions called for direct action on two specific demands—a political campaign to change the state laws relating to voting and inheritance rights, and an educational campaign to inform women of the rights and privileges accorded to women in other states. Despite the defensive and conciliatory tone of the resolutions, they covered four major areas—work, education, politics, and family law—and called for greater freedom for women in all aspects of their lives. The resolutions would serve as an agenda for over seventy years.

Of the letters read at the convention and the speeches delivered, it is noticeable that none mentioned antislavery. Although the *History of Woman Suffrage* later argued that antislavery activities "were the imitative steps to organized public action and the Woman Suffrage Movement" and we have seen the importance of the earlier movements, the conference of 1851 did not mention this reform. A letter from William H. and Mary Johnson, read at the convention, referred explicitly only to "those benevolent associations particularly for promoting temperance, in which the females of Chester County have borne such a conspicuous and effective part." This was particularly true, they reiterated, when male associations in the state had languished.

One theme throughout the years of antislavery and temperance movements and the emergence of the women's rights movement had been the increasing emphasis on egalitarianism. This was evidenced in appeals to "sisters," to sibling equality rather than authority. The sibling tie was a central image in each movement and provided a persistent theme in the 1830s and 1840s: "Am I not a woman and a sister," was an antislavery motto, "sisters" were called to the temperance standard, and "sisters" were not to be dependent on "brothers" but to achieve an equal status with them through the women's rights movement. With this theme came a rejection of hierarchical and patriarchal authority. Those who espoused this egalitarianism were a small minority, but they left the practice, and some theory, of an alternative to a patriarchal basis for society.

The theme crops up repeatedly in letters and statements. If women were vague on womanhood, female character, sexual differences, and the desire for harmony, they spoke clearly

on their denunciation of the doctrine of inequality. In a sense, the final speeches and resolutions reflected that careful balance that Darlington was determined to retain.

The resolutions upheld the possibility of "true womanhood" surviving women's entrance into politics. They said if women's province was to soothe passions no better place existed for that than in politics, that her "true sphere" was the one her nature and capability allowed her to fill and not "that appointed by man and bonded by his ideas of property"; and they dismissed the possibility of conflicting interests between the sexes. But they also offered special support for women in medical organizations and schools, and argued that property of "joint industry and economy" should go to the wife at a husband's death. With women's cooperation, predicted one speaker, women would be free in less than ten years.

This overoptimism was consistent with the strong belief in men's and women's natural rights, but resolutions were worded carefully to deal with the commonly held ideology of spheres, true womanhood, soothing passions, and cooperation of the sexes. Speeches emphasized the needs both for married women's rights and single women's opportunities. The claims were moderate and yet, for their time, politically progressive. They were a fitting culmination of the reform movement of the radical Hicksite Quakers.

Knowing what these reformers did and said, however, does not explain their motivation. Who were these people and why did they participate in a publicly unpopular reform, becoming a minority that advocated changes that would take so long to achieve in society? The names of seventy men and women appear in the documents of the women's rights conferences of 1851 and 1852, and some biographical material exists for over two-thirds of them. Detailed census data is available for thirty of the rural participants who lived in twenty-four households, and these necessarily will be the sample for analyzing these politically active females. A sample of Kennett Township, West Chester, and Kennett farm households were compared with the twenty-four households to see if the activists were representative of the Kennett community and of the rural town of West Chester. How did they compare in ethnic, economic, occupational, and family composition?

The most important difference to emerge is ethnic. The women's rights reformers reflected the ethnic monoculture of the Kennett farms rather than the growing number of black and Irish households in the township of Kennett and in West Chester. The leaders could have invited a black woman to speak—Sojourner Truth spoke when the progressive Quakers convened later that year at nearby Longwood. Mary Shadd might have welcomed an opportunity to speak in her hometown. Even the middle-class Forten sisters who attended a later Philadelphia conference were apparently not present. Black women as well as Irish may have attended the conference—no accounts have yet been found that describe the audience—but they were not officially represented. Nor did Darlington ever mention concern about ethnic or cultural representation. In fact, her desire to separate women's rights firmly from antislavery may have led her consciously to avoid asking women of color to participate. . . .

The figures indicate that the households from which the leaders came were relatively wealthy. Their wealth was far higher than the mean for West Chester, Kennett Township, or Kennett Farms. Although individual households, like the Darlingtons, may have had modest wealth, overall they had double that of either township or West Chester households. Over 50 percent had female live-in help compared to only about a third for township and town. These were not families, then, who were losing out in their communities. A few professionals in West Chester—lawyers, one doctor, and a school administrator—had impressively large incomes. Thus one cannot argue, as some historians of reform have argued, that

activism was the result of a general "status deprivation" of these families. It is possible that accumulation of wealth in Pennsylvania or other industrializing areas was bothering these reformers, for these rural households were enlightened enough to be concerned about economic differences.

It is more likely, however, that status deprivation of females within these families was a factor in their activism. The families exercising leadership had growing numbers of aging daughters in their households. The difference in mean age of the children in women's rights households and other households is large. These daughters and their families may have been apprehensive about the prospect of being unable to provide an income through marriage alliances. They would be concerned, then, with achieving flexible educational, vocational, and legal rights. Without an expansion of their options, the daughters could have suffered status deprivation in relation to their own cultural background—being dependent and a financial drain on their families.

The West Chester women's rights conference did not concern itself with the problems of women workers, as did the Rochester conference of 1849, which reported on the low wages of sewing women. A large percentage of women in Chester County were working outside their own homes, primarily as household workers, some as sewing women or proprietors of small shops in West Chester. Half of the reformers had at least one of these women working in their own homes. But the reformers seemed more concerned about their own work than that of others. Being a lady or a domestic, not a mill girl, were the main alternatives for these middle-class women. The radical Quakers rejected the role of the lady, but they also rejected the role of the domestic. They were not attractive alternatives for young middle-class rural women who chose not to marry. For that reason, Ann Preston, who delivered one of the main addresses, symbolized the possibilities for women in the profession of medicine.

Preston was exactly the type of young rural woman these reformers were thinking about when they spoke of educational, vocational, and political disabilities suffered by women. She came from a large Quaker Hicksite farm family of comfortable means. She had taught school and participated in the antislavery and temperance movements, but she could find no way to provide herself with a suitable income. There was no question that her brother would take over the family farm and provide for her aging parents, who were in their sixties. Other brothers had already left home to fend for themselves, and an only sister had died ten years earlier. At thirty-nine Ann Preston had just been able to embark on a professional career after the establishment of the Pennsylvania Medical School for Women. In a letter from Philadelphia shortly after the conference, she wrote that she did not want to depend on her brother.

Of course, other women faced the same problems quietly, saw no violation of rights, did become dependent upon their brothers, and withdrew within their spheres. Without the progressive Hicksite strain of reform, nourished by the late Enlightenment as well as selected romantic ideas reinforcing an older egalitarian spiritual base, these women could not have become the first feminists to challenge their destiny as dependent women in a proscribed sphere. The loosening of the bonds did not come easily, despite family support, economic security, and an egalitarian heritage.

What the women did was neither accepted nor accommodated outside their narrow reform circles. Rioters had burned down the Philadelphia hall where women had congregated to discuss antislavery. Philadelphia medical students had rioted when their sphere was threatened by women who wished to study medicine. Although the reformers came from a small unrepresentative group, they could have survived only within families and communities that nurtured their revolt.

That revolt and the extent to which it loosened the bonds of rural women should not be overemphasized. They did not challenge many roles. As Darlington had said, they considered social relations not a right but subject to compromise. They were concerned primarily with public institutions, and even there they chose their battleground carefully.

The issues of race, working women's conditions, and domestic relations were all subjects that would have to be addressed by later women's rights reformers. That they were omitted from the first struggle may have delayed the ability of white middle-class feminists to deal effectively with these issues in the next hundred years. Yet for all people struggling to loosen society's bonds, there was much to learn from these early feminists. The slow progress over the next hundred years was surely the responsibility of those who accepted their bonds rather than continuing the liberation process that had begun.

# 17

## "A MAID OF ALL TRAIDS": WOMEN IN THE WEST

### JULIE ROY JEFFREY

Between 1840 and the Civil War tens of thousands of families left the familiar surroundings of their homes, kin, and friends to travel into the trans-Mississippi West. For most, the midwestern prairies, the Rocky Mountains, and the valleys of the Pacific coast held out the promise of a new beginning, a second chance for winning the independence and moderate prosperity that was waning in the industrializing East. Across the country, men, women, and children loaded seed, tools, and a few personal belongings onto the "prairie schooners" that bumped and lurched across the Overland Trail. The journey lasted three to six months, and in the process men's and women's traditional roles blurred as the labor of the entire family became the only hedge against failure. Wind, rain, disease, and boredom were the constant companions of these early pioneers as they struggled to reach their destinations.

Every pioneer felt the burden of this transmigration, but perhaps none as fully as the frontier woman. Separated, often for life, from the female friends and relatives that were the center of her social and emotional world and forced by circumstance to engage in "unwomanly" work along the trail, the pioneer woman could only hope that the family dream of western settlement would bear fruit. In this essay, Julie Roy Jeffrey explores the life of westering women once they reached their destinations and set about the task of reconstructing homes and communities. As she reveals, the rigors of migration were only the beginning of women's travail.

"My heart arose in gratitude to God that we were spared to reach this land," Esther Hanna wrote in her journal a few days before ending it in September 1852. "I can scarcely realize that we are so near our contemplated home." For women like Esther Hanna, the journey's conclusion was a joyous event. Misgivings about the frontier evaporated as families began their new lives. For others, however, the period of adjustment to new surroundings was trying. Physical exhaustion from the trip's rigors, a reduced emotional resilience, and meager family resources contributed to a sense of desolation in the days after arrival. Clothes were tattered. The trail was littered with treasured possessions, discarded as animals had weakened, then died. No matter how carefully the trip had been planned, few arrived with much cash, and even the lucky ones found their reserves could not replace what they had thrown away in desperation. "There were no luxuries to be had even if we had ever so much money," one early pioneer recalled. But just as important as the physical and financial condition in which so many emigrants found themselves at the trip's end was the shock of confronting the reality of the frontier. Many women had survived the trip by fantasizing about their future "happy home in a happy land." When they reached their destination, they saw not a home but wilderness. "After the way we had suffered and struggled to get here," a Missouri woman wrote to her mother, "I had all I could do to keep from asking George to turn around and bring me back home." As dreams collapsed, some gave in to feelings. One band of women arriving in Puget Sound in November 1851 spent a long dreary afternoon helping their husbands carry possessions up the beach beyond the reach of the tide. Then, overwhelmed by their situation, one of the husbands later recalled, "the women sat down and cried." It was not long, of course, before some sort of shelter, however rudimentary, was constructed. But a permanent "home" often proved elusive. Journals, letters, and census data suggest several moves

during the early years of settlement, as families sought the right claim or the right job.

Women settling the farming frontier, far from the Pacific coast, also found adjustment difficult in the early months and years after their trip. Although they were not so fatigued after a journey ending in Nebraska or western Iowa, their situation initially seemed bleak. Prairies and plains struck many women as depressing. "As long as I live I'll never see such a lonely country," was how one woman described her reaction to the Texas plains, while a Nebraska pioneer reflected, "These unbounded prairies have such an air of desolation—and the stillness is very oppressive." Like settlers of Oregon and Washington, emigrants pushing the frontier west from the Mississippi arrived at their destination with little capital to soften the burdens of homesteading. Like their counterparts in the Far West, emigrants found their dreams of a permanent home illusory.

The early years of settlement on the farming frontier, of course, differed according to time, location, and settlers' backgrounds. The mid-century plains and prairie frontier offered emigrants coming from Europe and the Mississippi Valley not only fertile soil and sufficient rainfall, for example (unlike the arid plains, sweeping from the Dakotas south to Texas, settled later in the century, where the rainfall could not support traditional farming), but also special problems stemming from the region's geography and climate. Although emigrants could use familiar agricultural methods, the weather, with its extremes of temperature and its high winds, could mean low yields, crop failure, and the destruction of valuable livestock. Timber for building and fuel, so abundant in the Far West, was rare on the prairies and plains, and its scarcity compounded problems of settlement. Hunger, poverty, and ruin hovered closer to the pioneers of this frontier than those of the Far West. There, however, though subsistence was assured, poor transportation and inadequate markets meant a continuing shortage of capital, which affected the quality of life.

Although different parts of the frontier challenged settlers in different ways, there were enough common threads to the pioneering experience to make it possible to generalize about pioneer life and women's response to it. During the initial period of settlement, women on all frontiers shared crude living conditions and similar domestic situations. Because of the shortage of capital and labor, early farming efforts were on a small diversified scale and demanded the participation of the entire family, especially women. The first years of settlement, therefore, continued the trail experience by demanding that women depart from cultural and social behavioral norms for the sake of their family's survival. The sense of dislocation some felt initially stemmed from this enforced departure from familiar behavior. The early years of settlement, in fact, would test many facets of the cultural framework which women had brought west with them. The test suggested how firmly women clung to the framework and the meaning which it could provide for their lives even on the frontier.

As one Oregon woman noted, the frontier was "a hard country for woman." It was hard, she knew, because "things . . . are rather in a primitive state." Crude housing was part of this "primitive state," which all women shared no matter where they settled on the farming frontier. A dugout or sod house on the plains, a small shack, cabin, or hole in the Far West served for shelter. Other more exotic alternatives appeared. "During father's trip he had seen two stumps standing a few feet apart," recollected one pioneer later, "and he laughingly told mother she might live in them . . . She insisted that father clean them out, put on a roof, and we moved in, a family of eight persons." Whatever the arrangements, home was often open to the weather, uncomfortable, crowded, with little privacy. Families lived for months in these dwellings, sometimes for years, as money and time went into other improvements. Early homes challenged domestic

ideals and the concept of gentility, and women were sometimes discouraged. "What a contrast to the wheels of time unrolle to our view, compared with our home in Ill. one year since," sighed one.

The preparation of food, an important domestic duty, was arduous without the familiar ingredients and utensils. An Oregon pioneer of the 1840s described setting up housekeeping with her new husband with only one stew kettle (for making coffee, bread, and cooking meat) and three knives. Since the stoves with which many pioneer families had set out over the Oregon Trail had been too heavy to survive the trip, this woman, like so many others, did all her cooking over an open fire. No wonder some pioneers looked back to this initial period with distaste. "I assure you," Maria Cutting wrote, "we had many privations and Hardships to endure and O such makeouts sometimes having to use shorts instead of flour, sometimes sugar sometimes none."

Yet others took great pride in preparing tasty food despite all the obstacles; women's response to difficult living conditions often seemed related to their early attitude to emigration. As one Iowa pioneer explained, "I came here willingly believing it to be for the best and am determined to try with the assistance of Providence to make the best out of it." In any case, they knew they had no options beyond making "the best out of it." There was no returning home. As Margaret Wilson told her mother in a letter written in 1850, "You will wonder how I can bear it, but it is unavoidable, and I have to submit without complaining."

No matter how women reacted to primitive living conditions, few cared for their primitive neighbors. Oregon Trail diaries revealed that many women feared Indians, especially males. On the trail, however, the wagon train offered fainthearted women the protection of numbers; in any case, offensive natives were always left behind as the company moved on. Now settled, however temporarily, women on many parts of the frontier found themselves living in the midst of Indians.

They didn't like it. "I suppose Mother had

more trouble there [in Oregon], really, than she had on the road; because we were surrounded by Indians," one daughter explained. Even friendly Indians made women anxious by their way of silently appearing, wanting food or just a look at the white woman and her children. Even though their accounts show them dealing directly and even courageously with Indian visits, women felt vulnerable in these meetings. Many were persuaded that the Indian men were particularly aggressive when their husbands were away. Whether this was true or merely reflected the women's view of themselves as the weaker sex is unclear. Certainly, their actions showed few signs of weakness. Sarah Sutton was typical. When Indians came for food when her men were absent, she dealt with them by jerking "a tent pole and laying it about her with such good effect that she had her squat of Indians going on a double quick in a very short time." At other times, she wielded a pistol rather than the tent pole. Still, the incidents were unpleasant, and unnerving.

Although women sometimes trained Indians as servants, they described them at best as shiftless and curious, at worst as treacherous, savage, and cruel. Only rarely could white women reach across the barriers of race and culture to establish sympathetic contact with Indian women. Most accepted cultural generalizations and were convinced that "the native inhabitants must soon submit to 'manifest destiny.'" Pioneer women were unsympathetic to the clash between cultures and unaware that white behavior often provoked the Indian behavior they disliked so much. In one sense they were right to be suspicious and fearful, since the settlement period was punctuated by Indian violence and hostility. The Indian Wars in Oregon from 1855 to 1858 were only one example that the so-called inferior race could strike out in a deadly fashion against white settlers and their families. But women's negative attitudes increased their sense of vulnerability and isolation. "We had no neighbors nor company save a straggling land hunter, or the native Indians," recalled Susannah Willeford, an Iowa pioneer. "The latter were seldom if

ever welcome visitors as far as I was concerned."

Isolation from white women also shaped most women's responses to the earliest period of settlement. Although women had their own domestic circles, they missed female friends. A husband might be no substitute for a close friend or relative of their own sex, as Nellie Wetherbee discovered. "I have been very blue," she wrote in her journal, "for I cannot make a friend like mother out of Henry . . . It's a bore—and Mother is so different and home is so different . . . Oh dear dear." The difficulty of finding female friends stemmed, of course, from the scattered pattern of settlement (the Oregon Donation Law, for example, provided each family with 640 acres, thus ensuring isolation) and also from the fact that there were fewer women than men on the frontier in the first years. As Mollie Sanford noted in her diary, "I do try to feel that it is all for the best to be away off here [Nebraska]. I can see and feel that it chafes mother's spirit. . . . If the country would only fill up . . . We do not see a woman at all. All men, single or bachelors, and one gets tired of them."

But the sexual imbalance was not so great as many popular accounts have suggested. The 1850 male-female ratio for the country as a whole was 106 men to every 100 women, while in rural Oregon that same year, there were approximately 137 men to every 100 women. By 1860, however, the sex ratio in frontier counties approximated that in the East. Various studies of frontier settlements show, then, that the frontier was not overwhelmingly masculine. But given the role female friendship played in women's lives and the difficulties which made it hard for women to meet, the loneliness they felt was understandable.

Real isolation was, however, a short-lived phenomenon, usually lasting only two or three years on most parts of the frontier. Some of the men turning up in the census or in Mollie Sanford's diary were preparing homesteads for their families. The immigration pattern of Whidbey Island, near the coast of Washington, suggests the rapidity of the settlement process.

Attracted by its fertile prairie land and pleasant climate, Isaac Ebey, an 1848 pioneer from Missouri, selected the island for his future home. By the time his wife, Rebecca, and their two sons joined him three years later, there were several other families on Whidbey and more coming. In June 1852 Rebecca was writing, "We have plenty of company  four families of us here  12 children." Although her guests eventually moved to their own claims on the island, Rebecca's diary catalogues numerous visitors, both new emigrants and old. After Rebecca died in 1853, emigrants to Whidbey included the Ebey cousins, her husband's father, mother, brother, his two sisters, some children, and a single man who eventually married her daughter the next year. Nor was the Ebey clan the only one on the island, for other families as well as some unmarried settlers also migrated to Whidbey during these few years. Loneliness may have been a very real part of the frontier experience for women, but total isolation for an extended length of time usually was not.

If women shared common physical and social conditions on the farming frontier, they also shared a similar family environment. The stereotypical view of the frontier family suggests a familial experience which modern women would find oppressive and burdensome. Most historians have casually asserted that women on the frontier routinely married at fourteen or fifteen and that they then proceeded to bear children with monotonous regularity. Families with ten or twelve children are pictured as the norm. With such heavy maternal responsibilities, to say nothing of the arduous nature of pioneer life itself, pioneer women not only worked harder than women in the East, this interpretation implies, but differed from them culturally. Census data shows that throughout the nineteenth century the size of American families was shrinking, not because of reduced mortality rates, but because women bore fewer and fewer children. In 1800 white women who reached menopause

bore on the average 7.04 children. Forty years later the figure had fallen to 6.14, reaching 4.24 in 1880. A dramatic difference in family size on the frontier would imply a "frontier" set of values.

Unfortunately, there are not enough studies of the frontier family in the trans-Mississippi West to allow a definitive description of frontier family structure, but the stereotype appears to be misleading. Western women's fertility patterns were not very different from those of other women in the country. One study based on the 1860 census returns ranging from New Hampshire to Kansas, for example, revealed lower fertility rates in frontier townships than those in the more populated areas directly to the east. Young children who were unable to contribute to the frontier family's welfare in those crucial early years were not an asset but a burden.

"Will I be a happy beloved wife, with a good husband, happy home, and small family," Mollie Sanford, a Nebraska pioneer, had mused, "or an abused, deserted one, with eight or nine small children crying for their daily bread?" Scattered studies of different parts of the trans-Mississippi frontier suggest that Mollie Sanford's chances for marital satisfaction in the terms in which she posed them were good. The typical frontier household, though somewhat larger than those in the East, was made up of parents and a few children living together. An analysis of Iowa frontier families showed families with one to four children living at home, while a detailed study of a Texas pioneer area with 896 families turned up only twelve families with ten or more children. The "average" family household in this part of Texas contained four children, but fully *half* of the families had three children or fewer living at home. The 1850 manuscript for Oregon yielded similar results. Since none of these figures take into account children who were grown and on their own or include infant mortality figures, they do not disclose how many children women actually conceived and bore, but the figures suggest that pioneer households in the West were comparable in size with the American experience elsewhere.

Women on the frontier were, then, most often wives and mothers. Their small households suggest they believed in limiting the size of their families. Certainly contraceptive information was available. Newspapers between 1820 and 1873 advertised both contraceptives and abortifacients, while pamphlets, birth-control circulars, popular health books, and books also told women how to control conception. Contraceptive practices were long described in folklore. Although personal testimony concerning the use of birth control on the frontier is rare, a few references show that frontier women knew of and practiced birth control. An Oregon midwife, for example, described an abortion, a method of family limitation which increased during the nineteenth century. "I went to the woman's place several times," she recollected. "She had staged several sham battles. You see, they didn't do what was right, and had tried, too soon, to have the baby and get rid of it. When it was far along, it was a killing job. Hot salt water was what they used, and it sometimes passed. After the woman herself would be about to die as well as the baby, they'd call for help."

If pioneer women were not the fecund breeders of popular history, neither they nor their husbands were the excessively youthful group so often described. Most studies of pioneer families show husbands typically in their thirties or forties, with wives several years younger. Nor did women marry routinely in their early teens. One pioneer woman recalled a proposal when she was thirteen. "I said, *no!* Why I'm only a *child.* I have never given marriage a thought yet." Studies of age of marriage in Oregon and Texas turn up little evidence of early unions. Information which exists on the frontier family seems to suggest that married women on the farming frontier did not have the burdens of youthful inexperience or swarms of young children added to the diffi-

culties of creating a new life in the wilderness.

These relatively small families, of course, provided the context for women's emotional and work lives during the initial years of settlement, when the interaction with outsiders was limited. Many pioneer women resolved consciously, as did Susannah Willeford, "to devote my time, life and energies to the welfare and interest of my family." This was no small resolve; women's work for and with their families was extraordinary. Since few pioneers arrived with substantial financial or material resources, and since hired help was unavailable, every family was thrown back on itself in the struggle to get started. All cooperated in the work of establishing the farm, but because women often were the only adults besides their husbands, they had to contribute more than a woman's share.

"I am maid of all traids," one woman remarked in her diary in 1853. As had proved true on the trail, necessity blurred the relationship between men's and women's work. The tasks seemed endless. Women did heavy outside "male" chores, helping to dig cellars, to build cabins, "as there was no other man . . . [Father] could get to help him," helped with the plowing and planting, again since "there were neither man nor boy that we could hire in the county." Then there were the conventional female jobs, sewing, "sweeping dusting churning ironing baking bread and pies dishwashing &c." And always there was laundry, an arduous undertaking which many women seem to have particularly disliked. "Dreaded washing day," wrote one, and added, "And as Mr. Taylor is not well he brings me water I finish by noon then scrub in the after noon feeling quite tired." Women cared for vegetable gardens, cows, chickens. As farmers, cooks, seamstresses, and laundresses, their labor contributed to the family's well-being and survival in almost every way.

But women did more than these tasks, since they shared "a strong desire to provide the necessary comforts for our family." In many cases they seem to have become small-scale economic entrepreneurs. One resourceful but not unusual woman, for example, started out by cutting up wagon covers to make shirts to sell to the Indians. Then she moved on to making gloves for soldiers stationed nearby, a task with which her husband helped. "So, before spring, they were turning out very handsome gloves, also buckskin money belts." Later, as emigrants began to come into Oregon, she baked bread, pies, and cookies to sell. Female enterprises changed as opportunities changed, though the sale of butter and eggs seems to have provided a fairly steady source of income for women. These funds were especially important because of the chronic shortage of capital on the frontier. And as one observer pointed out, women often supported their families while their husbands learned how to farm. Occasionally women viewed their earnings as their own, but most often they were not a source of economic independence but rather a means of supplementing the family's income.

"Female hired help was not to be obtained," one man pointed out when reflecting on his pioneer years. "I assisted my wife all I could— probably did as much housework as she did." Continuing the pattern emerging on the journey west, men performed some female chores. Letters and journals show them helping with the washing, the cooking, and caring for children. But as on the trip west, men usually assumed these responsibilities only occasionally, when their wives were tired, ill, or in childbirth.

Much of the heavy labor women did initially could also be categorized as helping husbands out in the absence of male assistance. But wives more routinely assumed male responsibilities than their husbands took on female responsibilities. When men left their homesteads, as they did when gold was discovered, or when they went off to fight Indians, do political business, or herd cattle, they were often gone for months at a time. The women who stayed behind were left in charge. "As we live on a farm," wrote one, "whatever is done I have got to attend to and so I have a great deal of out doors work." As she listed her chores, they included caring for hogs, hens, milking the cows, and running the dairy. A hired man worked on the grain. On the plains, men often hired themselves out for cash, leaving their wives to oversee the crops and animals for weeks.

As their economic enterprises, their letters, and journals indicate, women were both practically and emotionally involved in economic matters as they sought to improve the family economic status. Even Kate Blaine, a Methodist minister's wife from the Northeast, wished she could be making some money. "If I were not the preacher's wife I should take in [washing] . . . It is very profitable," she confessed. Despite the claim of nineteenth-century culture that there was a gap between woman's world, the home, and man's world, the workplace, the two coincided on the frontier. Nor were women "disinterested" in economic matters. As women shared men's work, they adopted men's perspectives.

Home was not the quiet and cozy retreat that nineteenth-century culture envisioned, but a busy center of endless chores and economic ventures. Moreover, women were determined to defend it. One who recounted how a flood destroyed her family's investment added, "It did seem almost hopeless to start practically from the beginning again, but I was willing to do it." Destitution on the plains in the 1870s produced the same kind of female resolution when women refused to admit economic defeat. A spectacular case of courage and devotion to property was provided by the illiterate widow of a California squatter. When the rightful claimant to the land (who had killed her squatter husband) tried to drive her off the property, gun in hand, the widow seized her own pistols, approached her opponent, and dared him shoot her dead. Her defiance proved too much for him, and the woman retained the land to which she was so devoted.

If the frontier blurred sexual distinctions in

the world of work, it also tolerated other departures from the female sphere. Women were occasionally involved in politics. Widow Sims of Arkansas noted, "The papers are full of Politics as this is the year for the Presidential election . . . of course I take sides as every one does so I espouse the cause of Filmore." At least one woman did more than talk. "During these years," David Staples, an early pioneer on the West Coast recalled, "Mrs. Staples cast as many votes as any man. Voters from Arkansas and Missouri, who could not read would walk around . . . and ask her for whom they should vote. She would take the ballot, and running her pencil across certain names, would say I would not vote for that man. By this means, she very materially altered the complexion of results." Women occasionally conducted religious services in the absence of preachers. They filed claims, took care of business, and, as one wrote, "I had a gun and could shoot with any of them."

The activities of these self-reliant pioneer women defied a number of nineteenth-century stereotypes about women. But this did not necessarily mean that pioneer women abandoned the larger conception of women's nature or that they ceased to value female culture. Nor did it mean that they attempted to work out a new definition of woman's sphere. Their behavior and their attitude toward their family, their attempts to replicate female culture suggest that their new environment, although it changed what they did, had only a limited impact on their views.

One might expect, for example, that women's economic importance to the family enterprise might result in a reordering of family relations and the reallocation of power within the family. Ideology, of course, characterized the nineteenth-century family as a patriarchy, with men making decisions and women obediently accepting them. Actually, all American women probably had considerably more power than this model implied. As foreign visitors to the United States noted, "Woman is the centre and lawgiver in the home of the New World." Ideology never tells all.

If ideology does not describe reality, the nature of power relations in families of the past is elusive. Power is difficult to measure at any time. Who wins or loses family confrontations obviously reveals something about the allocation of power and can more easily be observed than the ways in which family members may influence or modify decisions. Yet any judgment about who wields power and how much depends on the latter process as well as the former. In dealing with the nineteenth-century frontier family, the normal problems of analysis are compounded by the lack of direct information about the day-to-day decision process. The privacy of family life, symbolized by the notion of home as retreat, worked against recording situations which might reveal power dynamics. As Elizabeth Lord, reminiscing about her pioneer life in Oregon, pointed out, "Of many things connected with our family I do not care to speak in these pages, such as my marriage, the loss of my first child and the birth of my second, which meant much to all of us and was a great event in our lives, and is something that especially belongs to ourselves."

Conclusions about the power structure of frontier families are, thus, drawn from hints rather than from direct evidence. Census data provide a few uncertain clues. They show, for example, that there was no great disparity of age between frontier husbands and wives, which may suggest some limitations of male authority. The small surplus of males on the frontier gave single women some freedom to pick and choose before marriage, which could have affected the nature of the marriage relation. And the falling birth rate may signify female power or a process of mutual decision-making. Certainly we know that when husbands were away in the mines, at the legislature, or on the range, women had real authority in their families.

But what evidence there is suggests that though women were co-partners in the frontier adventure, husbands still made major decisions. Men seem to have determined whether the family would move on to a better piece of land or pursue a business opportunity just as they had decided to bring their family west. Yet, in both cases, men initiated discussions but did not dictate. They consulted their wives, and it may be that female power was really the right of consultation. Both men and women testify to the interaction. Milo Smith, a Colorado pioneer, pointed out, "There is not an enterprise that I have ever gone into that I have not talked the details over with my wife before hand," while another pioneer described a lengthy period of negotiation between herself and her husband, who wanted to take up a new claim. "Finally, after much deliberation on my part, and persuasion on the part of my husband, I consented to taking up a . . . claim," she reported, but only after learning that there would be a colony of thirty settlers from Baltimore nearby.

Women on the frontier did make many minor decisions, although they still deferred to men, negotiated with them, and often worked for their goals indirectly. A revealing account of an Iowa pioneer family shows how many women operated. Although the husband planned to support the family by doing carpenter work, "Mother had different ideas. During his absence she had accumulated nine cows. . . . She was able to support the family nicely . . . But milking cows did not appeal to father; one week from the time he returned there was only one left." Yet this was not the end of dairying after all, even though a definitive male decision appeared to have been made. The woman did not block her husband, but with an inheritance she again invested in cows. With the proceeds from dairying she bought winter clothing and supplies. The message was clear. Eventually the family acquired hogs to help consume the milk; stock raising ended as the family's main economic activity. Female deference and patience succeeded.

Throughout, women were careful to maintain the idea of male superiority. As Kate Robins explained to her mother in New England,

"Abner would not like it if he knew I sent for you to send me things." The implication was that women would work behind men's backs and avoid direct confrontations with male authority. Frontier women were not attempting to upset the traditional male-female relationship; they did not consciously covet male power. Women's letters and journals describing the ways in which they managed when their husbands were away make this point explicitly. "My husband was absent so much of the time," wrote one woman, "engrossed in mining or in politics, that the care of the family and the farm was left entirely to me, and I was physically unequal to this double burden." Since her reminiscences show her to be a woman with great physical energy, one suspects that it was the constant responsibility which she disliked. Women were reluctant to take on the burden of decision-making alone, and when they did, it was with the expectation that they would do so only temporarily.

Mary Ann Sims, a widow at twenty-five, expressed her anguish at having to play a man's role on a more permanent basis. "I have been busy all day casting up accounts and attending to business," she wrote in January 1856. "I had no idie that it was as much trouble to superentend and take care of a family as it is I feel tired sometimes." A few weeks later she added, "Allway beeing accostum to have someone to depende on it is quite new to attend to business transactions and it pesters me no little." Two years later she observed, "I see a woman cannot fill the sphere of a woman and man too." By 1859 her thinking had crystallized. "It has often been a source of regret to me that my daughters were not sons a man can change his station in life but a woman scarsely ever arrives at more exalted station than the one which she is born in if we ecept those whose minds are mascaline enough to cope with men, a woman whose mind is supirior and whose feelings has been cast in a more exquisit mould to be compell to associate with *courser* minds who cannot understand is compill to feel loanly." Cultural prescriptions were so strong that the widow found herself physically and emotionally exhausted by male responsibilities. On the other hand, despite many offers of marriage, she remained single for several years. A study of frontier Texas illustrates a similar reluctance on the part of propertied widows to remarry. Perhaps the burden of decision-making lessened as women learned "to live alone and act for [themselves]."

Possibly women's fundamental importance in the early years of settlement set definite limits to female deference. "The women were not unaware" of their role in helping to support the family, one reminiscence noted, "and were quite capable of scoring a point on occasion when masculine attitudes became too bumptious." Though there may have been limits to deference and though women may have felt an underlying tension because of the contrast between the passive female stereotype and their own lives, most tried to observe cultural prescriptions concerning familial behavior. Direct confrontations occurred but appear to have been unusual. The evidence is, of course, weighted toward literate women, the very ones exposed to cultural role definitions. But studies of peasant women who prove to be less independent than educated women suggest that a dramatic reallocation of power within humble pioneer families was unlikely.

An examination of letters, journals, and memoirs which touch upon marriage and courtship also indicate how many women carried conventional ideals west with them. Although it has been suggested that frontier women were drab work partners with few sentimental illusions, many of them held to romantic views appropriate for any true woman. Nineteenth-century society had glorified romantic love as a necessary precondition for marriage. Advice books, novels, and schooling described the rapture which a potential husband could be expected to inspire. The rigors of frontier life modified but did not undercut the value of romance.

In fact, the situation of single women on the frontier encouraged romantic fancy. Scattered studies of pioneer families indicate that single women married not in their early teens but in their late teens and early twenties. The sex ratio on the frontier meant that young women did not have to accept the first available suitor who presented himself but could bide their time and choose among several. Frontier demography made romantic ideas and love and courtship meaningful for a woman could wait for "one of those purely spiritual and intelectual creatures" to appear rather than accepting a humdrum and unworthy admirer.

The selection of a mate was not without a functional aspect, however, which it may have lacked in settled urban areas (but probably not in farm communities). "Young women were really sincere when they sought to excel in the preparation of household articles," one pioneer woman commented. "Their teaching was such that such excellence brought its reward in desirable matrimonial favor and the final fulfillment of woman's mission in life." Both sexes agreed that industriousness and competence were desirable for a marriage. A series of letters from a young Nebraska pioneer to his mother reveals this perspective. "You wanted to know," he wrote, "when I was going to get married. Just as quick as I can get money ahead to get a cow and to get married. I want to before I commence shucking corn if I can to Aunt Jennie's oldest girl. She is a good girl and knows how to work . . . A fellow cant do much good on a place when he has everything to do both indoors and out both. She says if we marry right away, she is going to do the work in the house and shuck down the row when I am gathering corn, but I will be glad enough to get rid of the housework." After his marriage, he reported with satisfaction, "She makes everything look neat and tidy and is willing to help me all she can."

The realization that marriage represented a working partnership hardly precluded romantic ecstasy, at least on the part of women. Capable as she was of seeing through some of romantic ideology ("How pleasant it would be to have a comfortable little home with one I *love.*

I am afraid the anticipation is more pleasant than the participation would be"), Elizabeth Wardall faithfully recorded her raptures in a courtship lasting several years. "O: what a blessed thing is *love,*" she wrote, while Harriet Strong told her future husband, "How glad I am *love* is indiscribable. I would dislike to think anything that *could be fathomed* could effect you and me as it does."

Nor did marriage necessarily dull tender feelings. Women did not see their husbands merely as work partners, although this aspect of the relationship may well have provided a strong basis for their affection. Susannah Willeford described her husband as "my first and only choice. The man to whom I had first given my heart and confidence. The man with whom I had sacrificed my home and friends, the man with whom I had shed tears and shared his gladness and with whom I had shared many difficulties and by whom I had borne eight children." Her words convey their warm relationship, as do the testimonials of many others about their marriage. Pioneer wives both expected and experienced the feelings which nineteenth-century literature suggested were part of married life. Separation often led women to express these emotions in romantic terms. Roselle Putnam called her husband "the idol of my heart" and remarked, "Never did I know what it was to sufer anciety untill I knew what it was to be seperated from [him]," while the long-married Mrs. Stearns spoke of her husband's "dear face." When husbands finally returned, women like Rebecca Ebey captured the emotional tone of their marriages: "And one thing which made [the day] . . . seem more exceedingly delightful, My dear husband arrived safe at home."

Nor was love without a sexual component. Although an argument has been made that nineteenth-century women neither wanted nor enjoyed physical affection, scattered evidence from married and single women on the frontier shows that passion had a place. Since nineteenth-century women were reticent about sex, these references are all the more remarkable. Wrote one woman to her husband in 1867, "Dear Husband you say you think that I could get plenty to hug me well I don't know whether I could or not I don't think I look very hugable now at least to any but your self as there is no-one knows how well I can hug but you." That a chaste hug was perhaps not what she meant is suggested by a letter written a few weeks later when she revealed, "I dreamed of seeing you last night and I thought I had a pair of twins." In a similarly suggestive manner, Kate Blaine told her mother she missed her absent husband as a bedfellow. "Now when I sleep alone the bed is so cold and my feet will not keep warm." A few women were less ambiguous than Kate. Mary Ann Sims lamented she had not met a suitable marriage partner and acknowledged the sexual satisfactions she missed. "I know that there is not a woman . . . that is capable of feeling a more devoted affection than [I] I am naturely impolsive and affectionate and I loved my husban[d] with all the intencity that my nature was capable of feeling but I must confess it was more the passionate ideial love of youth," she wrote. Though she implied that passion should disappear with maturity, it was not so for her. Her final diary entries show her struggling to overcome her feelings for a man she described as wild and dissipated.

It is certainly true, as Phoebe Judson pointed out, that "the inconveniences of our environment and the constant drudgery eventually took all the romance and poetry out of our farm life." Phoebe was, of course, talking not of marriage but of her idealized vision of farming life, but her comment raises a valid point. Pioneer women worked hard most of the time, and their difficult life certainly put limits on flights of romantic fancy. But they were more than work drudges and their occasional references to love suggest that the romantic revolution had affected their attitudes and expectations.

The majority of frontier women were wives and mothers during the early years of settlement; primitive conditions and women's workloads complicated motherhood. But the idea that frontier women had no time for the luxury of maternal feelings, considered so central to the conception of motherhood, and even less time to lavish attention on their children, needs some modification. Frontier women obviously worked hard, but this did not mean that they did not take their role of mother seriously or that they were unconscious of a nineteenth-century mother's duty. "How forsably I feel the responsibility of a Mother," sighed one.

Only rarely did frontier women reveal how they felt about pregnancy and birth (which they called a time of sickness). Giving birth was, however, part of a "female ritual" which called for the involvement and support of other women on the frontier as it did in the East. To be alone at such a moment was a dreadful fate to be avoided. "I do not know what they will do when she is *confined* not having any Neighbours," wrote one woman, expressing the common fear of being without female support at such a moment. When it was at all possible, frontier women gathered round during childbirth, with little thought of monetary reward. The ritual had rules. "A woman that was expecting had to take good care that she had plenty fixed for her neighbors when they got there," explained one frontier woman. "There was no telling how long they was in for. There wasn't no paying these friends so you had to treat them good."

If women were reticent before birth, and gave few indications of what their views of motherhood were, not so afterward: "Well, old journal," Almira Beam exclaimed in 1861. "You have been rather silent these few months past: but it could not be helped. You have great cause to be thankful that we ever met. Arthur is asleep in his cradle below, and mother is getting dinner." In their letters east, women indicated their deep emotional concern for their children, recording the smallest details about their babies—their clothes, habits, small achievements. "I would tell you that he is the prettiest baby in the world," wrote Sarah Ever-

ett from Kansas, "if I was not intending to send his likeness." Occasionally mothers expressed ambivalent feelings about their female children. Two years earlier Sarah had described another baby as "the newcomer who seems to cause more rejoicing among her distant relatives than those at home—we think of calling [her] Clara Elizabeth . . . It isn't of much consequence however seeing it's nothing but a girl anyway."

Yet four months later Sarah reported the death of "*sweet little Clara*—She brought a great deal of sunshine into our homely cabin this summer, and when she was carried out of it, it certainly seemed very dark to me." Whatever Sarah's earlier comment meant, Clara's death revealed the way in which her mother saw the maternal relationship as central and emotionally absorbing. A child's death robbed the mother of one "more dear to me than any thing ever had been." The sentimentalism of such testimonials strikes the twentieth century as maudlin, but it was typical in the nineteenth century. Though children's death on the frontier was a fact (twenty of the thirty-five reported deaths in Cass County on the Nebraska frontier in 1860 were children six or younger), the attitude was anything but pragmatic.

The nineteenth century defined the regulation of children and the formation of their characters as a mother's central tasks. Life on the frontier complicated them, as Mollie Sanford suggested. "Mother . . . fears I am losing all the dignity I ever possessed." "I know I am getting demoralized, but I should be more so, to mope around and have no fun." The pressure of other duties and the lure of the wilderness made regulating children difficult. Children remembered running "wild in the woods without any restraints," "carefree all through the woods and . . . hills." Mother, noted Wilda Belknap in her autobiography, seemed to have little time to devote to the children after infancy. But this hardly signified an abnegation of maternal responsibility. Children also remembered punishments and disciplinary measures. In later years pioneer women often pointed to their children as symbols of their lifework, testifying to the importance they attributed to their work as mothers.

When they could, then, pioneer mothers molded and educated their children. Rebecca Ebey, a pioneer from Virginia, taught her children lessons, but not just in reading and writing. "We . . . spend our time in training the young minds of our children in the principles of Christ and creating within them a thirst for moral knowledge," she explained. If knowledge of Christian principles was one goal, the inculcation of the habits of steady industry was another. Women expressed disapproval of idleness and indolence in children and sought to encourage them to be useful. On the frontier mothers expected their children to work, so much so that one recollection of a pioneer childhood stated the obvious, "You will gather from what I have related that work and plenty of it was the lot of pioneer children."

Tasks were not assigned solely on the basis of sex. Girls recalled plowing, herding cows, carrying wood and water, while boys helped mothers wash clothes and dishes. "I think the boys ought to do something," explained one mother. Just as responsibilities of the sexes overlapped in the adult world, so, too, did they in the children's world. But as time passed and children grew, sex distinctions were stressed. Daughters recalled mothers clarifying appropriate female behavior. Both sexes acquired knowledge of sexual boundaries, as records show. One reminiscence tells of "Margaret Isabell's sons, . . . teenagers . . . [who] had held their mother up so she could milk the cow. She was still weak from the birth of the baby, but milking a cow was 'woman's work' so they would not do it." Girls recalled their introduction to domesticity as they acted as a "mother's right hand." This was an apprenticeship for marriage, as Amanda Gaines explained. "I assist Mother in house-hold duties which are various. She is preparing me for a Farmer's wife." Another daughter wondered whether she had any existence aside from the domestic routine, for her life was "so pre-scribed for me by my family environment that I do not know who I am." She did know what she did, however: washing, cooking, and assisting "dear old mother." Even recreation could be sex-bound, with girls riding, visiting, and picking wildflowers, while the "boys swam with Father . . . and trapped animals."

Since the frontier family worked together, it was natural that women shared child care with their husbands, a departure from nineteenth-century theory, which assigned child care exclusively to women. Women expected and wanted assistance, not only because of the work involved, but because of the need to clarify standards. Women assumed that their husbands would introduce sons to the male world and take responsibility for their development at the appropriate time. This might occur relatively early in the child's development. As one woman explained, one of her boys was a problem. "His pa is gone so much that he is becoming a great deal of trouble to me I have often heard it said that little boys would not be industrious about everything under their mother's controll . . . I find it so, They become so accustomed to their mother's commands . . . that they get so they do not mind it." Her conclusion was predictably, "When little boys become old enough to do some work they need a father to show them and to push them forward to make them industrious."

In the first few years following emigration to the West, frontier women helped create a new life for their families. The ways in which they went about their duties and the ways in which they related to other members of their families were influenced by their culture just as much as by the new environment. Tired and overworked as they were, many of them still seem to have had the energy to worry about standards and norms. Necessary modifications were, of course, made. The concept of gentility was clearly inappropriate on the frontier, as was the notion of woman as ornamental (an extension of the concept of domesticity much criticized by its advocates, like Sarah Hale). Child rearing demanded encouraging traits not usually stressed in safer environments. "Children here have to learn self reliance and independence as well as their parents," explained one parent.

But the truth was that female culture shaped the ways in which women perceived the frontier experience and provided a means of orientation to it. Even though frontier conditions forced them into manly pursuits and led them to modify some of their standards, they hardly pressed for a liberation from female norms and culture. For much of the "freedom" which women' experienced was the freedom to work even harder than they had before, with dramatic results. "I am a very old woman," wrote twenty-nine-year-old Sarah Everett. "My face is thin sunken and wrinkled, my hands bony withered and hard." Why should women lay claim to male tasks in addition to their own? The domestic ideal was a goal toward which women could direct their efforts, the promise of a day when their lives would not be so hard, their tasks so numerous. Domesticity, with its neat definition of woman's place, helped women bear what they hoped were temporary burdens and reestablished their sense of identity and self-respect. It served as a link with the past.

Frontier women gave many indications of their desire to hold on to the conventions of female culture no matter how unfavorable the circumstances seemed. "Home," crude and impermanent though it might be, received the kind of attention which would have pleased the proponents of domesticity. Though the cabin or sod house might not be the cozy nook pictured in stories of Western life, women hoped to make it one as they papered their walls with old newspapers or tacked up cloth to make the house snug and cheery. Old rags became rugs, old dresses curtains. A keg might become a footstool, upholstered with an old pair of pants. Thread turned into lace doilies. Outside, women planted flowers and trees from seeds they had brought with them and generally tried to maintain the standards of

domesticity and hospitality with which they had been familiar before emigration. Although they often wore rough and rugged clothing, even buckskin trousers, pioneer women found "all these things . . . dreadfully annoying." As one pointed out, "We were always wishing for enough money to buy better clothes." The interest in fashion and the attempts to dress in style were symbolic of the intention to remain feminine. The "career" of a mid-century Oregon pioneer is typical. "Although I had now been absent from civilization—otherwise Ohio—for more than a year," she wrote, "I was still considered an authority on the matter of dress and fashion. I was consulted and acted as adviser whenever a new cloak or gown was made . . . I trimmed hats, literally, for the entire neighborhood, and I knew less than nothing about millinery."

The determination to maintain ties to the traditional female world and to create a female community where, in fact, there was none, was apparent in the energy with which frontier women sustained old friendships and associations. Mrs. Coe remarked in a letter to a friend in 1863 that she had written hundreds of letters, so many "that my Diary has dwindled away to almost nothing—All my romance has become reality—and as for poetry—it has vanish'd, resolved itself into and, mingled with the landscape around me." Pioneer women wrote letters to female relatives and friends in the East, detailing their lives, providing all the vital information which was the basis for an intimate female dialogue. They enclosed material of their dresses, described dress patterns, sent pictures of their children; they asked scores of minute questions about the health of family and friends, marriages and deaths, fashion, religion. "The most trivial things that you can mention about each other have a great interest to us way out here," Mary Ann Adair explained to her mother and sister.

Bonds of affection sustained the dialogue between pioneer women and their Eastern friends and relatives, but that dialogue had emotional costs. Slow and irregular mails which could take up to a year contributed to the natural anxiety women felt for the health and well-being of those far away. "My dear mother," wrote one woman, "you do not know how miserable I feel about you, for I have not received a line from any of my family." And as years passed, a new fear appeared. "Everything has changed so much at home since I left, that I expect I should feel like a stranger now." And with time, it was also possible that those at home would cease to care. "I have waited almost a year and a half hoping to receive a letter from you," Elisabeth Adams wrote from Iowa to her sister. "Why do you do so? Do you not wish to have intercourse with me? Do you not *love me?* I am sure I love you, and the longer I live the more I feel the want of affection from others, the more my heart yearns for kindness and love from my own family, I mean my *father's family.*"

A common theme runs through the correspondence. "I want you to come if you can and as soon as you can for no doubt I shal feel my self very lonesome." Women's letters are filled with urgent invitations to friends and relatives to emigrate. Often over a period of years, encouragement and advice about the trip poured out of the West in hopes that friends from the old life could become part of the new. "I want you all here, then I would be perfectly contented," explained Louise Swift, while another woman told her sister, "When we get together again we will not be parted so easy."

If relatives and friends did not come West, women sustained ties with them by nourishing hopes of an Eastern visit. Eventually this hope was realized for a lucky few; other women remembered that, in the end, all would meet in heaven. Although some of their discussions about a heavenly meeting sound strange to modern ears, the emotional well-being of many pioneer women was sustained by their faith that the network of friends and relatives could be eternal. There is, perhaps, no greater testimony to the importance women far in the wilderness placed on female culture than the conviction that parts of it would be replicated in heaven.

While many women on the frontier devoted considerable energy to keeping alive the home network, feeling, as one young woman put it, "Tis true we may have friends among strangers; but, ah, they are not parents, brothers nor sisters," most naturally attempted to establish new ties with other women as soon as possible. The trip overland had provided one opportunity for a new beginning. "Ever since I saw you in camp at Iowa (in '54)," Anna Goodell told Mary Bozarth, "you have looked and acted like my good Auth Sarah." Proximity (which was a relative term) also determined friendships. Although the nearest neighbor might be miles away, women made a special point of visiting one another. Reciprocity was understood. "Mrs. Terry came this morning," wrote Almira Beam in her diary. "She says she will not come again until I come to see her." Soon Mrs. Terry had become "the best neighbor I ever saw, or heard of." Although women might go for days or even weeks without visitors, when they came, they stayed. The visits provided a relief from work and the opportunity for mutual support and sharing experiences. Rebecca Ebey's diary revealed the many rewards of female friendship. "I have been busy all day ironing cleaning up and mend the children's clothes Mrs. Alexander came over this evening to spend the night I was very much pleased to see her and had been look[ing] for her for a long time . . . Mrs. Alexander is very cheerful and makes me feel much better than I have done to be awhile in her company."

Yet creating the new web of friendships on the frontier was difficult. Distance was an obstacle, at least at first. And cultural or social differences, usually overlooked, could stand in the way of intimacy. "Oh how I pine for association [of] some kindred mind," a young widow in Arkansas reflected. "All of my neighbours are good honest kind people but they seem to have no idie beyond their little s[p]here of action they do not appear to have a feeling nor aspiration higher than the things of life satisfying their physical wants." Aware of such distinctions on the frontier, she decided, "I had rather be aloan for I feel aloan." Loneliness for another woman made "my mind meditate upon former scenes in my life when I had doting loving relatives all around me."

With time, however, the new network took shape. Ties became warm as marriage bound families together and family, relatives, and old friends emigrated to swell the circle of love. A recent study of kinship in Oregon suggests that this process could be relatively rapid. At least 40 percent of the households listed in the 1850 census had kinship ties with one other household and perhaps more. Census figures can only suggest the emotional significance of these relationships.

Despite the trials the frontier posed for them, many frontier women continued to see themselves as women within the mainstream of nineteenth-century culture. Although their courage, persistence, and physical endurance seem extraordinary to a later time, none of these women viewed themselves as extraordinary. Their diaries and letters show they expected to labor hard and long to achieve their goals. Though notes of weariness often creep into their accounts, they appear to have grumbled very little, at least on paper. Some complained of the monotony of farming life, though others seemed to enjoy the fact that there was "no bustleling crowd as in City or town to marr our peaceful happiness." They expressed discontent if family fortunes wavered. But they did not see themselves as drudges. Comments about Indian women invariably contrasted their own lot with that of the long-suffering Indian woman, who toiled like a slave for her husband.

The attitude of women during the early period of settlement was conditioned not only by their belief in hard work but also by limited expectations for personal happiness. Writing to her mother about a young niece's birthday, one woman advised telling the girl to remain a child "as long as she can, for the troubles of a woman, will come upon her soon enough!" The phrase "troubles of a woman" suggests something of the female frame of reference. Nineteenth-century ideology promised women fulfillment through marriage and motherhood, yet most knew the physical pains and dangers associated with bearing children and the disruption of female culture which marriage so often signified. In a highly mobile society, they witnessed the anguished separations which so frequently parted family and friends for life. The disparity between ideology and reality made it risky to assume happiness in any setting. The religious knew, of course, that God assigned both blessings and trials in life; Christians had to expect both. With such a frame of reference, nineteenth-century women were equipped to deal with the realities of their lives on the frontier far more easily than women of the present era could.

Their letters to friends and families in the East are good evidence of their plucky attitude to pioneer life. "Tell father I am not discourage and am not sorry I came," wrote Kate Robins to her brother, while Kate Blaine told her mother, "I could not have believed that I should have been as well contented as I am situated and must needs be here. We are deprived of all the conveniences I had considered indispensable before we came." Although most women were candid about the work required (Kate said, "A woman that can not endure almost as much as a horse has no business here, as there is no such thing as getting help") and frankly acknowledged their homesickness, they often were satisfied with their situation. "If our friends were here, we should be very contented, notwithstanding as we are deprived of many conveniences and comforts we might have enjoyed at home," Kate explained. Domestic triumphs, home improvements, new clothes, preaching in the vicinity were duly described and appreciated in the context of creating culture in the wilderness. The ultimate objective of many of the letter writers was, of course, persuasion. Still, the satisfactions cannot be discounted, nor can the women's underlying assumption of steady progress on the frontier. The future was promising in the West. So Phoebe Judson recalled, "The letters written back to our eastern friends gave such glowing descriptions of our fair dwelling place that some of them were encouraged to make arrangements to cross the plains the following year."

Women also told friends of the beauty of the West, of its good climate and healthy way of life. They noted the disappearance of old ail-ments and the feeling of bodily well-being they derived from the activities of outdoor life. And to their single relatives they described the "western gallant" perhaps not "dressed up gentlemen" but perhaps "better than anything you ever saw or heard of before."

Of course, it was in the interest of these women to attract friends and family to the West to aid in the task of building society anew. "I promise you a hearty welcome to my house" was a refrain of female letter writers. Yet the lures were real. As Pop from Arkansas pointed out, "If she was back and new as much as she does she would endure as much more as she has to get back to Oregon."

# 18

## "COME BY HERE, LORD"

### CHARLES JOYNER

The last decade of the eighteenth century and the first three decades of the nineteenth century witnessed an intense revival of religion in America. One of the most important aspects of this Second Great Awakening was the attempt by preachers, many of them laymen, to reach out and spread the gospel to those in the lower ranks of society. As the revival spirit spread from the North to the South at the turn of the century, this message of popular redemption was carried to the most oppressed of American peoples: the black slaves.

In the beginning southern slaveholders welcomed the revivalists, seeing in the conservative aspects of Protestantism a means to augment their control over their slaves. But as many slave owners quickly learned, revivalism was a double-edged sword. While Protestantism could communicate a message of otherworldliness and reconciliation with one's lot in life, it could also transmit a powerful message of redemption and deliverance from oppression. In spite of slaveholder attempts to suppress the redemptive side of Protestantism, many southern revivalists preached the full gospel to slaves, including in their sermons tales of Moses, Daniel, and other biblical leaders who sought the liberation of their people. As slaves listened to the preachings of these revivalists, they began to construct their own interpretation of Christian religion, drawing parallels between their own customary African beliefs and the new message of Christian revivalists. By the nineteenth century, as Charles Joyner reveals, Afro-Christianity was a complex amalgam of Old World practices such as conjuring, spiritualism, and expressive emotionality and New World Christian beliefs.

From Charles Joyner, *Down by the Riverside: A South Carolina Slave Community* (Urbana, Ill.: University of Illinois Press, 1984). Reprinted by permission of Charles Joyner and the University of Illinois Press.

**1**

Visitors to the Waccamaw rice plantations were struck by the religious fervor of the slave community—the slaves' active participation in church services, their ecstatic prayers and energetic shouts, and especially their spirituals. Of the origins and beliefs of that religion, as well as its meaning to the slaves, most of the visitors knew nothing. They never reflected that they were witnessing a remarkable cultural transformation: from a diversity of African beliefs and a multiplicity of African rites and practices to a distinctive Afro-Christianity that voiced the slaves' deepest ancestral values as they responded to a new and constricting environment. The All Saints slaves, uprooted from a culture in which religion applied to all aspects of life, were objects of intense proselytizing efforts on the part of their masters. They did not so much adapt to Christianity (at least not to the selective Christianity evangelized to them by their masters) as adapt Christianity to themselves. Just as the masters converted Christianity to their own culture, so the slaves converted Christianity to theirs. It was not God the judge of behavior—God the master or overseer—who was the object of worship in Afro-Christianity, but a God more like African deities: God the transcendant spirit. They worshipped this new Christian deity in traditional African ways, and they made European religious forms serve African religious functions. Christianity did, as the masters hoped, promote both a certain amount of slave forbearance and a faith that those who suffered most on earth would be rewarded in heaven. But Afro-Christianity also demonstrated that the slaves were as concerned with freedom in this world as with salvation in the next.

Slave religion on the Waccamaw may be examined as a process of cultural interaction between acquired Christianity and inherited African religious traditions. It is important to draw a distinction between the religious instruction of the slaves and the religious behavior of the slaves, although the two are by no means unrelated. The masters' attempts to indoctrinate the slaves with the tenets of Protestant Christianity, especially those which would promote their contentment with present conditions, met with considerable success. But African religious beliefs and practices continued to flourish in All Saints Parish in three distinct streams. One stream, which included such practices as ecstatic trances and spirit possession as a part of religious services, merged with Christianity, giving the slaves' religion a distinctive cast. Another stream, which included belief in hags and witches as well as certain malign spirits, continued to exist among slave Christians as a sort of parallel consciousness, neither part of their Christianity nor completely outside it. Yet another stream, which included conjuration and sorcery, flourished as an underground alternative religious system in ways that ran quite counter to the doctrines of Christianity. What had been a unified religious outlook in Africa, in which virtually all experience was religious, had become fragmented and diversified in the new environment.

That unified religious outlook had served important needs in Africa, and those needs continued to exist on the plantations of the New World. Belief in occult phenomena and efforts to manipulate them were not merely irrational and eccentric but also were a natural manifestation of a human world view in pre-industrial societies. In a world at the mercy of harvest and weather, of disaster and disease, lacking technology and education, acceptance of magic and conjuration as a means of attempting to control natural forces was understandable. Such an outlook among Africans and their descendants in the New World was considered primitive and superstitious; but it was part of the mentality of Europe as well, where not that long before belief in ghosts and fairies was more common than belief in Christianity and where witches and astrologers were more influential than priests. If Africans brought with them to All Saints Parish beliefs that the spirits of the ancestors regulated life in this world, Europeans brought with them beliefs in omens and witchcraft; both learned and common folk attempted to regulate their lives with signs, charms, and exorcisms.

Enslaved Africans in the South Carolina low country continued what an observer called "a strong attachment to their native country, and to those friends and relations with whom they spent the early years of life." Afro-American slaves maintained African ethnic distinctions on All Saints rice plantations well into the mid-nineteenth century; and they may have stolen away in the evenings to join with slaves of the same ethnic group from neighboring plantations to celebrate their African religions away from the masters' prying and unbelieving eyes. It would be absurd to minimize the African component in slave religion; however, one must not forget that enslaved Africans in the South Carolina low country came from widely separated areas of Africa. To stress their cultural similarities too much is inevitably to oversimplify. West African religions comprised a deeply complex reality, with diverse religious expression. But a theological affinity among African ethnic groups transcended differences in rites and practices and reflected a common bond, an overall spirit, which stressed the African's mystical relationship to God and the supernatural, as well as the role of the shaman—magician, sorcerer, or conjuror—in the social order. Moreover, the very diversity of African religious practices promoted an acceptance of cultural differences and an openness to cultural interaction. Even large and widespread ethnic groups, such as the Bantu, showed a tendency toward cultural fusion as a basic cultural characteristic. Such tendencies gave African cultural grammars an integral dynamism, an expectation of culture change as a fundamental trait. It is not surprising, then, that Afro-American continuities with African religion are found not so much in static and archaic reten-

tions, but in distinctive modes of expression that were the product of the slaves' creative response to a new environment in which they had to adapt to both Christianity and slavery.

## 2

The decline and breakup of a unified African religion into separate fragments were especially marked among the slaves of All Saints Parish. While other streams of African religion either converged or co-existed with Christianity, belief in magical shamanism—called voodoo or hoodoo in the New World—continued an underground existence outside of and hostile to the Christian tradition. Conjuration was, of course, practiced in secret, and documentation is inevitably scanty. Discussion of this aspect of slave religion is, therefore, necessarily more tentative and more speculative than one would wish. The role of slave conjuration in All Saints Parish remains both largely unknown and at least partly unknowable. Nevertheless, there is sufficient evidence to assert with confidence the continuity of an underground stream of magical shamanism throughout the slavery period and beyond. James R. Sparkman, the master of Mt. Arena, was astounded to learn that "on one plantation, where more than ordinary attention had been given to their religious training, there was an open relapse into Feticism or *Voodooism*" following emancipation. Appalled by having "been brought into personal contact with the devil" and having found themselves "powerless," the planters had to invoke "military interference," according to Sparkman, "before the outbreak could be contained."

Voodoo—or hoodoo—involved rituals whereby sorcerers called up the spirits of the dead to offer advice or to perform cures. The process of dying, according to West African belief, was not complete for up to five years. The spirits of the ancestors, the living dead, were the closest links between the world of the living and the world of the spirits, because they were beings who straddled both worlds. Since illness was regarded as supernatural in origin, it was necessary—through sorcery—to call up the spirits for protection. Magical shamanism could be used for either protective or malevolent purposes: it could cure an illness, kill an enemy, or secure someone's love. All misfortune was regarded as the result of sorcery—including, presumably, slavery. One's only protection was stronger magic. Such were the similarities in Afro-American occultism; with considerable variation it existed throughout the slave societies of the New World.

The perpetuation of hoodoo seems to have been most pronounced in areas where slaves were concentrated in large numbers. It arose with the arrival of slaves from the Caribbean or directly from Africa who adapted African snake cults to a new environment. The African connection in hoodoo was unmistakable. High in the pantheon of African deities, the snake god of so many African cultures—the Ewe, Fon, Bantu, Dahomey, Whydah, and Yoruba—symbolized the cosmic energy of nature, the arbiter of fortune and misfortune. His protective power could be invoked only by his sorcerers. Initiation rites featured snakeskins, and snake-charming was sometimes used in hoodoo. All sorts of supernatural powers were attributed to serpents in the snakelore of All Saints Parish, from little green snakes that made spring water cool and sweet to garter snakes that could break themselves into joints and put themselves back together again to coach-whips that could catch their tails in their mouths and roll like a hoop in pursuit of their victims. A coach-whip killed by wrapping its body around a victim, tying him to a tree, and whipping him to death with its tail. Snakes on the Waccamaw were said to eat eggs out of hen nests and to suck cows dry. If one attempted to kill snakes, they did not die until the sun went down. And they could multiply themselves virtually at will: an ex-slave recalled that someone had come upon "a whoppin' big rattler quiled [coiled] by a old dead, live-oak harricane. When that snake found somebody messin' 'round, she made a kind of strange noise

and opened her mouth and that man counted eighteen little ten inch rattlers that run right in that Mammy snake's mouth." The only cure for snakebite was a black chicken, "fer tie on ter dreen out de pizen ef dem rattler pop yuh on yuh laig" (to tie on to drain out the poison if those rattlers pop you on your leg). At no time did voodoo—or hoodoo—on the Waccamaw rice plantations approach the level or internal organization of Haitian Vodun, but it does appear to have achieved a distinctive character that raised it to a level beyond simple, unorganized conjuring.

All Saints slaves did not always go to their masters when they were troubled by physical or personal problems. Many of them took such complaints to local conjurers, the plantation priests or medicine men of the old religion. Such conjurers often enjoyed considerable influence and power among the slave community, even among some of the Christians. They gained and exercised their powers over the slaves in diverse ways and by various methods, but always by fear and awe. They were relied upon by their patrons both for protection or relief from spells and for laying spells upon their enemies. The conjurers were often marked not merely by an unusual mentality but also by some physical peculiarity that set them apart from other slaves, a peculiarity that typically suggested a relationship with the world of the spirits. One such All Saints conjurer, Obie Hines, was said to "look lak a witch—funny shapted [shaped]."

The position of conjurer was sometimes inherited, but more often was the result of peculiar circumstances of birth, such as being born feet-foremost or with a caul over the face. Such children were considered to have special powers. Babies born with a caul were believed to be gifted—or cursed—with second sight. They would always be able to see spirits and other supernatural phenomena: "Ain't I fer tell yuh Julie ain fer born wid caul but George gal, Zena is? Dat gal bin born wid caul. She kin see w'at de ornary, common run cain't see." Children thought to have been born with second sight were often taught the special lore of the conjurers. Some slave midwives, however, used a countercharm to lift the "curse" of second sight. Hagar Brown said of the caul: "Take that off. Make tea outer um. Feed baby till he all gone. Take the spell off. Can't see 'um. Can't see hant. When born take 'um from he face. Make tea. Feed 'um till he all gone. Drink 'em all. Spell take off. Can't see 'um." Lillie Knox explained to Genevieve Chandler that "Aunt Hagar does that so they won't grow up scared. When anyone like that they all the time seeing things and it'll scare them."

Other conjurers in All Saints Parish were said to have received their powers by selling themselves to the devil in exchange for the ability to conjure and cast spells. After meeting with the devil at a crossroads for nine consecutive nights, a novice conjurer would procure a lucky black cat bone, which would thereafter be used in conjuration and what was called "rich craft." Minnie Knox recalled to Chandler, "They does say black cat has een 'um uh lucky bone. Doan kill th' cat. Get yuh uh cat ain got on 'um no white hair. Doan kill 'um. Jess drap 'em een uh pot uh biling wautuh (water) en bil 'um till hit all bile tuh pieces. Wan leetle bone will stay on top." There were also reports of marriage between humans and the devil. Ellen Carolina told of one case in which the hapless groom did not know he was riding with the devil until it was too late: "Eber mile pos' day git to, gal countenance change. Ebery mile pos' gettin uglier and uglier. Git to las' mile pos' she tun to Debil wid long tail on em! No gal now."

The conjurers were assisted in their efforts by various combinations of common and uncommon substances that were held to be magical. "Peoples conjers wid grabe yard dirt," one ex-slave told Chandler. "Yuh can tek dat dirt en all kind ob ting en mek conjur bag. Dey bin some kind ob debilmint yuh mix wid dat stuff." An uninitiated person looked into a conjure bag at risk of life. Hagar Brown said, "I know I ain't goin' be the one peep in there. 'Cause I ain't make my peace yet. Know it will make you fall dead. Wouldn't have time to crook." A woman on Sandy Island told Chandler, "I hear tell bout a man ober de ribbah what jus looked

on a conjure man bag, and he died." She did describe, however, what a woman she knew found when she looked into a conjure bag. "What dat debbilment look like?" she exclaimed. "It wuz de terriblest lookin sight she eber has saw! She say it wuz all mixin up. De ting fuzz up like a baby head an wukkin up and mixin. Hab eye. Hab nose. Hab mout'. Red eye. Fuzz on em. An de mind come tuh Lutella. 'Stroy dat devil wuk!' And she done what de spirit say." Armed with such charms conjurers made powerful impressions on other slaves. They were said to possess all manner of malign powers.

Not all of the conjurers' spells had sinister intent. If they were considered the perpetrators of most misfortunes, they were also highly regarded as healers. The positive role played by the conjurers (or conjure-doctors as they were often called by the slaves) in the treatment of slave illnesses exemplified the role of religion in every aspect of slave life. The precise role of the medical profession in the treatment of slaves remains controversial, but white physicians did not enjoy a high reputation among All Saints slaves, and the white man's medicine was regarded with suspicion. Depending upon the complaint, conjure doctors might take a pharmaceutical approach to treatment. Africans had brought their highly esteemed pharmacopoeia with them to South Carolina as part of their oral traditions. They found the semitropical low country environment similar enough to that of West Africa that such knowledge was easily adapted to somewhat new flora and fauna. To cure a child of worms, for instance, Margaret Bryant said they would "git the gipsy (gypsum) weed. Beat 'em up for worm. Give 'em when the moon change." Rheumatism was treated by massaging the affected area with eelskin or having the patient ingest a decoction of oakbark or pokeberry tea, which did in fact possess medical properties. Other ailments might call for a sort of psychotherapy, as expressed in divination. The persistent headaches of Lillie Knox's grandmother, Kit, were diagnosed by conjurer Obie Hines as having been caused by a lizard in her head (a common diagnosis among conjurers): "En ole man Obie ax fuh uh hankercher. En he shake it en say, 'Kit! Blow yuh nostril!' 'Can't, man!' 'Blow, Kit, blow!' En she blow! En if she wuz here live ter-day, she'd tell you. She blow en blow out uh lizard out her nose—small, slick black lizard! She kept it en show it tuh us young'uns." If illness were caused by sorcery, it could only be removed by countersorcery: "I had a half-brother like to been run crazy. Pain in the head. Fix! They took some kinder rattlesnake dust and fix him. Nobody didn't know how. Didn't know whether somebody lay something cross that man path or put poison in his cap or what been done." But countersorcery could remove the evil spell: "Mother just give Rich that root woman treatment and turn that spell in time." Conjurers on the Waccamaw sometimes turned spells back upon their perpetrators. Zackie Knox told Chandler of a conjure doctor who was accused of giving a woman the "wandering sickness" by turning a spell back on her when she failed to pay him for putting a charm on her husband. Occasionally conjurers even attempted to "lay a trick" on the master or overseer. Ex-slave Ella Small recalled that at Wachesaw plantation a "conjur been throw at the obersheer (overseer) and hit my Brudder Frank."

Not all slaves believed in conjure, of course. "Conjur?" asked ex-slave Sabe Rutledge. "Wouldn't burn a hucks [crust of] bread for 'em." Lillie Knox recalled that her slave grandmother "didn't b'lieve in nuthin lak goopherin ner conjurin ner nuthin." Some of the ex-slaves were even more emphatic in their expressions of disbelief. "Now, me, I don't b'lieve in no conjur ball ner ritch-craft," said a former slave on Sandy Island. "I don't b'lieve in no coo-coo nor hoo-doo ner nuthin." While the Waccamaw conjurers were never able to command universal adherence, and while they never approached the political power of the Caribbean priests of Obeah, Myalism, or Vodun, it is clear that they exercised influence over the lives of the slaves out of proportion

to any power in their charms and spells. It is equally clear that they could neither have gained nor held such influence over other slaves had they not served a real function on the rice plantations. Even if the conjurers are acknowledged to have been frauds and extortionists, one must recognize that they also served the slave community as healers in time of sickness and as comforters in time of suffering, as interpreters of those unobservable spirits whose activities directed everyday life, and as awesome beings whose supernatural powers could be enlisted in the redress of grievances. For the Waccamaw slaves, their conjurers—the underground priests of voodoo—bridged the precarious servitude of the all-too-real world and the mysterious uncertainties of the spirit world. In so doing, they created for even the most credulous slaves a buffer against mental and emotional submission to the slave system. Many, perhaps most, of the All Saints slaves abandoned their adherence to this aspect of their African heritage. Those who did not, by helping to preserve and extend an autonomous African heritage, were making a contribution to community and survival.

### 3

Voodoo had a continuing appeal to some slaves; most slave Christians, when they did not totally reject that stream of African cosmology, considered the conjurers' powers to be evil and inimical to Christianity. Another stream, the venerable African distinction between hags and haunts, proved to be more compatible with the slaves' new religious outlook. Haunts were the spirits of the dead, returned to trouble the living: a low country version of the Congo zumbi or the Haitian zambi, although carrying a somewhat different connotation on the Waccamaw. Hags, on the other hand, were not spirits of the dead, but rather the disembodied spirits of witches who would shed their skins at night and "ride" people— that is, give them nightmares. "Hag a REAL PER-

SON," the old-timers emphasized. "They jus' learn dat trade." Slave Christians neither abandoned such beliefs nor incorporated them into Afro-Christianity. Hags, haunts, and plateyes—malevolent, shape-changing spirits—persisted in a parallel stream of belief.

Hags were particularly troublesome creatures who could fly through the air and who were given to vampirism: "Dey say hag sperit can go troo de keyhole of de do' en ef dey lak you dey goes in en sucks your blood troo yer nose. Nobody scusin a hag lak dat kin' o' diet, but dey eats dat fer de syrup on dey bread. When hag rides you, you mek noise same lak er little shiverin owl. You can't wake up en you won't wake up twell somebody tech you. You calls dat de hag ridin you." The very young and the very old were particularly susceptible to being victimized by hags. Ex-slave Liza Small believed that a hag was responsible for the death of her grandson: "My daughter have the two boy. Lose one. I low [allow] hag musser lock he jaw. Couldn't suck." Another aged slave personally struggled with hags until "she ole bones bin gib out." "Maum Nellie she try 'em. She fight hag seben year. Jes she wan. She wressel wid 'em. . . . But atter seben year dey run she. She say she too ole fer de hag fer ride. She say she too tired. She wuk so hard. She hoe. She plant. She harbest. En night come en she crabe fer res'." There were precautions that the slaves might take to keep hags from riding them. Maum Nellie employed traditional preventive measures: "She bed down she fire, en she fall in she bunk. But she ain't fer out she light. She light burn low fer keep hag out. En de sifter bin hang ober de key-hole. Dat, too, fer keep out hag. W'en hag come tru de keyhole en git en dat sifter, he hab de culiosity. En he stay right dere twell he count de hole in dat sifter. En he lose count. En he start ergin [again]. En he git mix. En daylight kotch 'em. En he hab for go." The only certain means of preventing a hag from riding one was to catch the hag, which could best be done by the traditional African method of salting and peppering her skin while she was out of it. "Ef you is

marry wid a hag, she gits up en slips out'n she skin an' hide it under de stairsteps or back doorsteps, en when she come back she gits back in en lays back down. Now, when you wife go, you git up en look under de staircase. Ef ye fin' she skin, you salt en pepper it good same lak you salt en pepper fish what you goin fry. Ef she gone haggin, she sho lef' it, en if you salts it, she kain't git back in." Once the hag was caught she must be destroyed: "Put 'em in a barrel o' tar an' B'UN EM UP." As Lillie Knox told Chandler, "Ain' nuttin else ter do."

Whether haunts were more fearsome creatures than hags was a matter of dispute among the slaves. According to one ex-slave the hags were worse: "Dey say de ded can't fer hurt yuh. Hit de libe ones do dat." But another judged haunts to be more sinister: "De hag cain't trouble she. Hag jes human. But she ain't fer manage dem hant." Those who reported having seen haunts described them in inhuman terms. "Dey all two bofe hab on long white robe en er hair hang down, en he face been red same lak de brick en de chimbley," one reported. He added that the haunts possessed inhuman mobility. "Dey walks right in tru de do', en hit barred!" Haunts were more likely to appear at certain times, such as a full moon, than at others: "De hant woorser at de full o' de moon. Maum Nellie fer testify it start way cross de fiel'. It bark lak fox. It howl lak dawg. It hoot lak squinch owl. It soun lak at de beas' ob de woods. En fuss news it hit de house. It circle. It prowl same lak stray dawg. En while she hol' she bref [breath], de door what she done bolt mube [move] open. De pot lid lif. De rockin chair rock." Since the spirits of the dead exercised such a disquieting effect on the living, efforts were made to contain them. Slave funerals, for example, tried to propitiate the spirits of the ancestors. If the deceased were considered likely to remain as a malign spirit, the living sought to prevent it. "Ef hit er wicked wan us bin fer bury us doan want 'e sperrit lebe behin. Us keep tight circle roun de grabe 'twell 'e well cober."

Perhaps the most hideous and most malevolent of the occult creatures of this stream of African cosmology was the plat-eye, a malign spirit that took various shapes in order to lure its victims into danger and rob them of their wits. "Maum Addie," an aged ex-slave in All Saints Parish, recalled, "De ole folks is talk bout Plat-eye. Dey say dey takes shape ob all kind de critter—dawg, cat, hawg, mule, varmint, an I is hear tell ob plat-eye takin form ob gator. I ain' see dem scusin wan leetle time [except for one little time]." Hagar Brown described how the plat-eye "turn bull and turn all kinder sumpting nudder. Right there that muster shed. Dat been Plat-eye!" Matthew Grant declared that plat-eyes could "turn to dog, turn to horse, turn back to people. Turn to lil' bird! The old head tell me if you try to run from dem they trip you up! Throw you down. See 'um better on a old moon and a new moon. Stay round graveyard and all them cross road. 'Specially a road where they carry dead body cross. When Plat-eye show he self to you, you got to see dem!"

"Maum Addie," a former slave, told Chandler of her encounter with a plat-eye: "En mah short handle leetle clam rake been in mah hand en I sing, 'Gawd will take care ob me.' . . . En den de mine come ter me, 'De Lawd heps dem what heps deysef.' W'en I raise up mah rake en I come right cross dat critter haid. Ef dat had bin a real cat, I'd er pin him ter dat lawg. My rake bin bury deep en de lawg hol' em. En I clare ter Gawd, Miss Jin, dat he up en prances right onder mah feets, dem eyes burning holes in me en he tail swish, swish lak ole Sooky tail when de flies bad." "Maum Addie" knew of but one means of keeping plat-eyes at bay: "Gunpowder en sulphur. Dey is say Plat-eye can' stan' dem smell mix." Since adopting that preventive measure, "dey ain fer trubble me sense dat wan time." She learned the remedy from a conjurer; but her description of him aptly illustrates the complexities of cultural creolization in the New World: "Uncle Murphy he witch doctor en he bin tell me how fer fend 'em off. Dat man full ob knowledge. He mus hab Gawd mind in 'em." Her defense against

plat-eyes was a fascinating blend of tradition and creativity, of conjuration, Christianity, and common sense: "So I totes mah powder en sulphur en I carries mah stick in mah han en puts mah truss in Gawd."

As one might expect of a once-unified religious cosmology shattered into diverse and sometimes mutually exclusive streams, belief in the various components was by no means uniform. Some abandoned belief in all forms of non-Christian supernaturalism. An ex-slave named Hackless recalled a slave preacher who spurned hags, haunts, and plat-eyes with equal disdain. "Dat wan brabe man. 'E all de time fer say Plat-eye ner hag ner hant ner ghos ain fer harm 'em. 'E ain fear de dark no*how*. . . . 'E truss Gawd." But many slaves selectively adhered to some beliefs and abandoned others, as, for example, Liza Small's skepticism regarding the efficacy of the widespread belief that painting the door and window facings blue would ward off hags. Chandler asked her why she had all her doors and windows painted blue. She answered simply, "Board tak' em." When Chandler asked why she used the color blue, she said, "Old man buy 'em." Finally, when Chandler said she had always heard blue would keep the hags out, she exclaimed, "That ain't so! That ain't so! I prove that. Sometimes they ride me till I can't keep up next day!"

**4**

A third stream of inherited cosmology—which included African ideas regarding polytheism, rebirth, and spirit possession in religious ritual—combined with elements of Christianity to form an influential, and distinctly black, religion on the rice plantations of the Waccamaw. Since this new slave religion was the result of a convergence of African and European religious orientations, it may be helpful for a moment to examine the Christianity evangelized to the slaves in order to gain some perspective on the creolization process by which the slaves blended elements of African religions with elements of Christianity and adapted them to the conditions of rice plantation life. The originality of slave religion on the plantation streets and in the plantation chapels resides neither in its specifically African features nor in its specifically Christian features, but in its unique and creative synthesis in response to the reality of slavery.

While early South Carolina slaveholders had only reluctantly tolerated efforts to Christianize their slaves, the rice planters of antebellum All Saints Parish eagerly supported and participated in missionary efforts on their plantations. James L. Belin, a Methodist pastor at Murrells Inlet, began a forty-year mission to the slaves in 1819. Most of the rice planters were Episcopalians and members of All Saints Church, Waccamaw. They began their own mission to the slaves in 1832 under the leadership of their newly ordained rector, a twenty-eight-year-old Englishman named Alexander Glennie. Glennie preached to slaves on one plantation each Sunday afternoon and another on Sunday evening, and he held services three or four evenings a week as well. He was thus able to visit each plantation in the parish once or twice a month. When he began his mission, he had ten black communicants; by 1862 there were 529. Ex-slave Sabe Rutledge recalled, "Before freedom Parson Glennie—he was piscopal—he would come give us a service once a month on the plantation—so mother said." J. Motte Alston described Glennie's visits to Woodbourne in his memoirs:

> The Reverend Alexander Glennie and his wife would come to us once every fortnight. He always came to dinner, after which he would teach the negro children their catechism and preach to all of my negroes at night. They always had a half holiday on these occasions, so as to let them brush up and make a respectable appearance. It was a law that all should attend.
>
> I had a Church built conveniently, and my family, myself, and guests always attended. It was quite wonderful what retentive memories they had, for few could read. The minister would always read the evening services of the Episcopal Book of Common Prayer and always,

too, the same Psalter so as to enable the congregation to respond, which they did most accurately and devoutly.

> But I do well remember one evening when the Bishop (Davis) accompanied Mr. Glennie and was to preach that evening, and all were rigged out in their Sunday's best, when in the midst of the service, while all were standing, one of the men, full six feet in height, went fast asleep and fell over the benches, and all came down with a crash to the floor, to the amusement of the congregation and to the mortification of the performer, whose specific gravity so greatly outweighed his spiritual zeal.

Perhaps such lapses in spiritual zeal were at least partly explained by the recollections of another ex-slave, Mariah Heywood, who remembered that "Parson Glennie come once a month to Sunnyside. Parson Glennie read, sing, pray. Tell us obey Miss Minna."

Between Glennie's visits the planters held morning devotionals for the house servants. A northern visitor described one such morning at Henry Buck's Woodbourne plantation: "a signal from the mistress caused the sounding of a bell in the hall, and some ten or twelve men and women house-servants, of remarkably neat and tidy appearance . . . entered the apartment. They took a stand at the remote end of the room and our host, opening a large, well-worn family *Bible,* read the fifty-fourth chapter of Isaiah. Then, all kneeling, he made a short extemporaneous petition, closing with the Lord's Prayer; all present, black as well as white, joining in it. Then Heber's beautiful hymn, 'From Greenland's Icy Mountains,' was sung; the negroes, to my ear, making much better music than the whites."

The rice planters supported such attempts at religious instruction of the slaves in part out of genuine concern for the slaves' spiritual welfare. The religion they taught to the slaves, however, was a highly selective form of Christianity, which stressed obedience in the here and now as much as salvation in the hereafter. When Buck held family devotions for his house servants, when John Hyrne Tucker and J.

Motte Alston compelled their slaves to attend chapel services, when Plowden C. J. and Emily Weston catechized their slaves and taught them to read the Bible, they did so out of a sincere Christian concern for the slaves' salvation. But they were also aware that religion was a more subtle, more humane, and more effective means of control than the whip.

Glennie eloquently emphasized this aspect of Christianity in his sermons to the slaves:

> "Servants, be obedient to them that are your masters according to the flesh, with fear and trembling, in singleness of your heart, as unto Christ; not with eye service as men pleasers; but as the servants of Christ, doing the will of God from the heart: with good will doing service, as to the Lord and not to men; knowing that whatsoever good thing any man doeth, the same shall he receive of the Lord, whether he be bond or free." This passage from the Bible shews to you, what God requires from you as servants; and there are many other passages which teach the same things. You should try and remember these parts of the Bible, that you may be able "to do your duty in that state of life, unto which it has pleased God to call you." For although a bad servant may not wish to know what God requires of him, yet a Christian servant will desire to know this, and to do his will in every thing.

"Here," Glennie told the slaves, "is a very plain command: 'servants be obedient': be obedient to your masters." Bad servants would neglect this command, "but you, who call yourselves children of God, will do his will" and "every day give proof that you wish to serve God, by your ready, your cheerful obedience." He cautioned them against "giving offence by any conduct that look like disobedience; for, by disobedience, you not only offend your earthly master, but you sin against God" and "bring reproach on Him whose name you bear." Servants should look upon their daily tasks as "the will of God." "Do not attend to your work only while your earthly master's eye is upon you; but remember that the eye of your heavenly Master is always upon you." A bad servant would only work "so long as his master's eye is upon him," but "you, who call yourselves the servants of Christ," will "do service' cheerfully, 'as to the Lord, and not to men.' " And, in the day of judgment, "it matters not whether we be bond-servants or free men: it matters not whether we be among the high and the rich, or among the low and the poor: we shall in that day receive according as we now live. If we now live as obedient followers of our Lord and Savior Jesus Christ, we shall, through him who loved us, inherit everlasting life."

It would be unfair to Glennie, and untrue to history, to suggest that he cynically reduced Christianity to patience, humility, and the fear of sin, or that he was more concerned with the slaves' discipline than with their salvation. Nevertheless, slaveholders believed his preaching had a significant effect on discipline in All Saints Parish. James R. Sparkman reflected on the success of the slaves' religious instruction in 1858: "The moral and social condition of the Slave population in this district has vastly improved within 20 years. The control, management, and entire discipline has materially changed, crime and rebellion are much less frequent. They have learned in many instances to govern themselves and to govern each other and through this section, *'Runaways'* are fewer and *'less lawless.'* " Colonel Thomas Pinckney Alston, a leading Waccamaw rice planter until his retirement in 1858, tacitly conceded that some planters were less interested in the slaves' understanding of the Christian gospels than with the effect of religious indoctrination on keeping order on the plantations.

The dilemma that Glennie and other ministers had to face was that the Christianity they preached was potentially subversive to the institution of slavery. He and the planters both realized this. During the 1834 legislative debate, which prohibited teaching slaves to read and write, a planter had noted that anyone who wanted slaves to read the *entire* Bible belonged in "a room in the Lunatic Asylum."

Glennie was no mere sycophant of cynical rice planters. He did not select merely the texts that promoted order and discipline among the slaves. But he did realize that the same religion that so effectively promoted order on Waccamaw rice plantations contained the seeds of disorder. He did not preach to his congregations that Pharoah had enslaved the children of Israel and held them in bondage in Egypt. He did not tell them that the Lord visited plagues on the slaveholders or that Moses led them in a mass escape from slavery to the promised land.

But Glennie did preach the equality of all in the sight of God. He spoke of "our first parents, Adam and Eve," and told slave and master alike that "all mankind are descended from them." He preached the equality of sinfulness. "All are born in sin," he said, "and if it were not for the love and mercy and goodness of God, all would live in sin, and would suffer the pains of hell forever." But "we sinners" are saved because "Christ Jesus came into the world." Glennie identified Jesus with the slaves. "And he did not appear as a great and rich man, but he took the form of a servant." Christianity imposed obedience not merely upon the slaves, but upon their earthly masters as well. Glennie preached that "in the day of judgment, the inquiry will be: What have we done in this world; how did we live in this world? It matters not," he told his congregations, "in what condition we have been here," whether slave or free, high or low, rich or poor. All would be held to the same account before God's judgment. "If we are disobedient to his word, we can inherit only everlasting misery." As servants were taught in the Bible how they must obey their masters, so masters were taught in the Bible how they must rule their servants, and the rich were taught how they must do good with their riches. Masters and slaves alike Glennie admonished to "remember the account which we shall all have to give before his judgment seat."

Here was the dilemma for the rice planters. As Christians, they were committed to the religious instruction of their slaves. But the religion to be taught to the slaves also called the masters to account. That the masters were as subject as the slaves to the requirements of Christianity created a problem of role boundaries on the rice plantations and emphasized internal tensions and anomalies that could not be ignored. Many, perhaps most, of the Waccamaw masters took Glennie's admonitions quite seriously. Plowden C. J. Weston prayed in the chapel at Hagley that God would "give to all masters grace to keep order and discipline in their families, and to treat their servants with mercy, kindness, gentleness, and discretion; knowing that thou has made of one flesh all the nations of the earth. Give to all servants grace to obey their masters, and please them well in all things; knowing that in thus doing they shall please thee who art the Master over all." Robert F. W. Allston believed that the "best inducement" to win the slaves to Christianity was "example on our own part; next a just, consistent, systematic administration of domestic government."

## 5

The missionary efforts of Glennie and others were an important source of Afro-Christianity among the slaves of All Saints Parish. But the slaves did not simply adopt Glennie's God and his faith. In their efforts to establish a spiritual life for themselves, they interpreted the elements of Christianity taught by Glennie in terms of deep-rooted African cognitive orientations. In stressing the significance of the African conribution to slave Christianity, it would be a mistake to leave the impression that Africa was culturally homogeneous or that it bequeathed to its exiles in the New World a legacy of static survivals. On the contrary, African religious expression was so diverse that borrowings were common among various ethnic groups. But rising above the plethora of rites and practices was a common bond—the concept of a sacred cosmos in which nearly all experience was religious, from the naming of children to beliefs regarding when to plant and how to hunt and fish. And underlying the various African cultures were shared cognitive or "grammatical" orientations—mental rules governing appropriate behavior—which affected the slaves' adoption, adaptation, and application of Christianity. Since slaves could no longer find on Waccamaw rice plantations anything approximating the African context of their sacred cosmos, they worshiped their new Christian God with the kind of expressive behavior their African heritage taught them was appropriate for an important deity.

The persistence of African expressive behavior in slave religion was manifested in a high degree of emotional involvement in worship, including the use of dances and chants to rhythmic accompaniment, culminating in trances and spirit possession. Unlike hoodoo and conjuration, spirit possession was incorporated into Afro-Christianity and reinterpreted in Christian terms. According to one of the Waccamaw rice planters, "Their whole religious worship is proverbially emotional, frequently running into boisterous shoutings, with noisy demonstrations of hands and feet, and extravagant, wild, hysterical gyrations of the body, which are contagious and Exhaustive, sometimes ending in a swoon or semicataleptic condition." At night many slave families went to one another's houses to hold prayer meetings and to sing and "shout." The shout was a series of body motions (usually described as a dance by outsiders) that the slaves performed to the accompaniment of spirituals. It exemplified the creative Afro-Carolinian adaptation of a West African ring dance performed to complex drum rhythms. In the New World the drums, upon which Africans had relied to articulate their spiritual life, were lost; but a substitute was improvised with polyrhythmic hand-clapping and foot-stamping. The slaves called the adaptation "shouting," after the African *saut,* meaning to walk or run around. Similar expressive behavior was widespread among blacks in the Caribbean and elsewhere in the South Carolina low country.

While many slave Christians frowned upon dancing itself, they participated in the shouts with great enthusiasm. "Fire take the church! Heart commence to turn over!" recalled Hagar Brown, describing her response as the spirit filled the church. "Great Lord! The whole thing been jump!" As she shouted up and down the aisles, she felt that "anything I want, I hold out my hand and say, 'Jehovah, I pend on you!'" In such prolonged religious fervor many became so stiff from trances that they "cannot buckle."

The phenomenon of spirit possession was the central fact of expressive behavior in the spiritual life of All Saints slaves. The necessity of experiencing spirit possession for conversion marked the continuation in Afro-Christianity of one of the most persistent features of African religion (especially pronounced among the Bantu, the Yoruba, and the Fante-Ashanti) in the New World. Conversion was characterized by a spiritual journey, or retreat, called "seeking." The seeker's prolonged praying and meditating during this period induced an ecstatic trance without which conversion was not considered authentic: "Fore he convert—like any other else man. Had to be borned again." Eventually the seeker "came through" and "found peace." Hagar Brown recalled her own conversion to Chandler: "I 'member and I 'member well when I wuz on my prayin' ground! 'Member when I get my thing!" she said. "I come through. Right there to old Laurel Hill been my prayin' ground." "Coming through" was in itself an ecstatic experience, as Hagar Brown described it: "How happy are the child of God when he know he sin forgiven! Somebody kept tryin' to tech me. I walkin'! Walkin'! And a big man with he hands folded jest so say, 'Let her 'lone! Leave her 'lone. Been that-a-way myself! He layin' down! 'Layin down hands cross he breast! No common head o' man! Spirit of God! Then I feel somebody tech me. My jaw been lock Thursday night twelve o'clock. Saturday I come through! Couldn't eat; couldn't eat! Them old timey people, couldn't fool em." Only after such an experience was one accepted as a member of the church. Others were considered sinners.

When slave Christians gathered at one another's houses for praise meetings, their expressive behavior provided a release for pent-up emotions in the soaring rhetoric of the prayers, the antiphonal singing, and the ecstatic shouts, unlike the sedate, unemotional Episcopal services that Glennie conducted for the planters at All Saints Church, Waccamaw. A white visitor, observing one such South Carolina praise meeting, remarked that "none can move a negro but a negro." This was not altogether true, but white preachers had to realize that sermons were no more passive experiences for blacks than was singing. A religious service was not a relationship between a performer and an audience, but a mutual performance. Just as songs were characterized by the strong call-and-response antiphony of West African music, so prayers and sermons were punctuated by congregational responses. Glennie "lined out" hymns for his black congregations, who responded antiphonally. A northern visitor described the scene: "We all went to a negro church. . . . The congregation responded and sang the Te Deum with Mr. G[lennie]. Some had books and could read, but as all could not, he would read two lines of a hymn & then they would all sing them & so on!!" Glennie tailored the catechismal style of his Anglican sermons to suit the stylistic expectations of the slaves. "Now do you, all of you, my brethren, receive this saying, that Christ Jesus came into the world to save sinners!" he would ask, and the congregation would respond. "Do you receive this, and live according to it, in the hope of going to heaven?" Again the congregation would respond—and so on through the series of questions and congregational answers that built to a powerful climax: "Do you look upon yourselves as among the sinners that Jesus came to save; and in consequence, are you so repenting of your sins as to forsake them? Do you kneel down upon your knees everyday before the holy God, and confess to him that you are miserable sinners, de-

serving his anger; and at the same time look to Jesus who was crucified for you, and pray that for his sake your sins may all be forgiven, that they may all be blotted out in his most precious blood? Is it your care too to pray, that the Holy Spirit may abide in your hearts, making you faithful followers of Jesus Christ, willing servants of God, obedient to him in all things?" This long series of questions, answered by the congregation whenever the preacher paused, was followed by three repetitive sentences. "That is what you ought to be doing, if you would have your souls to be saved," Glennie would say, and the congregation would respond. "That is what you ought to be doing, if you would have Jesus Christ to save you from living in sin in this world, and from suffering the punishment which your sins deserve in the next," he would say, and the congregation would respond. "Seriously think of these things, I pray you," Glennie concluded, "and may God bless you, and make you true followers of Jesus Christ, who came into this world to save sinners."

So powerful was the expressive behavior of the African religious heritage that white ministers ignored it at their peril if they wished to preach successfully to plantation slaves on the Waccamaw.

## 6

It was not merely in expressive behavior, however, that the religion of the slaves was distinctive. Afro-Christianity embodied a broader theology than just the selected portions taught them by Glennie and other white preachers. The slaves did not reject the Christian call to renounce sin and follow Jesus. Many of the slave songs from All Saints Parish reflected the emphasis of Glennie's sermons. There were songs that glorified Jesus:

*The Roman soldier 'round Him*
*A thousand army wide*
*If He had not been die for us*
*We all might not have been save*

*Now I just want to told you*
*How He went down in the grave*
*With the burden of nation*
*And sinner for to save*

And there were songs that urged the renunciation of sin:

*God sent Jonah to Ninevy [Ninevah] land.*
*Jonah disobey my God command*
*Paid his fare and he got on board.*
*Children, don't you do that!*

*Don't you do that!*
*Don't you do that!*

*God got His eye on you!*
*Don't you do that!*
*Don't you do that!*
*Don't you idle your time away!*

But the slaves also found in Christianity analogies to their own situation in the enslavement and persecution of the Israelites. And they found in Christianity the heroes and the hopes that could make life in bondage bearable.

If Glennie's sermons concentrated exclusively on the gospels and the epistles of the New Testament, the Afro-American spirituals from All Saints Parish were filled with Old Testament imagery—Daniel in the lion's den; Gabriel's blowing his horn; Ezekiel in the wilderness, chewing on dry bones; the shepherd boy David's felling of the mighty Goliath; God's rescuing Jonah from the whale; God's calling Moses to lead the Israelites out of slavery; God's sending a flood to destroy the wicked world. Such themes had immediate appeal to a people held in bondage and exile. And New Testament references in the All Saints spirituals ran heavily to revelation and to that final judgment day when God would redeem the righteous and punish the wicked for their misdeeds on earth.

There is a haunting quality about the spirituals that partly echoes African continuities in their music and performance style and partly reflects the trials and suffering, the sorrows and tribulations of life in bondage. Despite their inevitable sadness, however, the spirituals were also songs of hope and of affirmation. They reflected an awareness that slavery was an unnatural—and temporary—condition:

*God call Moses! (Ay Lord!)*
*God call Moses! (Ay Lord!)*
*God call Moses! (Ay Lord!)*
*Time is a-rollin on!*

*Moses free the people! (Ay Lord!)*
*Moses free the people! (Ay Lord!)*
*Moses free the people! (Ay Lord!)*
*Time is a-rollin on!* [41]

They reflected an awareness that God wreaks vengeance on the wicked who have oppressed his people:

*I'm looking for the stone*
*That rolling through Babylon!*
*I'm looking for the stone*
*That rolling through Babylon!*
*I'm looking for the stone*
*That rolling through Babylon!*
*Down from the kingdom of the world!*

They reflected an awareness that God can work miracles to bring about immediate change, as when the Syrian commander Naaman was cleansed of leprosy by washing in the Jordan River and became a follower of Jehovah:

*God told Naaman to go to Jordan!*
*Halleloo!*
*God told Naaman to go to Jordan!*
*Halleloo!*
*Halleloo! Halleloo!*

They reflected, too, belief that persistence would be rewarded:

*Joshua was the son of Nun*
*He never stop till the work was done!*

and

*Lord, I've started for the kingdom!*
*Lord, I've started for the kingdom!*
*Lord, I've started for the kingdom!*
*I ain't gon' turn back! I ain't goin' turn back!*

They called upon the Lord for strength to face the burdens of the present:

*Come by here, Lord! Come by here!*
*Come by here! my Lord! Come by here!*
*Come by here, Lord! Come by here!*
*Oh Lord, come by here!*

*Need your power, Lord, Come by here!*
*Need your power, Lord, Come by here!*
*Need your power, Lord, Come by here!*
*Oh, Lordy, Come by here!*

*Sinners moanin' Lord! Come by here!*
*Sinners moanin' Lord! Come by here!*
*Sinners moanin' Lord, Come by here!*
*Oh, Lordy, Come by here.*

But they expressed full confidence that heaven awaits them in the life beyond death. No one can enter heaven on the labor of others:

*I got to stand*
*Before the judgment bar!*
*Oh, there's nobody here*
*To stand there for me!*
*Oh, I got to stand there*
*For myself!*

But just as God delivered Daniel from the lion's den and the fiery furnace, He could also deliver His followers from the House of Bondage:

*I'm goin' home!*
*I'm goin' home!*
*I will overcome some day!*
*I'm goin' home!*
*I'm goin' home!*
*I will overcome some day!*

*I do believe!*
*I do believe!*
*I will overcome some day!*

*I do believe!*
*I do believe!*
*I will overcome some day.*

If the specific deities of Africa were left behind, the Christian doctrine of the Trinity was readily comprehensible to slave converts; and legions of saints and angels kept alive the spirit of African polytheism:

*I believe I'll count the angel!*
*I do believe I'll count the angel!*
*I do believe I'll count the angel!*
*How many angels in the band?*

Since the African cognitive grammar underlying the slaves' religion did not make a sharp distinction between the sacred and secular worlds, the perceptions and beliefs expressed in these songs were applied directly to the world of the rice plantations. As they labored in the rice fields under the broiling Carolina sun, they lightened their burdens with songs such as "Don't Get Weary, We're Almost Done." When slaves were sold away from the plantation, those remaining behind would face their grief with the help of such songs as

*Oh my sister done move!*
*My sister done move!*
*My sister done move her campin' ground!*
*Ah Lord! Lord have mercy!*
*My sister done move her campin' ground!*

and

*Gwine meet my Mother over there!*
*Gwine meet my Mother over there!*
*We gwine have a good time!*
*Way by-and-by!*

Other songs, such as this one taken down by an English visitor in 1856, could have served as a kind of code to inform the slaves of a secret religious gathering or a clandestine frolic:

*Oh, I takes my text in Matthew,*
*And some in Revelation,*
*Oh, I know you by your garment—*
*There's a meeting here to-night.*

And when the slaves sang of "Going over Jordan," or "I Done Started for the Kingdom," or celebrated the glory of "Canaan's Happy Shore," it is likely that the specific geography in their minds was not always biblical. Such songs as "If You See John the Writer" seem even more explicitly concerned with escape from the House of Bondage:

*If you see John the writer, tell him you saw*
*    me!*
*Tell him you saw me!*
*If you see John the writer, tell him you saw*
*    me*
*When you saw me I was on my way!*

*I'm travelin' up the King Highway!*
*I'm travelin' up the King Highway!*
*I'm travelin' up the King Highway!*
*When you saw me I was on my way!*

*I was on my way to a heavenly land when*
*    you saw me!*
*When you saw me!*
*I was on my way to a Heavenly land*
*When you saw me I was on my way!*

The old King's Highway, which George Washington had followed on his presidential visit in 1790, runs north and south through All Saints Parish. The slaves knew that route led to the free states.

At the outbreak of the Civil War several slaves were imprisoned in Georgetown for singing

*We'll soon be free*
*We'll soon be free*
*We'll soon be free*
*When de Lord will call us home*

*My brudder how long*
*My brudder how long*
*My brudder how long*
*'Fore we done sufferin' here*

*We'll fight for liberty*
*We'll fight for liberty*
*We'll fight for liberty*
*When de Lord will call us home*

Thomas Wentworth Higginson, who learned this song from Georgetown soldiers in the black regiment that he commanded, the First South Carolina Volunteers, speculated that " 'De Lord will call us home' was evidently thought to be a symbolic verse; for, as a little drummer boy explained to me, showing all his white teeth as he sat in the moonlight by the door of my tent, 'Dey tink *de Lord* mean for say de Yankees.' " Higginson's friend William Francis Allen remarked that "in this case the suspicion was unfounded." Presumably he regarded the suspicion as unfounded because the song was an old one, but the assumption that slaves only began to dream of freedom at the outbreak of the Civil War is spurious. Accepting for the moment the dubious proposition that the song initially meant freedom from sin rather than freedom from slavery, it is difficult to believe it did not take on the latter meaning during the Civil War. The slaves of All Saints Parish understood perfectly well what was at stake in the fighting. Welcome Beese told Chandler, "Yankee fight for free WE. . . . THEY FIGHT TO FREE NIGGER!" In the altered context of the Civil War—as later during the civil rights movement—old spirituals could take on more specific meanings.

## 7

The shouts, spirituals, and religious fervor of the slaves excited and alarmed their masters. They were encouraged that the slaves held family prayers and gathered at house meetings to sing and shout and to be moved by such slave preachers as Jemmy, a house servant at Hagley. Wyndham Malet, an English visitor to Hagley (and himself an Anglican priest), vividly rendered the cadence and imagery of one of Jemmy's prayers:

*O Lord,*
*in whose palm of his hand be the waters of*
*    the ocean—*
*who can remove mountains—*
*who weights the earth in a balance—*
*who can still the waves of the storm—*
*who can break the pines of the forest—*
*who gives us a land of rivers of waters—*
*O Jesus!*
*who died on the cross for us—*
*O forgive us our sins;*
*help us in this time of trial and need.*
*Protect our massa far away;*
*protect our brothers "Hector" and "Caesar"*
*    with him;*
*defend us now we are away from home;*
*defend our friends and relatives at home, &c.*

Jemmy was a man of status within the slave community, held in high regard as a man of words. The continuing social importance of the man of words marked the adaptation of African tradition to Afro-Christianity. Jemmy, who straddled the sacred and secular worlds, was regarded as having the ability to employ the powers of the sacred world within the secular domain.

Such "gifted" men—as Malet termed them—often acted as mediators between Christian belief and the everyday world of the plantation. One example of the African sense of the total involvement of religion in everyday life was the role of the slave preachers as arbiters in settling disputes among the slaves. As a Sandy Island slaveholder put it, the "mandates and decrees" of Afro-Christianity were regarded by the slaves to be "more authoritative & binding than the laws of the commonwealth or, as they express it, the laws of the white man." If the decision was not accepted, the offender might be ostracized by slave Christians as a "sinner," but repentant sinners were easily accepted back into the group, often enjoying extra attention in the process. "Here's the wandering sheep come back in the fold," the preacher said when Ben Horry repented. His return is illustrative: "Poor old Uncle Ben! In church after services he stay in. Tears just

pour out his eyes. Th' pitifulest thing in this world. Pitiful! Pitiful! He make you cry. Realize he doing wrong and turn back. And they read the scripture bout the prodigal son have returned." Through such mediation, the slave preachers not only promoted social order on the plantations but also helped to solidify a sense of slave community and served as role models with strong cultural identities not dependent upon their positions as slaves.

Furthermore, while Glennie and other white ministers preached Christianity at least partly to promote contentment, the slave preachers often sowed the seeds of discontent in the community. Much of the slaves' spiritual life was hidden from the masters' eyes. According to Sparkman, the black church was "regarded by many of its members as a *social but secret* society." The slaves of All Saints Parish often held religious services independently of the whites, and sometimes without their knowledge. Mariah Heywood recalled that they held secret prayer meetings throughout the Civil War in which they prayed for freedom from slavery. Such slave revolts as those of Gabriel Prosser, Nat Turner, and—closer to home— Denmark Vesey had been planned under cover of religious associations (although the conjurer Gullah Jack figured prominently in the Vesey plot). Slave preachers may also have played a role in slave revolts in Georgetown District in 1802 and 1829. Certainly charismatic slave preachers seem to have been involved in virtually every known slave revolt. In any event such spirituals as "We'll Soon Be Free" gave evidence not only that enslavement could not crush the love of freedom from the hearts and minds of the slaves but also that Afro-Christianity provided an appropriate vehicle for expressing that love of freedom.

Of course, Christianity did not take with every slave. For one thing, at least a few African-born slaves in the South Carolina low country retained their belief in Islam as late as the mid-nineteenth century. Some low country planters substituted a ration of beef instead of pork for Moslem slaves. Other slaves simply regarded Christianity as a nuisance. One African-born slave in the eighteenth century was reported to have said to another: "I am no such bad man as you think. . . . True I love dance and frolic;—sure Sambo, it's no harm, for make merry now and then. . . . Is nobody good but them praying sort a people? . . . I don't love this praying and going to meeting. What have we black people for do with that? The minister he never say any thing to us." But for others Afro-Christianity played an important role in their day-to-day lives on the rice plantations of the Waccamaw. Through their active participation in praise meetings, in their preservation of African traditions of spirit possession and expressive behavior in ecstatic prayers and energetic shouts, and especially in their transcendant spirituals, the slaves of All Saints Parish voiced their deepest values and proclaimed—and partly shaped—their sense of community.

# 19

## "GREASERS" IN THE DIGGINGS: CALIFORNIANS AND SONORANS UNDER ATTACK

### LEONARD M. PITT

The American victory in the Mexican War of 1846–1848 brought to the United States those territories that were to become Texas, Arizona, New Mexico, and California. The American victory also raised the question of the status of the Mexican and native-born inhabitants of these territories. Were they to retain their lands? Were they to have the same rights as citizens of the United States? Nowhere was this question more sharply posed than in California where descendants of the Spanish conquistadores had been living for three centuries. These native-born Californios composed the elite of Spanish California, owning huge haciendas and holding the reins of power in the territory. With the end of the Mexican War there was little sign that the power of the Californios would be significantly diminished.

Then, in the same year that the war ended, gold was discovered in the Sierra Nevada. As news of the unprecedented scale of the discovery and the ease with which it could be mined reached the outside world, thousands of Americans, Mexicans, and Europeans flocked to the California "Mother Lode" in search of quick fortunes. As Leonard Pitt shows in this essay, the California gold rush brought forth some of the worst of American traits. From the beginning American miners ignored the Californios' hereditary claims to the land and through intimidation and force drove them from the goldfields. They offered the same treatment to Mexican and European prospectors who dared to encroach upon "their" claims. This rampant nativism of the early years did not diminish once statehood was declared in 1850; instead prejudicial laws were written onto the books by a legislature in which only white Americans were represented. It was only when groups defined as "outsiders" began to offer armed resistance to these attacks that more moderate forces prevailed in early California.

From Leonard M. Pitt, *The Decline of the Californios: A Social History of the Spanish-Speaking Californians, 1846–1890* (Berkeley, Calif.: University of California Press, 1966). © 1966 The Regents of the University of California.

Why did the Spaniards and Mexicans fail to discover gold before 1848? What would have happened to them had they done so? These are two of the "iffiest" questions in all of California history.

The Mexicans had, in fact, discovered minor deposits of gold in southern California more than a decade prior to the historic Coloma discovery, but they did miss the big find in the Sierra. The causes of their oversight include a fear of Indian attack in the interior and a decision to hug the coast for protection; no population pressure ever drove them inward. The Spanish tradition of looking for signs of *oro* among the Indians, as in Hernán Cortés' conquest of the Aztecs, also played a role, although a negative one, for the California Indians did not manipulate gold. Another cause may have been that the contentment of rancho life after 1834 had sapped the rancheros' energy necessary to explore new territory. Or perhaps the trouble was, simply, bad luck: Captain Gabriel Moraga's forty-six expeditions before 1820 had brought him near, if not directly atop, the Mother Lode, yet no gleam caught his eye. The Spanish Americans generally did not want for daring as explorers or for skill as miners; centuries of experience in both had equipped them ideally for the fateful discovery they somehow failed to make.

As to what might have been their history had they chanced upon the Sierra gold, the possibilities are numerous. They range from the attainment of genuine cultural maturity and political independence to an even more crushing defeat than the one they received after 1849. Perhaps California would have become one of the most populous and heavily defended places in the Spanish Empire or in the Mexican Republic. The Californios might have had genuine Mexican military support in a war with the Yankees, and thus also a better treaty settlement. Conquest by a European power would not have been entirely out of the question either. The answer, of course, depends upon *when* one supposes the gold to have been discovered: the earlier the better

for the Californios, from the standpoint of the growth of Yankee expansionism in the 1840's. One suspects, however, that Manifest Destiny somehow was bound to triumph along the Pacific Coast and eventually convert California into a Yankee province.

The Californios themselves scarcely ever engaged in such ruminations, for they were not a people to pine over lost opportunities and were faced with realities that gave them enough food for thought. The discovery of gold in 1848 made an enormous impact on them—the greatest in their brief experience: it brought them riches, for one thing; it threw them together with other Latin Americans, for another; and, most important, it opened them to full-scale Yankee penetration and conquest.

As news of the discovery spread in 1848, Californios speedily converged on the Sierra from all directions and, in a sense, made up for lost time. The experience of the Angeleños was typical. With Don Antonio Coronel taking on the function of patrón, the thirty Californios, Sonorans, and Indian servants had good luck from the outset. They immediately enticed some mountain tribesmen to accept baubles in exchange for gold nuggets and, after spying out the Indians' trove and plying them with more trinkets, they obtained their digging labor into the bargain. In one day Antonio himself ended up with 45 ounces of gold; Dolores Sepúlveda found a 12-ounce nugget; and Señor Valdez discovered a boulder buried only 3 feet down which had once blocked the flow of an ancient alluvial stream and produced a towelful of nuggets in a short time. He sold his claim to Lorenzo Soto, who took out a whopping 52 pounds of gold in eight days and then sold it to Señor Machado, who also became rich. Even a Sonoran servant became fabulously wealthy overnight.

In all, about 1,300 native Californians mined gold in 1848, the year of the bonanzas. If they had missed the opportunity to discover Sierra gold in the past, they did not do so now; nearness to the placers gave them the head start on the thousands of prospectors still getting their wits together for the voyage halfway around the world. The Californios had additional advantages in knowing precisely where and how to find gold and in gladly pooling their resources and dividing their labor. As a result, the organized Californians, though less numerous than the 4,000 individualistic Yankees in the mines that year, probably extracted as much gold as they. Coronel, a struggling Mexican schoolteacher, had pocketed enough gold to become a prominent landowner, viticulturist, and community leader. He and many other Californios resolved to make a second expedition the next year. They dismissed the news that a few Californios had been harried from their claims by fist-swinging Oregon Yankees, who refused to acknowledge that the Treaty of Guadalupe Hidalgo granted some Mexicans full citizenship: in 1848 "everything ended peacefully."

In the year that followed, the story changed drastically. Coronel's return trip to the mines began badly, with a near-fatal brawl in a Sonoma saloon. One day he and *compadre* Juan Padilla were waiting for the wet January weather to clear, when a former Bear Flagger began to bully Padilla for having served as Bernardo Garcia's henchman in the wartime atrocity against Cowie and Fowler. Padilla insisted that the charge was a lie, and the American replied with an assault. After a severe beating, Padilla lay in an upstairs room, hovering near death for several weeks, while below his accuser continued to threaten his life. Only Coronel's good reputation and the intercession of friendly Americans restrained the former Bear Flagger.

After nursing his friend back to life, Coronel returned to the Sierra. He fell in among Chileans, Mexicans, and Germans doing well at dry diggings until confronted with posters declaring that foreigners had no right to be there and must leave the mines at once; resistance would be met by force. Although this threat never materialized, excitement mounted. In a nearby camp, a Mexican gambler's tent had been raided, and some Yankees accused five foreigners of stealing 5 pounds of gold. Coronel's associates doubled the accusation against at least one apparently honorable man and raised 5 pounds of gold to offer as ransom. Coronel conferred with a Yankee delegation and gave them the gold. The delegates then retired to consider the offer but never reemerged from the drunken and agitated crowd, which by then numbered into the hundreds. The money did no good; all five prisoners were convicted and flogged at once, and two of them, a Frenchman and a Chilean, were charged with a previous murder and robbery. Guilty or not, the pair scarcely understood enough of the proceedings to reply to the accusations. When Coronel next saw them they were standing in a cart, lashed together back to back and pinned with a note warning away defenders such as might come from Coronel's camp. A horse then jolted the cart from under the men, and California had witnessed its first lynching. That incident resulted, Coronel thought, from a declining gold supply and the Yankees' increasing jealousy of successful Spanish Americans.

As quickly as possible Don Antonio led his group away from the newly named "Hangtown," and resettled in the remote northern mines. But even there a hundred gringos appeared with the gruff announcement that the entire riverbed belonged exclusively to Americans who would tolerate no foreigners. Furious, some of Coronel's people who had reached the limit of their endurance planned armed resistance, even at the cost of their lives, but Coronel held back and sadly announced, "For me gold mining is finished."

By July many other Californios had cause to echo Coronel's words. As the only true native-born citizens they did have a legitimate place in the mines, yet they knew no way to convince 100,000 hostile strangers of this truth. Fisticuffs or hand combat simply was not the Californians' style. Consequently, one of them carried into the field of combat a safe-conduct pass, signed by the army's secretary of state, which certified him as a bona fide citizen deserving of every right and privilege, of every lawful aid and protection. What good the pass did is not recorded, but the attacks mounted. For most Californios, the best answer was to go home and stay there: "Don't go to the mines on any account," one *paisano* advised another. Out of pride, which prevented them from being converted into aliens by Yankee rogues and upstarts, few Californians ventured back into the maelstrom after 1849.

Musing over the gold rush from a safe distance, the Californians once more concluded that outsiders were, by and large, despicable. Mariano Vallejo said of the forty-niners without sparing any nationality, "The good ones were few and the wicked many." Hugo Reid ticked off the list of troublemakers:

> . . . vagabonds from every quarter of the globe. Scoundrels from nowhere, rascals from Oregon, pickpockets from New York, accomplished gentlemen from Europe, interlopers from Lima and Chile, Mexican thieves, gamblers of no particular spot, and assassins manufactured in Hell for the expressed purpose of converting highways and biways into theatres of blood; then, last but not least, Judge Lynch with his thousand arms, thousand sightless eyes, and five-hundred lying tongues.

The Californians now simply reverted to their customary circular logic, which held that evil came from outsiders, that outsiders were mostly evil, and that evil mothered evil. In no other way could they explain the ugly behavior of so many people, especially Americanos.

After a century of slow population growth, during which the arrival of twenty-five cholos or fifty Americans seemed a momentous occasion, suddenly and without warning California faced one of the swiftest, largest, and most varied folk migrations of all time. More newcomers now arrived each day in California than had formerly come in a decade. Briefly told, the story of the Californians in the gold rush is their encounter with 100,000 newcomers in the single year of 1849—80,000 Yankees, 8,000 Mexicans, 5,000 South Americans, and several thousand miscellaneous Europeans—and with numbers that swelled to a quarter million by 1852. Even assuming the goodwill of every last one of these strangers, they outnumbered the Californians ten and fifteen times over and reduced them to feelings of insignificance.

It is the destiny of ethnic groups in the United States to be thrown together with people of "their own kind" whom they neither know nor particularly like—perhaps even despise. This was the lot of the Californios in 1849, with the massive migration of Latin Americans. It was bad enough that by 1850 the Mexican cholos outnumbered the 15,000 Californios; even worse, angry Yankees simply refused to recognize any real distinctions between Latin Americans. Whether from California, Chile, Peru, or Mexico, whether residents of twenty years' standing or immigrants of one week, all the Spanish-speaking were lumped together as "interlopers" and "greasers." In this molding, the Californians, who had always kept aloof from cholos and earlier had won some grudging respect from the Yankees, lost most heavily. Their reputation as a people more heroic, handsome, and civilized than other "Spaniards" now dissolved. Their proximity to the greasers between 1849 and 1852 put them in actual jeopardy of their lives. In essence then, the Latin-American immigrants were a sort of catalyst whose presence caused the sudden and permanent dissolution of the social elements.

The biggest waves of Latin Americans came from Chile and northern Mexico. The Chileans excelled in baking and bricklaying and other skills and thus found themselves in especially great demand in California. They settled down at the foot of San Francisco's Telegraph Hill, in a place called "Little Chile," or went into the mines to dig, until expelled by the Yankees.

Even more prominent and numerous were the northern Mexicans. Distinguishable from other Latin Americans by their billowy white pantaloons, broad sandals, and sombreros, the

"Sonoranians" or "Sonorans," as the Yankees called them, first entered the Sierra late in 1848, after either trudging across the Colorado deserts or sailing via Mazatlán. Some had sojourned in California earlier; in 1842, well before the advent of James Marshall, a Sonoran had discovered gold near San Fernando Mission. More visibly mestizo, less consciously Spanish than the Californians, they seemed "primitive" by local standards. Apache raiders kept them from their own mines and pastures, so that the Sonorans pounced on the California discovery as a panacea. The northern Mexican patróns themselves encouraged the migration of the peons by sponsoring expeditions of twenty or thirty underlings at a time, giving them full upkeep in return for half of their gold findings in California. The migration included so broad a spectrum of the population of Sonora and Sinaloa and was so large and continuous throughout 1850, that it compelled the governors of northern Mexico to admonish repeatedly about the dangers of life on gringo soil.

The Sonorans came on swiftly, heedless of any warnings, knowing that they had vital services to offer California—as prospectors and hired hands, as supply merchants and mule skinners, also as monte gamblers and prostitutes. The leading merchants of Altar and Horcasitas, Sonoran towns near the international boundary, stripped their shelves in the spring of 1849, loaded up every available pack animal, and scurried for the mines. There they sold everything they had brought, dug some gold, and shortly left their followers to return to Sonora for new stock or for quick investment in Mexican securities—much of this accomplished before most of the Yankee Argonauts had even arrived.

Sonorans gravitated mainly toward the San Joaquin River tributaries, called the "southern mines" or "dry diggings," especially near a spot named in their honor, Sonora. Here they introduced Yankees to many of the rudimentary mining techniques that typified the early gold rush era. Sonorans somehow could probe the topsoil with knives and bring up nuggets, or work the *batea* (pan) to great advantage. Where water was scarce and quartz plentiful, as in the southern mines, they had the endurance to sit for hours and winnow dirt in their serapes, sometimes using their own gargantuan breath if the wind died down. They could also improvise the *arastra* (mill), consisting of a mule harnessed to a long spoke treading in a circle and grinding ore under a heavy, flat boulder. Others eventually caught on to those techniques and machines and later surpassed them, but the Sonorans' sixth sense for finding gold and their willingness to endure physical hardship gave them great advantages. Talent made them conspicuously "lucky" and, therefore, subject to attack by jealous Yankees.

Although the Californios quietly withdrew from the Sierra and left the field to the Mexicans and the Yankees, the scene in the mines deserved their closest attention. For, the mines became the staging ground for widespread attacks on their ranchos and pueblos, the rehearsal place for broad-scale assaults on the Spanish-speaking.

The problem of precisely how to react to the remaining "Spaniards" made the Yankees squirm. They shifted from violence to legislation, from legislation to litigation, and back again to violence. Some wished to exploit, others to expel, and still others to control the Latin Americans. On occasion, some Yankees even proposed allowing them completely free access to the mines.

It would have given small comfort to Coronel, Vallejo, Reid, and other Californios to learn that good and decent men had inspired the purge trials of the winter and spring of 1849. Yet, in truth, a great deal of antiforeigner agitation originated from the most reputable new citizens—army officers, lawyers, merchants, clergy, and public officials. It is a fact that the first organized and officially sanctioned outburst against Spanish Americans came from three hundred "white-collar" Yankees. While stranded in Panama in January 1849, on their way to San Francisco, they heard distressing rumors that "foreign plunderers" from all over the Pacific littoral had already siphoned off $4 million worth of gold in California; how much remained for "true citizens" thus was problematic. On a slight provocation, the Yankees called a public meeting to deal sternly with the interlopers. No less a dignitary than the justice of the Oregon Territory presided over the gathering, and in the background hovered General Persifor F. Smith, traveling to Monterey to take charge of the army. Smith drafted a circular declaring that, in California, he would "consider everyone who is not a citizen of the United States, who enters upon public land and digs for gold as a trespasser." This declaration won him three hundred vows of support.

The miners, who twice confronted Coronel with the charge that "foreigners" had "no right" to dig gold, were simply enforcing Smith's hastily improvised "doctrine of trespass." In April, vigilantes at Sutter's Mill drove away masses of Chileans, Mexicans, and Peruvians; and during a similar purge along the Sacramento River on the Fourth of July lives were lost, property was destroyed, and foreigners' goods were sold at auction. More than a thousand victims, mainly Chileans, came pouring down into San Francisco shortly afterward, many of them embarking for home. "General Smith is blamed by everyone as the sole cause of the outrage."

Smith beat a hasty retreat when he discovered that the consequences of the plunderers' activities had been grossly overrated: gold was still plentiful, and most of the dust already exported from California had found its way into the hands of American supply merchants. His successor, Brigadier General Bennett Riley, rode through the mines trying to undo some of the damage caused by the doctrine of trespass by telling Americans that technically all diggers were guests on government land, and that thereafter none should be denied access to its bounty.

Resentment against the "greasers" mount-

ed, however, a product of deep and abiding feelings of nationalism, racism, and despair over the debasement of free labor. The nationalism was partly a hangover from the war. Some men imagined seeing whole battalions, armed to the teeth . . . moving through the heart of Mexico . . . gotten up by the great capitalists and friends of Santa Anna . . . rising in one solid mass whose cry is 'California's recovery or death!' " Yankee veterans unhappy in the diggings and nostalgic for army comradery saw in the coming of the "greasers" the pretext for a "muss," whether for mayhem or for merriment. Northern Europeans—the Irish in particular—and Australians became implacable foes of the Spanish Americans, more so perhaps than many native-born citizens of the United States. The notorious San Francisco gang, the "Hounds," for example, which was staffed by former New York Volunteers and Australians, took particular delight in attacking the Chileans who came to San Francisco after fleeing enemies in the mountains.

The forty-niner's xenophobia also stemmed from fear of unfair economic competition. Back home, one could normally see who became rich, how rich, and by what means; a community could use institutional means to regulate the process and keep it fair. But on the periphery of civilization, controls broke down: men sometimes prospered by unfair means; the population upsurge, the ceaseless shuffling of men from camp to camp, and their scrambling for the top of the social ladder defied control by ordinary methods. Thus the forty-niner improvised new devices, even vigilante justice.

Fear of economic competition had some basis in reality. Sonoran peddlers marched into the mines and sold 10,000 pack mules in three years, thereby depressing the prices of mules (from $500 to $150 a head in a matter of weeks) and of freight rates (from $75 to $7 per hundredweight in two months). This reversal of fortunes evoked no complaint from the Yankee miners, who could buy onions, potatoes, and other supplies all the more cheaply and had come to associate Mexican mule bells with savory cooking odors and a few cheap comforts of life; but it brought, in 1850, a pained outcry from Stockton entrepreneurs, who sought mass expulsion of their business rivals. Moreover, when the Mexicans set to work as peons in the employ of their patróns, they did make themselves the target of the prospectors. Miners who began muttering against the Mexicans and plotting violence felt keenly conscious that the Spanish Americans were cheapening the value of labor.

The treatment of immigrant Spanish Americans in the mines hinged also on the slavery question. They came into California precisely when the Yankees felt most irritated on this score and could see most clearly the parallels between Negroes and their masters, on the one hand, and peon and patróns, on the other. Yankee prospectors ejected from the mines with equal vigor any combination of bondsmen and masters. In July a prominent Texan, Thomas Jefferson Green, and his slaves were unceremoniously tossed out of Rose Bar on the Yuba River. The prospectors put into effect a local code prohibiting the mining operations of all master-servant teams, whatever their relationship. Three months later this provision cost the life of a Chilean and led to the ear cropping and whipping of Chileans and Mexicans who tried to oppose it.

With California's entry into the Union as a free state, the plight of the Spanish Americans in the mines worsened momentarily. Their protagonists proclaimed that, if slaves were prohibited from the mines, then so should be the "refuse population from Chile, Peru and Mexico and other parts of the world [who are] . . . as bad as any of the free negroes of the North, or the worst slaves of the South." The apparent inconsistency in immigration policy annoyed both the friends and the enemies of slavery. In the first California legislature, nativists freely categorized the Pacific immigrants as a race whose morality and intelligence stood "but one degree above the beasts of the field." The State Assembly, in no uncertain terms (by a vote of twenty-two to two), asked Congress to bar from the mines all persons of foreign birth, *even* naturalized citizens.

This extreme nativism soon brought about its own backlash. A fraction of the entrepreneurs in the mines began to worry less about the alleged dangers of unlimited immigration or of competition from "foreign capitalists" and more about the "disgregated, fractioned, broken up" techniques of mining; more about the possibilities of investing capital and hiring Mexican laborers, and less about expelling the interlopers. Usually outshouted at public meetings and outvoted in the legislature, this Yankee faction nonetheless had on its side the logic of economy and the ear of a few outspoken politicians who began a campaign to exploit, rather than exclude, aliens.

Advocates of this new position were most numerous and effective in the southern mines. There, the Sonorans evicted from the northern placers late in 1849 found relative safety, hiring themselves out to Yankees who maintained loaded pistols, "cool eyes . . . [and] steady nerves" against possible opposition by other Yankees. The Yankee patróns especially appreciated the Sonorans' skill and willingness to work for a daily wage of a dollar in food and a fraction of gold. "Greasers" worked speedily, when prompted, although work itself—and riches or savings—bored them, and gambling, drinking, dancing, and indolence cut down their work time. The argument ran as follows: The American, "with all his impatience of control, his impetuous temperament, his ambitions and yearning will . . . [never] be content to deny himself the pleasure of civilized life in the states for the sake of $4.00 to $3.00 per day, to develop the resources of the dry diggings"; the Mexican, on the other hand, is "milder in spirit, more contented to endure more willing to suffer, more weak spirited, if you please," but for those very reasons he is the man for the job. Although a mere "hewer of wood and drawer of water," he would unlock California's wealth much as the Negro had done in the South. American freight shippers at the same time learned that the Mexican *arrieros* (mule skinners) were the most reliable of hired hands—skillful, proud of their work, and sure to get the pack train through the worst blizzard, over the toughest mountain trail. A genuine paternal fondness sometimes linked the arriero and his new Yankee patrón.

Yankee tradesmen of the southern mines came to see the Spanish Americans as particularly good customers. It occurred to them that, in contrast with the stingy Yankee who saved his money and sent it home, the Latin American invariably wanted to take home goods, not money; he spent all he had. Just as the Spaniard's eccentric work habits could be turned to the operator's profit, so could his spendthrift tendencies be turned to the advantage of the merchant. General Riley discovered that "Americans, by their superior intelligence and shrewdness in business, generally contrived to turn to their own benefit the earnings of Mexicans, Chileans and Peruvians."

The tension between Yankee and Latin-American miners climaxed in the Foreign Miners' Tax Law of 1850, one of the most original if benighted laws ever passed in a California legislature.

Thomas Jefferson Green, its author, boasted that he personally could "maintain a better stomach at the killing of a Mexican" than at the crushing of a body louse. A Texan, he had come to this opinion in a Mexican prison while brooding over the failure of a filibustering expedition. After a harrowing escape from the prison, Green published an account of his exploits, together with a tirade against all things Mexican (and Negro) and a proposal that the United States swallow up all of Mexico. He had come to California in the hope of using slaves to plant cotton, although the episode at the Yuba River smashed that idea completely. Because he had served in three Southern legislatures, however, and had a good reputation among Southerners, he easily won election as state senator from Sacramento.

Green had legendary powers of persuasion,

even over men who disliked his social ideals. It was he who always gained adjournment of the California Senate to "more comfortable surroundings"—namely, his own bar—and thus earned his colleagues the sobriquet, "Legislature of the Thousand Drinks." In his tax bill—a kind of personal rejoinder to the men who had expelled him from Rose Bar for attempting to use Negro bondsmen—he proposed to issue mining permits to foreigners at a cost of $20 monthly (he later reduced it to $16). This tax, he thought, would bolster the bankrupt state treasury by $200,000 each month and would also encourage Yankee operators to buy licenses for their operatives, and to employ them "at a fair rate . . . until the labor is performed according to contract." The law would delight Americans no end and discourage mob action, or what Green grandly called "the interruption of the stronger power which is in the people." This possibility so neatly wrapped up all the nagging problems of labor competition, foreign monopolies, taxation, bondage, immigration, and mob violence that the Assembly passed it nineteen to four and the Senate seven to four; the latter house, by a vote of eleven to two, also gave Green a special commendation for originating so "splendid" a plan.

Although later condemned as an intemperate and malicious act, "conceived in drink and brought forth in jollity," the Foreign Miners' Tax Law actually had quite sober intentions. Its main difficulty was that instead of flatly trying to either exploit, expel, or give free rein to the foreign-born, it tried to straddle the issue. It promised something for everybody: the prospector would be able to evict all "unprotected" aliens, the operator would be able to undercut the "agents of foreign bankers" who sponsored immigration, the government would receive money to pay its bills (among them, the expense vouchers of the legislature), the collectors would make a commission of $3 on each permit sold, and the immigrants themselves could claim the protection of the law if they paid their tax. On the face of it, one could hardly have asked for a more equitable solution.

Yet the Foreign Miners' Tax Law hardly worked that way at all. In Tuolumne County, where most of the potential taxpayers were entrenched, the impost caused outright defiance. Printed posters immediately denounced the tax and implored its intended victims to "put a bridle in the mouths of that horde who call themselves citizens of the United States, thereby profaning that country." Two French radicals, schooled in the Revolution of 1848, engineered a rebellion and for its success needed the cooperation of the Mexicans. Although the Mexicans were gun-shy, they nevertheless went to tell the Yankees what was on the mind of all non-Yankees. An impressive array of 4,000 "aliens"—mostly Mexicans—congregated on the outskirts of Sonora on Sunday, May 19, to consider proper action against the law, which was to take effect the next day. To the collector's face the delegation flatly declared that the foreign-born might pay $3 or even $5 monthly, but not $20—a token sum for protection against rowdies, but not an entire fortune monthly. When the collector held his ground and demanded the full amount, most foreigners fled the town. One remaining Mexican threatened the sheriff, or so it seemed to the bystander who killed him with a bowie knife. Local officials prohibited merchants from selling supplies to any foreign miners and spread an alarm to nearby camps to call up reinforcements for the forthcoming "war" at the county seat.

One hundred and fifty war veterans promptly stopped work at Mormon Gulch, selected a captain, put on the remains of their uniforms, and, with regimental colors high, marched to Sonora for action. Sonora received them warmly with fulsome speeches, food, and free liquor. By nightfall the town seethed with inevitable rumors of Mexican incendiarism, assassination, and massacre. Officers posted pickets, stored weapons, and briefed the men for the next day's action. Sonora was under martial law.

Next morning, into the diggings marched four hundred Americans—a moving "engine of terror"—heading for Columbia Camp, the foreigners' headquarters. They collected tax money from a few affluent aliens and chased the rest away, with a warning to vacate the mines. One trooper recalls seeing "men, women and children—all packed up and moving, bag and baggage. Tents were being pulled down, houses and hovels gutted of their contents; mules, horses and jackasses were being hastily packed, while crowds were already in full retreat." The posse finally arrested the two "hot-headed Frenchmen . . . of the red republican order," who started everything, fined them $5 for "treason," and dismissed them. Thus ended the "muss." The men liquored up for the road, hoisted the Stars and Stripes to the top of a pine tree, fired off a salute, and headed for home. Next day, about five hundred French and German forty-eighters stormed into Sonora shouting revolutionary slogans and vowing to liberate the Frenchmen. Upon hearing that the pair had been freed, the would-be liberators dispersed sheepishly.

Sonora had just about recovered from the excitement of this "French Revolution" when a new attack broke over the heads of the Spanish-speaking. A series of robberies and violent deaths came to light near town in which the victims were Yankees and the murder weapons *riatas;* this made it easy to blame "foreigners of Spanish-American origin." Next, a Sonoran and his three Yaqui Indian retainers were caught burning two bodies and would have been lynched, but for the timely intervention of the justice of the peace and the sheriff, who remanded the prisoners to the district court. On the morning of the court trial (July 15), the Mormon Gulch veterans again descended on Sonora in military order and spoiling for action. Informed that the prisoners might be hirelings of a "notorious Mexican chief" at Green Flat, they marched there, rounded up practically every male in sight, herded them back to Sonora, and literally corralled them for safekeeping overnight. In the morning, the justice of the peace investigated the "caze of murther against 110 Greasers . . . captured by 80 brave Americans," but, having determined that the Mexicans were innocent newcomers, he let them go. After a momentary riot scene in the courtroom, the Sonoran, on bended knees, convinced the jury that he and his Indians had killed no one but had accidentally discovered the bodies and were trying to dispose of them according to Yaqui burial custom. The crowd dispersed grudgingly.

Unhappily, another gruesome death, uncovered the very next day, again made Sonora the prey of every rumor incriminating Latin Americans. Since all previous measures had failed to stop the atrocities, it was proposed to cleanse the hillsides thoroughly of every Spanish American with the least tinge of "evil." The present emergency demanded that "all Mexicans should suffer for a few." The "better element" of Yankees in the southern mines, who normally recoiled from drastic measures, now feared that their territory was fast acquiring the reputation of a bandit refuge, which was bad for business, and felt impelled to join the broadside attack. Outshouting one dissenting voice, a large public meeting in Sonora voted to force all foreigners to deposit their arms with Americans and apply for permits of good conduct. All Latin Americans, except "respectable characters," were given fifteen days in which to depart. The Mormon Gulch veterans set to work enforcing these dicta with gusto.

The screening plan to expel the "obnoxious" Spanish Americans worked well. It reduced the danger of *bandido* attack and frightened off economic rivals. Between May and August, from five to fifteen thousand foreign-born diggers scattered from the southern mines. Mexicans went elsewhere looking for surcease of trouble but were dogged everywhere; eventually, they came streaming out of the Sierra, some showing signs of "pinching want." Even those who paid the extortionate

$20 found that it bought very little protection, for if the collector neglected his monthly rounds their certificates lapsed, and if the Americans of one county refused to honor permits bought in another, the Spanish-speaking had little recourse but to leave. They knew that they alone of all foreign miners were being subjected to the tax: when they taunted the collectors to tax Irishmen, Frenchmen, and other Europeans they received no satisfactory reply. Masqueraders posing as collectors came into Mexican camps, solemnly tore up valid permits, and demanded money for new ones; when rebuffed, they auctioned off the victim's dirt and installed in his claim a "loyal citizen." One imposter carried off his charade so well at Don Pedro's Bar that he convinced a posse to help him chase away forty peons and their patrón and killed two Mexicans in the action, before his identity was uncovered.

Even when seeking an escape from California, Mexicans found the Americans lying in wait for them. On the Colorado River, a United States Army lieutenant had express orders "to make all Sonorans passing out of California with gold, pay a duty . . . and for my trouble, to put the whole of it in my pocket." A troop of California militiamen blandly confiscated from homebound Sonorans more than a hundred "stolen" mules and horses, ignoring the brand marks, proving ownership and compelling the Mexicans to walk 300 miles, including 100 miles across desert.

In the preceding year misunderstanding, fear, and hatred had created an atmosphere so hostile to "Sonorans" as to sanction fraud and murder. Nonetheless, the argument for both protecting and exploiting the foreign miners once more gathered strength. The earliest and most effective counterattack against prejudice was made by the San Francisco Vigilance Committee of 1849, which summarily expelled the "Hounds" from town and made amends to the Chileans who had been tormented by them. Thereafter many individuals took up the cause, speaking in behalf of civil law or laissez-faire competition or on grounds of simple re-vulsion against mob violence. Among those spokesmen were judges, editors, lawyers, a sheriff, a brigadier general, merchants, mine operators, and the French consul. Several sympathetic collectors ceased selling permits. Even the state attorney general disliked the tax so thoroughly that he refused to defend the collector prosecuted in the California Supreme Court and ignored the governor's threat to prosecute him for dereliction of duty.

Xenophobia had injured its perpetrators as well as its victims. As Mexicans fled the southern mines in 1850, the profits of Yankee merchants plunged alarmingly. Eight-dollar crowbars in one afternoon dropped to fifty cents; a plot of land worth several thousand dollars went begging "for a few bits." Out of sheer dollars-and-cents self-interest, if nothing else, businessmen collected money, hired a lawyer to sue the local collector, and circulated a mass petition asking the governor to lower the impost to $5; all but one merchant signed the document. In July and August, after the second wave of expulsions caused retail losses as high as $10,000 a day in three southern counties, merchants who had helped expel the "evil characters" during the bandit scare became aware that *all* Mexicans were fleeing, not merely the undesirables. A crowd gathered at Georgetown, down the road from Sonora, and went on record as denouncing antiforeigner vigilantes and as supporting civil law. As a result the Stockton *Times* reported that the screening plan enforced at Mormon Gulch and elsewhere was "speedily held in contempt."

These forces had planned to persuade the governor to reduce the tax, the legislature to repeal it, or, best of all, the courts to nullify it. In the state Supreme Court they pleaded that it infringed the exclusive right of the federal government to govern federal lands and abridged the protection granted to aliens by the state constitution and by two treaties with Mexico. Neither of these arguments, however, swayed the high tribunal, which advanced a philosophy of states' rights in all matters relat-

ing to the federal government. Two Southern attorneys convinced the court that a state (1) could rightfully tax federal lands, unless specifically prohibited from doing so, and (2) had police powers to defend itself against undesirables. The court, in effect, agreed with the author of the tax act, Green, who had grandly declared that congressional inaction on the California mines had thrown the state back onto "universal laws . . . higher, greater, and stronger than the written constitution." Gratuitously, the court added that even had the law violated a treaty—which had not been demonstrated—it might still be valid, for state laws could take precedence over treaties. Thus, the Spanish Americans had unknowingly become the victims of the imponderable and pervasive sectional controversies of the day.

Notwithstanding its new judicial seal of approval, the tax was a practical failure, as even its original supporters admitted. The Mexican was not the Negro slave; California was not Texas. The governor, aware that the tax was reaping more resentment than revenue, cut the rate to $20 for four months. Even after this corrective, however, the state obtained only $30,000 instead of an expected $2,400,000. The collector in a county that had 15,000 potential taxpayers, sold only 525 permits and was so harassed on his job that he resigned. By 1851 Stockton's leading citizens had developed such loathing for the tax—"a law for the killing of children to get their fat"—that they decided to rally the entire county and lobby in the state capital to obtain its repeal. This they accomplished early in 1851.

The tax had failed to make the state wealthy, to prevent mob action, and to convert immigrants into hirelings as promised. It had eliminated the Latin Americans already in California and curtailed new immigration, a result that did not altogether fill the original bill. Now, having pushed the tax aside, the boosters of the foreign miners hoped to summon them back and make amends. The Yankees had a sudden vision that with the law gone, tens of thousands of Latin Americans would come flooding out of Mexico and Chile and the California towns and wash up into the southern mines, thus opening a new era in gold mining.

That dream failed to materialize, however, since the Spanish Americans by now mistrusted the Yankees and suspected that gold was giving out. They withdrew to Los Angeles and other villages or returned home, informing their countrymen of the dangers of venturing forth into California. Of course, small parties of Spanish Americans continued to enter the diggings, rummaging about on their own hook and staying alert to the possibility of trouble. The one lone Mexican patrón who dared bring in peons in 1852 stood out so conspicuously that he became the center of an international incident. His case made the complete circuit to Mexico City, Washington, and back to California. The district attorney investigated it for the United States Secretary of War, who determined that, although the crowd of Americans who stopped the Mexican was "wholly unprincipled and deserving of punishment," Mexican nationals should seek reparations in the state courts, since the federal government took no responsibility for riots. Thereafter, no patrón was courageous or indiscreet enough to enter the mines, and the Yankee triumph over "foreign capitalists" and "slaves" was complete.

In the long view of California history, the Mexican miners represent merely a link in a long chain of migrants who reach across the "Spanish borderland." They unwittingly followed the trail blazed by the Spanish soldier Juan Bautista Anza and used later by Mexican cholos and colonists. They foreshadowed the coming of the "wetbacks" and the braceros in the twentieth century. As ever, the Mexicans met with mixed success in California, often defeat. They did find some gold, but had to fight for every ounce. That they escaped Yankee bondage was perhaps the most fortunate thing that happened to them.

The migration of the Mexican forty-niners affected the Californios in two ways: for one thing, it put the Yankees in an ugly frame of mind toward all the Spanish-speaking, including the native-born; for another, it sent the newcomers into the established old communities of California, where they fused imperceptibly with those born there. This tended to break down the old and somewhat artificial distinction between "native Californians" and "Mexicans." The fusion went on continuously thereafter.

The Mexican newcomers had, however, one major advantage over their California-born brethren; whereas they could ultimately evade the gringo enemy by returning home, the Californios, attacked on their own soil, could not.

# 20

# ADVOCATE OF THE DREAM

## STEPHEN B. OATES

No American president has been as mythologized as Abraham Lincoln. Whether revered as the savior of the Union or condemned as the cause of the Civil War and the subsequent decline of the South, the sixteenth president has appeared larger than life since he took the oath of office in 1861. In this reconsideration of the man behind the myth, Stephen B. Oates examines Lincoln's commitment to a moral vision of national prosperity and political equality open to all Americans. The "American dream" of material reward for individual effort was Lincoln's guiding philosophy, Oates suggests, from his early days as a young politician in Illinois through his final days as leader of the victorious Union.

The greatest challenge to this dream of moderate mobility was the continued existence of slavery in the southern states, and it haunted Lincoln throughout his public life. From his unsuccessful senatorial campaign of 1858, during which he declared that the nation could not exist "half slave and half free," through his wartime emancipation of southern slaves, Lincoln dealt with the complex moral, economic, and political issues raised by slavery with a mixture of principle and pragmatism. Ultimately, Oates argues, it was Lincoln's creative struggle with the conundrum of slavery and individual liberty that led to his greatness as a leader.

Part III from Stephen B. Oates, *Abraham Lincoln: The Man Behind the Myths* (New York: Harper & Row, 1984). Copyright © 1984 by Stephen B. Oates. Reprinted by permission of Harper & Row, Publishers, Inc.

## 1. THE BEACON LIGHT OF LIBERTY

In presidential polls taken by *Life* magazine in 1948, the *New York Times Magazine* in 1962, and the *Chicago Tribune Magazine* in 1982, historians and political scholars ranked Lincoln as the best chief executive in American history. They were not trying to mythologize the man, for they realized that errors, vacillations, and human flaws marred his record. Their rankings indicate, however, that the icon of mythology did rise out of a powerful historical figure, a man who learned from his mistakes and made a difference. Indeed, Lincoln led the lists because he had a moral vision of where his country must go to preserve and enlarge the rights of all her people. He led the lists because he had an acute sense of history—an ability to identify himself with a historical turning point in his time and to articulate the promise that held for the liberation of oppressed humanity the world over. He led the lists because he perceived the truth of his age and embodied it in his words and deeds. He led the lists because, in his interaction with the spirit and events of his day, he made momentous *moral* decisions that affected the course of humankind.

It cannot be stressed enough how much Lincoln responded to the spirit of his age. From the 1820s to the 1840s, while Lincoln was growing to manhood and learning the art and technique of politics, the Western world seethed with revolutionary ferment. In the 1820s, revolutions broke out not only in Poland, Turkey, Greece, Italy, Spain, and France, but blazed across Spain's ramshackle South American empire as well, resulting in new republics whose capitals rang with the rhetoric of freedom and independence. The Republic of Mexico even produced laws and promulgations that abolished slavery throughout the nation, including Mexico's subprovince of Texas. In that same decade, insurrection panics rocked the Deep South, especially the South Carolina tidewater, as America's disinherited Africans reflected the revolutionary turbulence sweeping the New World. In 1831, in an effort to liberate his people, a visionary slave preacher named Nat Turner incited the most violent slave rebellion in American history, a revolt that shook the South to its foundations and cleared the way for the Great Southern Reaction against the human-rights upheavals of the time. In the 1830s, a vociferous abolitionist movement sprang up in the free states; Great Britain eradicated slavery in the Empire; and impassioned English emancipators came to crusade in America as well. In distant Russia, Czar Nicholas I established an autonomous communal structure for Russia's millions of serfs—the first step in their eventual emancipation two decades later. In the 1840s, while Lincoln practiced law and ran for Congress, reformist impulses again swept Europe. Every major country there had liberal parties that clamored for representative government, self-rule, civil liberties, and social and economic reform. In 1848, the year Congressman Lincoln denounced "Mr. Polk's War" against Mexico, defended the right of revolution, and voted against slavery expansion, revolutions again blazed across Europe, flaring up first in France against the July Monarchy, then raging through Italy and central Europe. These were revolutions against monarchy, despotism, exploitation by the few, revolutions that tried to liberate individuals, classes, and nationalities alike from the shackles of the past. In sum, it was an age of revolution, a turbulent time when people throughout the Western world were searching for definitions of liberty, fighting and dying for liberty, against reactionary forces out to preserve the status quo.

Out in Illinois, Lincoln identified himself with the liberating forces of his day. In fact, he became the foremost political spokesman for those impulses in the United States, a man with a world view of the meaning and mission of his young country in that historic time.

From earliest manhood, Lincoln was a fervent nationalist in an age when a great many Americans, especially in Dixie, were aggressive localists. His broad outlook began when he was an Indiana farm boy tilling his father's mundane wheatfield. During lunch breaks, when he was not studying grammar and rhetoric, Lincoln would peruse Parson Weems's eulogistic biography of George Washington, and he would daydream about the Revolution and the origins of the Republic, daydream about Washington, Jefferson, and Madison as great national statesmen who shaped the course of history. By the time he became a politician in the 1830s, Lincoln idolized the Founding Fathers as apostles of liberty (never mind for now that many of those apostles were also southern slaveowners). Young Lincoln extolled the Fathers for beginning a noble experiment in popular government on these shores, to demonstrate to the world that a free people could govern themselves without hereditary monarchs and aristocracies. And the foundation of the American experiment was the Declaration of Independence, which in Lincoln's view proclaimed the highest political truths in history: that all men were created equal and entitled to liberty and the pursuit of happiness. This meant that men like Lincoln were not chained to the conditions of their births, that they could better their station in life and realize the rewards of their own talent and toil.

A good example, Lincoln believed, was his political idol, Whig national leader Henry Clay of Kentucky. Born into a poor farm family, Clay lifted himself all the way to the United States Senate and national and international fame. For Lincoln, this taught a "profitable lesson"—"it teaches that in this country, one can scarcely be so poor, but that, if he *will,* he *can* acquire sufficient education to get through the world respectably." Thanks to the Declaration, which guaranteed Americans "the right to rise," Lincoln himself had acquired enough education to "get through the world respectably." Thus he had a deep, personal reverence for the Declaration and insisted that all his political sentiments flowed from that document.

All his economic beliefs derived from that document, too. Indeed, Lincoln's economics were as nationalistic and deeply principled as his politics. Schooled in the Whig doctrine of order and national unity, Lincoln advocated a strong federal government to maintain a prosperous, stable economy for the benefit of all Americans—"the old and the young, the rich and the poor, the grave and the gay, of all sexes and tongues, and colors and conditions," as he would say. Thus he championed a national bank, internal improvements financed by the federal government, federal subsidies to help the states build their own canals, turnpikes, and railroads, and state banks whose task was to ensure financial growth and stability. "The legitimate object of government," Lincoln asserted later, "is to do for the people what needs to be done, but which they can not, by individual effort, do at all, or do so well, for themselves."

Lincoln's national economic program was part of his large vision of the American experiment in popular government. By promoting national prosperity, stability, and unity, his economics would help guarantee his "American dream"—the right of all Americans to rise, to harvest the full fruits of their labors, and so to better themselves as their own talent and industry allowed. Thus the American experiment ensured two things essential to liberty: the right of self-government and the right of self-improvement.

Nor was the promise of America limited to the native-born. Her frontier, Lincoln said, should function as an outlet for people the world over who wanted to find new homes, a place to "better their conditions in life." For Lincoln, the American experiment was the way of the future for nations across the globe. A child of the Enlightenment, the American system stood as a beacon of hope for "the liberty party throughout the world."

Yet this beacon of hope harbored a monstrous thing, a relic of despotism in the form of Negro slavery. In Lincoln's view, bondage was the one retrograde institution that disfigured the American experiment, and he maintained that he had always hated it, as much as any abolitionist. His family had opposed slavery, and he had grown up and entered politics thinking it wrong. In 1837, in his first public statement on slavery, Lincoln contended that it was "founded both on injustice and bad policy," and he never changed his mind. But before 1854 (and the significance of this date will become clear), Lincoln generally kept his own counsel about slavery and abolition. After all, slavery was the most inflammable issue of his generation, and Lincoln observed early on what violent passions Negro bondage—and the question of race that underlay it—could arouse in white Americans. In his day, slavery was a tried and tested means of race control in a South dedicated to white supremacy. Moreover, the North was also a white supremacist region, where the vast majority of whites opposed emancipation lest it result in a flood of southern "Africans" into the free states. And Illinois was no exception, as most whites there were anti-Negro and anti-abolition to the core. Lincoln, who had elected to work within the American system, was not going to ruin his career by trumpeting an unpopular cause. To be branded as an abolitionist in central Illinois—his constituency as a legislator and a U.S. congressman—would have been certain political suicide.

Still, slavery distressed him. He realized that it should never have existed in a self-proclaimed free and enlightened Republic. He who cherished the Declaration of Independence understood only too well how bondage mocked and contradicted that noble document. Yes, he detested slavery. It was a blight on the American experiment in popular government, the one institution that robbed the Republic of its just example in the world, robbed the United States of the hope it should hold out to oppressed people everywhere.

He opposed slavery, too, because he had witnessed some of its evils firsthand. In 1841, on a steamboat journey down the Ohio River, he saw a group of manacled slaves on their way to the cruel cotton plantations of the Deep South. Lincoln was appalled at the sight of those chained Negroes. Fourteen years later he wrote that the spectacle "was a continual torment to me" and that he saw something like it every time he touched a slave border. Slavery, he said, "had the power of making me miserable."

Again, while serving in Congress from 1847 to 1849, he passed slave auction blocks in Washington, D.C. In fact, from the windows of the Capitol, he could observe the infamous "Georgia pen"—"a sort of Negro livery stable," as he described it, "where droves of negroes were collected, temporarily kept, and finally taken to southern markets, precisely like droves of horses." The spectacle offended him. He agreed with a Whig colleague that the buying and selling of human beings in the United States capital was a national disgrace. Accordingly Lincoln drafted a gradual abolition bill for the District of Columbia. But powerful southern politicians howled in protest, and his own Whig support fell away. At that, Lincoln dropped the bill and sat in gloomy silence as Congress rocked with debates—with drunken fights and rumbles of disunion—over the status of slavery in the territories. Shocked at the behavior of his colleagues, Lincoln confessed that slavery was the one issue that threatened the stability of the Union.

Yet Attorney Lincoln had to concede that bondage was a thoroughly entrenched institution in the southern states, one protected by the U.S. Constitution and a web of national and state laws. This in turn created a painful dilemma for Lincoln: a system he deeply loved had institutionalized a thing he abominated. What could be done? Lincoln admitted that the federal government had no legal authority in peacetime to harm a state institution like slavery. And yet it should not remain in what he considered "the noblest political system the world ever saw."

Caught in an impossible predicament, Lincoln persuaded himself that if slavery were confined to the South and left alone there, time would somehow solve the problem and slavery would ultimately die out. Once it was no longer workable, he believed, southern whites would gradually liberate the blacks on their own. They would do so voluntarily.

And he told himself that the Founding Fathers—that Washington, Jefferson, and Madison—had felt the same way, that they too had expected slavery to perish some day. In Lincoln's interpretation, the Fathers had tolerated slavery as a necessary evil, one that could not be removed where it already existed without causing wide-scale chaos and destruction. But, Lincoln contended, they had taken steps to restrict the growth of bondage (had prohibited it in the old Northwest Territories, had outlawed the international slave trade) and thus to place the institution on the road to extinction. And he decided that this was why the Fathers had not included the words *slave* or *slavery* in the Constitution. When bondage did disappear, "there should be nothing on the face of the great charter of liberty suggesting that such a thing as negro slavery had ever existed among us."

So went Lincoln's argument before 1854. Thanks to the Founding Fathers, slavery was on its way to its ultimate doom. And he believed that southerners and northerners alike accepted this as axiomatic. The task of his generation, Lincoln thought, was to keep the Republic firmly on the course charted by the Fathers, guiding America toward that ultimate day when slavery would finally be removed, the nation righted at last with her own ideals, and popular government preserved for all humankind. It was this vision—this sense of America's historic mission in the progress of human liberty—that shaped Lincoln's beliefs and actions throughout his mature years.

Still, despite his passionate convictions about popular government and human liberty, Lincoln before the Civil War did not envision black people as permanent participants in the great American experiment. On the contrary, he feared that white Americans were too prejudiced to let Negroes live among them as equals. If it was impossible for blacks to be completely free in America, then he preferred that they be free somewhere else. Once slavery died out in Dixie, he insisted that the federal government should colonize all blacks in Africa, an idea he got from Henry Clay.

Of course, emancipation and colonization would depend entirely on the willingness of southerners to cooperate. Lincoln hoped and assumed that they would. Before the Civil War,

he always sympathized with the mass of southern whites and thought them inherently humane and patriotic. After all, Lincoln himself was a native Kentuckian, and *he* loved the American experiment and tried to be a fair-minded man. He said of southern whites and slavery, "They are just what we would be in their situation. When it is said that the institution exists, and that it is very difficult to get rid of . . . I can understand and appreciate the saying." Yet he thought the great majority of southern whites "have human sympathies, of which they can no more divest themselves than they can of their sensibility to physical pain." Because of their human sympathies, he assumed that they would abolish slavery when it became necessary to do so.

Assumptions aside, though, Lincoln had no evidence that southerners would ever voluntarily surrender their slaves, voluntarily give up their status symbols and transform their cherished way of life founded on the peculiar institution. In 1832, the year Lincoln entered politics, Virginia had actually considered emancipation and colonization (in the aftermath of Nat Turner's insurrection), but had rejected colonization as too costly and complicated to carry out. And neither they nor their fellow southerners were about to emancipate their blacks and leave them as free people in a white man's country. As a consequence, they became adamantly determined that slavery should remain on a permanent basis, not just as a labor device, but as a means of race control in a region brimming with Negroes.

Yet Lincoln clung to the notion that slavery would eventually perish in Dixie, that southerners were rational men who would gradually liberate their blacks when the time came. And he clung to the belief that somehow, when the time did come, the Republic would pay out all the millions of dollars necessary to compensate slaveowners for their losses and ship more than three million blacks out of the country. And he assumed, too, that southerners would consent to the deportation of their entire labor force.

Students often ask me, "Was Lincoln serious? How could a logical and reasonable man like him embrace such fantastic notions?" I can only guess at the answer. Given the tenacious existence of slavery in Dixie and the white supremacist attitudes that prevailed all over his country, what other choices did Lincoln have? His whole idea of southern-initiated emancipation and federal colonization may seem chimerical to us. But in his view it appeared to be the only course short of war that had the slightest chance of working. And he *had* to believe in something. He could not accept the monstrous possibility that southern slavery might continue indefinitely. No, he told himself, it must and would die out as he figured. And so he said in 1852: if the Republic could remove the danger of slavery and restore "a captive people to their long-lost father-land," and do both so gradually "that neither races nor individuals shall have suffered by the change," then "it will indeed be a glorious consummation."

## 2. THIS VAST MORAL EVIL

Then came 1854 and the momentous Kansas-Nebraska Act, brainchild of Senator Stephen A. Douglas of Illinois. Douglas's measure overturned the old Missouri Compromise line, which excluded slavery from the vast northern area of the old Louisiana Purchase territory. The act then established a new formula for dealing with slavery in the national lands: now Congress would stay out of the matter, and the people of each territory would decide whether to retain or outlaw the institution. Until such time as the citizens of a territory voted on the issue, southerners were free to take slavery into most western territories, including the new ones of Kansas and Nebraska. These were carved out of the northern section of the old Louisiana Purchase territory. Thanks to the Kansas-Nebraska Act, a northern domain once preserved for freedom now seemed open to a proslavery invasion.

At once a storm of free-soil protest broke across the North, and scores of political leaders branded the Kansas-Nebraska Act as part of a sinister southern plot to extend slave territory and augment southern political power in the national capital. Had not the pro-southern Pierce administration and powerful southern politicians like Senator David R. Atchison of Missouri helped Douglas ram the measure through Congress? Had not every southern senator but two voted in favor of it? Were not Missouri border captains vowing to make Kansas a gateway for proslavery expansion to the Pacific?

There followed a series of political upheavals. The old Whig party disintegrated, and in its place emerged the all-northern Republican party, dedicated to blocking slavery extension, saving the cherished frontier for free white labor, and dismantling southern power in Washington. At the same time, a civil war blazed up in Kansas, as proslavery and free-soil pioneers came into bloody collisions on the prairie there—proof that slavery was far too volatile ever to be solved as a purely local matter.

No one was more upset about Kansas-Nebraska than Lincoln. In his view, the southern-controlled Democratic party—the party that dominated the presidency, the Senate, and the Supreme Court—had launched a revolt against the Founding Fathers and the entire course of the Republic as far as slavery was concerned. Now bondage was not going to die out in the South. It was going to grow and expand and continue indefinitely, as slaveholders dragged manacled black people across the West, adapting slave labor to mines and farms and whatever conditions they found there. Now southern leaders would create new slave states on the frontier and make bondage powerful and permanent in America. Now the Republic would never remove the cancer that afflicted its political system—would never remove a "cruel wrong" that marred her global image and made a mockery of the Declaration.

Lincoln plunged into the antiextension fight. He campaigned for the national Senate. He joined the Republicans and became head of the new party in Illinois. He inveighed against the "Slave Power" and its insidious "new designs" to place bondage on the road to expansion and perpetuity. He spoke with an urgent sense of mission that gave his speeches a searching eloquence—a mission to save the American experiment, turn back the tide of slavery expansion, restrict the peculiar institution once again to the South, and place it back on the road to extinction, as Lincoln believed the Founding Fathers had so placed it.

Still, he could not believe that the southern people were involved in the new slave policy. No, they were beguiled by scheming Democratic politicians—by Douglas and southern leaders in Washington and back in Dixie, who were out to enlarge slave territory under the guise of popular sovereignty, under the pretext that it was all "a sacred right of self-government." On the stump in Illinois, Lincoln engaged in a rhetorical dialogue with the southern people, speaking as though they were in his audiences. He did not fault them for the origin of slavery; he bore them no ill-will of any kind. He still believed in their intrinsic decency and sense of justice, still believed that they too regarded slavery as wrong—that they too felt there was humanity in the Negro. Do you deny this? he asked them at Peoria in 1854. Then why thirty-four years ago did you join the North in branding the African slave trade as an act of piracy punishable by death? "Again," Lincoln went on, "you have amongst you, a sneaking individual, of the class of native tyrants, known as the 'SLAVEDEALER.' He watches your necessities, and crawls up to buy your slave, at a speculating price. If you cannot help it, you sell to him; but if you can help it, you drive him from your door. You despise him utterly. You do not recognize him as a friend, or even as an honest man. Your children must not play with his; they may rollick freely with the little negroes, but not with the 'slave-dealers' children. If you are obliged to deal with him, you try to get through the job without so much as touching him. It is common with you to join hands with the men you meet; but with the slave dealer you avoid the ceremony—instinctively shrinking from the snaky contact."

Now why is this? Lincoln asked southern whites. Is it not because your human sympathy tells you "that the poor negro has some natural right to himself—that those who deny it, and make mere merchandise of him, deserve kickings, contempt and death?" He beseeched southerners not to deny their true feelings about slavery. He beseeched them to regard bondage strictly as a necessity, as the Fathers had so regarded it, and to contain its spread as those "old-time men" had done.

"Fellow countrymen—Americans south, as well as north," Lincoln cried, let us prevent the spirit of Kansas-Nebraska from displacing the spirit of the Revolution. "Let us turn slavery from its claims of 'moral right,' back upon its existing legal rights . . . and there let it rest in peace. Let us re-adopt the Declaration of Independence, and with it, the practices, and policy, which harmonize with it. Let north and south—let all Americans—let all lovers of liberty everywhere—join the great and good work. If we do this, we shall not only have saved the Union; but we shall have so saved it, as to make, and to keep it, forever worthy of the saving."

But Lincoln's entreaties fell on deaf ears in Dixie. Across the region, in an age of revolutionary agitation, proslavery apologists disparaged the Declaration of Independence and the idea of human equality as "a self-evident lie." They trumpeted Negro bondage as a great and glorious good, sanctioned by the Bible and ordained by God throughout eternity. They contended that Negroes were subhuman and belonged in chains as naturally as cattle in pens. Cranky George Fitzhugh even exhorted southerners to destroy free society (or capitalism), revive the halcyon days of feudalism, and enslave all workers—white as well as black. And he ranted at abolitionists for allying themselves with the "uncouth, dirty, naked little cannibals of Africa." Because "free society" was "unnatural, immoral, unchristian," the proslavery argument went, "it must fall and give way to a slave society—a system as old as the world." For "two opposite and conflicting forms of society cannot, among civilized men, co-exist and endure. The one must give way and cease to exist—the other become universal." "Free society!" shrieked one Alabama paper. "We sicken of the name! What is it but a conglomeration of greasy mechanics, filthy operatives, small-fisted farmers, and moon-struck theorists?"

Such pronouncements made Lincoln grimace. They convinced him that a contemptible breed of men had taken over in the South and "debauched" the public mind there about the moral right of slavery. "The slave-breeders and slave-traders are a small, odious and detested class, among you," he wrote a southern friend; "and yet in politics, they dictate the course of all of you, and are as completely your masters, as you are the masters of your own negroes." But to Lincoln's despair, proslavery, anti-northern declarations continued to roar out of Dixie. Worse still, in 1857 the pro-southern Supreme Court handed down the infamous Dred Scott decision, which sent Republicans reeling. In it, the court decreed that Negroes were inferior beings who were not and never had been United States citizens and that the Constitution and Declaration were whites-only charters that did not apply to them. What was more, the court ruled that neither Congress nor a territorial government could outlaw slavery in the national lands, because that would violate southern property rights as guaranteed by the Fifth Amendment. As Lincoln and other Republicans observed, the net effect of the decision was to legalize slavery in all federal territories from Canada to Mexico.

The ominous train of events from Kansas-Nebraska to Dred Scott shook Lincoln to his foundations. By 1858, he and a lot of other Republicans began to see a treacherous conspiracy at work in the United States—a plot on the part of southern leaders and their northern Democratic allies to reverse the whole course of modern history, to halt the progress of human liberty as other reactionary forces in the world were attempting to do. As Lincoln and his colleagues saw it, the first stage of the conspiracy was to betray the Fathers and expand bondage across the West, ringing the free

North with satellite slave states. At the same time, proslavery theorists were out to discredit the Declaration and replace the idea of the equality of men with the principles of inequality and human servitude. The next step, Lincoln feared, would be to nationalize slavery. The Supreme Court would hand down another decision, one declaring that states could not exclude slavery either because that too violated the Fifth Amendment. Then the institution would sweep into Illinois, sweep into Indiana and Ohio, sweep into Pennsylvania and New York, sweep into Massachusetts and New England, sweep all over the northern states, until at last slavery would be nationalized and America would end up a slave house. At that, as Fitzhugh advocated, the conspirators would enslave all American workers regardless of color. The northern free-labor system would be expunged, the Declaration of Independence overthrown, self-government abolished, and the conspirators would restore despotism with class rule, an entrenched aristocracy, and serfdom. All the work since the Revolution of 1776 would be annihilated. The world's best hope—America's experiment in popular government—would be destroyed, and humankind would spin backward into feudalism.

For Lincoln, the Union had reached a monumental crisis in its history. If the future of a free America was to be saved, it was imperative that Lincoln and his party block the conspiracy in its initial stage—the expansion of slavery onto the frontier. To do that, they demanded that slavery be excluded from the territories by federal law and once again placed on the road to its ultimate doom. In 1858 Lincoln set out after Douglas's Senate seat, inveighing against the Little Giant for his part in the proslavery plot and warning Illinois—and all northerners beyond—that only the Republicans could save their free-labor system and their free government.

Now Lincoln openly and fiercely declaimed his antislavery sentiments. He hated the institution. Slavery was "a vast moral evil" he could not but hate. He hated it because it degraded blacks and whites alike. He hated it because it violated America's *"central idea"*—the idea of equality and the right to rise. He hated it because it was cruelly unjust to the Negro, prevented him from eating "the bread that his own hands have earned," reduced him to "stripes, and unrewarded toils." He hated slavery because it imperiled white Americans, too. For if one man could be enslaved because of the color of his skin, Lincoln realized, then any man could be enslaved because of skin color. Yet, while branding slavery an evil and doing all they could to contain it in Dixie, Lincoln and his Republican colleagues would not, legally could not, molest the institution in those states where it already existed.

Douglas, fighting for his political life in free-soil Illinois, lashed back at Lincoln with unadulterated race baiting. Throughout the Great Debates of 1858, Douglas smeared Lincoln and his party as Black Republicans, as a gang of radical abolitionists out to liberate southern slaves and bring them stampeding into Illinois and the rest of the North, where they would take away white jobs and copulate with white daughters. Douglas had made such accusations before, but never to the extent that he did in 1858. Again and again, he accused Lincoln of desiring intermarriage and racial mongrelization.

Lincoln did not want to discuss such matters. He complained bitterly that race was not the issue between him and Douglas. The issue was whether slavery would ultimately triumph or ultimately perish in the United States. But Douglas understood the depth of anti-Negro feeling in Illinois, and he hoped to whip Lincoln by playing on white racial fears. And so he kept warning white crowds: Do you want Negroes to flood into Illinois, cover the prairies with black settlements, and eat, sleep, and marry with white people? If you do, then vote for Lincoln and the "Black Republicans." But *I* am against Negro citizenship, Douglas cried. I want citizenship for whites only. I believe that this government "was made by the white man, for the benefit of the white man, to be administered by white men." "I do not question Mr. Lincoln's conscientious belief that the negro

was made his equal, and hence his brother"—great laughter at that—"but for my own part, I do not regard the negro as my equal, and positively deny that he is my brother or any kin to me whatever."

Such allegations forced Lincoln to take a stand. It was either that or risk political ruin in white-supremacist Illinois. What he said carefully endorsed the kind of racial discrimination then enforced by Illinois law. Had he not done so, as one scholar has reminded us, "the Lincoln of history simply would not exist." At Charleston, Illinois, Lincoln conceded that he was not and never had been in favor "of making voters or jurors of Negroes, nor of qualifying them to hold office, nor to intermarry with white people." There was, he said at Ottawa, "a physical difference" between the black and white races that would "probably" always prevent them from living together in perfect equality. And Lincoln wanted the white race to have the superior position so long as there must be a difference. Therefore any attempt to twist his views into a call for perfect political and social equality was "but a specious and fantastic arrangement of words by which a man can prove a horse chestnut to be a chestnut horse."

We shall probably never know whether Lincoln was voicing his own personal convictions in speeches like these, given in the heat of political debate before all-white audiences. To be sure, this is one of the most hotly disputed areas of Lincoln scholarship, with several white historians siding with Bennett and Harding and labeling Lincoln a white supremacist. Certainly in the 1850s he had ambivalent feelings about what specific social and political rights black people ought to enjoy. But so did a good many principled and dedicated white abolitionists. When compared to the white-supremacist, anti-Negro attitudes of Douglas and most other whites of that time, Lincoln was an enlightened man in the matter of race relations. In those same 1858 debates, he consistently argued that if Negroes were not the equal of Lincoln and Douglas in moral or intellectual endowment, they *were* equal to Lincoln, Douglas, and "every living man" in their right to liberty, equality of opportunity, and the fruits of their own labor. (Later he insisted that it was bondage that had "clouded" the slaves' intellects and that Negroes were capable of thinking like whites.) Moreover, Lincoln rejected "the counterfeit argument" that just because he did not want a black woman for a slave, he therefore wanted her for a wife. He could just let her alone. He could let her alone so that she could also enjoy her freedom and "her natural right to eat the bread she earns with her own hands."

While Douglas (like the Supreme Court) emphatically denied that the Declaration of Independence applied to Negroes, Lincoln's position held that it did. The Negro was a man; Lincoln's "ancient faith" taught him that all men were created equal; therefore there could be no "moral right" in one man's enslaving another. As historian Richard N. Current has said, Lincoln left unstated the conclusion of his logic: that there was no moral right in one man's making a political and social inferior of another on grounds of race.

In the debate at Alton, Lincoln took his reasoning even further as far as the Declaration was concerned. "I think the authors of that notable document intended to include *all* men," Lincoln said, "but they did not intend to declare all men equal in *all respects.* They did not mean to say all were equal in color, size, intellect, moral development, or social capacity." What they meant was that all men, black as well as white, were equal in their inalienable rights to life, liberty, and the pursuit of happiness. When they drafted the Declaration, they realized that blacks did not then have full equality with whites, and that whites did not at that time have full equality with one another. The Founding Fathers did not pretend to describe America as it was in 1776. "They meant to set up a standard maxim for free society,"

Lincoln said, "which should be familiar to all, and revered by all; constantly looked to, constantly labored for, and even though never perfectly attained, constantly approximated, and thereby constantly spreading and deepening its influence, and augmenting the happiness and value of life to all people of all colors everywhere."

By stressing "to all people of all colors everywhere," Lincoln reminded his countrymen that the American experiment remained an inspiration for the entire world. But he reminded them, too, as historian Current has noted, that "it could be an effective inspiration for others only to the extent that Americans lived up to it themselves." No wonder Lincoln said he hated Douglas's indifference toward slavery expansion. "I hate it because of the monstrous injustice of slavery itself," Lincoln explained at Ottawa. "I hate it because it . . . enables the enemies of free institutions, with plausibility, to taunt us as hypocrites."

Exasperated with Douglas and white Negrophobia in general, Lincoln begged American whites "to discard all this quibbling about this man and the other man—this race and that race and the other race as being inferior," begged them to unite as one people and defend the ideal of the Declaration of Independence and its promise of liberty and equality for all humankind.

Lincoln's remarks, however, aggravated a lot of common people in Illinois; they voted for Douglas candidates in 1858 and helped return Lincoln's rival to the Senate.* The historical Lincoln even lost Springfield and Sangamon County, because his controversial views on slavery and the Negro, as one historian has argued, were too advanced for his neighbors. If we are to understand Lincoln's attitudes on slavery and race, it is imperative that we weigh them in proper historical context. We can learn nothing, nothing at all, if his words are

---

*In those days, state legislatures chose U.S. Senators. Lincoln hoped to win by persuading Illinois voters to elect Republican rather than Democratic candidates to the legislature.

lifted from their historical setting and judged only by the standards of another time.

## 3. MY DISSATISFIED FELLOW COUNTRYMEN

We return to why Lincoln still ranks as the best President Americans have had. In large measure, it was because of his sense of history and his ability to act on that. It was because he saw the slavery problem and the future of his country in a world dimension. He saw that what menaced Americans of his day affected the destinies of people everywhere. On the stump in Illinois, Ohio, and New York, he continued to warn free men of the heinous efforts to make bondage permanent in the United States. He would not let up on his countrymen about the *moral* issue of slavery. *"If slavery is not wrong,"* he warned them, *"nothing is wrong."* He would not let up on "the miners and sappers" of returning despotism, as he called proslavery spokesmen and their northern allies, and on the historical crisis threatening his generation, a crisis that would determine whether slavery or freedom—despotism or popular government, the past or the future— would triumph in his impassioned time.

Yet in the late 1850s Lincoln's goal was not the presidency. One of the more popular misconceptions about him was that he had his eye on the White House even in the Great Debates. Yet there is not a scintilla of reliable evidence to support this. What Lincoln wanted, and wanted fervently, was a seat in the national Senate, because in the antebellum years it was the Senate that featured the great orators of the day—men like Daniel Webster, John C. Calhoun, and especially Lincoln's idol, Henry Clay. The presidency, by contrast, was a mundane administrative job that offered little to a man of Lincoln's oratorical abilities. No, he preferred the national Senate, because in that august body he could defend the containment of slavery, defend free labor, defend popular government and the American experiment, in speeches that would be widely read and pre-

served for posterity in the *Congressional Globe*. As a loyal Republican, he would take any respectable national office that would simultaneously "advance our cause" and give him personal fulfillment. But throughout 1859 and early 1860, he kept his eye on Douglas's Senate seat in 1864.

So it was that Lincoln kept assailing Douglas for his role in the proslavery plot Lincoln saw at work in his country. And he reminded northerners of the Republican vision of a future America—a better America than now existed—an America of thriving farms and bustling villages and towns, an America of self-made agrarians, merchants, and shopkeepers who set examples and provided jobs for self-improving free workers—an America, however, that would never come about if slavery, class rule, and despotism triumphed in Lincoln's time.

Meanwhile, he kept trying to reach the southern people, to reason with them about slavery and the future of the Union, to woo them away from their reactionary leaders. He observed how ironic it was that the Democrats had abandoned their Jeffersonian heritage and that the Republicans—supposedly the descendants of the old Federalists—now defended Jeffersonian ideals. He warned southerners that "This is a world of compensations; and he who would *be* no slave, must consent to *have* no slave. Those who deny freedom to others, deserve it not for themselves."

"I think Slavery is wrong, morally, and politically," he told southern whites at Cincinnati in 1859, still speaking to them as though they were in his audience. "I desire that it should gradually terminate in the whole Union." But "I understand you differ radically with me upon this proposition." You believe that "Slavery is a good thing; that Slavery is right; that it ought to be extended and perpetuated in this Union." But we Republicans not only disagree with you; we are going to "stand by our guns" and beat you in a fair election. Yet we will not hurt you. We will treat you as Washington, Jefferson, and Madison treated you, and will leave slavery alone where it already exists among you. "We mean to remember that you are as good as we are; that there is no difference between us other than the difference of circumstances. We mean to recognize and bear in mind always that you have as good hearts in your bosoms as other people, or as we claim to have, and treat you accordingly. We mean to marry your girls when we have a chance— the white ones I mean—[laughter] and I have the honor to inform you that I once did have a chance that way."

But he cautioned southerners about their threats to disrupt the Union should the Republicans win the government in 1860. How will disunion help you? Lincoln demanded. If you secede, you will no longer enjoy the protection of the Constitution, and we will no longer be forced to return your fugitive slaves. What will you do—build a wall between us? Make war on us? You are brave and gallant, "but man for man, you are not better than we are, and there are not so many of you as there are of us." Because you are inferior in numbers, "you will make nothing by attempting to master us."

Despite Lincoln's reassurances, southern spokesmen derided the Republicans as warmongering abolitionists out to destroy the southern way of life based on slavery. In October, 1859, they got all the evidence they needed that this was so. Old John Brown and a handful of revolutionaries—most of them young, five of them black—invaded Harpers Ferry in an attempt to incite a full-scale slave rebellion. Though the raid failed and Brown was captured and hanged, the South convulsed in hysteria, as rumors of slave uprisings and abolitionist invasions pummeled the region. For their part, southern politicians pronounced the raid a Republican conspiracy, a mad and monstrous scheme to drown the South in rivers of blood. During a tour of the embattled Kansas Territory, Lincoln denied such accusations and argued that hanging Brown was just. But he warned southerners that "if constitutionally we elect a President, and therefore you undertake to destroy the

Union, it will be our duty to deal with you as old John Brown has been dealt with."

At Cooper Union the following year, Lincoln responded to continued southern imputations about the Republicans and John Brown. "You charge that we stir up insurrections among your slaves," Lincoln said. "We deny it; and what is your proof? Harper's Ferry! John Brown!! John Brown was no Republican; and you have failed to implicate a single Republican in his Harper's Ferry enterprise." But he saved his most eloquent remarks for his fellow Republicans. Since they intended southerners no harm and promised over and over to leave their slaves alone, what then was the dispute about? "The precise fact upon which depends the whole controversy" was that southerners thought slavery right and Republicans thought it wrong. "Thinking it right, as they do, they are not to blame for desiring its full recognition, as being right; but, thinking it wrong, as we do, can we yield to them? Can we cast our votes with their view, and against our own? In view of our moral, social, and political responsibilities, can we do this?" No, the Republicans' sense of duty would not let them yield to southern demands about slavery. Nor would Republicans be frightened from their duty by threats of disunion and destruction to the government. "LET US HAVE FAITH THAT RIGHT MAKES MIGHT, AND IN THAT FAITH, LET US, TO THE END, DARE TO DO OUR DUTY AS WE UNDERSTAND IT."

Impressed by his impassioned oratory and firm commitment to party principles, and impressed too by his availability, the Republicans chose Lincoln to be their standard bearer in 1860, to run for President on their free-soil, free-labor platform. In the countdown to the Republican nomination, Lincoln insisted that he preferred the Senate to the White House. But as his chances for the nomination brightened he confessed that "the taste *is* in my mouth a little," and he let a cadre of zealous lieutenants work to secure his nomination. Contrary to a persistent popular misconception, they did not do so simply by making bargains with Republicans from other states, promising Cabinet positions and other offices if they would throw their delegations to Lincoln. Modern scholarship has thoroughly demolished this claim. While Lincoln's managers may have made conditional overtures (as any manager would do), they followed Lincoln's own instructions and did not bind him to any convention deals. Moreover, supporters of William H. Seward, the front-running candidate before the convention, had as many offices to disseminate as Lincoln's men. What won Lincoln the nomination was not the peddling of spoils but a hard decision on the part of the Republican delegates that Seward "could not win and must give way to someone who could," as one historian has phrased it. And that someone was Abraham Lincoln, who was available, who was a loyal party man, who came from a crucial state, and who was more likely than any other candidate to carry the populous lower North, which was indispensable for a Republican victory.

Lincoln, for his part, accepted the nomination because he was as ambitious as he was deeply principled. While he preferred to serve the Republican cause on Capitol Hill, he would work for it wherever the party wanted to put him so long as it was a meaningful national office. And in 1860 that was the White House. In Lincoln, as it turned out, the Republicans chose a candidate more unbending in his commitment to Republican principles than anybody else they might have selected. As the Republican standard bearer, Lincoln was inflexible in his determination to prohibit slavery in the territories by national law and to save the Republic (as he put it) from returning "class," "caste," and "despotism." He exhorted his fellow Republicans to stand firm in their duty: to brand slavery as an evil, contain it in the South, look to the future for slavery to die a gradual death, and promise colonization to solve the question of race. Someday, somehow, the American house must be free of slavery. That was the Republican vision, the distant horizon Lincoln saw.

Yet, for the benefit of southerners, he repeated that he and his party would not interfere with slavery in Dixie. The federal government had no constitutional authority in peacetime to tamper with a state institution like slavery.

But southerners in 1860 were in no mood to believe anything Lincoln said. In their eyes, he was a "horrid looking wretch," another John Brown, "a black-hearted abolitionist fanatic" who lusted for Negro equality. There were, of course, a number of loyal Unionists in the South who pleaded for reason and restraint, who beseeched their fellow southerners to wait for an overt Republican act against them before they did anything rash. For most, though, Brown's Harpers Ferry invasion was all the overt action they intended to tolerate. For all classes in Dixie, from poor whites in South Carolina to rich cotton planters in Mississippi, Lincoln personified the feared and hated *Yankee*—the rapacious entrepreneur, the greasy mechanic, the mongrel immigrant, the frothing abolitionist, the entire "free-love, free-nigger" element, all of whom in southern eyes had combined in Lincoln's party. In him, southerners saw a monster who would send a Republican army into Dixie to free the slaves by gunpoint and whip up a racial storm that would consume their farms and plantations, their investments, their wives and daughters. Even if the South had to drench the Union in blood, exclaimed an Alabama paper, "the South, the loyal South, the Constitutional South, would never submit to such humiliation and degradation as the inauguration of Abraham Lincoln."

For Lincoln, the slavedealers had indeed assumed leadership in Dixie, and he would never compromise with them over a single plank in the Republican platform. Anyway, he still refused to believe that the South's blustery spokesmen truly reflected popular sentiment there. "The people of the South," he remarked during the obstreperous 1860 campaign, "have too much good sense, and good temper, to attempt the ruin of the government." He agreed with his advisers that southern Unionism was too powerful for secession to triumph. Surely, he reasoned, the southern people shared his own sentiments about the future of the American experiment. Surely, like the powerful southerners who helped found the country, like Washington, Jefferson, and Madison, the southern people of his day believed in the Declaration of Independence, which was their charter of liberty as much as his own and that of the Republicans. Surely the southern people would reject the forces of reaction in the world and come around to Lincoln's view, to stand with those who sought the liberation and uplift of the human spirit.

On election day, November 6, telegraph dispatches across the country carried the crucial news: Lincoln had defeated his three leading opponents—John Breckinridge of the southern Democrats, Douglas of the northern Democrats, and John Bell of the Constitutional Union ticket—and was to be the sixteenth President. Lincoln had won, not because his foes were split, but because he carried California and Oregon and every northern state except New Jersey, which divided its electoral votes between him and Douglas. In the electoral college, where Lincoln gained his triumph, his total vote exceeded that of his combined opponents by a margin of 187 to 123. In popular votes, though, Lincoln was a minority President, with 1,866,452 ballots compared to 2,815,-617 for his combined foes. Many factors were involved in this confusing and raucous contest, but the fact remains that the majority of Americans in 1860 regarded Lincoln as too radical and dangerous to occupy the White House. Of course, you don't learn about this in the story of Lincoln as Man of the People.

In the Deep South, newspapers screamed with headlines about Lincoln, and people thronged the streets of southern cities with talk of secession everywhere. "Now that the black radical Republicans have the power," asserted a South Carolinian, "I suppose they will [John] Brown us all." Of course, Lincoln and his party did not have the power. They had only won the presidency. The Democrats, though divided,

still controlled the Supreme Court and both houses of Congress, and would have demolished any abolition bill the Republicans might have introduced there. But for southerners that stormy winter, the nation had reached a profound turning point: an all-northern party avowedly hostile to slavery had gained control of the executive branch of the government. In the Deep South, a white man reading his newspaper could rehearse what was bound to follow. With the North's supremacy in population and drift toward abolition and revolutionary violence, that party was certain to win the rest of the government one day and then attack slavery in Dixie. Better, then, to strike for southern independence now than to await the Republican blow. Thus, even before Lincoln could be inaugurated, the seven states of the Deep South—with their heavy slave concentrations—left the Union and established the slave-based Confederacy. As a South Carolina resident explained to President Buchanan: "Slavery with us is no abstraction—but a *great* and *vital fact.* Without it our every comfort would be taken from us. Our wives, our children, made unhappy—education, the light of knowledge—all *all* lost and our *people ruined for ever. Nothing short of separation from the Union can save us."* The editor of the Montgomery *Mail* agreed. "To remain in the Union is to lose all that white men hold dear in government. We vote to get out."

In Springfield, President-elect Lincoln admitted that there were "some loud threats and much muttering in the cotton states," but insisted that the best way to avoid disaster was through calmness and forbearance. What reason did southerners have to be so incensed? What had the Republicans done to them? What southern rights had they violated? Did not southerners still have the fugitive slave law? Did they not have the same Constitution they had lived under for seventy-odd years? "Why all this excitement?" Lincoln asked. "Why all these complaints?"

With the border states also threatening to secede, Lincoln seemed confused, incredulous, at what was happening to his country. He seemed not to understand how he appeared in southern eyes. He kept telling himself that his advisers were right, that southern Unionism would somehow bring the errant states back. He could not accept the possibility that *his* election to the presidency might cause the collapse of the very system which had enabled him to get there. The irony of that was too distressing to contemplate.

In his Inaugural Address of March 4, 1861, Lincoln pleaded for southern whites to understand the Republican position on slavery. He assured them once again that he would not molest slavery in Dixie, that he had no legal right to molest it there. He even approved the original Thirteenth Amendment, just passed by Congress, that would have explicitly guaranteed slavery in the southern states. Lincoln endorsed the amendment because he deemed it consistent with Republican ideology. And in his conclusion he spoke personally to the southern people, as he had done so often since 1854: "In *your* hands, my dissatisfied fellow countrymen, and not in *mine,* is the momentous issue of civil war. The government will not assail *you.* You can have no conflict, without being yourselves the aggressors. *You* have no oath registered in Heaven to destroy the government, while *I* shall have the most solemn one to 'preserve, protect and defend' it."

"I am loth to close. We are not enemies, but friends. We must not be enemies. Though passion may have strained, it must not break our bonds of affection. The mystic chords of memory, stretching from every battlefield, and patriot grave, to every living heart and hearthstone, all over this broad land, will yet swell the chorus of the Union, when again touched, as surely they will be, by the better angels of our nature."

In Dixie, excitement was so great that men read in Lincoln's words, not conciliation, but provocation. The feverish Charleston *Mercury* even blasted it as a declaration of war. At that very moment, in fact, war threatened to break out in Charleston harbor, where hostile rebel cannon ringed Fort Sumter and its lonely Union flag. The Confederates had already seized every U.S. fort in Dixie except for Sumter and one other in the Florida Gulf. Now Sumter became a symbol for both sides, as the rebels demanded that Lincoln surrender it and angry Union men exhorted him to hold.

In the ensuing crisis, Lincoln clung to the belief that the southern people would overthrow the secessionists and restore the southern states to the Union. But he had little time to wait, for the Sumter garrison was rapidly running out of provisions. Should he send a relief expedition? But what if that betrayed southern Unionists and detonated a civil war? In "great anxiety" about what to do, Lincoln consulted repeatedly with his Cabinet and with high-ranking officers of the army and navy, but they gave him conflicting advice. Far from being an aggressive tyrant who forced the innocent South to start the war, the historical Lincoln vacillated over Sumter, postponed a decision, suffered terribly. He told an old Illinois friend that "all the troubles and anxieties" of his life could not equal those that beset him during the Sumter nightmare. They were so great, Lincoln said, that he did not think it possible to survive them.

Then a report from an emissary he had sent to Charleston smashed his hope that the crisis could be peacefully resolved. The emissary reported that South Carolinians had "no attachment to the Union," and that some wanted a clash with Washington to unite the Confederacy. Moreover, Unionism was equally dead everywhere else in Dixie, and the seceded states were "irrevocably gone." There was no conceivable way that Lincoln could avoid an armed collision with southern rebels: if he did not hold Sumter, he would have to stand somewhere else or see the government collapse.

It was a rude awakening for Lincoln, who had placed great faith in the potency of southern Unionism, who had always thought that southern white people loved the country as much as he and shared his faith in the American promise. Well, he had been wrong. Out of that sobering realization, out of everything he held dear about the Union, out of all his suffering, came a decision to stand firm. After all, he had won the presidency in a fair and legal contest. He would not compromise his election mandate. He would preserve the Union and the principle of self-government on which the Union was based: the right of a free people to choose their leaders and expect the losers to acquiesce in that decision. If southerners disliked him, they could try to vote him out of office in 1864. But he was not going to let them separate from the Union, because that would set a catastrophic precedent that any unhappy state could leave the Union at any time. For Lincoln, the philosophy of secession was "an ingenious sophism" southerners had contrived to vindicate their rebellion. This sophism held that each state possessed "some omnipotent, and sacred supremacy," and that any state could lawfully and peacefully leave the Union without its consent. "With rebellion thus sugar coated," Lincoln complained, southern leaders "have been drugging the public mind of their section for more than thirty years." Yet it was a preposterous argument. The Constitution specifically stated that the Constitution and the national laws made under it were the supreme law of the land. Therefore the states could not be supreme as the secessionists claimed; the Union was paramount and permanent, and could not be legally wrecked by a disaffected minority. The principle of secession was disintegration, Lincoln said. And no government based on that principle could possibly endure.

Yes, he would hold Fort Sumter. In that imperiled little garrison in Charleston Harbor, surrounded by rebel batteries and a hostile population, Lincoln saw the fate of popular government hanging in the balance. He would send a relief expedition to Sumter, and if the Confederates opened fire, the momentous issue of civil war was indeed in their hands.

And so the fateful events raced by: the firing on the fort, Lincoln's call for 75,000 troops, the secession of four border states, and the beginning of war. Deeply embittered, Lincoln grumbled about all the *professed* Union men" in Dixie who had gone over to the rebellion. And he looked on in distress as one supposedly loyal southerner after another resigned from the United States Army and headed south to enlist in the rebel forces. It depressed him immeasurably. He referred to Robert E. Lee, Joseph E. Johnston, John Bankhead Magruder, and all like them as traitors. And in his public utterances he never again addressed the southern people as though they were in his audiences. Instead he spoke of them in the third person, calling them rebels and insurrectionaries—a domestic enemy engaged in treason against his government.

And so the Civil War had come—a war that no reasonable man in North or South had wanted. What began as a ninety-day skirmish on both sides swelled instead into a vast inferno of destruction with consequences beyond calculation for those swept up in its flames. For Lincoln, the country was out of control, threatening to annihilate everyone and everything, all promise and all hope, and he did not think he could bear the pain he felt. His election had provoked this madness, and he took it personally. Falling into a depression that would plague him throughout his embattled presidency, he remarked that the war was the supreme irony of his life: that he who sickened at the sight of blood, who abhorred stridency and physical violence, who dreamed that "mind, all conquering *mind*," would rule the world someday, was caught in a national holocaust, a tornado of blood and wreckage with Lincoln himself whirling in its center.

# 21

# HEROES AND COWARDS

## BELL I. WILEY

The drama and sacrifice of war has occupied an important place in the American popular imagination for more than a century. Ironically, this fascination with the travails of warfare exists despite the fact Americans have seldom experienced warfare directly. The free security offered by the Atlantic and Pacific oceans as well as the relative military weakness of its northern and southern neighbors have largely allowed Americans to escape the debilitating effects of wars fought on their own territory. Only in the Revolutionary War, the War of 1812, and the Civil War did Americans find their farms, towns, and cities turned into battlefields and the civilian population menaced by contending armies.

The greatest of these internal wars was the Civil War of 1861–1865. Not only did the war claim over 600,000 American lives, destroy millions of dollars in property, and end a whole way of life, but it was in addition the only war in which American fought American. In this essay, Bell I. Wiley takes us beyond the exploits of military leaders and the movements of whole armies to the gritty experiences of the ordinary Confederate soldier. Wars are a collection of battles, and it was the danger and anarchy of conflict that tested the resolve of the ordinary soldier. Some, as Wiley poignantly reveals, became heroes and others cowards in the process, but none escaped the experience of combat unchanged.

Reprinted with permission of Louisiana State University Press from *The Life of Johnny Reb* by Bell I. Wiley. Copyright © 1970 by Bell I. Wiley.

While it may be granted that there were significant changes in the reactions of soldiers as they became accustomed to combat, the fact remains that the experiences and behavior of those taking part in Confederate battles followed the same general pattern. These more or less common characteristics must be described in some detail.

When an encounter with the Yankees was expected certain preliminaries were necessary. One of these was the issue of extra provisions, accompanied by the order to "cook up" from three to five days' rations, so that time would not have to be taken for the preparation of food during the anticipated action. This judicious measure generally fell short of its object because of Johnny Reb's own characteristics: he was always hungry, he had a definite prejudice against baggage, and he was the soul of improvidence. Sometimes the whole of the extra ration would be consumed as it was cooked, and rarely did any part of it last for the full period intended. About the same time that food was dispensed the general in command would address his men for the purpose of firing their spirit and inspiring them to deeds of valor. Soldiers en route to Shiloh, for example, were thus charged by Albert Sidney Johnston:

> "I have put you in motion to offer battle to the invaders of your country. With the resolution and disciplined valor becoming men fighting, as you are, for all worth living or dying for, you can but march to a decisive victory over the agrarian mercenaries sent to subjugate and despoil you of your liberties, property, and honor. Remember the precious stake involved; remember the dependence of your mothers, your wives, your sisters, and your children on the result; remember the fair, broad, abounding land, the happy homes, and the ties that would be desolated by your defeat.
>
> "The eyes and the hopes of eight millions of people rest upon you. You are expected to show yourselves worthy of your race and lineage; worthy of the women of the South, whose noble devotion in this war has never been exceeded in any time. With such incentives to

brave deeds and with the trust that God is with us, your general will lead you confidently to the combat, assured of success."

Presently each man would be given a supply of ammunition. This was delayed as long as possible, so that the powder would not become dampened through carelessness of the men. If Confederates held the initiative, the issue of ammunition would take place the night before the attack; but if the Rebs were on the defensive, without any definite knowledge of the time of assault, the issue of cartridges had to take place at an earlier stage. The customary allotment to each fighter was from forty to sixty rounds, a round being a ball and enough powder for a single shot.

Prior to their issue lead and powder for each load had, for convenience, been wrapped in a piece of paper with the bullet at one end, the powder behind it, and the other end closed with a twist or a plug to hold the powder in place. This improvised cartridge was cylindrical in shape, somewhat resembling a section of crayon. When Johnny Reb loaded his gun— usually a muzzle loader—he bit off the twisted end so that the powder would be exploded by the spark when the trigger was pulled, dropped the cartridge in the muzzle, rammed in a piece of wadding and waited for the opportunity to draw bead on a Yankee. Surplus rounds were kept in a cartridge box—a leather or metal container that hung from the belt—or in a haversack, or in trouser pockets.

Knapsacks and other baggage not actually needed on the field were supposed to be left in the rear with the quartermaster, but officers always had trouble preventing their men from throwing aside their equipment at random. After Bull Run and Shiloh most soldiers did not have to be cautioned about their canteens, as the acute suffering from thirst experienced in those engagements was a sufficient reminder to carry well-filled water tins into subsequent fights.

The day of battle finally comes. The men are roused from sleep at a very early hour, perhaps two or three o'clock. The well-known call to arms is an extended beat of the snare drum known as the "long roll." After the lines are drawn up officers inspect equipment, giving particular attention to ammunition, to see that all is in readiness.

Then a few words of advice and instruction: Do not shoot until you are within effective musket range of the enemy; fire deliberately, taking care to aim low, and thus avoid the over-shooting to which you have been so markedly susceptible in previous battles. If you merely wound a man so much the better, as injured men have to be taken from the field by sound ones; single out a particular adversary for your fire, after the example of your sharpshooting forefathers at Bunker Hill and New Orleans. When possible pick off the enemy's officers, particularly the mounted ones, and his artillery horses. Under all conditions hold your ranks; avoid the natural but costly inclination to hud-dle together under heavy fire. When ordered to charge, do so at once and move forward rapidly; you are much less apt to be killed while going steadily forward than if you hesi-tate or retreat; but in case you have to fall back, do so gradually and in order; more men are killed during disorganized retreat than at any other time; if your objective is a battery, do not be terrorized—artillery is never as deadly as it seems; a rapid forward movement reduces the battery's effectiveness and has-tens the end of its power to destroy. Do not pause or turn aside to plunder the dead or to pick up spoils; battles have been lost by indul-gence in this temptation. Do not heed the calls for assistance of wounded comrades or stop to take them to the rear; details have been made to care for casualties, and the best way of pro-tecting your wounded friends is to drive the enemy from the field. Straggling under any guise will be severely punished. Cowards will be shot. Do your duty in a manner that becomes the heroic example your regiment has already set on earlier fields of combat.

Orders to march are now given, and to the waving of colors and the stirring rhythm of fife and drum the regiments proceed to their ap-pointed place in the line of battle. As the dawn mist clears away, a scene of intense activity is revealed on all sides. Surgeons are preparing their kits; litter bearers and ambulances are ominously waiting. Arrived at their place in line, the men wait for what seem interminable hours while other units are brought into posi-tion. There is some talk while they wait, though less than earlier in the war. Comrades quietly renew mutual pledges to seek out those who are missing at the battle's end—for help if they are wounded and for protection of belongings and notification of homefolk if they are dead. A few men read their testaments, some mutter soft prayers—a devout captain is observed standing with Bible in hand reading aloud to his Mississippians, but this scene is unusual. Here and there a soldier bites off a chew of tobacco and joins a host of comrades whose jaws are already working. Very rarely an offi-cer or a private sneaks a swig of "How Come You So" to bolster his spirit for the ordeal ahead. Everywhere suspense bears down with crushing force, but is indicated largely by si-lence.

Presently the rattle of musketry is heard in front. Skirmishers must have made contact with enemy pickets. All are alert. A signal gun is fired and the artillery joins in with ac-cumulating fury. At last the command—"For-ward!"—and an overpowering urge to make contact with the enemy. Soon lines of blue are discernible. Comrades begin to fall in increas-ing numbers. Now the shout, lost perhaps in the din of battle—"Charge!"—accompanied by a forward wave of officer's saber and the line leaps forward with the famous "Rebel yell."

This yell itself is an interesting thing. It was heard at First Manassas and was repeated in hundreds of charges throughout the war. It came to be as much a part of a Rebel's fighting equipment as his musket. Once, indeed, more so. Toward the end of an engagement near Richmond in May 1864, General Early rode up to a group of soldiers and said, "Well, men, we must charge them once more and then we'll be through." The response came back, "General, we are all out of ammunition." Early's ready retort was, "Damn it, holler them across." And, according to the narrator, the order was literally executed.

The Confederate yell is hard to describe. An attempt to reproduce it was made a few years ago when Confederate veterans re-enacted battle scenes in Virginia. But this, by the very nature of things, was an inadequate representation. Old voices were too weak and incentive too feeble to create again the true battle cry. As it flourished on the field of combat, the Rebel yell was an unpremeditated, unrestrained and utterly informal "hollering." It had in it a mixture of fright, pent-up nervousness, exultation, hatred and a pinch of pure deviltry. Yelling in attack was not peculiar to Confederates, for Yanks went at Rebels more than once with "furious" shouts on their lips. But the battle cry of Southerners was admittedly different. General "Jube" Early, who well understood the spirit of his soldiers, made a comparison of Federal and Confederate shouting as a sort of aside to his official report of the battle of Fredericksburg. "Lawton's Brigade, without hesitating, at once dashed upon the enemy," he said, "with the cheering peculiar to the Confederate soldier, and which is never mistaken for the studied hurrahs of the Yankees, and drove the column opposed to it down the hill." Though obviously invidious, the general's observation is not wholly inaccurate.

The primary function of the rousing yell was the relief of the shouter. As one Reb observed after a fight in 1864, "I always said if I ever went into a charge, I wouldn't holler! But the very first time I fired off my gun I hollered as loud as I could, and I hollered every breath till we stopped." At first there was no intention of inspiring terror in the enemy, but the practice soon attained such a reputation as a demoralizing agent that men were encouraged by their officers to shout as they assaulted Yankee positions. In the battle of Lovejoy's Station, for instance, Colonel Clark cried out to his Mississip-

pians, "Fire and charge with a yell." Yankees may not have been scared by this Rebel throat-splitting, but they were enough impressed to set down in their official reports that the enemy advanced "yelling like fiends," or other words to the same effect.

Naturally a thing of such informal character as the Rebel yell varied considerably with the time and circumstance. Mississippians had a note quite different from that of Virginians. Rebs attacking Negro troops injected so much hatred into their cry as to modify its tonal qualities. A most interesting variant was that of the trans-Mississippi Indians organized by the Confederacy. Colonel Tandy Walker, commander of the Second Indian Brigade, reporting an action of his troops in Arkansas, said that when the Federals retreated Private Dickson Wallace was the first man to reach their artillery, "and mounting astride one of the guns gave a whoop, which was followed by such a succession of whoops from his comrades as made the woods reverberate for miles around."

But those Rebs who are now charging at the Yankees know that yelling is only a small part of their business. Yankee lines loom larger as the boys in gray surge forward. Now there is a pause for aiming, and the roar of countless muskets, but the individual soldier is hardly conscious of the noise or the kick of his weapon. Rarely does he have time to consider the effectiveness of his shot. He knows that scores of Yankees are falling, and his comrades as well, but he cannot attend to details of slaughter on either side. He drops to his knee, fumblingly bites off and inserts a cartridge, rams it home with a quick thrust of the rod, then rises and dashes forward with his fellows. On they go, these charging Rebs, feeling now that exaltation which comes after the fight gets under way. "There is something grand about it—it is magnificent," said Robert Gill of his experience under fire near Atlanta. "I feel elated as borne along with the tide of battle."

Presently there is an obvious slowing down

of the advance, as resistance increases and attacking ranks become thin. Artillery fire comes in such force as to shatter good-sized trees, and men are actually killed by falling limbs. The lines of gray seem literally to bend beneath the weight of canister and grape, and yelling soldiers lean forward while walking as if pushing against the force of a wind. Slaughter becomes so terrible that ditches run with blood. The deafening noise is likened by one Reb to "a large cane brake on fire and a thunder storm with repeated loud thunder claps." The flight of shells (called "lamp posts" and "wash kettles" according to their size and shape) reminds Robert Gill of "frying on a large scale only a little more so"; and Maurice Simons thinks of a partridge flying by, "only we would suppose that the little bird had grown to the size of an Eagle." Some of the men, unable to confront this holocaust, seek the protection of rocks, trees and gullies. Others of stronger nerve close the gaps and push onward.

The overwhelming urge to get quickly to the source of danger brings an end to loading and shooting. With one last spurt the charging troops throw themselves among their adversaries, gouging with bayonets, swinging with clubbed muskets, or even striking with rocks, fence rails and sticks. Presently one side or the other gives way, and the charge is over.

But not the battle. Before the day's fighting is completed there will be several charges, each followed by lulls for reorganization. And perhaps the conflict, as at Gettysburg, will extend to a second and third day, each characterized by repetitions of attack over various portions of the field; or perhaps the main action, as at Fredericksburg, will be defensive, staving off repeated Federal assaults.

Moving to the charge, though by far the most dramatic part of the fighting, actually made up only a small portion of a soldier's experience in battle. There were hours of lying on the ground or of standing in line, perhaps under the heat of a broiling sun, while troops on other parts of the field carried out the tasks assigned them. Then there was endless shift-

ing, to bolster a weak spot here, to cut off an enemy salient there, or to replenish ammunition. These and many other activities, coupled with repeated advances on enemy positions, took a heavy toll of the soldier's strength.

As the day wore on he was increasingly conscious of exhaustion. Though accustomed before the war to long hours of labor on the farm or extended jaunts in pursuit of game, he found fighting the hardest work he had ever done. Fatigue was sharpened by the fact that rest and food had been scarce during the days before the battle. By midafternoon his strength was often so depleted that he could hardly load and fire his gun, if indeed he was able to stand at all. Those who fought at Shiloh may have joined in the postwar criticism of Beauregard for not pushing the battle as Sunday's sun sank in the west, but officers' reports made soon after the fight show that most of the men were so exhausted that further aggression was impossible.

Increasing with the combatant's fatigue came intolerable thirst. Sweating in the grime and dust, he had emptied his canteen early in the day, hoping to refill it from some stream. But rarely was there any such chance. If he were lucky enough to reach a pond he was apt to find it so choked with the dead and wounded as to be unfit for use. But even so, that soldier considered himself lucky who could sweep aside the gory scum and quench his thirst by greedy draughts of the muddy water underneath.

If the battle happened to be in winter, as at Murfreesboro, Fredericksburg, or Nashville, the suffering from thirst was not so intense. But the exposure to cold was hardly less severe. Discomfort was increased by damp weather, scarcity of clothing, and the inability to make fires. At Murfreesboro, for instance, soldiers lay in line of battle for nearly a week under a cold rain without fire.

When the combat extended over several days, as was frequently the case, hunger was added to other discomforts. At Gettysburg Washington Artillerymen became so famished that a captain sent a detail to gather food from the haversacks of Federal dead. Many other hungry soldiers were not so fortunate as to have this opportunity.

The coming of night usually brought a rest from fighting, but not from suffering. The disorganization which characterized Confederate battles often separated the soldier from his regiment. The command of duty, plus a desire to know the lot of his friends, would cause him, tired to the point of prostration though he was, to set out on a tedious search for his fellows. When he found the scattered remnants of his company he would probably discover that some messmate, committed to his care by mutual pledge before the battle, was missing. Then he must make a round of the battlefield and the emergency hospitals, inquiring patiently, calling out the name of his friend, and scanning by candlelight the ghastly faces of dead and wounded. The quest might end in happy discovery, but more likely it would prove futile. At last the weary soldier would fall down on the ground. And in spite of the piteous cries of the wounded he would sink at once into heavy slumber.

The morrow of a battle, whether its duration was for one or several days, was in some respects more trying than the conflict itself. Scenes encountered in the burial of the dead were strange and appalling: there a dead Yankee lying on his back "with a biscuit in his hand and with one mouthful bitten off and that mouthful still between his teeth"; here "the top of a man's Skull Hanging by the Hair to a Limb some 8 or 9 feet from the ground"; yonder another "man Siting behind a large oak tree his head . . . shot off"; to the right a small, whining dog curled up in the arms of a dead Yankee, refusing to be coaxed from its erstwhile master; to the left a lifeless Reb sprawled across the body of a well-dressed Federal, the gray-clad's hand in the Northerner's pocket—a gruesome warning to those who are tempted to plunder during battle; farther on, the field is strewn with nude figures blackened and mutilated by a fire that swept across the dry foliage in the

wake of the fight. One of the burying party working in Federal-traversed territory is shocked to find that before his arrival "the hogs got a holt of some of the Yankey dead." In any direction one chances to gaze lie heaps of disfigured bodies; to a rural-bred Georgian the scene following Fredericksburg suggested "an immense hog pen and then all killed."

After a prolonged summer encounter the task was unusually repulsive. Wrote a soldier who helped in the burial of the Gettysburg dead:

> "The sights and smells that assailed us were simply indescribable—corpses swollen to twice their original size, some of them actually burst asunder with the pressure of foul gases and vapors. . . . The odors were nauseating and so deadly that in a short time we all sickened and were lying with our mouths close to the ground, most of us vomiting profusely."

While some were burying the dead, others were walking about picking up spoils. Trinkets of all sorts, such as Yankee letters, diaries, photographs, and pocket knives are much in demand as souvenirs to be sent home to relatives. "I am going to send you a trophie that come off the battle field at Gettysburg," wrote a Reb to his sister. "I got three pictures out of a dead Yankees knapsack and I am going to send you one. . . . The pictures are wraped up in a letter from the person whose image they are. . . . She signed her name A. D. Spears and she lived in Main somewhere, but I could not make out where she lived." Occasionally Rebs laughed over the sentimental contents of such letters. Some soldiers profited financially from their plundering of battlefields. Following the Franklin engagement of December 1864 George Athey wrote:

> "I got agood knapsack fuol of tricks whitch I sold $4.5 dolars worth out of it and cepe as mutch as I wanted."

Articles essential to personal comfort were eagerly gathered up. After the Seven Days' Battles a Reb wrote exultantly:

"We have had a glorious victory with its rich Booty A many one of our boys now have a pair of Briches a nice Rubber cloth & a pair of Blankets also a pair or more of Small Tent Cloths."

The avidity with which an impoverished Confederate might pounce upon the riches left in the wake of Federal defeat, as well as the unhappy consequence of overenthusiasm, is evidenced by an entry in a Tennessean's diary following the battle of Seven Pines:

"I awoke quite early yesterday morning, and everything seemed very quiet, I went over the field seeing what I could see. Here were Sutlers' tents, filled with luxuries, oranges, lemons, oysters, pineapples, sardines, in fact, almost everything that I could think of. My first business was to eat just as much as I possibly could, and that was no small amount, for I had been living on hard tack several days. I then picked out a lot of stationery, paper, envelopes, ink, pens and enough to fill one haversack, then I found a lot of puff bosomed linen shirts, and laid in a half dozen together with some white gloves and other little extras enough to fill another haversack. Then I filled another with nuts and candies and still another with cheese. With this load, I wandered around picking up some canteens to carry back to the boys. Then adding to my load such articles as a sword, an overcoat, etc. . . . I quickened my pace and before I had gone twenty steps, the Yankees opened fire . . . and the balls whistled around me in a perfect shower. I had about two hundred yards to go before reaching my regiment, and by the time I reached it, I had thrown away all my plunder."

If the battle ended in defeat, falling back might be so hurried as to leave the dead and wounded in Federal hands. This, added to the increased hardships of retreat and the disappointment of being whipped, caused the soldier's cup to overflow with bitterness.

But whether victorious or not, Johnny Reb began within a remarkably short time to recall and to enjoy the interesting and humorous detail of the combat. Campfire groups must have delighted in teasing Private Joseph Adams about losing his pants when a shell exploded near him at Murfreesboro; and there was doubtless plenty of laughter when M. D. Martin told how a shell cut off his two well-stocked haversacks and scattered hardtack so promiscuously that "several of the boys were struck by the biscuits, and more than one thought he was wounded."

James Mabley could always get a good laugh with his story of the Reb at Chancellorsville who while in the act of drawing a bead on a Yank was distracted by a wild turkey lighting in a tree before him; the Federal was immediately forgotten, and in an instant the crack of this Reb's gun brought the turkey to the ground.

The men of Gilmor's Battalion never tired of asking their colonel after a valley engagement of 1864 "if spades are trumps"; for during this fight a ball went all the way through an unopened deck of cards that he was carrying in his inside coat pocket, stopping only at the last card, the ace of spades.

Almost everyone could tell of a "close shave" when a bullet hit a knapsack, perforated a hat, or spent itself by passing through a bush immediately in front, to fall harmlessly to the ground in plain view. One soldier marveled at hearing through the din of battle the cry of John Childress as he fell: "I am killed, tell Ma and Pa goodbye for me."

Then someone may have mentioned the tragic case of Jud and Cary Smith, Yale-educated brothers from Mississippi. While in the act of lying down under fire, the younger, Cary, putting his hand under his coat found his inner garments covered with blood; and with only the exclamation "What does this mean?" he died. Jud was so overwhelmed with grief that he spent the entire night muttering affectionate words over his brother's corpse. He passed the next day and night in unconsolable solitude. The third day was that of Malvern Hill, and when the first charge took place Jud kept on going after his comrades fell back under the murderous fire, and he was never seen or heard of again. After the father learned of the fate of his two sons he joined Price's army as a private soldier; when his regiment charged at Iuka, he followed the example set by Jud at Malvern Hill, and he likewise was never heard of again.

But there was not much lingering on tragic notes. It was more pleasant to talk of how Jeb Stuart at Second Manassas beguiled the Yankees into exaggerated ideas of Rebel strength by having his men drag brush along the roads to stir up huge clouds of dust; or of how the Yankee General Banks was duped into abandoning several strong positions during his Red River campaign by such Confederate ruses as sending drummers out to beat calls, lighting superfluous campfires, blowing bugles, and "rolling empty wagons over fence rails"; or of how George Cagle, while lying on a ridge at Chickamauga, kept at work four or five muskets gathered from incapacitated comrades, and as Yankee bullets whistled overhead he simulated the activity of an artillery unit, giving such commands as "attention Cagle's Battery, make ready, load, take aim, fire"; of how Sergeant Nabors scared nervous Yankee prisoners who asked him at Atlanta if he were going to kill them by replying, "That's our calculation; we came out for that purpose."

By no means was all of the fighting in the open field. Warring in trenches—Johnny Reb usually called them "ditches"—made its appearance in the spring of 1862 on the Virginia peninsula where Magruder's army was entrenched for a month. At Vicksburg, where Pemberton's troops were under siege for forty-seven days, soldiers spent most of the time in earthworks along the line, or in caves to the rear. During the Atlanta campaign Rebs of the Army of Tennessee saw considerable trench warfare. But by far the longest stretch of this sort of campaigning was done by Lee's troops, who spent the greater part of the war's

last year in the ditches around Petersburg.

Occasionally the routine of trench fighting was broken by an assault of one army or the other, but the time was mostly spent in desultory exchanges of artillery and musket fire. The Federals, being the besiegers and having vastly superior resources, did the larger part of the firing. So unlimited, indeed, were their supplies of ammunition that they could make the countryside reverberate with repeated discharges of their heavy cannon.

The defenders of Vicksburg were subjected to heavier fire than any other trench fighters in the war. Back of them lay the Mississippi, dotted with gunboats, and before them were the troops of Grant and Sherman well equipped with artillery. The besieged were deficient in both guns and ammunition. Hemmed in thus by superior forces and equipment, conscious of their inability to give effective retaliation, living on ever dwindling rations, suffering from a shortage of drinking water, and cut off largely from their friends, they were subjected day after day and night after night to a cannonading that was so severe at times as to make heads ache from the concussion. One of the defenders wrote in his diary at the midpoint of siege:

> "The fighting is now carried on quite systematically . . . in the morning there seems to be time allowed for breakfast, when all at once the work of destruction is renewed. There is about an hour at noon & about the same at sunset, taking these three intervals out the work goes on just as regularly as . . . on a well regulated farm & the noise is not unlike the clearing up of new ground when much heavy timber is cut down! Add to that the nailing on of shingles by several men & one has a pretty good idea of the noise. It might be supposed that a score of villages had sprung up all round him & that the inhabitants were vieing with each other to see who could be the most industrious."

The caves dug in the hillside were poor protection against the heavy shells that came screeching through the air with varying notes of terror. If one lifted his head ever so little above the earthworks, the crack of a sharpshooter's rifle, followed instantly by a dull thud, would announce the doom of another Reb. A man who was slightly wounded in the trenches stood in considerable danger of being more seriously injured, if not killed outright, as he traversed the open space between battle line and hospital. Life under such conditions became a torturing ordeal, and the situation was not helped by jesting speculation as to the prospective comforts of Johnson's Island, Camp Chase and Camp Douglas.

In the trenches before Atlanta and Petersburg existence was not so perilous nor so gloomy as at Vicksburg. Common to all, however, was the intolerable heat of the summer sun. Some men sought alleviation by building little brush arbors along the trenches. The sultriness of the ditches became so unbearable at night that some of the men resorted to sleeping on the edge—and when the Federal batteries opened they would simply roll over to safety. But immunity from danger in the Atlanta and Petersburg trenches was only comparative. The killing and wounding of men by Federal sharpshooting and artillery fire were of such common occurrence as hardly to elicit notice save by the company to which the casualty belonged.

The number of killed and wounded would have been much greater but for the skill of the men in side-stepping arched shots. "The mortars are thrown up a great height," wrote an Alabamian from Petersburg, "and fall down in the trenches like throwing a ball over a house—we have become very perfect in dodging them and unless they are thrown too thick I think I can always escape them at least at night." He added that the dugouts which they contrived at intervals along the trenches and which they were wont to call bombproofs were not impervious at all to mortar shells, and that "we always prefer to be out in the ditches—where by using strategy and skill we get out of their way." So confident did the troops become

of their ability to escape these lobbed shots of the Yankees that they would keep up a derisive yelling throughout a bombardment.

During periods of truce ladies from Petersburg made several visits to the lines, walking down the ditches in their cumbersome hoop skirts to see how bombproofs were made, climbing upon the parapets to get a look at the Yankees, giggling and oh-ing at the strange sights confronting them. Both Federals and Rebs enjoyed these interludes in crinoline but some of the latter could not refrain from mischievously expressing the wish that the Yanks would throw a few shells over to see if the fair visitors would shake with terror or raise the Rebel yell.

But these tantalizing glimpses of Petersburg belles afforded only brief respite from the terrible filth, the smothering heat of summer and the cold of winter, the rain and mud of all seasons, the restricted movement and the countless other deprivations that made trench warfare the most unpleasant aspect of Confederate soldierhood. Open fighting with all its dangers was immeasurably preferable to such existence as this.

But what of valor and of cowardice on the field of battle? There were numerous manifestations of both, though many more of the former than of the latter. Deeds of Rebel bravery, individual and collective, were of such common occurrence as to be quite beyond all estimation. A few definite instances will serve as examples of the glory that lighted up the fields of Manassas, of Shiloh, of Antietam, of Gettysburg, of Spottsylvania—and of countless others.

At Shiloh Private Samuel Evans refused to go to the rear when a ball passed through both cheeks, "but remained and fought for a considerable length of time, cheering on the men and loading and shooting as fast as he could." An officer who saw his men reduced from twenty-eight to twelve as he led them into the ravaging fire at Seven Pines cried out as he fell pierced through the heart, "Boys, I am killed, but you press on." Private Ike Stone was severely wounded at the beginning of the Murfreesboro fight, but he paused only to bind up his injuries, and when his captain was incapacitated Stone took charge of the company and led it valorously through the battle, this despite a second wound. In the thick of this same fight Sergeant Joe Thompson was overwhelmed with the impulse to take a prisoner; leaping ahead of his comrades he overtook the retreating Federal column, seized a Yank and started to the rear with him; but this man having been shot down in his grasp, Thompson ran back to the still-retreating lines, seized a second Federal and brought him away safely. When Private Mattix's left arm was so seriously injured that he could no longer fire his musket, he went to his commanding officer and said, "Colonel, I am too badly wounded to use my gun but can carry the flag; may I?" Before this three standard-bearers had been shot down in succession, but when the requested permission was given him, Mattix seized the staff, stepped boldly in front of the regiment, and carried the colors throughout the remainder of the contest.

In his official report of Second Manassas Major J. D. Waddell, commanding Toombs' Georgians, said that he "carried into the fight over 100 men who were barefoot, many of whom left bloody foot-prints among the thorns and briars through which they rushed, with Spartan courage and really jubilant impetuosity, upon the serried ranks of the foe." Colonel E. C. Cook of the Thirty-second Tennessee Infantry reported after Chickamauga that one of his men, J. W. Ellis, who had marched for six weeks without shoes, "went thus into battle and kept up with his company at all times till wounded."

At Chickamauga Private Mayfield was wounded in the thigh by a Minié ball and at the same time dazed by a shell. Litter bearers picked him up and were carrying him to the rear when he recovered from the shock and sprang to the ground with the remark, "This will not do for me," and rushed back to continue the fight. In this same engagement Private McCann fought gallantly until his ammunition was exhausted; then he picked up cartridge boxes of the dead and wounded and coolly distributed ammunition among his comrades. When the colonel commended his heroic conduct McCann asked that his bravery be cited in the official report of the battle. Shortly afterward he received a mortal wound and as he was borne dying to the rear, he turned smiling to his colonel and reminded him of the promise of honorable mention.

Of all the brave those who were entrusted with the colors had the most consistent record. Almost every official report of regimental commanders mentions the courageous action of standard-bearers. To keep the flag flying was a matter of inestimable pride, and its loss to the enemy was an incalculable disgrace. Consequently men vied with each other for the honor of holding the cherished emblem aloft in the thickest of the fight. The Federals, knowing the close association of morale and colors, and being easily able to single out standard-bearers because of their conspicuousness, were wont to concentrate an unusually heavy fire upon them. Literally thousands of those who aspired to the honor of carrying and guarding the flags paid for the privilege with their lives.

"In my two color companies," reported Colonel Jenkins of the Palmetto Sharpshooters after Seven Pines, "out of 80 men who entered 40 were killed and wounded, and out of 11 in the color guard, 10 were shot down, and my colors pierced by nine balls passed through four hands without touching the ground." At Antietam the First Texas Infantry lost eight standard-bearers in succession, and at Gettysburg, the Twenty-sixth North Carolina lost fourteen. At Antietam also, the flag of the Tenth Georgia—which regiment lost fifty-seven per cent of its men and officers in this one engagement—received forty-six shots. The standard of Lyle's Regiment was torn to tatters at Corinth, and color-bearer Sloan when last seen by his comrades was "going over the breast works waving a piece over his head and shouting for the Southern Confederacy."

Color Sergeant Rice of the Twenty-eighth

Tennessee Infantry, downed by a bullet at Murfreesboro, still clung to the flag, holding it aloft as he crawled on his knees until a second shot brought death and delivered him of his trust. On another part of this bloody field Color Sergeant Cameron advanced too far ahead of his comrades and was captured. He tore the flag from its staff, concealed it on his person, carried it to prison with him, escaped, and brought it back to be unfurled anew above its proud followers.

Murfreesboro likewise afforded the setting for perhaps the most extraordinary of all color-bearer feats. While this contest raged at its greatest fury the opposing lines came very near each other in that portion of the field occupied by the Nineteenth Texas Cavalry (dismounted). A Yankee standard carrier stood immediately to the front of the Texas Color Sergeant, A. Sims, waving his flag and urging the blue column forward. Sergeant Sims, construing this as something of a personal insult, rushed forward, planted his own flag staff firmly on the ground with one hand and made a lunge for that of his exhorting adversary with the other. At the moment of contact, both color-bearers, Yankee and Rebel, "fell in the agonies of death waving their banners above their heads until their last expiring moments." The Texas standard was rescued, but not until one who rushed forward to retrieve it had also been shot down.

Confederate authorities sought to stimulate the men by offering medals and badges to those who were cited by officers. Unable to supply these emblems, Congress passed an act in October 1862 providing for the publication of a Roll of Honor after each battle which should include the names of those who had best displayed their courage and devotion. Such lists were read at dress parades, published in newspapers and filed in the adjutant general's office. As a further inducement commissions were offered to those who should distinguish themselves, and special inscriptions were placed on flags of those regiments that captured artillery or gave other proof of unusual achievement. But the most effective incentive was probably that of personal and family pride. This was strikingly evidenced by the remark of a Georgian to his brother after Franklin: "I am proud to say that there was no one between me and the Yankees when I was wounded."

Cowardice under fire, being a less gratifying subject than heroism, has not received much attention from those who have written or talked of the Confederate Army. Of the various sources of information on this obscure point the most fertile are the official reports of battles by commanders of units ranging from regiments to armies. But the most numerous of these reports—those submitted by regimental commanders—are characterized by a reluctance to admit wholesale cowardice because of possible reflections on the conduct of the commanders themselves. This reluctance sometimes resulted in misrepresentation of the rankest sort, as in the following case: After the attack on Battery Wagner, Morris Island, South Carolina, July 18, 1863, Colonel Charles W. Knight, commanding the Thirty-first North Carolina Regiment, said in closing his report, "It is useless to mention any officer or man, when all were acting coolly and bravely." In the body of his report he mentioned being repulsed, but there is absolutely no suggestion of bad conduct on the part of the regiment. But when Knight's superior, General William B. Taliaferro, reported the battle, he said: "The Thirty-first North Carolina could not be induced to occupy their position, and ingloriously deserted the ramparts. . . . I feel it my duty to mention . . . [their] disgraceful conduct."

In the reports of higher ranking officers, who could admit bad conduct of portions of their commands with more impunity than colonels, and in the wartime letters and diaries of the common soldiers, much testimony on the subject may be found. This evidence shows clearly that Confederate soldiers were by no means immune to panic and cowardice.

At First Manassas a few Rebs fled into the woods when shells began to fly. There was disgraceful conduct at the beginning of Mc-

Clellan's peninsula campaign, when General D. H. Hill wrote that "several thousand soldiers . . . have fled to Richmond under pretext of sickness. They have even thrown away their arms that their flight might not be impeded." At Seven Pines there were a few regiments that "disgracefully left the battle field with their colors." General W. H. C. Whiting in reporting the battle of Gaines's Mill said: "Men were leaving the field in every direction and in great disorder . . . men were skulking from the front in a shameful manner; the woods on our left and rear were full of troops in safe cover from which they never stirred." At Malvern Hill, General Jubal Early encountered "a large number of men retreating from the battle-field," saw "a very deep ditch filled with skulkers," and found a "wood filled with a large number of men retreating in confusion."

Men ran, skulked and straggled by the hundreds at Shiloh. A Tennessee regiment took fright during an advance, ran back on supporting lines crying, "Retreat! Retreat!" and caused great confusion; but they were rallied and set in motion toward the Federal position; again they were overcome with fear, and this time they rushed back so precipitately that they ran over and trampled in the mud the color-bearer of the regiment behind them. A Texas regiment behaved in the same manner; placed in line of battle it began firing, but before the guns had all been discharged, "it broke and fled disgracefully from the field." An officer who attempted to bring back the fugitives and threatened to report them as "a pack of cowards" was told that "they did not care a damn" what they were called, they would not follow him. When General W. J. Hardee tried to rally another demoralized regiment he was fired on by its members. Some of the straggling for which Shiloh was notorious was due to circumstances that exonerate those involved, but there can be no doubt that a large part of those who found various pretexts for leaving the firing line were playing the coward. Said Colonel O. F. Strahl in his official report: "On Monday morning we . . . had a great number of stragglers attached to us. The stragglers demonstrated very clearly this morning that they had strayed from their own regiments because they did not want to fight. My men fought gallantly until the stragglers ran and left them and began firing from the rear over their heads. They were then compelled to fall to the rear. I rallied them several times and . . . finally left out the stragglers." General Beauregard clinched this evidence in his official report: "Some officers, non-commissioned officers, and men abandoned their colors early in the first day to pillage the captured encampments; others retired shamefully from the field on both days while the thunder of cannon and the roar and rattle of musketry told them that their brothers were being slaughtered by the fresh legions of the enemy."

General Bushrod Johnson reported that at Murfreesboro troops on his right became demoralized and "men of different regiments, brigades, divisions, were scattered all over the fields," and that he was almost run over, so precipitate was their flight. Captain Felix Robertson said that he had never seen troops so completely broken as those demoralized at Murfreesboro. "They seemed actuated only by a desire for safety," he added. "I saw the colors of many regiments pass, and though repeated calls were made for men of the different regiments, no attention was paid to them."

At Chancellorsville and Gettysburg the conduct of the soldiers seems to have been exceptionally good. This may have been due in some part to vigorous efforts of General Lee and of the War Department early in 1863 to tighten up the discipline of the Army of Northern Virginia. The fighting before Vicksburg was marred by shameful conduct in the action of May 16, 1863, of which General Pemberton said: "We lost a large amount of artillery. The army was much demoralized; many regiments behaved badly," and Colonel Edward Goodwin reported of a small number of troops immediately in front of him:

"At this time our friends gave way and came rushing to the rear panic-stricken. . . . I brought my regiment to the charge bayonets, but even this could not check them in their flight. The colors of three regiments passed through. . . . We collared them, begged them, and abused them in vain."

The wholesale panic which seized Confederate troops at Missionary Ridge was as notorious as it was mystifying. A soldier who took part in the battle wrote in his diary, "In a few minutes the whole left gave way and a regular run commenced." After a retreat of several hundred yards, this Reb's battalion rallied momentarily, "but it was in such a confused mass that we made but a feeble resistance, when all broke again in a perfect stampede." His conviction was that the troops acted disgracefully, that they "did not half fight."

General Bragg in his official report of the fight said that "a panic which I had never before witnessed seemed to have seized upon officers and men, and each seemed to be struggling for his personal safety, regardless of his duty or his character." He added that "no satisfactory excuse can possibly be given for the shameful conduct of the troops on our left in allowing their line to be penetrated. The position was one which ought to have been held by a line of skirmishers against any assaulting column, and wherever resistance was made the enemy fled in disorder after suffering heavy loss. Those who reached the ridge did so in a condition of exhaustion from the great physical exertion in climbing, which rendered them powerless, and the slightest effort would have destroyed them." What stronger indictment could there be of any soldiery by its general-in-command!

But the woeful tale is not ended. In connection with Early's campaign of 1864 in the Shenandoah Valley occurred some of the most disgraceful running of Confederate history. After an engagement near Winchester on July 23, General Stephen Ramseur wrote his wife:

"My men behaved shamefully—They ran from the enemy. . . . The entire command stampeded. I tried in vain to rally them & even after the Yankees were checked by a few men I posted behind a stone wall, they continued to run all the way to the breastworks at Winchester—& many of them threw away their guns & ran on to Newtown 6 miles beyond. They acted cowardly and I told them so."

On September 19, 1864, during another hard fight near Winchester, a panic of unprecedented proportions struck the ranks of Early's army. Regiment after regiment broke and fled back toward the town. General Bryan Grimes, appalled by the demoralization and fearful that his brigade would succumb to it, threatened "to blow the brains out of the first man who left ranks," and then moved over to confront the fugitives, waving his sword and giving many a Reb the full weight of its flashing blade.[67] But fleeing regiments, increasing now in number, could not be stopped. They poured into the town, out the valley pike, and some continued their disordered course for miles beyond. "The Ladies of Winchester came into the streets and beged them crying bitterly to make a stand for their sakes if not for their own honor," wrote a captain who witnessed the rout; but "the cowards did not have the shame to make a pretense of halting."

A month later at Cedar Creek, plunder combined with cowardice to inflict upon Early's veterans one of the most shameful defeats of the war. In the morning, by brilliant action, the Confederates pounced upon the Federals and drove them from their camps. As the Southern lines advanced large numbers of soldiers and officers turned aside, against positive orders, and began to ransack the rich stores abandoned by the foe. While the victors were absorbed in pillage, the Federals rallied, and in the afternoon they counterattacked. The disorganized Confederates broke first on the left, and then all along the line. Efforts of division commanders and of others who attempted to stay the tide of panic was to no avail, and the field was utterly abandoned.

"It was the hardest day's work I ever engaged in," Grimes said, "trying to rally the men. Took over flags at different times, begging, commanding, entreating the men to rally—would ride up and down the lines, beseeching them by all they held sacred and dear, to stop and fight, but without any success. I don't mean my Brigade only, but all."

Price's Missouri expedition of 1864 was marked by an instance of large-scale panic. When the Federals attacked the Confederate rear on October 25, near Carthage, Missouri, demoralization set it. As Price rode rapidly to the point of danger he "met the divisions of Major-Generals Fagan and Marmaduke retreating in utter and indescribable confusion, many of them having thrown away their arms. They were deaf to all entreaties or commands, and in vain were all efforts to rally them."

While the Atlanta campaign seems to have been remarkably free of demoralization under fire, there were at least two instances involving a considerable number of men. In a skirmish on June 9, 1864, a Texas cavalry unit that had a distinguished record in battle broke upon slight contact with the Federal cavalry, and fled in a manner described as disorderly and shameful by General Ross. Later, in the Battle of Jonesboro, August 31, 1864, an advancing brigade of Confederates halted without orders when it came to the Federal picket line, the men seeking shelter behind piles of rails. They seemed "possessed of some great horror of charging breastworks," reported Colonel Bushrod Jones, "which no power of persuasion or example could dispel."

The last instance of large-scale panic during the war was at Nashville, December 16, 1864. On this occasion the division of General Bate, when assaulted about four o'clock in the afternoon by the Federals, began to fall back in great confusion and disorder. In a few moments the entire Confederate line was broken, and masses of troops fled down the pike toward Franklin. All efforts to rally the troops proved fruitless. General Bate in his official report leaves the impression that the rout, due to extenuating circumstances, cast little if any reproach upon his men. But General Hood, in chief command, was evidently of contrary opinion, as he says that Confederate loss in killed and wounded was small, implying that withdrawal took place without much resistance. He says further that the break came so suddenly that artillery guns could not be brought away. Captain Thomas J. Key says in his diary that "General Bate's division . . . shamefully broke and fled before the Yankees were within 200 yards of them," and that there "then ensued one of the most disgraceful routs" that it had ever been his misfortune to witness.

There were innumerable cases of individual cowardice under fire. When men are assembled in such large numbers, especially when many of them are forced into service, a certain proportion are inevitably worthless as fighters. Some of those who fled wanted earnestly to act bravely, but they had not the power to endure fire unflinchingly. This type is well exemplified by the Reb who covered his face with his hat during the battle of Fredericksburg, and who later, when told that his turn at the rifle pits was imminent, "made a proposition that he would go out from camp and strip" and let his comrades "get switches and whip him as much as they wanted" if they would obtain his release from the impending proximity to Federal fire. A similar case was encountered by Colonel C. Irvine Walker. A man had been reported for cowardly behavior on the field. Walker called him to task and told him that he would be watched closely during the next engagement. When the time came the colonel went over to check his performance as the regiment advanced. "I found him in his place," reported Walker, "his rifle on his shoulder, and holding up in front of him a frying pan." The man was so scared that he sought this meager protection, yet he moved forward with his company and was killed.

Another case of infamy converted to valor

was cited by Colonel William Stiles, of the Sixtieth Georgia Infantry. During a charge this officer saw a robust Reb drop out of line and crouch behind a tree; the colonel slipped up and gave him a resounding whack across the back with the flat of his sword, and shouted, "Up there, you coward!"

The skulker, thinking evidently that he was the mortal victim of a Yankee shot, "clasped his hands, and keeled over backwards, devoutly ejaculating, 'Lord, receive my spirit!' "

After momentary bafflement, Stiles kicked the prostrate soldier violently in the ribs, exclaiming simultaneously, "Get up, sir! The Lord wouldn't receive the spirit of such an infernal coward."

The man sprang up with the joyful exclamation, "Ain't I killed? The Lord be praised," grabbed his musket, rejoined his comrades, and henceforth conducted himself with courage.

Other officers had less success. Men who had no shoes were often excused from fighting, and a good many soldiers took advantage of this rule by throwing away their shoes on the eve of conflict. Others left the field under pretext of helping the wounded to the rear, and this in spite of strict orders against removal of casualties by anyone except those specifically detailed for the purpose. Still others feigned sickness or injury. A favorite ruse was to leave one's own regiment during the confusion of battle, and then to evade duty by a pretense of endless and futile searching for the outfit intentionally abandoned.

Infuriated officers would curse these shirkers, beat them with swords and even threaten them with shooting, and on occasion carry out their threats on the spot. Commanders would place file-closers in the rear with instructions to arrest, and in some instances to shoot down, those who refused to do their duty. Courts-martial sentenced great numbers to hard and disgraceful punishments. Private soldiers covered spineless comrades with scorn and ridicule. But these measures were only partially effective.

There can be no doubt that the trying conditions under which Confederate soldiers fought contributed to the bad performance of some on the field of battle. Men often went into combat hungry and remained long under fire with little or nothing to eat. Sometimes, as at Antietam and Gettysburg, they fought after exhausting marches. Many of those who participated in the routs at Chattanooga and at Nashville were without shoes. Often the Confederate artillery protection was inadequate. The superior number of the Federals made Rebel flanks unduly vulnerable, and flank sensitiveness was the cause of more than one panic. Casualties among line officers were unusually heavy, and replacement with capable men was increasingly difficult after 1863.

When all of these factors are considered, it is rather remarkable that defection under fire was not more frequent than it actually was. Those soldiers who played the coward, even granting that the offenders totaled well up in the thousands, were a very small proportion of the Confederate Army. Taken on the whole of his record under fire, the Confederate private was a soldier of such mettle as to claim a high place among the world's fighting men. It may be doubted that anyone else deserves to outrank him.